R. Gupta's®

POPULAR MASTER GUIDE

Indian Army SOLDIER Technical Trade

(Soldier Technical, Ammunition & Aviation)

Recruitment Exam

PREVIOUSLY KNOWN AS **MER – TECHNICAL TRADE**

M.L. Batura (Ex. AEC)
(Retd. Army Officer)
& RPH Editorial Board

2019
EDITION

RAMESH PUBLISHING HOUSE, New Delhi

Published by
O.P. Gupta *for* Ramesh Publishing House

Admin. Office
12-H, New Daryaganj Road, Opp. Officers' Mess,
New Delhi-110002 ✆ 23261567, 23275224, 23275124

E-mail: info@rameshpublishinghouse.com
Website: www.rameshpublishinghouse.com

Showroom
• Balaji Market, Nai Sarak, Delhi-6 ✆ 23253720, 23282525
• 4457, Nai Sarak, Delhi-6, ✆ 23918938

Book Code: R-130

ISBN: 978-93-87918-24-5

HSN Code: 49011010

INFORMATION RELATED TO THE EXAMINATION AND SYLLABUS

For the recruitment of Soldier Technical Trade in the Indian Army, the application forms are no longer invited. Now on a fixed place and fixed time, an open recruitment rally is conducted, in which, Physical Test is held and the eligible candidates are called for the Written Examination.

Educational Qualification: 10+2 with 50% or above marks.

SYLLABUS

There would be one question paper in the Written Examination.

Time : 1 hour ***M.M.: 100***

Science (25 questions)	:	Physics (15 Qs.) & Chemistry (10 Qs.)
Mathematics (15 questions)	:	The questions of Mathematics will cover Arithmetic, Algebra, Mensuration, Trigonometry, Geometry and Statistics etc. You will have to give the answers only and not to solve.
G.K. (10 questions)	:	There will be questions on General Knowledge covering History, Geography, Constitution of India, UNO including Abbreviation and General Awareness etc.

Note: *In the beginning of the book, previous paper and model paper, have been given. The candidate would find it easy to understand the syllabus if he goes through them carefully.*

CONTENTS

Chemistry

GENERAL KNOWLEDGE 1-48

India

World

Previous Paper (Solved)

Indian Army Soldier (Technical Trade) Recruitment Examination

PART-I : GENERAL KNOWLEDGE

1. When was the Arjuna Award started?

A. 1952 B. 1961

C. 1965 D. None of these

2. The number of Union Territories in India is........... .

A. 7 B. 8

C. 9 D. None of these

3. Who drafted the Indian Constitution?

A. Pandit Jawaharlal Nehru

B. Dr. Bhim Rao Ambedkar

C. Sarojini Naidu

D. None of these

4. Which river is called 'Salt River'?

A. Godavari B. Luni

C. Krishna D. None of these

5. Where is the Birth place of Lord Mahavira?

A. Patliputra B. Vaishali

C. Kapilvastu D. None of these

6. The book 'Raghuvansha' was written by.............

A. Tulsi Das B. Kali Das

C. Soor Das D. Valmiki

7. Which two countries signed the Panchsheel agreement?

A. India-China B. India-Pak

C. India-Nepal D. Pak-China

8. Where the famous Hazratbal Mosque (Dargaha) is situated?

A. Shimla B. Srinagar

C. Chandigarh D. None of these

9. Which City is known as the 'Queen of Arabian Sea'?

A. Cochi B. Bengluru

C. Mumbai D. Pune

10. Where is the Tomb of Humayun?

A. Agra B. Delhi

C. Bhatinda D. Ludhiana

PART-II : PHYSICS

11. A red ribbon placed in green light will look:

A. Black B. Green

C. Orange D. None of these

12. Heat is transmitted from higher to lower temperature through actual mass motion of the molecules in:

A. Conduction B. Convection

C. Radiation D. All of these

13. ....absorbs the harmful UV radiation from the Sun and prevents it from reaching the earth.

A. Ozone layer
B. Exosphere
C. Magnetosphere
D. None of these

14. The SI unit of current is.......... .

A. Ampere B. Coulomb
C. Ohm D. Mho

15. The central point of the surface of the mirror is known as ....

A. Focus B. Pole
C. Radius D. None of these

16. What is the name of the fuel specially used in rockets?

A. Propellant B. Special Oil
C. Solar D. None of these

17. A pendulum is undergoing simple harmonic motion. The velocity of the bob in mean position is 'v'. If now its amplitude is doubled, keeping length same, its velocity in mean position will be:

A. $\frac{v}{2}$ B. $2v$
C. $4v$ D. None of these

18. What is the escape velocity from the earth's surface?

A. 11.2 km/sec B. 12.2 km/sec
C. 16 km/sec D. None of these

19. Which property do all bodies have while falling?

A. Gravity B. Acceleration
C. Speed D. None of these

20. The lightest metal is ....

A. Na B. Li
C. Mg D. None of these

21. An electric bulb is rated 220 V – 100 W. If it is operated at 110 V, then power consumed by it will be:

A. 100 W B. 25 W
C. 400 W D. None of these

22. Dyne/cm is the unit of ....

A. Surface Tension
B. Work
C. Force
D. None of these

23. The instrument for the accurate measurement of emf of a cell is ....

A. Voltmeter
B. Potentiometer
C. A slide wire bridge
D. None of these

24. Two resistances 1 ohm and 2 ohm are connected in parallel. The equivalent resistance of the combination is equal to ....

A. $\frac{1 \times 2}{1+2}$
B. $\frac{1+2}{1+2}$
C. $1 - 2$
D. None of these

25. Nuclear fusion occurs in ....

A. Hydrogen bomb
B. Neutron bomb
C. Nuclear reactor
D. None of these

PART-III : MATHEMATICS

26. The radius and height of a cylinder are in the ratio 5 : 7 and its volume is 550 cm^3. Find its radius:

A. 3 cm B. 4 cm

C. 5 cm D. 6 cm

27. The common root of the equation $x^2 - 5x + 6 = 0$ and $x^2 - 6x + 8 = 0$ is ....

A. $x + 3$ B. $x - 2$

C. $x + 4$ D. $x + 5$

28. The perimeter of a rhombus is 100 cm. If one of its diagonals is 14 cm, then the area of the rhombus is ....

A. 144 cm^2 B. 225 m^2

C. 336 cm^2 D. None of these

29. The diameter of a circle whose area is 3850 m^2 is:

A. 70 m B. 65 m

C. 75 m D. None of these

30. A polygon has 44 diagonals the number of its sides is ....

A. 9 B. 10

C. 11 D. None of these

31. If the radius of a cylinder is doubled, then how many times the volume will increase?

A. 2 B. 3

C. 8 D. None of these

32. A bicycle is purchased at ₹ 800 and sold at a profit of 12%. Its selling price is ....

A. ₹ 896 B. ₹ 704

C. ₹ 788 D. None of these

33. What is the 70% of 449?

A. 314.3 B. 333.3

C. 349.3 D. 339.3

34. $8 \times 6\left(\frac{2}{3} \div \frac{4}{9}\right) \times \frac{2}{3} = ?$

A. 42 B. 38

C. 43 D. None of these

35. 2 cubes each of volume 64 cm^3 are joined end to end. Find the surface area of the resulting cuboid:

A. 160 cm^2 B. 192 cm^2

C. 224 cm^2 D. None of these

36. Find the cost of papering the walls of a room 10 mtr long, 5 mtr breadth and 5 mtr height with paper 75 cms wide @ ₹ 10 per mtr.

A. ₹ 1000 B. ₹ 2000

C. ₹ 3000 D. ₹ 3500

37. The value of (cos 70° cos 40° + sin 70° sin 40°) is ....

A. $\frac{\sqrt{3}}{2}$ B. 1

C. cos 80° D. sin 80°

38. The angle of elevation to the top of a tower from a point on the ground, which is 30 m away from the foot of the tower, is 30°. Find the height of the tower?

A. $30\sqrt{3}$ B. 15 m

C. $15\sqrt{3}$ D. $20\sqrt{3}$

39. If simple interest is ₹ 36 @ of 3% per annum and time is 3 years, then find the Principal?

A. ₹ 400

B. ₹ 500

C. ₹ 600

D. None of these

40. Find the value of $\left(\frac{25}{81}\right)^{\frac{1}{2}}$:

A. $\frac{9}{25}$

B. $\frac{5}{9}$

C. $\frac{9}{5}$

D. $\frac{25}{9}$

PART-IV : CHEMISTRY

41. Isotopes are atoms showing same ....

A. Atomic Number

B. Atomic mass

C. Number of Neutrons

D. P_2O_5

42. The most stable configuration of n-butane is:

A. Skewed

B. Eclipsed

C. Staggered or anti

D. None of these

43. A crystal which is hard and has high melting point is ....

A. Covalent

B. Ionic

C. Metallic

D. Molecular

44. The compressibility factor for an ideal gas is ....

A. 1.5

B. 1.0

C. 2.0

D. ∞

45. In which orbital region is the probability for finding electron in nucleus finite:

A. 1*s*

B. 2*p*

C. 2*s*

D. 3*d*

46. Zinc oxide is called ....

A. Philosopher's wool

B. Epsom salt

C. Tartar emetic

D. Gobar gas

47. In a chemical equation what does the symbol (↑) signify?

A. Gas State

B. Liquid State

C. Solid State

D. Colloidal State

48. Considering the elements B, C, N, F and Si, the correct order of their non-metallic character is:

A. B > C > Si > N > F

B. Si > C > B > N > F

C. F > N > C > B > Si

D. None of these

49. Among metals, the poorest conductor of heat is............ .

A. Lead

B. Tin

C. Bismuth

D. Mercury

50. Which gas is used in extinguishing fire?

A. CO_2

B. NH_3

C. OK

D. None of these

ANSWERS

1	2	3	4	5	6	7	8	9	10
B	A	B	B	B	B	D	B	A	B
11	**12**	**13**	**14**	**15**	**16**	**17**	**18**	**19**	**20**
A	B	A	A	B	A	B	A	A	D
21	**22**	**23**	**24**	**25**	**26**	**27**	**28**	**29**	**30**
B	A	B	A	A	C	B	C	A	C
31	**32**	**33**	**34**	**35**	**36**	**37**	**38**	**39**	**40**
D	A	A	D	A	B	A	A	A	B
41	**42**	**43**	**44**	**45**	**46**	**47**	**48**	**49**	**50**
A	C	B	B	A	A	A	C	A	A

SOME SELECTED EXPLANATORY ANSWERS

15. The central point on the surface of the mirror is called the pole of the mirror. It is represented by the letter P. A pole of the mirror can be found by drawing a straight line from the centre C to the largest distance on the surface from C. Where the line cuts the mirror, you will find the pole P.

16. Rocket propellant is a material used by a rocket as, or to produce in a chemical reaction, the reaction mass (propulsive mass) that is ejected, typically with very high speed, from a rocket engine to produce thrust, and thus provide space craft propulsion. Each rocket type requires different kind of propellant: chemical rockets require propellants capable of undergoing exothermic chemical reactions, which provide the energy to accelerate the resulting gases through the nozzle. Thermal rockets instead use inert propellants of low molecular weight that are chemically compatible with the heating mechanism at high temperatures, while cold gas thrusters use pressurized, easily stored inert gases. Electric propulsion requires propellants that are easily ionized or made into plasma, and in the extreme case of nuclear pulse propulsion the propellant consists of debris from nuclear explosions.

21. We know that power of the electric bulb

$$(W) = \frac{\{\text{Volt}(V)\}^2}{\text{Resistance}(R)}$$

According to the question,

Rating of the bulb = 220 V – 100 W

$$\therefore \quad 100 = \frac{(220)^2}{R}$$

$$R = \frac{(220)^2}{100} = \frac{48400}{100}$$

$$= 484\ \Omega.$$

Again, when use voltage = 110 V

Then, $W = \frac{(110)^2}{484} = \frac{12100}{484}$

$= 25$ W.

24. $R_1 = 1\ \Omega$, $R_2 = 2\ \Omega$

When R_1 and R_2 are in parallel series then, total resultant Resistance

$= \frac{R_1 \times R_2}{R_1 + R_2} = \frac{1 \times 2}{1+2}$.

26. According to the question,

Radius of the cylinder = $5x$

Height of the cylinder = $7x$

Volume of cylinder $V = \pi r^2 h$

$$550 = \pi(5x)^2.(7x)$$

$$550 = 175x^3.\pi$$

$$x^3 = \frac{550}{175\pi}$$

$$x^3 = \frac{550 \times 7}{175 \times 22}$$

$$x = 1$$

Radius of the cylinder $5x = 5$ cm.

27. For common roots

$$x^2 - 5x + 6 = x^2 - 6x + 8$$

$$6x - 5x = 8 - 6$$

$$x = 2$$

Hence, common root = $x - 2$.

28. Perimeter of the rhombus

= 4 × length of the side

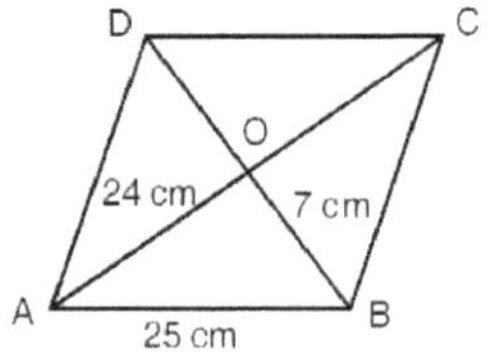

$\therefore$ Length of the side = $\frac{\text{Perimeter}}{4}$

$= \frac{100}{4} = 25$ cm.

From ΔAOB, $\angle AOB = 90°$

(Diagonals of rhombus bisect each other at right angle)

$\therefore \quad AO = \sqrt{(AB)^2 - (OB)^2}$

$= \sqrt{(25)^2 - \left(\frac{14}{2}\right)^2}$

$= \sqrt{576} = 24$ cm.

Diagonal $AC = 2 \times AO$

$= 2 \times 24 = 48$ cm.

Area of the rhombus

$= \frac{1}{2} \times$ Product of diagonals

$= \frac{1}{2} \times 14 \times 48 = 336\ \text{cm}^2$

29. Area of the circle

$$A = \pi\left(\frac{d}{2}\right)^2$$

Where, d = diameter of the circle

Then, $d = 2\left(\frac{A}{\pi}\right)^{\frac{1}{2}}$

$= 2\left(\frac{3850}{22} \times 7\right)^{\frac{1}{2}}$

$= 2 \times 35 = 70$ cm.

30. Number of diagonals in n sides of polygon = ${}^nC_2 - n$

Here, $\frac{n(n-1)}{2} - n = 44$

$n^2 - n - 2n = 88$

$n^2 - 3n - 88 = 0$

$(n - 11)(n + 8) = 0$

$\therefore \quad n = 11.$

31. Volume of cylinder

$V = \pi r^2 h$

$V \propto (r)^2$

When radius is double then volume will increase four times

32. S.P. = C.P. × (1 + Profit %)

$= 800 \times \left(1 + \frac{12}{100}\right)$

= 800 × 1.12 = ₹ 896.

33. $449 \times \frac{70}{100} = 314.3$.

34. $8 \times 6\left(\frac{2}{3} \div \frac{4}{9}\right) \times \frac{2}{3}$

$= 8 \times 6\left(\frac{2}{3} \div \frac{9}{4}\right) \times \frac{2}{3} = 8 \times 6\left(\frac{3}{2}\right) \times \frac{2}{3}$

= 8 × 6 = 48.

35. Length of each side of cube

$= \sqrt[3]{64} = 4$ cm.

When two cubes joint together then Length of the cuboid = 8 cm.

Total surface area of cuboid

$= 2(l \times b + b \times h + h \times l)$

= 2 (8 × 4 + 4 × 4 + 4 × 8)

= 160 cm^2

36. Cost of paper

$= \frac{2(10 \times 5 + 5 \times 5)}{75} \times 100 \times 10$

= ₹ 2000.

37. We know that

cos A . cos B + sin A . sin B

= cos (A – B)

Here, A = 70°,

B = 40°

$\therefore$ cos (70 – 40) = cos 30° = $\frac{\sqrt{3}}{2}$.

38. Height of the tower = AB

Angle of elevation ∠ACB = 30°

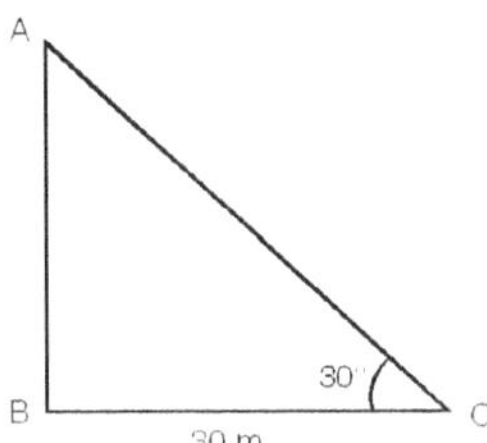

From ΔABC,

$\tan 30° = \frac{AB}{BC}$

$\frac{1}{\sqrt{3}} = \frac{AB}{30}$

$\therefore \quad AB = \frac{30}{\sqrt{3}}$

$= 10\sqrt{3}$ m.

39. From Formulae $P = \frac{\text{S.I.} \times 100}{r \times t}$

$= \frac{36 \times 100}{3 \times 3}$

= ₹ 400.

40. $\left(\frac{25}{81}\right)^{\frac{1}{2}} = \left(\frac{5 \times 5}{9 \times 9}\right)^{\frac{1}{2}}$

$= \left(\left(\frac{5}{9}\right)^2\right)^{\frac{1}{2}} = \frac{5}{9}$.

Model Test Paper (Solved)

Time : 60 Minutes *Max. Marks : 100*

Note: *Attempt all questions.*

MATHEMATICS

1. Complete the following series:
3, 6, 12, 15, 30
(*a*) 33 (*b*) 35 (*c*) 38 (*d*) 42

2. A vendor sells 10 toffees for a rupee, gaining thereby 20%. How many did he buy for a rupee?
(*a*) 12 (*b*) 8 (*c*) 14 (*d*) 11

3. A man spends 35% of his income on house rent, 75% of the remaining on other items, what percentage of income does he save?
(*a*) 16.25 (*b*) 48.75
(*c*) 34.50 (*d*) None of these

4. A, B and C are employed to do a piece of work for ₹ 529. A and C are supposed to finish 19/23 of the work together. How much shall be paid to B?
(*a*) ₹ 72 (*b*) ₹ 80
(*c*) ₹ 92 (*d*) ₹ 98

5. A cylindrical piece of metal of radius 2 cm and height 6 cm is shaped into a cone of same radius. The height of the cone is:
(*a*) 16 cm (*b*) 12 cm
(*c*) 18 cm (*d*) 24 cm

6. The circumference of two concentric circles forming a ring are 88 cm and 66 cm respectively. The width of the ring is:
(*a*) 10.8 cm (*b*) 3.5 cm (*c*) 5.3 cm (*d*) 7 cm

7. The difference between simple interest and compound interest on ₹ 1200 for one year at 10% per annum reckoned half-yearly is:
(*a*) ₹ 13.30 (*b*) ₹ 8.60 (*c*) ₹ 3 (*d*) ₹ 9.30

8. A boy goes to school from village at 3 km/hr and return 2 km/hr. If he takes 5 hours in all, the distance between the village and the school is:
(*a*) 6 km (*b*) 8 km (*c*) 9 km (*d*) 5 km

9. The value of $\sum_{j=0}^{n}\left({}^{4n+1}C_j + {}^{4n+1}C_{2n-j}\right)$ *is*

(*a*) $2^{4n} + {}^{4n+1}C_n$

(*b*) 2^{4n+1}

(*c*) $2^{4n+1} + {}^{4n+1}C_n$

(*d*) 2^{4n}

10. If $A = \{(x, y) \mid x^2 + y^2 \leq 4\}$ and $B = \{(x, y) \mid (x-3)^2 + y^2 \leq 4\}$ and the point $P\left(a, a-\frac{1}{2}\right)$ belongs to the set B – A then the set of possible real values of a is:

(*a*) $\left(\frac{1+\sqrt{31}}{4}, \frac{7+\sqrt{7}}{4}\right)$

(*b*) $\left[\frac{7-\sqrt{7}}{4}, \frac{1+\sqrt{31}}{4}\right]$

(*c*) $\left(\frac{1-\sqrt{31}}{4}, \frac{7-\sqrt{7}}{4}\right)$

(*d*) None of these

11. If the first and the $(2n-1)^{\text{th}}$ terms of an AP, a GP and an HP are equal and their n^{th} terms are a, b, and c respectively then:

(*a*) $a = b = c$

(*b*) $a \geq b \geq c$

(*c*) $a + c = b$

(*d*) $ac - b^2 = 0$

12. The solution set of $\frac{x^2 - 3x + 4}{x+1} > 1, x \in \mathrm{R}$, is:

(*a*) $(3, +\infty)$

(*b*) $(-1, 1) \cup (3, +\infty)$

(*c*) $[-1, 3]$

(*d*) None of these

13. If α, β be two complex numbers then $|\alpha|^2 + |\beta|^2$ is equal to

(*a*) $\frac{1}{2}\left(|\alpha+\beta|^2 - |\alpha-\beta|^2\right)$

(*b*) $\frac{1}{2}\left(|\alpha+\beta|^2 + |\alpha-\beta|^2\right)$

(*c*) $|\alpha+\beta|^2 + |\alpha-\beta|^2$

(*d*) None of these

14. In a polygon no three diagonals are concurrent. If the total number of points of intersection of diagonals interior to the polygon be 70 then the number of diagonals of the polygon is:

(*a*) 20

(*b*) 28

(*c*) 8

(*d*) None of these

15. The value of the determinat $\begin{vmatrix} bc & ca & ab \\ p & q & r \\ 1 & 1 & 1 \end{vmatrix}$, where a, b, c are the pth, q^{th} and r^{th} terms of an HP, is:

(*a*) $ap + bq + cr$ (*b*) $(a + b + c)(p + q + r)$
(*c*) Zero (*d*) None of these

GENERAL KNOWLEDGE

16. 'Dispur' is the capital of the Indian State of:
(*a*) Arunachal Pradesh (*b*) Tripura
(*c*) Assam (*d*) Manipur

17. The term of a member of the Rajya Sabha is:
(*a*) 5 years (*b*) 6 years
(*c*) 4 years (*d*) None of these

18. Knesset is the name of Parliament of:
(*a*) Bosnia (*b*) Japan
(*c*) Pakistan (*d*) Israel

19. The Central Rice Research Institute (CRRI) is located at:
(*a*) Kohima (*b*) Agra (*c*) Cuttak (*d*) Nasik

20. Which blood group is known as Universal donor?
(*a*) AB (*b*) A (*c*) O (*d*) B

21. Operation Flood pertains to:
(*a*) Construction of dams (*b*) Fisheries development
(*c*) Narcotics smuggling (*d*) Dairy product

22. Who has written 'My Country : My Life"?
(*a*) Jaswant Singh (*b*) L.K. Advani
(*c*) Kuldip Nayar (*d*) Sonia Gandhi

23. Inflation is measured through:
(*a*) Price Index
(*b*) Bank rate
(*c*) Money circulated by the Reserve Bank
(*d*) None of these

24. Gautam Buddha's Mahapariniravana or Shedding of his body took place in:
(*a*) Kushinagar (*b*) Sarnath
(*c*) Lumbini (*d*) Gaya

25. When was the Nobel Prize started?

(*a*) 1905 (*b*) 1934

(*c*) 1900 (*d*) 1901

PHYSICS

26. Einstein has given the formula, $E = mc^2$ where c stands for:

(*a*) velocity of light (*b*) velocity of sound

(*c*) a constant (*d*) a curvature

27. Devices used to change the voltage of alternating current are:

(*a*) Transformers (*b*) Solenoids

(*c*) Galvanometer (*d*) Dynamo

28. What happens when you blink?

(*a*) the iris changes size (*b*) the cornea is washed

(*c*) your sight is focussed (*d*) your sight is rested

29. The sky is blue because:

(*a*) there is more blue light in the sunlight

(*b*) scattering of sunlight by air molecules in the atmosphere

(*c*) scattering of sunlight by polution in the atmosphere

(*d*) other colours are absorbed by heavenly bodies

30. The purpose of fuse wire in electric installations is:

(*a*) to prevent the building from damage when high voltage current flows

(*b*) to protect the building from lightning discharge

(*c*) to save electricity

(*d*) None of these

31. Given a tumbler full of water upto its brim and also having a piece of ice floating inside:

(*a*) will the water level fall

(*b*) will the water level overflow

(*c*) will the water level remain the same

(*d*) will the water disappear

32. In the pressure cooker, the vegetable boils quickly because:

(*a*) steam is good for all digestion

(*b*) vegetables get crushed under the impact of steam

(*c*) pressure increases due to the steam and vegetable boil faster

(*d*) None of these

33. A far-sighted object can be seen with the help of:
(*a*) Periscope (*b*) Microscope
(*c*) Binoculars (*d*) None of these

34. Microscope is used to:
(*a*) identify distant object (*b*) magnify very minute particles
(*c*) destroy bacteria (*d*) None of these

35. One mole of CO_2 contains:
(*a*) 6.02×10^{23} atoms of C (*b*) 6.02×10^{23} atoms of O
(*c*) 18.1×10^{23} molecules of CO_2 (*d*) None of these

36. Choose the correct answer.
Naphthalene can be easily purified by:
(*a*) sublimation (*b*) crystallisation
(*c*) distillation (*d*) extraction with a solvent

37. Refining of petroleum involves the process of:
(*a*) simple distillation (*b*) steam distillation
(*c*) distillation under reduced pressure (*d*) fractional distillation

38. If two compounds have the same empirical formula but different molecular formulae they must have:
(*a*) different percentage composition (*b*) different molecular weight
(*c*) same viscosity (*d*) same vapour density

39. Which of the following fertilisers has the highest nitrogen percentage?
(*a*) Ammonium sulphate (*b*) Calcium cyanamide
(*c*) Urea (*d*) Ammonium nitrate

40. The property which serves as a criterion of purity of an organic compound is:
(*a*) Solubility in water (*b*) Melting point
(*c*) Density (*d*) Crystalline nature

CHEMISTRY

41. Which of the following elements has a definite volume but no shape?
(*a*) Hg (*b*) Fe (*c*) Sn (*d*) Br

42. Which of the following is the strongest acid?
(*a*) H_2SO_4 (*b*) $HClO_4$ (*c*) HNO_2 (*d*) HBr

43. *Kajal* is the form of:
(*a*) coke (*b*) charcoal
(*c*) carbon-black (*d*) asphalt

44. Which one of the following gas will turn the lime water milky?
(*a*) CO_2 (*b*) CO (*c*) N_2 (*d*) Cl_2

45. Diamond and graphite are:
(*a*) isotopes (*b*) allotropes (*c*) coal (*d*) charcoal

46. Washing soda is:
(*a*) sodium sulphate (*b*) sodium carbonate
(*c*) calcium carbonate (*d*) sodium bicarbonate

47. Which of the following metals has very low melting point and melts even in hand?
(*a*) Sodium (*b*) Gallium (*c*) Potassium (*d*) Graphite

48. The unwanted material in an ore is known as:
(*a*) flux (*b*) gangue (*c*) slag (*d*) mineral

49. Hydrogen gas is not liberated when which of the following metal is added to dil HCl?
(*a*) Ag (*b*) Mg (*c*) Zn (*d*) Sn

50. In the brown ring test, the brown colour of the ring is due to:
(*a*) ferric nitrate (*b*) ferrous nitrate
(*c*) a mixture of NO and NO_2 (*d*) nitrosoferrous sulphate

EXPLANATORY ANSWERS

Mathematics

1. (*a*) 33, the sequence in series is + 3, × 2, + 3 × 2 etc.

2. (*a*) S.P. of 10 toffees = Re. 1
Gain = 20%

$$\therefore \text{ C.P. of 10 toffees} = \text{Re.} \left(\frac{100}{120} \times 1\right) = \text{Re. } \frac{5}{6}$$

$$\because \text{ Re. } \frac{5}{6} \text{ is the C.P. of 10 toffees}$$

$$\therefore \text{ Re 1 is the C.P. of } 10 \times \frac{6}{5} = 12$$

Therefore, he bought 12 toffees for a rupee.

3. (*a*) $\text{House rent} = \frac{35}{100}x = \frac{7x}{20}$

$$\text{Remaining} = \left(x - \frac{7x}{20}\right) = \frac{13x}{20}$$

Other expenditures = $\left(\frac{75}{100}\times\frac{13x}{20}\right)=\frac{39x}{80}$

Saving = $\left(\frac{13x}{20}-\frac{39}{80}\right)=\frac{13x}{80}$

$\therefore$ Saving per cent = $\left(\frac{13x}{80}\times\frac{1}{x}\times 100\right)=\frac{65}{4}\%=16.25\%$

4. *(c)* Work done by

B = $\left(1-\frac{19}{23}\right)=\frac{4}{23}$

$\therefore (A+C):B=\frac{19}{23}:\frac{4}{23}=19:4$

$\therefore$ B's share = Rs. $\left[529\times\frac{4}{23}\right]$ = Rs. 92

5. *(c)* Let the height of cone be h cm. $\pi\times 2^2\times 6=\frac{1}{3}\pi\times 2^2\times h$

$\Rightarrow$ h = 18 cm

6. *(b)* Let, inner radius = r and outer radius = R cm

Then $2\times\frac{22}{7}\times R=88\Rightarrow R=\left(88\times\frac{7}{44}\right)=14$ cm

Again, $2\times\frac{22}{7}\times r=66\Rightarrow r=\left(66\times\frac{7}{44}\right)=\frac{21}{2}$ cm = 10.5 cm

$\therefore$ Width of the ring = (14 – 10.5) cm = 3.5 cm

7. *(c)* S.I. = Rs. $\left(\frac{1200\times 10\times 1}{100}\right)$ = Rs. 120

C.I. = Rs. $\left[1200\times\left(1+\frac{5}{100}\right)^2-1200\right]$ = Rs. 123

$\therefore$ (C.I.) – (S.I.) = Rs. (123 – 120) = Rs. 3

8. *(a)* Let the required distance be x km

Then, $\frac{x}{3}+\frac{x}{2}=5$ or, $2x+3x=30$ or, $x=6$ km

9. *(a)* Value $= \left({}^{4n+1}C_0 + {}^{4n+1}C_1 + \ldots + {}^{4n+1}C_n\right) + \left({}^{4n+1}C_{2n} + {}^{4n+1}C_{2n-1} + \ldots + {}^{4n+1}C_n\right)$

$= \left({}^{4n+1}C_0 + {}^{4n+1}C_1 + \ldots + {}^{4n+1}C_{2n}\right) + {}^{4n+1}C_n = 2^{4n} + {}^{4n+1}Cn.$

10. *(b)* P $\in$ B but P $\notin$ A.

So, $a^2 + \left(a - \frac{1}{2}\right)^2 > 4$ and $(a-3)^2 + \left(a - \frac{1}{2}\right)^2 \leq 4.$

$\therefore$ We get $8a^2 - 4a - 15 > 0$ ...(1)

$8a^2 - 28a + 21 \leq 0$ ...(2)

Solving (1) and (2), we get the set of possible values of a.

11. *(d)* n^{th} term is the middle term in each case. So, a, b, c are the AM, GM, HM respectively of the same two numbers. For any two numbers AM, GM and HM are in GP.

12. *(b)* $\frac{x^2 - 3x + 4}{x+1} > 1$

$\Rightarrow \frac{x^2 - 4x + 3}{x+1} > 0$

$\Rightarrow (x-1)(x-3)(x+1) > 0, x \neq 1$

{multiplying by $(x+1)^2$}

$\therefore$ From general sign scheme:

(–) (+) (–) (+)
–1 1 3

{$\because$ For $x = 0$, expression > 0}

13. *(b)* $|\alpha + \beta|^2 = (\alpha + \beta)\left(\overline{\alpha + \beta}\right)$

$= (\alpha + \beta)\left(\overline{\alpha} + \overline{\beta}\right) = \alpha\overline{\alpha} + \beta\overline{\beta} + \alpha\overline{\beta} + \overline{\alpha}\beta = |\alpha|^2 + |\beta|^2 + \alpha\overline{\beta} + \overline{\alpha}\beta$

$\Rightarrow |\alpha = \beta|^2 = (\alpha - \beta)\left(\overline{\alpha} - \overline{\beta}\right)$

$= \alpha\overline{\alpha} + \beta\overline{\beta} - \alpha\overline{\beta}\ \overline{\alpha}\beta = |\alpha|^2 + |\beta|^2 - \alpha\overline{\beta} - \overline{\alpha}\beta$

14. *(a)* A selection of four vertices of the polygon gives an interior intersection.

$\therefore$ The number of side $= n$

$\Rightarrow {}^nC_4 = 70 \Rightarrow n(n-1)(n-2)(n-3)$

$= 24 \times 70 = 8 \times 7 \times 6 \times 5$

$\therefore n = 8$

$\therefore$ The number of diagonals $= {}^8C_2 - 8 = 20$

15. *(c)* $\Delta = abc\begin{vmatrix} \frac{1}{a} & \frac{1}{b} & \frac{1}{c} \\ p & q & r \\ 1 & 1 & 1 \end{vmatrix} = abc\begin{vmatrix} x+(p-1)d & x+(q-1)d & x+(r-1)d \\ p-1 & q-1 & r-1 \\ 1 & 1 & 1 \end{vmatrix}$

$= \quad abc\begin{vmatrix} x & x & x \\ p-1 & q-1 & r-1 \\ 1 & 1 & 1 \end{vmatrix} = abc\begin{vmatrix} 1 & 1 & 1 \\ p-1 & q-1 & r-1 \\ 1 & 1 & 1 \end{vmatrix} = 0$

$= \quad (R \rightarrow R_1 - d \times R_2)$

General Knowledge

16	**17**	**18**	**19**	**20**	**21**	**22**	**23**	**24**	**25**
(c)	*(b)*	*(d)*	*(c)*	*(c)*	*(d)*	*(b)*	*(a)*	*(a)*	*(d)*

Physics

26	**27**	**28**	**29**	**30**	**31**	**32**	**33**	**34**	**35**
(a)	*(a)*	*(b)*	*(b)*	*(a)*	*(c)*	*(c)*	*(c)*	*(b)*	*(a)*
36	**37**	**38**	**39**	**40**					
(a)	*(d)*	*(b)*	*(c)*	*(b)*					

Chemistry

41	**42**	**43**	**44**	**45**	**46**	**47**	**48**	**49**	**50**
(a)	*(a)*	*(b)*	*(a)*	*(b)*	*(b)*	*(b)*	*(b)*	*(a)*	*(d)*

MATHEMATICS

ARITHMETIC

1

Number System

The development of the number system started with natural numbers. These are generally known as counting numbers.

Natural Numbers

Numbers which start from 1 are known as natural numbers. It is denoted by N. The smallest natural number is 1. It is written as, N = {1, 2, 3, ..., ∞}

Whole Numbers

A number which starts from zero (0) is known as whole number. It is denoted by W. It is written as, W = {0, 1, 2, 3, ..., ∞}

Integers

Natural numbers along with 0 and their negatives are known as integers. It is denoted by I. It is written as, I = {..., –4, –3, –2, –1, 0, 1, 2, 3, 4, ...}

Even Numbers

A number which is divisible by 2 is known as even numbers. Such as, 2, 4, 6, 10, 12, 128, 432 etc.

Odd Numbers

A number which is not divisible by 2 is known as odd numbers: Such as, 1, 3, 5, 7, 9, 11, 13, 21, 29, 123 etc.

Prime Numbers

A number which is divided by itself is known as prime numbers. The smallest prime number is 2. Such as, 2, 3, 5, 7, 11, 13, 17, 19, 23, ... etc.

The formulae given below are quite useful for quick multiplication:

(*i*) $(a + b)^2 = a^2 + 2ab + b^2$

(*ii*) $(a - b)^2 = a^2 - 2ab + b^2$

(*iii*) $a^2 - b^2 = (a + b)(a - b)$

(*iv*) $a^2 + b^2 = (a + b)^2 - 2ab$

(*v*) $(a + b)^3 = a^3 + b^3 + 3ab(a + b)$

(vi) $(a-b)^3 = a^3 - b^3 - 3ab(a-b)$
(vii) $a^3 + b^3 = (a+b)(a^2 - ab + b^2)$
(viii) $a^3 - b^3 = (a-b)(a^2 + ab + b^2)$

Example : Simplify the following : $\dfrac{261 \times 261 \times 261 - 77 \times 77 \times 77}{261 \times 261 + 261 \times 77 + 77 \times 77}$

Solution : $\dfrac{261 \times 261 \times 261 - 77 \times 77 \times 77}{261 \times 261 + 261 \times 77 + 77 \times 77}$

Let $261 = a$
and $77 = b$

$$\therefore \quad \frac{a^3 - b^3}{a^2 + ab + b^2} = \frac{(a-b)(a^2+ab+b^2)}{(a^2+ab+b^2)} = a - b$$

$$\therefore \quad 261 - 77 = 184.$$

MULTIPLE CHOICE QUESTIONS

1. The face value of 8 in the numeral 458926 is:
A. 8000 B. 8 C. 1000 D. 458000

2. $106 \times 106 + 94 \times 94 = x$, the value of x is:
A. 21032 B. 20032 C. 23032 D. 20072

3. If $m \times 48 = 173 \times 240$ then the value of m is:
A. 545 B. 685 C. 865 D. 495

4. $\left(1-\frac{1}{3}\right)\left(1-\frac{1}{4}\right)\left(1-\frac{1}{5}\right)\ldots\left(1-\frac{1}{n}\right) = x$, then the value of x is:
A. $\frac{1}{n}$ B. $\frac{2}{n}$ C. $\frac{2(n-1)}{n}$ D. $\frac{2}{n(n+1)}$

5. When simplified the product $\left(2-\frac{1}{3}\right)\left(2-\frac{3}{5}\right)\left(2-\frac{5}{7}\right)\ldots\left(2-\frac{997}{999}\right)$ is equal to:
A. $\frac{5}{999}$ B. $\frac{1001}{999}$ C. $\frac{1001}{3}$ D. None of these

6. Which number should replace both the asterisks in $\left(\frac{*}{21}\right) \times \left(\frac{*}{189}\right) = 1$?
A. 21 B. 63 C. 3969 D. 147

7. In a division sum, the divisor is 12 times the quotient and 5 times the remainder. If the remainder be 48, then the dividend is:

A. 240 B. 576 C. 4800 D. 4848

8. What least number must be subtracted from 1294 so that the remainder when divided by 9, 11, 13 will leave in each case the same remainder 6?

A. 0 B. 1 C. 2 D. 3

9. If $\sqrt{\left(1+\frac{27}{169}\right)} = \left(1+\frac{x}{13}\right)$, then the value of x is:

A. 1 B. 3 C. 5 D. 7

10. If $\frac{x}{y} = \frac{3}{4}$, then the value of $\left(\frac{6}{7}+\frac{y-x}{y+x}\right)$ equals:

A. $\frac{5}{7}$ B. $1\frac{1}{7}$ C. 1 D. 2

11. The largest natural number by which the product of three consecutive even natural numbers is always divisible, is:

A. 16 B. 24 C. 48 D. 96

12. The least number of five digits which is exactly divisible by 12, 15 and 18 is:

A. 10080 B. 10800 C. 18000 D. 81000

13. The least number which when divided by 8, 9, 12, 16 and 20 leaves the same remainder 1 in each case is:

A. 712 B. 271 C. 721 D. 720

14. The value of 0.8693 + 0.092 + 0.87 + 0.4 equals:

A. 2.3213 B. 2.2331 C. 3.2313 D. 2.2313

15. The prime numbers between 1 to 50 are:

A. 8 B. 12 C. 15 D. 10

16. If $\frac{a}{b} = \frac{4}{3}$, then $\frac{3a+2b}{3a-2b}$ equals:

A. 6 B. 3 C. 5 D. –1

17. If $\sqrt{3^n} = 81$, then n equals:

A. 2 B. 4 C. 6 D. 8

18. If $\sqrt{\frac{x}{196}} = \frac{72}{56}$, then x equals:

A. 18 B. 14 C. 324 D. 212

19. If $a \times 48 = 173 \times 240$, then the value of a is:
A. 545 B. 685 C. 865 D. 495

20. If $\frac{80}{x} = \frac{x}{20}$, then the value of x is:
A. 40 B. 400 C. 800 D. 1600

21. If 'x' and 'y' are both odd numbers, which of the following numbers must be an even number?
A. $x + y$ B. $x \times y$ C. $xy + 2$ D. $2x + y$

22. 'a' is less than 'b' then, which of the following numbers is greater than 'a' and less than 'b'?
A. $\frac{a+b}{2}$ B. $\frac{ab}{2}$ C. $b^2 - a^2$ D. ab

23. $a + b + c + d$ is a positive number, a minimum of 'x' of the number a, b, c and d must be positive, where 'x' is equal to—
A. –1 B. 2 C. 3 D. 4

24. There are four numbers A, B, C and D. Average of the first three i.e., A, B and C is 15 and that of B, C and D is 16. If the last number, i.e., D is 19, then the first number is—
A. 15 B. 16 C. 17 D. 18

25. Think of a number, divide it by 9 and add 9 to it, if the result is 27, the number is—
A. 18 B. 21 C. 100 D. 162

26. Of the three numbers, the first is twice the second and thrice the third. If the average of three is 22, the three numbers are—
A. 12, 18, 36 B. 18, 12, 36 C. 36, 12, 18 D. 36, 18, 12

27. The number which when added to itself 10 times gives 264. The number is—
A. 20 B. 22 C. 24 D. 26

28. If a person is standing on the sixth number in the queue from both the ends, the total persons in the queue are—
A. 9 B. 11 C. 12 D. 13

29. A number 'x' when multiplied by 5 and added to three times its own gives 64, the number is—
A. 8 B. 12 C. 14 D. 18

30. If the sum of two numbers 'x' and 'y' is equal to twice the first number, the second number 'y' is—
A. $> x$ B. $< x$
C. $= x$ D. negative number

ANSWERS

1	2	3	4	5	6	7	8	9	10
B	D	C	B	C	B	D	B	A	C
11	**12**	**13**	**14**	**15**	**16**	**17**	**18**	**19**	**20**
C	A	C	D	C	B	D	C	C	A
21	**22**	**23**	**24**	**25**	**26**	**27**	**28**	**29**	**30**
A	A	A	B	D	D	C	B	A	C

EXPLANATORY ANSWERS

1. The face value of 8 in the numeral 458926 is 8.

3. $\because m = \dfrac{173 \times 240}{48} = 865.$

7. Let quotient = Q and remainder = R
Then, divisor = 12Q = 5R   Now, R = 48
$\Rightarrow$ 12Q = 5 × 48 $\Rightarrow$ Q = 20 $\therefore$ Dividend = (20 × 240 + 48) = 4848

11. It is 2 × 4 × 6 = 48

15. The prime numbers between 1 to 50 are 2, 3, 5, 7, 11, 13, 17, 19, 23, 29, 31, 37, 41, 43, 47.
Hence, there are 15 prime numbers between 1 to 50.

17. $\because \sqrt{3^n} = 81 \Rightarrow 3^{\frac{n}{2}} = 3^4 \Rightarrow \dfrac{n}{2} = 4 \Rightarrow n = 8.$

20. $\because \dfrac{80}{x} = \dfrac{x}{20} \Rightarrow x^2 = 80 \times 20 \Rightarrow x^2 = 1600 \Rightarrow x = 40$

21. Since the sum of two odd numbers is always even number, therefore, $x + y$ is even number.

22. Average of two different numbers is always between the two numbers.

23. If all numbers were not positive, then the sum could not be positive. If a, b, c were all – 1 and d were 5, then $a + b + c + d$ would be positive, so *(b)*, *(c)*, *(d)* are incorrect.

25. Let the number is x.

$\therefore \dfrac{x}{9} + 9 = 27$ or, $\dfrac{x}{9} = 27 - 9 = 18$ $\therefore x = 18 \times 9 = 162.$

29. $5 \times x + 3x = 64 \Rightarrow 8x = 64$ $\therefore x = \dfrac{64}{8} = 8$

30. $x + y = 2x$ $\therefore y = 2x - x = x$

❖ ❖ ❖

2

HCF and LCM

Highest Common Factor

The HCF of two or more than two numbers is the greatest number that divides each of them exactly. The highest common factor is also known as Greatest Common Divisor or Greatest Common Measure.

There are two methods of determining the HCF of two or more numbers.

(*i*) HCF by Factorization method

(*ii*) HCF by Division method.

HCF by Factorization Method

Express each one of the given number as the product of prime factors. Now choose common factors and take the product of these factors to obtain the required HCF.

EXAMPLE : Find the HCF of 126, 396 and 5400.

SOLUTION :

$$126 = 2 \times 3 \times 3 \times 7$$
$$396 = 2 \times 2 \times 3 \times 3 \times 11$$
$$5400 = 2 \times 2 \times 2 \times 3 \times 3 \times 3 \times 5 \times 5$$

Common factors are 2, 3 and 3.

Hence, the HCF = $2 \times 3 \times 3 = 18$.

HCF by Division Method

Divide the larger number by the smaller one. Now, divide the divisor by the remainder. Repeat the process of dividing the preceding divisor by the remainder last obtained till zero is obtained as remainder. The last divisor is the required HCF.

EXAMPLE: Find the HCF of 48, 168 and 324.

SOLUTION: Firstly, we find the HCF of 48 and 168.

```
48) 1 6 8 (3
   -1 4 4
   ------
   24) 4 8 (2
      - 4 8
      -----
          0
```

Thus, HCF of 48 and 168 = 24.

Now, HCF of 24 and 324

```
24) 3 2 4 (13
   - 2 4
   -----
       8 4
       7 2
   -------
       1 2) 2 4 (2
            2 4
           -----
             0
```

Hence, HCF of 48, 168 and 324 = 12

Lowest Common Multiple

The LCM of two or more numbers is the lowest or least number which is exactly divisible by each of them.

LCM by Factorization

Resolve each one of the given numbers into a product of prime factors. Then LCM is the product of highest powers of all the factors.

EXAMPLE: Find the LCM of 72, 189 and 1026.

SOLUTION: $72 = 2^3 \times 3^2$

$189 = 3^3 \times 7$

and $1026 = 2 \times 3^3 \times 19$

$\therefore$ $\text{LCM} = 2^3 \times 3^3 \times 7 \times 19$

$= 8 \times 27 \times 7 \times 19 = 28728$

FORMULA

Product of two numbers = HCF × LCM.

$\text{LCM} = \dfrac{\text{Product of numbers}}{\text{HCF}}$ $\text{HCF} = \dfrac{\text{Product of numbers}}{\text{LCM}}$

$\text{First number} = \dfrac{\text{LCM} \times \text{HCF}}{\text{2nd number}}$ $\text{2nd number} = \dfrac{\text{LCM} \times \text{HCF}}{\text{First number}}$

HCF and LCM of Fractions

(*i*) $\text{HCF} = \dfrac{\text{HCF of numerators}}{\text{LCM of denominators}}$ (*ii*) $\text{LCM} = \dfrac{\text{LCM of numerators}}{\text{HCF of denominators}}$

MULTIPLE CHOICE QUESTIONS

1. HCF of 1485 and 4356 is:

A. 189 B. 89 C. 99 D. 83

2. LCM of 18, 24, 42, 63 is:

A. 302 B. 604 C. 504 D. 404

3. Which of the following fractions is the greatest of all? $\frac{7}{8}, \frac{6}{7}, \frac{4}{5}, \frac{5}{6}$

A. $\frac{6}{7}$ B. $\frac{4}{5}$ C. $\frac{5}{6}$ D. $\frac{7}{8}$

4. Which of the following is in ascending order?

A. $\frac{5}{7}, \frac{7}{8}, \frac{9}{11}$ B. $\frac{5}{7}, \frac{9}{11}, \frac{7}{8}$ C. $\frac{7}{8}, \frac{5}{7}, \frac{9}{11}$ D. $\frac{9}{11}, \frac{7}{8}, \frac{5}{7}$

5. HCF of three numbers is 12. If they be in the ratio 1 : 2 : 3, the numbers are:
A. 12, 24, 36 B. 10, 20, 30 C. 5, 10, 15 D. 4, 8, 12

6. The largest natural number which exactly divides the product of any four consecutive natural numbers is:
A. 6 B. 12 C. 24 D. 120

7. The traffic lights at three different road crossings change after every 48 seconds, 72 seconds and 108 seconds respectively. If they all change simultaneously at 8 : 20 : 00 hrs; then they will again change simultaneously at:
A. 8 : 27 : 12 hrs B. 8 : 27 : 24 hrs
C. 8 : 27 : 36 hrs D. 8 : 27 : 48 hrs

8. The HCF of two numbers is 16 and their LCM is 160. If one of the number is 32, then the other number is:
A. 48 B. 80 C. 96 D. 112

9. The HCF of two numbers is 12 and their difference is also 12. The numbers are:
A. 66, 78 B. 70, 82 C. 94, 106 D. 84, 96

10. The largest number which exactly divides 210, 315, 147 and 161 is:
A. 3 B. 7 C. 21 D. 4410

11. The least perfect square number which is divisible by 3, 4, 5, 6 and 8 is:
A. 900 B. 1200 C. 2500 D. 3600

12. The smallest number which is divisible by 12, 15 and 20 is a perfect square, is:
A. 400 B. 900 C. 1600 D. 3600

13. The sum of two numbers is 216 and their HCF is 27. The numbers are:
A. 54, 162 B. 108, 108 C. 27, 189 D. None of these

14. The HCF and LCM of two numbers are 44 and 264 respectively. If the first number is divided by 2, the quotient is 44. The other number is:
A. 33 B. 66 C. 132 D. 264

15. The number of prime factors in $2^{222} \times 3^{333} \times 5^{555}$ is:
A. 3 B. 1107 C. 1110 D. 1272

16. The number of prime factors in the expression $(6)^{10} \times (7)^{17} \times (11)^{27}$ is:
A. 54 B. 64 C. 71 D. 81

17. Three measuring rods are 64 cm, 80 cm and 96 cm in length. The least length of cloth that can be measured exact number of times using any one of the above rod is:
A. 0.96 m B. 19.20 m C. 9.60 m D. 96.00 m

18. The product of two numbers is 1600 and their HCF is 5. The LCM of the numbers is:
A. 320 B. 1605 C. 1595 D. 8000

19. About the number of pairs which have 16 as their HCF and 136 as their LCM, we can definitely say that:
A. Only one such pair exists B. Only two such pairs exist
C. Many such pairs exist D. No such pair exist

20. The total number of prime factors of the product $(8)^{20} \times (15)^{24} \times (7)^{15}$ is:
A. 59 B. 98 C. 123 D. 138

21. A number n is said to be perfect, if the sum of all its divisors (excluding n itself) is equal to n. A perfect number is
A. 21 B. 15 C. 9 D. 6

22. HCF of $4 \times 27 \times 3125$, $8 \times 9 \times 25 \times 7$ and $16 \times 81 \times 5 \times 11 \times 49$ is
A. 1260 B. 540 C. 360 D. 180

23. Which is of the following is a co-primes?
A. (23, 92) B. (21, 35) C. (18, 25) D. (16, 62)

24. The LCM of $2^3 \times 3^2 \times 5 \times 11$, $2^4 \times 3^4 \times 5^2 \times 7$ and $2^5 \times 3^3 \times 5^3 \times 7^2 \times 11$ is :
A. $2^5 \times 3^4 \times 5^3$ B. $2^3 \times 3^2 \times 5$
C. $2^5 \times 3^4 \times 5^3 \times 7^2 \times 11$ D. $2^3 \times 3^2 \times 5 \times 7 \times 11$

25. The G.C.D. of 1.08, 0.36 and 0.9 is
A. 0.108 B. 0.18 C. 0.9 D. 0.03

26. H.C.F. of 3240, 3600 and a third number is 36 and their L.C.M. is $2^4 \times 3^5 \times 5^2 \times 7^2$. The third number is
A. $2^3 \times 3^5 \times 7^2$ B. $2^5 \times 5^2 \times 7^2$ C. $2^2 \times 5^3 \times 7^2$ D. $2^2 \times 3^5 \times 7^2$

27. The ratio of two numbers is 3 : 4 and their H.C.F. is 4. Find their L.C.M.
A. 48 B. 24 C. 16 D. 12

28. Three numbers are in the ratio 1 : 2 : 3 and their HCF is 12. Find the numbers.
A. 12, 24, 36 B. 10, 20, 30 C. 5, 10, 15 D. 4, 8, 12

29. If the sum of two numbers is 55 and the H.C.F. and L.C.M. of these numbers are 5 and 120 respectively. Find the sum of their reciprocals.
A. $\frac{120}{11}$ B. $\frac{11}{120}$ C. $\frac{601}{55}$ D. $\frac{55}{601}$

30. The L.C.M. of two numbers is 495 and their HCF is 5. If the sum of the numbers is 100, then find their difference.
A. 90 B. 70 C. 46 D. 10

ANSWERS

1	2	3	4	5	6	7	8	9	10
C	C	D	B	A	C	A	B	D	B
11	**12**	**13**	**14**	**15**	**16**	**17**	**18**	**19**	**20**
D	D	C	C	C	B	C	A	D	C
21	**22**	**23**	**24**	**25**	**26**	**27**	**28**	**29**	**30**
D	D	C	C	B	D	A	A	B	D

EXPLANATORY ANSWERS

2.

2	18, 24, 42, 63
3	9, 12, 21, 63
3	3, 4, 7, 21
7	1, 4, 7, 7
	1, 4, 1, 1

LCM of 18, 24, 42, 63 = $2 \times 3^2 \times 7 \times 4 = 504$.

5. Let the numbers be x, $2x$ and $3x$.
Then, their HCF = x
According to the question, $x = 12$
$\therefore$ The numbers are 12, 24, 36.

6. $1 \times 2 \times 3 \times 4 = 24$
$\therefore$ Required number = 24.

10. HCF of 210, 315, 147 and 161 = 7 Hence, the required number = 7.

12. LCM of 12, 15 and 20 = 60
Hence, required number = $60 \times 60 = 3600$.

15. The number of prime factors in the given product
= (222 + 333 + 555) = 1110

19. HCF is always a factor of LCM. So no two numbers exist with HCF = 16 and LCM = 136.

24. $2^3 \times 3^2 \times 5 \times 11$; $2^4 \times 3^4 \times 5^2 \times 7$
and $2^5 \times 3^3 \times 5^3 \times 7^2 \times 11$
$\therefore$ LCM = $2^5 \times 3^4 \times 5^3 \times 7^2 \times 11$

25. GCD of 108, 36 and 90 = 18
Hence, GCD of 1.08, 0.36 and 0.9 = 0.18.

27. Let the numbers be $3x$ and $4x$; HCF = 4; Hence, $x = 4$
Then, numbers will be 12 and 16;
$\therefore$ Their LCM = 48.

28. Let the numbers are x, $2x$ and $3x$;
Their HCF = 12
Then, $x = 12$,
so the numbers will be 12, 24, 36.

29. Let the number be x and y.
Then, $x + y = 55$;
$xy = \text{HCF} \times \text{LCM} = 5 \times 120$

$\therefore$ Sum of their reciprocals = $\dfrac{1}{x} + \dfrac{1}{y} = \dfrac{x+y}{xy} = \dfrac{55}{5 \times 120} = \dfrac{11}{120}$

30. Let the number be x and $(100 - x)$
Now, $x(100 - x) = 5 \times 495$
$\Rightarrow x^2 - 100x + 2475 = 0$
$\Rightarrow x^2 - 55x - 45x + 2475 = 0$
$\Rightarrow x(x - 55) - 45(x - 55) = 0$
$\Rightarrow (x - 45)(x - 55) = 0$
Either, $x = 45$ or, $x = 55$
Hence, the numbers are 45 and 55
So, their difference = 55 – 45 = 10

3

Simplification

Simplification means expressing in a simpler form. In order to simplify an expression we use the operations in the following order which is easily remembered as "BODMAS".

(*i*) Bracket (*ii*) Of (*iii*) Division (*iv*) Multiplication (*v*) Addition (*vi*) Subtraction.

'Of' means multiplication but it is operated even before division.

While removing brackets, first of all bar bracket '—' and after that small bracket '( )' is removed. Thereafter curley bracket '{ }' and at last square bracket '[ ]' is removed.

EXAMPLE: Simplify: $10 - \left[6 - \left\{7 - \left(6 - \overline{8 - 5}\right)\right\}\right]$

SOLUTION: $10 - \left[6 - \left\{7 - \left(6 - 3\right)\right\}\right]$

$= 10 - [6 - \{7 - 3\}]$ $= 10 - [6 - 4] = 10 - 2 = 8.$

MULTIPLE CHOICE QUESTIONS

1. $\dfrac{48 - 12 \times 3 + 9}{12 - 9 \div 3}$ equals:

A. 3 B. 21 C. $\dfrac{7}{3}$ D. $\dfrac{1}{3}$

2. $\dfrac{69 - 14 \times 3 + 2}{9 \times 5 - (5)^2}$ equals:

A. 1.45 B. 2.75 C. 26.5 D. 265

3. If $\dfrac{17.28 \div x}{3.6 \times 0.2} = 2$ then, the value of x is:

A. 120 B. 1.20 C. 12 D. 0.12

4. $171 \div 19 \times 9$ equals:

A. 0 B. 1 C. 18 D. 81

5. $3120 \div 26 + 13 \times 30$ equals:

A. 2400 B. 3900 C. 536 D. None of these

6. $\frac{31}{10}\times\frac{3}{10}+\frac{7}{5}\div 20$ equals:

A. 0 B. 1 C. 100 D. $\frac{107}{200}$

7. The simplification of $1+\cfrac{1}{2+\cfrac{1}{1-\cfrac{1}{3}}}$ yields the result:

A. $\frac{2}{7}$ B. $\frac{7}{9}$ C. $\frac{9}{7}$ D. $\frac{13}{7}$

8. The value of $1+\frac{1}{4\times 3}+\frac{1}{4\times 3^2}+\frac{1}{4\times 3^3}$ up to four places of decimals is:

A. 1.1202 B. 1.1203 C. 1.1204 D. None of these

9. $\dfrac{\frac{1}{2}\div 4+20}{\frac{1}{2}\times 4+20}$ equals:

A. $\frac{81}{88}$ B. $2\frac{3}{11}$ C. $\frac{161}{176}$ D. 1

10. $3\div\left[(8-5)\div\left\{(4-2)\div\left(2+\frac{8}{13}\right)\right\}\right]$ equals:

A. $\frac{13}{17}$ B. $\frac{68}{13}$ C. $\frac{17}{13}$ D. $\frac{13}{68}$

11. $10-[9-\{8-(7-6)\}]-5$ is equal to:

A. –5 B. 1 C. 3 D. 9

12. $\dfrac{\frac{1}{5}\div\frac{1}{5}\text{ of }\frac{1}{5}}{\frac{1}{5}\text{ of }\frac{1}{5}\div\frac{1}{5}}$ is equal to:

A. 1 B. 5 C. $\frac{1}{5}$ D. 25

13. The value of $1+\cfrac{1}{1+\cfrac{1}{1+\cfrac{1}{9}}}$ is:

A. $\frac{29}{19}$ B. $\frac{10}{19}$ C. $\frac{29}{10}$ D. $\frac{10}{9}$

14. $\frac{3}{48}$ is what part of $\frac{1}{12}$?

A. $\frac{3}{7}$ B. $\frac{1}{12}$ C. $\frac{4}{3}$ D. None of these

15. How many $\frac{1}{8}$s are there in $37\frac{1}{2}$?

A. 300 B. 400
C. 500 D. Cannot be determined

16. $\frac{885 \times 885 \times 885 + 115 \times 115 \times 115}{885 \times 885 + 115 \times 115 - 885 \times 115}$ is equal to:

A. 115 B. 770 C. 885 D. 1000

17. The value of $\frac{9^2 \times 18^4}{3^{16}}$ is:

A. $\frac{2}{3}$ B. $\frac{4}{9}$ C. $\frac{16}{81}$ D. $\frac{32}{243}$

18. $\left(1\frac{3}{5} - \frac{2}{3} \div \frac{12}{13} + \frac{7}{5} \times \frac{1}{3}\right)$ is equal to:

A. $1\frac{31}{90}$ B. $\frac{19}{30}$ C. $\frac{11}{30}$ D. 30

19. The value of $48 \div 12 \times \left(\frac{9}{8} \text{ of } \frac{4}{3} \div \frac{3}{4} \text{ of } \frac{2}{3}\right)$ is:

A. $1\frac{1}{3}$ B. $5\frac{1}{3}$ C. 3 D. 12

20. $(20 \div 5) \div 2 + (16 \div 8) \times 2 + (10 \div 5) \times (3 \div 2)$ is equal to

A. 9 B. 12 C. 15 D. 18

21. The sum of 1/9, 1/3, 1/6 and 7/18 of a number is 150. The number is

A. 120 B. 130 C. 140 D. 150

22. Which is the greatest? .999, .1011, .1995, .9985

A. .999 B. .1011 C. .1995 D. .9985

23. In decimal system, $9\frac{1}{8}$ may be represented as

A. 9.18 B. 9.125 C. 9.025 D. 9.225

24. $2.205 \div 0.15 = ?$

A. 1.47 B. 14.7 C. 147 D. 0.147

25. G.C.M. of .24, 3.2 and 16.0 is
A. 80 B. 8 C. .8 D. .08

26. L.C.M. of .24, 3.2 and 16.0 is
A. .48 B. 4.8 C. 48 D. 480

27. A pole has 0.5 of its length in mud, 0.25 of its length in water and 2 metres above water. The total length of the pole is
A. 8 metres B. 5 metres C. 4 metres D. 2 metres

28. $\sqrt{1/3}$ is equal to
A. 0.57 B. 0.35 C. 0.30 D. 3.00

29. How many times does 2/3 of 1/2 go into half of third?
A. 2 B. 1/2 C. 1/3 D. 2/3

30. The eleventh part of $990\frac{990}{990}$ is
A. 99.0 B. 99.99 C. 90 D. 90.9

ANSWERS

1	2	3	4	5	6	7	8	9	10
C	A	C	D	D	B	C	B	C	A
11	**12**	**13**	**14**	**15**	**16**	**17**	**18**	**19**	**20**
C	D	A	D	A	D	C	A	D	A
21	**22**	**23**	**24**	**25**	**26**	**27**	**28**	**29**	**30**
D	A	B	B	D	C	A	A	B	C

EXPLANATORY ANSWERS

4. $171 \div 19 \times 9 = 9 \times 9 = 81.$

5. $3120 \div 26 + 13 \times 30 = 120 + 390 = 510.$

6. $\frac{31}{10} \times \frac{3}{10} + \frac{7}{5} \div 20 = \frac{31}{10} \times \frac{3}{10} + \frac{7}{5} \times \frac{1}{20}$

$= \frac{93}{100} + \frac{7}{100} = \frac{93+7}{100} = \frac{100}{100} = 1$

11. $10 - [9 - \{8 - (7 - 6)\}] - 5$
$= 10 - [9 - \{8 - 1\}] - 5$
$= 10 - [9 - 7] - 5$
$= 10 - 2 - 5 = 10 - 7 = 3$

22. .999 is the greatest.

23. $9\frac{1}{8} = 9 + \frac{1}{8} = 9 + .125 = 9.125$

26. L.C.M. of .24, 3.2 and 16.0 = L.C.M. of $\frac{24,\ 320 \text{ and } 1600}{100}$

$= \frac{4800}{100} = 48.$

27. Let total length of the pole = x
Pole above water = $x - [0.5x + 0.25x]$
= $0.25x$; But, $0.25x = 2$ metres

$\therefore\ x = \frac{2 \times 100}{25} = 8$ metres

28. $\sqrt{\frac{1}{3}} = \frac{1}{\sqrt{3}} \times \frac{\sqrt{3}}{\sqrt{3}} = \frac{\sqrt{3}}{3} = \frac{1.732}{3} = .57$

29. $\frac{2}{3} \text{ of } \frac{1}{2} = \frac{2}{3} \times \frac{1}{2} = \frac{1}{3}$

$\frac{1}{2} \text{ of } \frac{1}{3} = \frac{1}{6}$

$\therefore \quad \frac{1}{6} \div \frac{1}{3} = \frac{1}{6} \times \frac{3}{1} = \frac{1}{2}$

30. Eleventh part of $990\frac{990}{990} = 990\frac{990}{990} \div 11 = \frac{990}{11} = 90$

4

Surds and Indices

Surds

If 'a' is a rational number and n is a positive integer such that nth root of 'a', *i.e.*, $a^{1/n}$ or $\sqrt[n]{a}$ is an irrational number, then $a^{1/n}$ is called a surd or radical.

For example, $\sqrt{2} = 2^{1/2}$ = Square root of 2

$\sqrt[3]{5} = 5^{1/3}$ = Cube root of 5

Important Formulae Based on Surds

$\sqrt[n]{a} = a^{1/n}$ and it is called a surd of order n.

(*i*) $\sqrt[n]{a^n} = a$

(*ii*) $\sqrt[n]{ab} = \sqrt[n]{a}\,\sqrt[n]{b}$

(*iii*) $\sqrt{a} \times \sqrt{b} = \sqrt{ab}$

(*iv*) $\left(\sqrt{a} + \sqrt{b}\right)^2 = a + b + 2\sqrt{ab}$

(*v*) $\left(\sqrt{a} - \sqrt{b}\right)^2 = a + b - 2\sqrt{ab}$

(*vi*) $\left(\sqrt{a} + \sqrt{b}\right)\left(\sqrt{a} - \sqrt{b}\right) = a - b$ where a and b are positive rational numbers.

Indices

The expression a^n is termed as power function or simply power, a is called the base and n is called index or exponent of the power a^n.

For example, 2^2 = square of 2, 2^3 = cube of 2, etc.

Laws of Indices

(*i*) $a^m \times a^n = a^{m+n}$

(*ii*) $a^m \times a^n \times a^p \times \ldots = a^{m+n+p+\ldots}$

(*iii*) $\dfrac{a^m}{a^n} = a^{m-n}$, if $m > n$

(*iv*) $(a^m)^n = a^{mn}$

(*v*) $(ab)^n = a^n b^n$

(*vi*) $a^0 = 1$

(*vii*) If $a^m = a^n$ then $m = n$

(*viii*) If $a^m = b^m$ then $a = b$

MULTIPLE CHOICE QUESTIONS

1. If the infinite series is $x = \sqrt{6 + \sqrt{6 + \sqrt{6 + \ldots}}}$ then the value of x is:

A. 2.5 B. 3 C. 6 D. 8

2. If $\frac{9^n \cdot 3^2 \cdot 3^n - (27)^n}{3^{3m} \cdot 2^3} = \frac{1}{27}$, then the value of $(m - n)$ is:

A. 1 B. 2 C. $\sqrt{3}$ D. $\sqrt{\frac{2}{3}}$

3. If $x = \frac{\sqrt{5}+\sqrt{3}}{\sqrt{5}-\sqrt{3}}$ and $y = \frac{\sqrt{5}-\sqrt{3}}{\sqrt{5}+\sqrt{3}}$, then $(x + y)$ is equal to:

A. 8 B. 6 C. $2\sqrt{15}$ D. $2\left(\sqrt{5}+\sqrt{3}\right)$

4. $2^{x+1} + 2^{x+3} = 2560$, then x is equal to:

A. 12 B. 11 C. 8 D. 6

5. If $\frac{5+2\sqrt{3}}{7+4\sqrt{3}} = a + b\sqrt{3}$, then b is equal to:

A. –6 B. 6 C. –11 D. 11

6. If $\frac{(21)^{5.36}}{(21)^{3.47}} = (21)^x$, then the value of x is:

A. 8.88 B. 1.54 C. 9.32 D. 1.89

7. $\sqrt{24}+\sqrt{12}$ equal to:

A. $\sqrt{36}$ B. $2\sqrt{6}+2\sqrt{3}$ C. $6\sqrt{2}$ D. $\sqrt{288}$

8. If $a^b = 64$, where a and b are positive integers then $(a - b)^{a+b-4}$ is:

A. 0 B. 1 C. 2 D. $\frac{1}{2}$

9. The value of $\frac{5^{10+n} \cdot 25^{3n-4}}{5^{7n}}$ is:

A. 5 B. 8 C. 25 D. 16

10. $3^x - 3^{x-1} = 18$, then the value of x^x is:

A. 3 B. 8 C. 27 D. 216

11. If $x = \sqrt{10+\sqrt{25+\sqrt{121}}}$, then x is equal to:

A. –2 only B. 2 only C. ± 4 D. 4 only

12. If $a^x = b^y = c^z$ and $b^2 = ac$, then y is equal to:

A. $\frac{xz}{x+z}$ B. $\frac{xz}{2(x-z)}$ C. $\frac{xz}{2(z-x)}$ D. $\frac{2xz}{x+z}$

13. 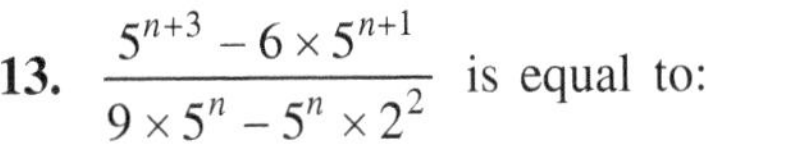 $\dfrac{5^{n+3} - 6 \times 5^{n+1}}{9 \times 5^n - 5^n \times 2^2}$ is equal to:

A. 5 B. 19 C. 25 D. 95

14. The value of $\left(\dfrac{x^a}{x^b}\right)^{(a+b)} \times \left(\dfrac{x^b}{x^c}\right)^{(b+c)} \times \left(\dfrac{x^c}{x^a}\right)^{(c+a)}$ is equal to:

A. 0 B. 2 C. 1 D. 3

15. If $\sqrt{3^n} = 729$, then the value of n is:

A. 12 B. 8 C. 10 D. 6

16. The value of $4\sqrt{3} - 3\sqrt{12} + 2\sqrt{75}$ is:

A. $2\sqrt{3}$ B. $4\sqrt{3}$ C. $6\sqrt{3}$ D. $8\sqrt{3}$

17. The value of $\sqrt{50} - \sqrt{98} + \sqrt{162}$ is:

A. $5\sqrt{2}$ B. $7\sqrt{2}$ C. $3\sqrt{2}$ D. $4\sqrt{2}$

18. If $x = 1 - \sqrt{2}$, the value of $\left(x - \dfrac{1}{x}\right)^3$ is:

A. 1 B. 4 C. 8 D. 2

19. If $a = 7 - 4\sqrt{3}$, then the value of $\sqrt{a} + \dfrac{1}{\sqrt{a}}$ is equal to:

A. 1 B. 4 C. 2 D. 3

20. The value of $\dfrac{4\sqrt{18}}{\sqrt{12}} - \dfrac{8\sqrt{75}}{\sqrt{32}} + \dfrac{9\sqrt{2}}{\sqrt{3}}$ is:

A. 0 B. 2 C. 1 D. 3

21. If $(625)^2 = 390625$, then the value of $\sqrt{.00390625}$ will be:

A. .0625 B. 0.625 C. .00625 D. .000625

22. $x \otimes y = \sqrt{(x+1)(y+1)^2}$, then the value of $3 \otimes 7$ will be:

A. 21 B. 16 C. 18 D. 28

23. The cube root of 8^4 is:

A. 16 B. 8 C. 4 D. 64

24. By what smallest number 270 be multiplied so that the resulting number becomes a perfect cube?

A. 121 B. 109 C. 100 D. 99

25. By what smallest number 675 be multiplied so that the product becomes a perfect square number?

A. 2 B. $\frac{3}{5}$ C. 4 D. 3

26. If the approximate square root of 80 is 8.94. What will be the value of $\sqrt{20}$?

A. 3.37 B. 4.47 C. 4.87 D. 4.40

27. What will be the value of $\sqrt[3]{32+\sqrt{1012+\sqrt{144}}}$?

A. 4 B. 6 C. 5 D. 8

28. What will be the square root of $\left(\sqrt[3]{0.00000064}\right) \times \sqrt{2.56}$?

A. .06 B. .08 C. .05 D. .04

29. If $\frac{\sqrt{?}}{4} = \frac{1}{3}$, what will be in place of (?)?

A. $\frac{16}{3}$ B. $\frac{16}{9}$ C. $\frac{21}{16}$ D. $\frac{4}{3}$

30. If 30% of $\sqrt{?}$ + 15% of 40 = 11, what should replace the sign of interrogation (?)?

A. $\frac{2500}{9}$ B. $\frac{2400}{7}$ C. $\frac{2300}{11}$ D. $\frac{2200}{7}$

ANSWERS

1	2	3	4	5	6	7	8	9	10
B	A	A	C	A	D	B	B	C	C
11	**12**	**13**	**14**	**15**	**16**	**17**	**18**	**19**	**20**
D	D	B	C	A	D	B	C	B	A
21	**22**	**23**	**24**	**25**	**26**	**27**	**28**	**29**	**30**
A	B	A	C	D	B	A	B	B	A

EXPLANATORY ANSWERS

6. $$\frac{(21)^{5.36}}{(21)^{3.47}} = (21)^x$$

$\Rightarrow \quad (21)^{5.36-3.47} = (21)^x$

$\Rightarrow \quad x = 1.89$

7. $\sqrt{24}+\sqrt{12} = 2\sqrt{6}+2\sqrt{3}$

8. $a^b = 64 = (4)^3 \Rightarrow a = 4,\ b = 3$

$\therefore\ (a-b)^{a+b-4} = (4-3)^{4+3-4} = (1)^3 = 1$

13. $$\frac{5^{n+3}-6\times 5^{n+1}}{9\times 5^n - 5^n\times 2^2} = \frac{5^n\times 5^3 - 6\times 5^n\times 5}{9\times 5^n - 4\times 5^n}$$

$$= \frac{5^n(125-30)}{5^n(9-4)} = 5^0\times\frac{95}{5}$$

$$= 1 \times 19 = 19.$$

15. $\sqrt{3^n} = 729 \Rightarrow 3^{n/2} = 3^6$

$\Rightarrow \quad \frac{n}{2} = 6$

$\Rightarrow \quad n = 12.$

25. $675 = 3\times 3\times 3\times 5\times 5 = 3\times 3^2\times 5^2$

From the above, we find that only a factor 3 is left unpaired

$\therefore$ If we multiply 675 by 3 the product would be $\underline{3\times 3}\times 3^2\times 5^2$ which is a perfect square.

$\therefore$ The required smallest number is 3.

27. $\because\ \sqrt[3]{32+\sqrt{1012+\sqrt{144}}} = \sqrt[3]{32+\sqrt{1012+12}}$

$= \sqrt[3]{32+\sqrt{1024}} = \sqrt[3]{32+32} = \sqrt[3]{64} = \sqrt[3]{4\times 4\times 4} = 4$

29. $\frac{\sqrt{?}}{4} = \frac{1}{3} \Rightarrow \sqrt{?} = \frac{4}{3} \qquad \Rightarrow ? = \frac{4}{3}\times\frac{4}{3} = \frac{16}{9}$

$\therefore$Sign of interrogation (?) should be replaced by $\frac{16}{9}$.

5

Ratio, Proportion & Partnership

Ratio

When comparison is made by dividing one quantity by another of the same kind, the result is called ratio. If a and b are two numbers, ratio of a to b is denoted by $a : b$ or $\frac{a}{b}$. The first term a is called antecedent and the second term b is called consequent.

Proportion

Equality of two ratios is called proportion. If $a : b = c : d$, then a, b, c, d are called in proportion. In a proportion $a : b : : c : d$, then a and d are called extremes and b and c are called means.

Product of extremes = Product of means

Comparison of Ratio: Suppose $\frac{a}{b} > \frac{c}{d}$ then we say that $a : b > c : d$.

Compounded Ratio: The compound ratio of the ratios $a : b$, $c : d$ and $e : f$ is $ace : bdf$.

Duplicate Ratio: The duplicate ratio of $a : b$ is $a^2 : b^2$.

Triplicate Ratio: The triplicate ratio of $a : b$ is $a^3 : b^3$.

EXAMPLE: If A : B = 3 : 4 and B : C = 8 : 9 then find A : C.

SOLUTION: $A : B = 3 : 4 \Rightarrow \frac{A}{B} = \frac{3}{4}$

$B : C = 8 : 9 \Rightarrow \frac{B}{C} = \frac{8}{9}$

$\frac{A}{C} = \frac{A}{B} \times \frac{B}{C} = \frac{3}{4} \times \frac{8}{9} = \frac{2}{3}$

$\Rightarrow A : C = 2 : 3$

Partnership

Partnership is a form of association of two or more persons who contribute resources like money together in order to carry on a business. It may be of simple or compound type.

Simple partnership is one in which the capitals of the partners are invested for the same time. The profits or losses are divided among the partners in the ratio of their investments.

Compound partnership is one in which the capitals of the partners are invested for different periods. In such cases, equivalent capitals are calculated for each partner by multiplying their capital contributions with time. The profits or losses are then divided in the ratio of these equivalent capitals.

The partner who invests the money in the business as well as takes part in its management, is known as **Working partner**.

The partner who only invests the money in the business and does not work, is known as **Sleeping partner**.

MULTIPLE CHOICE QUESTIONS

1. If A : B = 2 : 3 and B : C = 4 : 5, then C : A is equal to:
A. 15 : 8 B. 12 : 10 C. 8 : 5 D. 8 : 15

2. If 10% of x is the same as 20% of y, then $x : y$ is equal to:
A. 1 : 2 B. 2 : 1 C. 5 : 1 D. 10 : 1

3. The mean proportional to $6+\sqrt{27}$ and $6-\sqrt{27}$ is:
A. 3 B. 9 C. 10 D. $\sqrt{10}$

4. If $x : y = 9 : 11$, the value of $\dfrac{5x+3y}{3x+5y}$ is:
A. 45 : 55 B. 18 : 22 C. 37 : 41 D. 39 : 41

5. If $a + b : b + c : c + a = 6 : 7 : 8$ and $a + b + c = 14$, then the value of c is:
A. 14 B. 7 C. 8 D. 6

6. Two numbers are in the ratio 2 : 3. If 5 is added to each number, the ratio becomes 5 : 7. The bigger number is:
A. 30 B. 40 C. 60 D. 20

7. What should be added to each of the numbers 12, 30, 40 and 86, so that they are in proportion?
A. 6 B. 4 C. –6 D. –4

8. The ratio of males and females of a village is 5 : 3. If there are 800 males in the village, females are:
A. 240 B. 480 C. 840 D. 488

9. In a mixture of 60 litres, the ratio of ethanol to ether is 4 : 1. How much ether must be added to the mixture to make this ratio 2 : 1?
A. 10 litres B. 12 litres C. 18 litres D. 24 litres

10. The proportion of zinc and copper in a brass piece is 4 : 5. How much zinc will be there in 180 kg of such a piece?

A. 40 kg B. 80 kg C. 100 kg D. 120 kg

11. The prices of a scooter and a television set are in the ratio 3 : 2. If a scooter costs ₹ 6000 more than the television set, the price of the television set is:

A. ₹ 18000 B. ₹ 12000 C. ₹ 10000 D. ₹ 6000

12. The weight of a 13 metres long iron rod be 23.4 kg. The weight of 6 metres long of such rod will be:

A. 7.2 kg B. 12.4 kg C. 10.8 kg D. 18 kg

13. The ratio between the ages of Gayatri and Savitri is 6 : 5 and the sum of their ages is 44 years. The ratio of their ages after 8 years will be:

A. 5 : 6 B. 7 : 8 C. 8 : 7 D. 14 : 13

14. Two numbers are such that the ratio between them is 3 : 5 but if each is increased by 10, the ratio between them becomes 5 : 7. The numbers are:

A. 3, 5 B. 7, 9 C. 13, 22 D. 15, 25

15. A, B and C share the profit in the ratio of 3 : 5 : 7. If the gain is ₹ 2040, then C's share is:

A. ₹ 360 B. ₹ 600 C. ₹ 952 D. ₹ 120

16. A, B and C started a business with ₹ 47000. A puts in ₹ 5000 more than B and B ₹ 3000 more than C. The share of A out of the profit of ₹ 14100 will be:

A. ₹ 3600 B. ₹ 4500 C. ₹ 6000 D. ₹ 6300

17. A starts a business with ₹ 5000. After 4 months B joins him with a sum of ₹ 4000. In the end of the year there is a profit of ₹ 8970. The share of A in the profit will be:

A. ₹ 3120 B. ₹ 4020 C. ₹ 5850 D. ₹ 6360

18. A, B, C are three partners in a business. The profit share of A is $\frac{3}{16}$ of the profit and B's share is $\frac{1}{4}$ of the profit. If C receives ₹ 243, then the amount received by B will be:

A. ₹ 90 B. ₹ 96 C. ₹ 108 D. ₹ 120

19. A, B and C share the profit in the ratio 2 : 3 : 7. If the average gain is ₹ 8000, then B's share is:

A. ₹ 2000 B. ₹ 1000 C. ₹ 1500 D. ₹ 3000

20. Ashok started a business investing ₹ 90,000. After 3 months Shabir joined him with a capital of ₹ 1,20,000. If at the end of one year the total profit made by them was ₹ 96,000, what will be the difference between their shares?

A. ₹ 24000 B. ₹ 8000 C. ₹ 20000 D. None of these

21. If a : b = 2 : 3, b : c = 4 : 5 and c : d = 6 : 7, then a : d is equal to:

A. 2 : 7 B. 7 : 8 C. 4 : 13 D. 16 : 35

22. The mean proportional between 0.32 and 0.02 is:

A. 0.34 B. 0.3 C. 0.16 D. 0.08

23. The sum of three numbers is 98. If the ratio between the first and second be 2 : 3 and that between the second and third be 5 : 8, then what is the second number?

A. 20 B. 30 C. 10 D. 40

24. One man adds 3 litres of water to 12 litres of milk and another 4 litres of water to 10 litres of milk. What is the ratio of the strenghts of the milk in the two mixtures?

A. 15 : 25 B. 25 : 28 C. 28 : 25 D. None of these

25. ₹ 425 is divided among 4 men, 5 women and 6 boys such that the share of a man, a woman and a boy may be in the ratio of 9 : 8 : 4. What is the share of a woman?

A. ₹ 34 B. ₹ 24 C. ₹ 44 D. None

26. A vessel contains liquids P and Q in the ratio 5 : 3. If 6 litres of the mixture are removed and the same quantity of liquid q is added, the ratio becomes 3 : 5. What quantity does the vessel hold?

A. 40 litres B. 50 litres C. 30 litres D. None of these

27. A bucket contains a mixture of two liquids P and Q in the proportion 7 : 5. If 9 litres of the mixture is replaced by 9 litres of liquid Q, then the ratio of the two liquid becomes 7 : 9. How much of the liquid P was there in the bucket?

A. 11 litres B. 21 litres C. 31 litres D. None of these

28. Three glasses P, Q and R with their capacities in the ratio 2 : 3 : 4 are filled with a mixture of spirit and water. The ratio of spirit to water in P, Q and R is 1 : 5, 3 : 5 and 5 : 7 respectively. If the contents of these glasses are mixed together, what is the ratio of spirit to water in the mixture?

A. 14 : 27 B. 23 : 47 C. 25 : 47 D. None of these

29. A and B are two alloys of gold and copper prepared by mixing metals in proportions 7 : 2 and 7 : 11 respectively. If equal quantities of the alloys are melted to form a third alloy C, the proportion of gold and copper in C will be

A. 5 : 9 B. 5 : 7 C. 7 : 5 D. 9 : 5

30. Gold is 19 times as heavy as water and copper 9 times as heavy as water. The ratio in which these two metals be mixed so that the mixtures is 15 times as heavy as water is:

A. 1 : 2 B. 2 : 3 C. 3 : 2 D. 19 : 135

ANSWERS

1	2	3	4	5	6	7	8	9	10
A	B	A	D	D	A	A	B	B	B
11	**12**	**13**	**14**	**15**	**16**	**17**	**18**	**19**	**20**
B	C	C	D	C	C	C	C	A	D
21	**22**	**23**	**24**	**25**	**26**	**27**	**28**	**29**	**30**
D	D	B	C	A	A	B	C	C	C

EXPLANATORY ANSWERS

3. Mean proportional $= \sqrt{(6+\sqrt{27})(6-\sqrt{27})}$

$= \sqrt{36-27} = \sqrt{9} = 3$

8. Ratio of Males : Females = 5 : 3

$\Rightarrow \frac{800}{x} = \frac{5}{3} \Rightarrow 5x = 3 \times 800$

$\Rightarrow x = \frac{3 \times 800}{5} = 3 \times 160 = 480$

Hence, number of females = 480.

10. In 9 kg of brass, zinc = 4 kg

$\therefore$ In 180 kg of brass, zinc $= \frac{4}{9} \times 180 = 80$ kg.

12. Weight of 13 m long iron rod = 23.4 kg

Weight of 6 m long iron rod

$= \frac{23.4}{13} \times 6 \text{ kg} = 1.8 \times 6 = 10.8$ kg.

15. C's share = $\frac{7}{15} \times 2040$ = ₹ 952.

19. B's share = $\frac{3}{2+3+7} \times 8000 = \frac{3 \times 8000}{12}$ = ₹ 2000

22. Mean proportional = $\sqrt{0.32 \times 0.02} = \sqrt{0.0064} = 0.08$

23. The ratio among the three numbers is

	2	:	3		
			5	:	8
and	10	:	15	:	24

∴ The second number = $\frac{98}{10+15+24} \times 15 = 30$

25. The ratio of shares of group of men, women and boys

= 9 × 4 : 8 × 5 : 4 × 6 = 9 : 10 : 6

∴ Share of 5 women = $\frac{425}{9+10+6} \times 10$ = ₹ 170

∴ Share of 1 woman = $\frac{170}{5}$ = ₹ 34

29. Gold in C = $\left(\frac{7}{9} + \frac{7}{18}\right) = \frac{21}{18} = \frac{7}{6}$

Copper in C = $\left(\frac{2}{9} + \frac{11}{18}\right) = \frac{15}{18} = \frac{5}{6}$

∴ Gold : Copper = $\frac{7}{6} : \frac{5}{6}$ = 7 : 5

6

Average

The sum of all the quantities of same kind divided by their number is called average (or mean) of those quantities.

FORMULAE

1. Average = $\left(\dfrac{\text{Sum of observations}}{\text{Number of observations}}\right)$

2. Sum of the first n natural numbers = $1 + 2 + 3 + ... + n = \dfrac{n(n+1)}{2}$

3. Sum of the squares of the first n natural numbers

   $= 1^2 + 2^2 + ... + n^2 = \dfrac{n(n+1)(2n+1)}{6}$

4. Sum of the cubes of the first n natural numbers

   $= 1^3 + 2^3 + ... + n^3 = \left\{\dfrac{n(n+1)}{2}\right\}^2$

5. Sum of the first n odd numbers = $1 + 3 + 5 + ... + (2n - 1) = n^2$

Different kinds of mean or average:

(*a*) Arithmetic mean, (*b*) Geometric mean, (*c*) Harmonic mean

$$\text{A.M.} = \frac{x_1 + x_2 + x_3 + ... + x_n}{n}$$

$$\text{G.M.} = (x_1 \,.\, x_2 \,.\, x_3 \,...\, x_n)^{1/n}$$

$$\text{H.M.} = \frac{n}{\dfrac{1}{x_1} + \dfrac{1}{x_2} + ... + \dfrac{1}{x_n}}.$$

EXAMPLE 1. : Find the average of first ten prime numbers.

SOLUTION: First ten prime numbers are 2, 3, 5, 7, 11, 13, 17, 19, 23 and 29.

$$\therefore \text{ Average} = \frac{2+3+5+7+11+13+17+19+23+29}{10}$$

$$= \frac{129}{10} = 12.9$$

EXAMPLE 2. : The average of 11 results is 50. If the average of first six results is 49 and that of last six is 52, find the sixth result.

SOLUTION: Sum of 11 results = $11 \times 50 = 550$

Sum of first 6 results $6 \times 49 = 294$

Sum of last 6 results = $6 \times 52 = 312$

$\therefore$ 6th result = $294 + 312 - 550 = 56$

EXAMPLE 3. : The average age of three boys is 15 years. If their ages are in the ratio 3 : 5 : 7. What is the age of the youngest boy?

SOLUTION: Let the ages of the three boys be $3x$, $5x$ and $7x$.

$$\text{Average age} = \frac{3x + 5x + 7x}{3} = 5x \text{ and } 5x = 15 \Rightarrow x = 3$$

The age of the youngest boy = $3x = 3 \times 3 = 9$ years.

MULTIPLE CHOICE QUESTIONS

1. The average of first five multiples of 3 is:
   A. 3 B. 9 C. 12 D. 15
2. The average of 25 results is 18, that of first 12 is 14 and of the last 12 is 17. Thirteenth result is:
   A. 78 B. 85 C. 28 D. 72
3. Out of three numbers, the first is twice the second and is half of the third. If the average of the three numbers is 56, the three numbers in order are:
   A. 48, 96, 24 B. 48, 24, 96 C. 96, 24, 48 D. 96, 48, 24
4. The sum of three numbers is 98. If the ratio between first and second be 2 : 3 and that between second and third be 5 : 8, then the second number is:
   A. 30 B. 20 C. 58 D. 48
5. The average age of a committee of seven trustees is the same as it was 5 years ago; a young man having been substituted for one of them. The new man compared to the replaced old man, is younger in age by:
   A. 5 years B. 7 years C. 12 years D. 35 years
6. The average expenditure of a man for the first five months is ₹ 120 and for the next seven months is ₹ 130. His monthly average income if he saves ₹ 290 in that year, is:
   A. ₹ 160 B. ₹ 170 C. ₹ 150 D. ₹ 140
7. The average salary of 20 workers in an office is ₹ 1900 per month. If the manager's salary is added, the average becomes ₹ 2000 per month. The manager's salary is:
   A. ₹ 24000 B. ₹ 25200 C. ₹ 45600 D. None of these

8. The average temperature of first 3 days is 27°C and of the next 3 days is 29°C. If the average of the whole week is 28.5°C, the temperature of the last day is:

A. 31.5°C B. 10.5°C C. 21°C D. 42°C

9. A cricketer scored 180 runs in the first test and 258 runs in the second. How many runs should he score in the third test so that his average score in the three tests would be 230 runs?

A. 219 B. 242 C. 334 D. None of these

10. The average of first five prime numbers is:

A. 5.0 B. 5.2 C. 5.6 D. 6.0

11. The average weight of 3 men A, B and C is 84 kg. Another man D joins the group and the average now becomes 80 kg. If another man E, whose weight is 3 kg more than that of D, replaces A, then average weight of B, C, D and E becomes 79 kg. The weight of A is:

A. 70 kg B. 72 kg C. 75 kg D. 80 kg

12. The average age of A, B, C, D and E is 45 years. By including x, the present average of all the six is 49 years. The present age of x is:

A. 64 years B. 69 years C. 45 years D. 40 years

13. The average height of 30 boys, out of a class of 50, is 160 cm. If the average height of the remaining boys is 165 cm, the average height of the whole class (in cm) is:

A. 161 B. 162 C. 163 D. 164

14. The average age of an adult class is 40 years. 12 new students with an average age of 30 years join the class, thereby decreasing the average of the class by 4 years. The original strength of the class was:

A. 10 B. 18 C. 12 D. 15

15. If a, b, c, d, e are five consecutive even numbers, their average is:

A. $5(a + 4)$ B. $\frac{abcde}{5}$

C. $5(a + b + c + d + e)$ D. None of these

16. Of the three numbers, second is twice the first and is also thrice the third. If the average of the three numbers is 44, the largest number is:

A. 24 B. 36 C. 72 D. 108

17. The average of 50 numbers is 38. If two numbers namely, 45 and 55 are discarded, the average of remaining number is:

A. 36.50 B. 37.00 C. 37.50 D. 37.52

18. The average height of 30 girls out of a class of 40 is 160 cm and that of the remaining girls is 156 cm. The average height of the whole class is:

A. 158 cm B. 158.5 cm C. 159 cm D. 159.5 cm

19. The average of n numbers is x. If 36 is subtracted from any two numbers each, then new average is $(x - 8)$. The value of n is:

A. 6 B. 8 C. 9 D. 72

20. The average salary of male employees in a firm is ₹ 520 and that of female employees is ₹ 420. The mean salary of all the employees is ₹ 500. The percentage of female employees is:

A. 40% B. 30% C. 25% D. 20%

21. Out of three numbers, the first is twice the second and is half of the third. If the average of the three numbers is 56, the three numbers in order are

A. 48, 96, 24 B. 48, 24, 96 C. 96, 24, 48 D. 96, 48, 24

22. The average age of 30 students in a class is 12 years. The average age of a group of 5 of the students is 10 years and that of another group of 5 of them is 14 years. The average age of the remaining students is

A. 8 years B. 10 years C. 12 years D. 14 years

23. Out of four numbers, the average of first three is 15 and that of the last three is 16. If the last number is 19, the first is

A. 15 B. 16 C. 18 D. 19

24. The average age of an adult class is 40 years. 12 new students with an average age of 32 years join the class, thereby decreasing the average by 4 years. The original strength of the class was

A. 10 B. 11 C. 12 D. 15

25. The average age of 24 students in a class is 10. If the teacher's age is included, the average increases by one. The age of the teacher is

A. 25 B. 30 C. 35 D. 40

26. The average age of A, B, C and D five years ago was 45 years. By including X, the present age of all the five is 49 years. The present age of X is

A. 64 years B. 48 years C. 45 years D. 40 years

27. The average expenditure of a man for the first five months is ₹ 120 and for the next seven months it is ₹ 130. If he saves ₹ 290 in that year, his monthly average income is

A. ₹ 1000 B. ₹ 1800 C. ₹ 2000 D. ₹ 2500

28. The average weight of a class of 40 students is 40 kg. If the weight of the teacher be included, the average weight increases by 500 gms. The weight of the teacher is

A. 40.5 kg B. 60 kg C. 60.5 kg D. 62 kg

29. The average weight of 8 persons is increased by 2.5 kg when one of them whose weight is 56 kg is replaced by a new man. The weight of the new man is

A. 66 kg B. 75 kg C. 76 kg D. 86 kg

30. If a, b, c, d, e are five consecutive odd numbers, their average is

A. $5(a + 4)$ B. $\frac{abcde}{5}$

C. $5(a + b + c + d + e)$ D. None of these

ANSWERS

1	2	3	4	5	6	7	8	9	10
B	A	B	A	D	C	D	A	D	C
11	**12**	**13**	**14**	**15**	**16**	**17**	**18**	**19**	**20**
C	B	B	B	D	C	C	C	C	D
21	**22**	**23**	**24**	**25**	**26**	**27**	**28**	**29**	**30**
B	C	B	C	C	C	B	C	C	D

EXPLANATORY ANSWERS

1. Average $= \frac{3(1+2+3+4+5)}{5} = \frac{(3 \times 15)}{5} = 9$

6. Total income for 12 months = ₹ $(120 \times 5 + 130 \times 7 + 290)$ = ₹ 1800

Average monthly income = ₹$\frac{1800}{12}$ = ₹150

10. Average $= \frac{2+3+5+7+11}{5} = \frac{28}{5} = 5.6.$

13. Total height of 30 boys = $30 \times 160 = 4800$

Total height of 20 boys = $20 \times 165 = 3300$

Total height of 50 boys = 8100

Average height of 50 boys $= \frac{8100}{50} = 162.$

19. $\dfrac{nx - 36 - 36}{n} = x - 8$

$\Rightarrow nx - 72 = nx - 8n$

$\Rightarrow 8n = 72 \Rightarrow \quad n = 9$

23. Sum of four numbers = (15 × 3 + 19) = 64

Sum of last three numbers = (16 × 3) = 48

∴ First number = (64 – 48) = 16

24. Let the original strength = x

Then, $40x + 12 \times 32 = (x + 12) \times 36$

$\Rightarrow \quad 40x + 384 = 36x + 432$

$\Rightarrow \quad 4x = 48$

$\Rightarrow \quad x = 12$

25. Age of the teacher = (25 × 11 – 24 × 10) years = 35 years

26. Present age of x = [(49 × 5) – (4 × 45 + 4 × 5)] years

= 45 years

27. Total income = (120 × 5 + 130 × 7 + 290) = ₹ 1800

28. Weight of the teacher = (41 × 40.5 – 40 × 40) kg = 60.5 kg

29. Total increase = (8 × 2.5) kg = 20 kg

Weight of new man = (56 + 20)kg = 76 kg

30. Average $= \dfrac{a + (a+2) + (a+4) + (a+6) + (a+8)}{5}$

$= (a + 4)$

7 Percentage

The word 'per cent' or 'percentage' means 'for every one hundred'. In other words, it gives an indication of rate per hundred. It is denoted by the symbol %.

For example, 5% means 5 out of one hundred or $\frac{5}{100}$.

Important Facts:

For quickly solving the problems related to percentage, remember following rules:

(a) Of the given two numbers if the first is $x\%$ more than the second, then the second will be $\left(\frac{100 \times x}{100 + x}\right)\%$ less than the first.

(b) Of the given two numbers if the first is $x\%$ less than the second, then the second will be $\left(\frac{100 \times x}{100 - x}\right)\%$ more than the first.

(c) If two numbers are respectively $x\%$ and $y\%$ more than a third number, then the first number will be $\left(\frac{100 + x}{100 + y} \times 100\right)\%$ of the second.

(d) If two numbers are respectively $x\%$ and $y\%$ less than a third number, then the first number will be $\left(\frac{100 - x}{100 - y} \times 100\right)\%$ of the second.

Example 1. : A's income is 150% more than B's income. By how much per cent is B's income less than A's income?

Solution : Here, A's income is 150% more than B's income, *i.e.*, $x = 150$

$\therefore$ B's income will be $\left(\frac{100 \times 150}{100 + 150}\right)\%$ less than A's income,

$$\left(\frac{100 \times 150}{100 + 150}\right)\% = \frac{100 \times 150}{250}\% = 60\%$$

Example 2. : If a number is increased by 10% and thereafter decreased by 10%, then by how much per cent the number has been increased or decreased?

Solution : $\because$ The number is first increased by 10% and later the new number is decreased by 10%

$\therefore$ Percentage decrease in the number = $\left(\frac{(10)^2}{100}\right)\% = 1\%$

Example 3. : The population of a town is 40,000. If the population increases 20% every year, find the population after 3 years.

Solution: Population after 3 years = $40000\left(1+\frac{20}{100}\right)^3$

$= 40000 \times \frac{6}{5} \times \frac{6}{5} \times \frac{6}{5} = 69120$

MULTIPLE CHOICE QUESTIONS

1. If x is 90% of y, then what per cent of x is y?
A. 90 B. 190 C. 101.1 D. 111.1

2. A number exceeds 20% of itself by 40. The number is :
A. 50 B. 60 C. 80 D. 320

3. The price of an article is cut by 10%. To restore it to the former value, the new price must be increased by :
A. 10% B. $9\frac{1}{11}\%$ C. $11\frac{1}{9}\%$ D. 11%

4. The income of a broker remains unchanged though the rate of commission is increased from 4% to 5%. The percentage of slump business is :
A. 8% B. 1% C. 20% D. 80%

5. 5% income of A is equal to 15% income of B and 10% income of B is equal to 20% income of C. If income of C is ₹ 2000, then total income of A, B and C is :
A. ₹ 6000 B. ₹ 18000 C. ₹ 20000 D. ₹ 14000

6. A student who secures 20% marks in an examination fails by 30 marks. Another student who secures 32% gets 42 marks more than those required to pass. The percentage of marks required to pass is:
A. 20 B. 25 C. 28 D. 30

7. In a college election, a candidate secured 62% of the votes and is elected by a majority of 144 votes. The total number of votes polled is :
A. 600 B. 800 C. 925 D. 1200

8. What will be 80% of a number whose 200% is 90?
A. 144 B. 72 C. 36 D. None of these

9. p is six times as large as q. The per cent that q is less than p, is :
A. $83\frac{1}{3}$ B. $16\frac{2}{3}$ C. 90 D. 60

10. The price of an article has been reduced by 25%. In order to restore the original price, the new price must be increased by :
A. $33\frac{1}{3}\%$ B. $11\frac{1}{9}\%$ C. $9\frac{1}{11}\%$ D. $66\frac{2}{3}\%$

11. The price of cooking oil has increased by 25%. The percentage of reduction that a family should effect in the use of cooking oil so as not to increase the expenditure on this account is :
A. 25% B. 30% C. 20% D. 15%

12. In an organisation, 40% of the employees are matriculates, 50% of the remaining are graduates and the remaining 180 are postgraduates. How many employees are graduates?
A. 360 B. 240 C. 300 D. 180

13. In 40% of the people read newspaper X, 50% read newspaper Y, and 10% read both the papers. What percentage of the people read neither newspaper?
A. 10% B. 15% C. 20% D. 25%

14. The population of a town increases by 5% annually. If its population in 2008 was 138915, what it was in 2005?
A. 110000 B. 100000 C. 120000 D. 90000

15. The population of a village is 4500. $\frac{5}{9}$th of them are males and rest females. If 40% of the males are married, then the percentage of married female is :
A. 35 B. 40 C. 50 D. 60

16. A's income is 10% more than B's. How much per cent is B's income is less than A's?
A. 10% B. 7% C. $9\frac{1}{11}\%$ D. $6\frac{1}{2}\%$

17. A mixture of 40 litres of milk and water contains 10% water. How much water must be added to make water 20% in the new mixture?
A. 10 litres B. 7 litres C. 5 litres D. 3 litres

18. If $z = \frac{x^2}{y}$ and x, y both are increased in value by 10%, then the value of z is :

A. unchanged B. increased by 10%
C. increased by 11% D. increased by 20%

19. In an examination, 35% of the examinees failed in G.K. and 25% in English. If 10% of the examinees failed in both, then the percentage of examinees passed will be:

A. 40% B. 45% C. 48% D. 50%

20. If the price of a television set is increased by 25%, then by what percentage should the new price be reduced to bring the price back to original level?

A. 15% B. 20% C. 25% D. 30%

21. A candidate needs 35% marks to pass. If he gets 96 marks and fails by 16 marks, then the maximum marks are :

A. 250 B. 320 C. 300 D. 425

22. In an election one of the two candidates gets 40% votes and loses by 100 votes. Total number of votes is :

A. 500 B. 400 C. 600 D. 1000

23. If the income tax is decreased by 26%, a man's net income increases by $\frac{2}{3}\%$. The rate of income tax is:

A. $3\frac{1}{2}\%$ B. $2\frac{1}{2}\%$ C. $1\frac{1}{2}\%$ D. 3%

24. The gross income of a person is ₹ 20000. 10% of his income is exempted from income tax and his net income is ₹ 19100. The rate of income tax is :

A. 3% B. 2% C. 4% D. 5%

25. If the rate of income tax is 5%, the net income of a person is ₹ 17100. If the rate of income tax is 6%, how much will be the net income?

A. 15820 B. 16920 C. 17820 D. 18920

26. The gross income of a person is ₹ 15000, 20% of his income is exempted from income tax and the rate of income tax is ₹ 4%. The net income is :

A. 14520 B. 14620 C. 15520 D. 15620

27. The gross income of a person is ₹ 16000. A part of his income is exempted from income tax and his net income is ₹ 14480. If the rate of income tax is 8%, the income exempted from income tax is :

A. 1600 B. 1700 C. 1800 D. 1500

28. One-eight of a number is 17.25. What will 73% of number be?
A. 82.66 B. 96.42 C. 100.74 D. 138.00

29. If 58% of 960 – x% of 635 = 277.4, find the value of x.
A. 24 B. 36 C. 44 D. 58

30. There are 1225 employees in an organisation, out of which 40% got transferred to different places. How many such employees got transferred?
A. 490 B. 540 C. 630 D. 710

ANSWERS

1	2	3	4	5	6	7	8	9	10
D	A	C	C	B	B	A	C	A	A
11	**12**	**13**	**14**	**15**	**16**	**17**	**18**	**19**	**20**
C	D	C	C	C	C	C	B	D	B
21	**22**	**23**	**24**	**25**	**26**	**27**	**28**	**29**	**30**
B	A	B	D	B	A	D	C	C	A

EXPLANATORY ANSWERS

2. $x - 20\%$ of $x = 40$

$$\Rightarrow x - \frac{x}{5} = 40 \Rightarrow \frac{4x}{5} = 40$$

$$\Rightarrow x = \frac{40 \times 5}{4} = 50$$

3. Required percentage $= \dfrac{10}{100-10} \times 100$

$$= \frac{10}{90} \times 100 = 11\frac{1}{9}\%$$

7. (62% of x – 38% of x) = 144
$\Rightarrow$ 24% of x = 144

$$\Rightarrow x = \frac{144 \times 100}{24}$$

$= 600$

10. Required percentage $= \dfrac{25}{100-25} \times 100 = \dfrac{25}{75} \times 100 = 33\dfrac{1}{3}\%$

13. Number of people read either one or both = 40 + 50 – 10 = 80%
Hence, number of people read neither newspaper = 100 – 80 = 20%

16. Required percentage = $\left[\frac{10}{(100+10)} \times 100\right]\% = 9\frac{1}{11}\%$

21. 35% of x = 96 + 16 = 112

$$\Rightarrow \frac{35}{100} \times x = 112 \Rightarrow x = \frac{112 \times 100}{35} = 320$$

22. Out of 100, difference in votes = (60 – 40) = 20
20% of x = 100

$$\therefore\ x = \frac{100 \times 100}{20} = 500$$

25. Gross income = $\frac{100}{95} \times 17100$ = ₹ 18000

New net income = $\frac{94}{100} \times 18000$ = ₹ 16920

28. The number = 8 × 17.25 = 138.00

73% of the number = $\frac{73}{100} \times 138 = \frac{10074}{100} = 100.75$

30. The number of employess got transferred = $\frac{40}{100} \times 1225 = 490$

8

Profit & Loss

Cost Price (CP)

The price at which an article is purchased is called the cost price of the article.

Selling Price (SP)

The price at which an article is sold is called the selling price of the article.

Profit or Gain

If SP is greater than the CP, the seller is said to have a profit or gain.

Clearly, Gain = SP – CP

Loss

If SP is less than CP, the seller is said to have a loss.

Clearly, Loss = CP – SP

Profit or loss per cent is calculated on cost price.

$$\text{Profit \%} = \frac{\text{Profit}}{\text{CP}} \times 100$$

$$\text{Loss \%} = \frac{\text{Loss}}{\text{CP}} \times 100$$

If an article is sold at a gain of 20%,

then, SP = (120% of CP)

If an article is sold at a loss of 20%,

then, SP = (80% of CP)

Example 1. : Ravi buys an article for ₹ 5000 and sells it at 20% gain. Find it selling price.

Solution: Profit = 20% of CP $= \frac{20}{100} \times 5000$

⇒ Profit = ₹ 1000

SP = CP + Profit

= 5000 + 1000

= ₹ 6000

Example 2. : A man sells an article at 20% gain for ₹ 3600. Find its cost price.

Solution: Let CP = ₹ 100

then SP = 100 + 20 = ₹ 120

When SP ₹ 120 then CP = ₹ 100

When SP ₹ 3600 then CP = $\frac{100}{120} \times 3600$

Hence CP = ₹ 3000

MULTIPLE CHOICE QUESTIONS

1. A loss of 5% was suffered by selling a plot for ₹ 4085. The cost price of the plot was:
A. ₹ 4350 B. ₹ 4259.25 C. ₹ 4200 D. ₹ 4300

2. On selling an article for ₹ 240, a trader loses 4%. In order to gain 10%, he must sell that article for:
A. ₹ 264.00 B. ₹ 273.20 C. ₹ 275.00 D. ₹ 280.00

3. A man purchased a watch for ₹ 400 and sold it at a gain of 20% of the selling price. The selling price of the watch is:
A. ₹ 300 B. ₹ 320 C. ₹ 440 D. ₹ 500

4. If 5% more is gained by selling an article for ₹ 350 than by selling it for ₹ 340, the cost of the article is:
A. ₹ 50 B. ₹ 160 C. ₹ 200 D. ₹ 225

5. Profit after selling a commodity for ₹ 425 is same as loss after selling it for ₹ 355. The cost of the commodity is:
A. ₹ 385 B. ₹ 390 C. ₹ 395 D. ₹ 400

6. The cost price of an article, which on being sold at a gain of 12% yields ₹ 6 more than when it is sold at a loss of 12%, is:
A. ₹ 30 B. ₹ 25 C. ₹ 20 D. ₹ 24

7. The CP of an article which is sold at a loss of 25% for ₹150, is:
A. ₹ 125 B. ₹ 175 C. ₹ 200 D. ₹ 225

8. When the price of pressure cooker was increased by 15%, its sale fell down by 15%. The effect on the money receipt was:
A. no effect B. 15% decrease
C. 7.5% increase D. 2.25% decrease

9. A man sells 320 mangoes at the cost price of 400 mangoes. His gain per cent is:
A. 10% B. 25% C. 15% D. 20%

10. By selling 12 oranges for one rupee a man loses 20%. How many for a rupee should he sell to get a gain of 20%?
A. 5 B. 8 C. 10 D. 15

11. A man sells a car to his friend at 10% loss. If the friend sells it for ₹ 54000 and gains 20%, the original CP of the car was:
A. ₹ 25000 B. ₹ 37500 C. ₹ 50000 D. ₹ 60000

12. The loss incurred on selling an article for ₹ 270 is as much as the profit made after selling it at 10% profit. The CP of the article is:
A. ₹ 90 B. ₹ 110 C. ₹ 363 D. ₹ 300

13. An item costing ₹ 200 is being sold at 10% loss. If the price is further reduced by 5%, the selling price will be:
A. ₹ 179 B. ₹ 175 C. ₹ 171 D. ₹ 170

14. A trader lists his articles 20% above CP and allows a discount of 10% on cash payment. His gain per cent is:
A. 10% B. 6% C. 8% D. 5%

15. A discount series of 10%, 20% and 40% is equal to a single discount of:
A. 50% B. 56.80% C. 70% D. 70.28%

16. An umbrella marked at ₹ 80 is sold for ₹ 68, the rate of discount is:
A. 12% B. 15% C. $17\frac{11}{17}\%$ D. 20%

17. A reduction of 20% in the price of mangoes enables a person to purchase 12 more for ₹ 15. The price of 16 mangoes before reduction was:
A. ₹ 5 B. ₹ 6 C. ₹ 7 D. ₹ 9

18. Tarun bought a TV with 20% discount on the labelled price. Had he bought it with 25% discount, he would have saved ₹ 500. At what price did he buy the TV?
A. ₹ 5,000 B. ₹ 10,000 C. ₹ 12,000 D. None of these

19. If a commission of 10% is given on the marked price of a book, the publisher gains 20%. If the commission is increased to 15%, the gain is:
A. $16\frac{2}{3}\%$ B. $13\frac{1}{3}\%$ C. $15\frac{1}{6}\%$ D. None of these

20. There would be 10% loss if rice is sold at ₹ 5.40 per kg. At what price per kg should it be sold to earn a profit of 20%?
A. ₹ 7.20 B. ₹ 7.02 C. ₹ 6.48 D. ₹ 6

21. At what price must Kantilal sell a mixture of 80 kg sugar at ₹ 6.75 per kg with 120 kg at ₹ 8 per kg to gain 20%?
A. ₹ 7.50 per kg B. ₹ 8.20 per kg
C. ₹ 8.35 per kg D. ₹ 9 per kg

22. Subhash purchased a taperecorder at $\frac{9}{10}$ of its selling price and sold it at 8% more than its S.P. His gain is :

A. 8% B. 10% C. 18% D. 20%

23. A dealer marks his goods 20% above cost price. He then allows some discount on it and makes a profit of 8%. The rate of discount is :

A. 12% B. 10% C. 6% D. 4%

24. A trader lists his articles 20% above C.P. and allows a discount of 10% on cash payment. His gain per cent is :

A. 10% B. 8% C. 6% D. 4%

25. Tarun bought a T.V. with 20% discount on the labelled price. Had he bought it with 25% discount, he would have saved Rs. 500. At what price did he buy the T.V.?

A. ₹ 5000 B. ₹ 8000 C. ₹ 10000 D. ₹ 12000

26. While selling a watch, a shopkeeper gives a discount of 5%. If he gives a discount of 7%, he earns ₹ 15 less as profit. The marked price of the watch is :

A. ₹ 697.50 B. ₹ 712.50 C. ₹ 787.50 D. None of these

27. Kabir buys an article with 25% discount on its marked price. He makes a profit of 10% by selling it at ₹ 660. The marked price is :

A. ₹ 600 B. ₹ 700 C. ₹ 800 D. ₹ 885

28. A person bought an article and sold it at a loss of 10%. If he had bought it for 20% less and sold it for ₹ 55 more, he would have had a profit of 40%. The C.P. of the article is :

A. ₹ 200 B. ₹ 225 C. ₹ 250 D. None of these

29. The purchase tax on an article is levied at the rate of $66\frac{2}{3}\%$ of its wholesale price, while the retailer's profit amounts to 20% of the retail price of the article. What is the wholesale price of an article which is retailed at ₹ 12.50?

A. ₹ 4 B. ₹ 6 C. ₹ 8 D. ₹ 2

30. The catalogue price of a radio is ₹ 720. If it is sold at a discount of $16\frac{2}{3}\%$ of the catalogue price, the gain is 25%. Find the gain or loss per cent, if it is sold for ₹ 160 below the catalogue price.

A. $16\frac{2}{3}\%$ B. 16% C. 18% D. 20%

ANSWERS

1	2	3	4	5	6	7	8	9	10
D	C	D	C	B	B	C	D	B	B
11	**12**	**13**	**14**	**15**	**16**	**17**	**18**	**19**	**20**
C	D	C	C	B	B	A	D	B	A
21	**22**	**23**	**24**	**25**	**26**	**27**	**28**	**29**	**30**
D	D	B	B	B	D	C	C	B	A

EXPLANATORY ANSWERS

1. Loss = 5%, SP = ₹ 4085

Let CP = ₹ 100

$\therefore$ SP = ₹ 100 – 5 = ₹ 95

When SP ₹ 95 then CP = ₹ 100

When SP ₹ 4085 then CP = $\frac{100}{95} \times 4085 = 4300$

Hence, the cost price of the plot was ₹ 4300.

5. Let CP = ₹ x, then, $425 - x = x - 355 \Rightarrow 2x = 780 \Rightarrow x = 390$

Hence, the cost of commodity is ₹ 390.

7. 100 – 25 = 75

When SP 75 then CP = ₹ 100

When SP 150 then CP = ₹$\frac{100}{75} \times 150 =$ ₹ 200

9. Let CP of each mango be ₹ 1.

Then, CP of 400 mangoes = ₹ 400

$\therefore$ CP of 320 mangoes = ₹ 320

SP of 320 mangoes = ₹ 400

Profit = 400 – 320 = ₹ 80

$$\text{Profit\%} = \frac{80}{320} \times 100 = 25\%$$

11. SP = ₹ 54000 and gain earned = 20%

CP = ₹$\left(\frac{100}{120} \times 54000\right)$ = ₹ 45000

Now, SP = ₹ 45000 and Loss = 10%

$\therefore$ CP = ₹$\left(\frac{100}{90} \times 45000\right)$ = ₹ 50000

13. SP = 90% of ₹ 200 = ₹ 180
Further, SP = (95% of ₹180) = ₹ 171

16. Marked price = ₹ 80, SP = ₹ 68
Discount = MP – SP = 80 – 68 = ₹ 12

Discount % = $\frac{\text{discount}}{\text{MP}} \times 100 = \frac{12}{80} \times 100 = 15\%$

22. Let S.P. = ₹ 100; C.P. for Subhash = $\frac{9}{10} \times 100$ = ₹ 90 and S.P. = ₹ 108

Hence, gain % for Subhash = $\frac{108-90}{90} \times 100 = 20\%$

23. Let C.P. be ₹ 100; then Marked price = ₹ 120 and S.P. = ₹ 108

$\therefore$ Discount = $\left(\frac{12}{120} \times 100\right)\% = 10\%$

24. Let C.P. be ₹ 100
Then, marked price = ₹ 120

S.P. = ₹ $\left(\frac{90}{100} \times 120\right)$ = ₹ 108 $\therefore$ Gain % = $\left(\frac{8}{100} \times 100\right)\% = 8\%$

26. Let the marked price = ₹ x

Then, $\frac{7x}{100} - \frac{5x}{100} = 15$

$\Rightarrow \frac{x}{50} = 15$ $\qquad \therefore x =$ ₹ 750

27. C.P. = $\frac{100}{110} \times 660$ = ₹ 600

Hence, M.P. = $\frac{100}{75} \times 600$ = ₹ 800

❖ ❖ ❖

9

Simple & Compound Interest

In any money transaction there is a **lender** who gives money, and a **borrower** who receives money. The amount of loan borrowed, is called the principal (P). The borrower pays a certain amount for the use of this money. This is called **Interest (I)**. Interest is always calculated on the principal borrowed. The borrowing is for a specified **Time (t)** and on specified terms. The specified term is expressed as per cent of the principal and is called rate of interest. The sum of the principal and the interest is called the **Amount (A)**.

Interest is of two kinds—**Simple Interest and compound Interest**. If the interest is calculated only, on a certain sum borrowed it is called Simple Interest. The simple interest (SI) on a principal P at R% per annum for T years is given by: $SI = \frac{P \times R \times T}{100}$

Compound Interest differs from Simple Interest that in CI the interest for the future period is calculated not only on the principal but also on the interest earned until the previous period. The difference between the final amount (A) obtained at the last unit of time and the original principal is called the **Compound Interest**.

Important Relations

Principal	=	₹ P (in rupees)
Rate	=	R % (in per cent per annum)
Time period	=	T years (in years)
Amount	=	₹ A (in rupees)

When interest is compounded annually, $A = P\left[1 + \frac{R}{100}\right]^T$

When interest is compounded half-yearly,

$$A = P\left[1 + \frac{R/2}{100}\right]^{2T} = P\left[1 + \frac{R}{200}\right]^{2T}$$

[R is divided by 2 and T is multiplied by 2.]

CI = A – P

Example 1. : Find the simple interest on ₹ 1000 for 3 years at 10% p.a.

Solution: $SI = \frac{P \times R \times T}{100} = \frac{1000 \times 10 \times 3}{100} = ₹\ 300$

EXAMPLE 2. : Find the amount of ₹ 600 in 4 years at 3% p.a.

SOLUTION: $SI = \frac{P \times R \times T}{100} = \frac{600 \times 3 \times 4}{100} = ₹\ 72$

$\therefore$ Amount = P + SI = 600 + 72 = ₹ 672

EXAMPLE 3. : In what time will ₹ 7000 give ₹ 3675 as interest at the rate of 7% p.a. simple interest?

SOLUTION: $T = \frac{SI \times 100}{P \times R} = \frac{3675 \times 100}{7000 \times 7} = \frac{15}{2} = 7\frac{1}{2}$ years.

MULTIPLE CHOICE QUESTIONS

1. The simple interest on ₹ 500 for 6 years at 5% p.a. is:
A. ₹ 250 B. ₹ 150 C. ₹ 140 D. ₹ 120

2. A certain sum of money at SI amounts to ₹ 1012 in $2\frac{1}{2}$ years and to ₹ 1067.20 in 4 years. The rate of interest per annum is:
A. 2.5% B. 3% C. 4% D. 5%

3. ₹ 1200 amounts to ₹ 1632 in 4 years at a certain rate of simple interest. If the rate of interest is increased by 1%, it would amount to how much?
A. ₹ 1635 B. ₹ 1644 C. ₹ 1670 D. ₹ 1680

4. A man will get ₹ 87 as simple interest on ₹ 725 at 4% per annum in:
A. 3 years B. 3½ years C. 4 years D. 5 years

5. At simple interest, a sum doubles after 20 years. The rate of interest per annum is:
A. 5% B. 10%
C. 20% D. Data inadequate

6. A lent ₹ 600 to B for 2 years and ₹ 150 to C for 4 years and received altogether from both ₹ 90 as simple interest. The rate of interest is:
A. 12% B. 10% C. 5% D. 4%

7. Interest on a certain sum of money for $2\frac{1}{3}$ years at $3\frac{3}{4}\%$ per annum is ₹ 210. The sum is:
A. ₹ 2800 B. ₹ 1580 C. ₹ 2400 D. None of these

8. A certain sum of money at simple interest amounts to ₹ 1260 in 2 years and to ₹ 1350 in 5 years. The rate per cent per annum is:
A. 2.5% B. 3.75% C. 5% D. 7.5%

9. A sum of money doubles itself in 5 years. It will become 4 times itself in:
A. 10 years B. 12 years C. 15 years D. 20 years

10. The simple interest on a sum of money will be ₹ 600 after 10 years. If the principal is trebled after 5 years, the total interest at the end of 10 years will be:
A. ₹ 600 B. ₹ 900
C. ₹ 1200 D. Data inadequate

11. ₹ 800 amounts to ₹ 920 in 3 years at simple interest. If the interest rate is increased by 3%, it would amount to how much?
A. ₹ 1056 B. ₹ 1112 C. ₹ 1182 D. ₹ 992

12. A sum of money at simple interest amounts to ₹ 2240 in 2 years and ₹ 2600 in 5 years. The sum is:
A. ₹ 1880 B. ₹ 2000
C. ₹ 2120 D. Data inadequate

13. If ₹ 7500 are borrowed at CI at the rate of 4% per annum, then after 2 years the amount to be paid is:
A. ₹ 8082 B. ₹ 7800 C. ₹ 8100 D. ₹ 8112

14. Simple interest on a sum at 4% per annum is ₹ 80 in 2 years. The compound interest on the same sum for the same period is:
A. ₹ 81.60 B. ₹ 160 C. ₹ 1081.60 D. None of these

15. ₹ 800 at 5% per annum compound interest will amount to ₹ 882 in:
A. 1 year B. 2 years C. 3 years D. 4 years

16. What is the principal amount which earns ₹ 132 as compound interest for the second year at 10% per annum?
A. ₹ 1000 B. ₹ 1200 C. ₹ 1320 D. None of these

17. The difference between the compound interest and the simple interest on a certain sum at 5% per annum for 2 years is ₹ 1.50. The sum is:
A. ₹ 600 B. ₹ 500 C. ₹ 400 D. ₹ 300

18. The compound interest on a certain sum of money for 2 years at 10% per annum is ₹ 420. The simple interest on the same sum at the same rate and for the same time will be:
A. ₹ 350 B. ₹ 375 C. ₹ 380 D. ₹ 400

19. A sum amounts to ₹ 2916 in 2 years and to ₹ 3149.28 in 3 years at compound interest. The sum is :
A. ₹ 1500 B. ₹ 2000 C. ₹ 2500 D. ₹ 3000

20. A sum of money amounts to ₹ 10648 in 3 years and ₹ 9680 in 2 years. The rate of interest is:
A. 5% B. 10% C. 15% D. 20%

21. If the simple interest on a certain sum of money at 6% per annum for 3 years is ₹ 90, the sum will be:
A. ₹ 500 B. ₹ 450 C. ₹ 525 D. ₹ 560

22. If the simple interest on Re. 1 for 1 month is 1 paise, the rate per cent p.a. will be :
A. 10% B. 8% C. 12% D. 6%

23. A sum of money doubles itself in 20 years. In how many years will it triple itself at the same rate of simple interest?
A. 30 years B. 50 years C. 40 years D. 45 years

24. If the simple interest on Rs. 500 for 4 years is Rs. 40, find the rate per cent p.a.
A. 3½% B. 2% C. 2½% D. 3%

25. After what time will the sum of ₹ 2000 become ₹ 2240 at 4% per annum simple interest?
A. 3 years B. 2 years C. 5 years D. 4 years

26. What will be the compound interest on ₹ 8000 for 3 years at 5% p.a.?
A. ₹ 1361 B. ₹ 1261 C. ₹ 1260 D. ₹ 1250

27. What will be the amount if a sum of ₹ 2500 is invested for 1 year at 4% per annum compound interest, interest being compounded half-yearly?
A. ₹ 2625 B. ₹ 2601 C. ₹ 2830 D. ₹ 2901

28. Find the compound interest on ₹ 2560 for ½ year at 12½% per annum, interest payable quarterly.
A. ₹ 3720.50 B. ₹ 2722.50 C. ₹ 2752.50 D. ₹ 2250.50

29. After how many years will ₹ 3375 become ₹ 4096 at $6\frac{2}{3}\%$ per annum compound interest?
A. 4 years B. 2 years C. 2½ years D. 3 years

30. A certain sum of money placed at compound interest amounts to Rs. 110 in 1 year and to Rs. 121 in 2 years. The rate of interest per annum is :
A. 5% B. 10% C. 8% D. 4%

ANSWERS

1	2	3	4	5	6	7	8	9	10
B	C	D	A	A	C	C	A	C	C
11	**12**	**13**	**14**	**15**	**16**	**17**	**18**	**19**	**20**
D	B	D	A	B	B	A	D	C	B
21	**22**	**23**	**24**	**25**	**26**	**27**	**28**	**29**	**30**
A	C	C	B	A	B	B	B	D	B

EXPLANATORY ANSWERS

1. $SI = \frac{P \times R \times T}{100} = \frac{500 \times 5 \times 6}{100} = ₹\ 150$

3. $R = \frac{SI \times 100}{P \times T} = \frac{432 \times 100}{1200 \times 4} = 9\%$

New rate = (9 + 1)% = 10%

$$SI = \frac{P \times R \times T}{100} = \frac{1200 \times 10 \times 4}{100} = ₹\ 480$$

Amount = P + SI = 1200 + 480 = ₹ 1680

4. $T = \frac{SI \times 100}{P \times R} = \frac{87 \times 100}{725 \times 4} = 3$ years

5. Let P be ₹ x then A = ₹ $2x$

SI = A – P = $2x - x$ = ₹ x

$R = \frac{SI \times 100}{P \times T} = \frac{x \times 100}{x \times 20} = 5\%$

12. SI for 3 years = 2600 – 2240 = ₹ 360

SI for 2 years = $\frac{360}{3} \times 2$ = ₹ 240

∴ Sum = 2240 – 240 = ₹ 2000

13. $A = P\left(1 + \frac{R}{100}\right)^T = 7500\left(1 + \frac{4}{100}\right)^2$

$$= 7500 \times \frac{26}{25} \times \frac{26}{25} = ₹\ 8112$$

21. $P = \frac{90 \times 100}{6 \times 3} = ₹\ 500$

22. Rate $= \frac{1 \times 100}{100 \times \frac{1}{12}} = 12\%.$

23. Let principal = ₹ x; Amount = ₹ $2x$; then I = $2x - x$ = ₹ x

∴ $R = \frac{x \times 100}{x \times 20} = 5\%$

Again, if principal = ₹ x; Amount = ₹ $3x$; then I = $3x - x$ = ₹ $2x$

Hence, $T = \frac{2x \times 100}{x \times 5} = 40$ years

24. Rate $= \frac{40 \times 100}{500 \times 4} = 2\%$

25. Here, I = 2240 – 2000 = ₹ 240

$\therefore T = \frac{240 \times 100}{2000 \times 4} = 3$ years

26. $\therefore$ C.I. $= 8000\left[\left(1+\frac{5}{100}\right)^3 - 1\right] = 8000\left[\left(\frac{21}{20}\right)^3 - 1\right]$

$= \frac{8000 \times 1261}{8000}$ = ₹ 1261

27. $A = 2500\left(1+\frac{2}{100}\right)^2 = 2500\left(\frac{51}{50}\right)^2 = \frac{2500 \times 51 \times 51}{50 \times 50}$ = ₹ 2601

28. Amount $= 2560\left(1+\frac{25}{8 \times 100}\right)^2 = \frac{2560 \times 33 \times 33}{32 \times 32}$ = ₹ 2722.50

29. Here, $4096 = 3375\left(1+\frac{20}{3 \times 100}\right)^n \Rightarrow \frac{4096}{3375} = \left(1+\frac{1}{15}\right)^n$

$\Rightarrow \left(\frac{16}{15}\right)^3 = \left(\frac{16}{15}\right)^n \quad \therefore n = 3$ years

10

Time & Work

The problems on Time and Work can be solved by following two methods:

(*i*) **Ratio and Proportion Method:** Since problems concerning to Time and Work have proportional relation, these can be solved by this method.

(*ii*) **Unitary Method:** In this method, we first proceed to reduce the problem to either work done by one person or work done in 1 day and so on as per the requirement of the problem.

If M_1 persons can do W_1 works in D_1 days and M_2 persons can do W_2 works in D_2 days then we have a very general formula in the relationship of

$$M_1 D_1 W_2 = M_2 D_2 W_1$$

The above relationship can be taken as a very basic and all-in-one formula we also derive:

(*i*) More men less days and conversely more days less men.

(*ii*) More men more work and conversely more work more men.

(*iii*) More days more work and conversely more work more days.

$$M_1 D_1 T_1 W_2 = M_2 D_2 T_2 W_1$$

Example: 5 men can prepare 10 toys in 6 days working 6 hrs a day. How many days can 12 men prepare 16 toys working 8 hrs a day?

Solution: $M_1 D_1 T_1 W_2 = M_2 D_2 T_2 W_1$

$$5 \times 6 \times 6 \times 16 = 12 \times D_2 \times 8 \times 10$$

$$D_2 = \frac{5 \times 6 \times 6 \times 16}{12 \times 8 \times 10} = 3 \text{ days.}$$

Example: A and B together can do a piece of work in 12 days, B alone can finish it in 30 days. In how many days can A alone finish the work?

Solution: (A + B)'s 1 day's work $= \frac{1}{12}$

B's 1 day's work $= \frac{1}{30}$

$\therefore$ A's 1 day's work $= \frac{1}{12} - \frac{1}{30} = \frac{5-2}{60} = \frac{3}{60} = \frac{1}{20}$

Hence, A alone can finish the work in 20 days.

MULTIPLE CHOICE QUESTIONS

1. A and B can together do a piece of work in 15 days. B alone can do it in 20 days. In how many days can A alone do it?

A. 30 days B. 40 days C. 45 days D. 60 days

2. A can do a piece of work in 30 days while B can do it in 40 days. A and B working together can do it in:

A. 70 days B. $42\frac{3}{4}$ days C. $27\frac{1}{7}$ days D. $17\frac{1}{7}$ days

3. A can do $\frac{1}{3}$ of the work in 5 days and B can do $\frac{2}{5}$ of the work in 10 days. In how many days both A and B together can do the work?

A. $7\frac{3}{4}$ days B. $8\frac{4}{5}$ days C. $9\frac{3}{8}$ days D. 10 days

4. A, B and C can do a piece of work in 6, 12 and 24 days respectively. They altogether will complete the work in:

A. $3\frac{3}{7}$ days B. $\frac{7}{24}$ days C. $4\frac{4}{5}$ days D. $\frac{5}{24}$ days

5. A, B and C contract a work for ₹ 550. Together A and B are to do $\frac{7}{11}$ of the work. The share of C should be:

A. ₹ $183\frac{1}{3}$ B. ₹ 200 C. ₹ 300 D. ₹ 400

6. A and B finish a job in 12 days while A, B and C can finish it in 8 days. C alone will finish the job in:

A. 20 days B. 14 days C. 24 days D. 16 days

7. 12 men can complete a work in 8 days. Three days after they started the work, 3 more men joined them. In how many days will all of them together complete the remaining work?

A. 2 B. 4 C. 5 D. 6

8. Mahesh and Umesh can complete a work in 10 and 15 days respectively. Umesh starts the work and after 5 days Mahesh joins him. In all, the work would be completed in:

A. 9 days B. 7 days C. 11 days D. None of these

9. Sunil completes a work in 4 days whereas Dinesh completes the work in 6 days. Ramesh works $1\frac{1}{2}$ times as fast as Sunil. How many days it will take for the three together to complete the work?

A. $\frac{7}{12}$ B. $1\frac{5}{12}$ C. $1\frac{5}{7}$ D. None of these

10. A can complete a work in 6 days and B in 5 days. They work together, finish the job and receive ₹ 220 as wages. B's share should be:

A. ₹ 120 B. ₹ 110 C. ₹ 100 D. ₹ 90

11. 12 men and 8 children can finish a piece of work in 9 days. If each child takes twice the time taken by a man to finish the work, in how many days will 12 men finish the same work?

A. 8 days B. 15 days C. 9 days D. 12 days

12. A, B and C together earn ₹ 150 per day while A and C together earn ₹ 94 and B and C together earn ₹ 76. The daily earning of C is:

A. ₹ 75 B. ₹ 56 C. ₹ 34 D. ₹ 20

13. If 5 men or 9 women can finish a piece of work in 19 days, 3 men and 6 women will do the same work in:

A. 10 days B. 12 days C. 13 days D. 15 days

14. A can do a piece of work in 12 days. B is 60% more efficient than A. The number of days, it takes B to do the same piece of work, is:

A. $7\frac{1}{2}$ days B. $6\frac{1}{4}$ days C. 8 days D. 6 days

15. A and B can do a piece of work in 45 and 40 days respectively. They began the work together, but A leaves after some days and B finished the remaining work in 23 days. After how many days did A leave?

A. 6 days B. 8 days C. 9 days D. 12 days

16. 12 men can complete a work within 9 days. After 3 days they started the work, 6 men joined them to replace 2 men. How many days will they take to complete the remaining work?

A. 2 days B. 3 days C. 4 days D. $4\frac{1}{2}$ days

17. 10 men can finish a piece of work in 10 days whereas it takes 12 women to finish it in 10 days. If 15 men and 6 women undertake to complete the work, how many days will they take to complete it?

A. 2 days B. 4 days C. 5 days D. 11 days

18. A can do a piece of work in 80 days. He works at it for 10 days and then B alone finishes the work in 42 days. The two together could complete the work in:

A. 24 days B. 25 days C. 30 days D. 35 days

19. A and B can together finish a work in 30 days. They worked for it for 20 days and then B left. The remaining work was done by A alone in 20 more days. A alone can finish the work in:

A. 48 days B. 50 days C. 54 days D. 60 days

20. A can complete a job in 9 days, B in 10 days and C in 15 days. B and C start the work and are forced to leave after 2 days. The time taken by A alone to complete the remaining work is:

A. 13 days B. 10 days C. 9 days D. 6 days

21. 12 boys can do a piece of work in 16 days. In how many days can 6 boys do the same work?

A. 16 days B. 32 days C. 23 days D. 24 days

22. A can do a piece of work in 8 days while B can do the same work in 16 days. If they start working together, how long would they take to complete half portion of this work?

A. $2\frac{2}{3}$ days B. $3\frac{5}{7}$ days C. $4\frac{1}{2}$ days D. $3\frac{1}{2}$ days

23. A can do a piece of work in 4 days. B is 50% more efficient than A. How long would B alone take to finish this work?

A. $3\frac{1}{3}$ days B. $5\frac{1}{4}$ days C. $2\frac{2}{3}$ days D. $1\frac{2}{3}$ days

24. A and B working together complete a work in 35 days. If A takes 60 days to complete it, how long would B alone take to complete it?

A. 64 days B. 72 days C. 81 days D. 84 days

25. A few children working together can do a piece of work in 18 days. If the number of children employed on the work is made double, how long would they take to complete half of the work?

A. $4\frac{1}{2}$ days B. $2\frac{1}{3}$ days C. $8\frac{3}{4}$ days D. $6\frac{1}{2}$ days

26. 10 men or 18 boys can do a piece of work in 15 days. In how many days would 25 men and 15 boys complete the same work working together?

A. $5\frac{1}{2}$ days B. $4\frac{1}{2}$ days C. $6\frac{2}{3}$ days D. $2\frac{1}{3}$ days

27. A can do a piece of work in 40 days. He starts working, but having some other engagements he drops out after 5 days. Thereafter B completes this work in 21 days. How many days would A and B take to complete this work working together?

A. 15 days B. 16 days C. 17 days D. 11 days

28. Two persons A and B can complete a piece of work in 8 hours and 16 hours respectively. If they work at it alternately for an hour, A starting first, in how many hours will the work be finished?

A. $9\frac{1}{3}$ hours B. $10\frac{1}{2}$ hours C. $11\frac{1}{2}$ hours D. $8\frac{1}{2}$ hours

29. 15 men can complete a work in 210 days. They started the work but at the end of 10 days 15 additional men, with double efficiency, were inducted. How many days, in whole, did they take to finish the work?

A. $76\frac{2}{3}$ days B. $84\frac{3}{4}$ days C. $72\frac{1}{2}$ days D. 70 days

30. A and B working together can complete a piece of work in 12 days and B and C working together can complete the same work in 16 days. A worked at it for 5 days and B worked at it for 7 days. C finished the remaining work in 13 days. How many days would C alone take to complete it?

A. 10 days B. 24 days C. 32 days D. 40 days

ANSWERS

1	2	3	4	5	6	7	8	9	10
D	D	C	A	B	C	B	A	D	A
11	**12**	**13**	**14**	**15**	**16**	**17**	**18**	**19**	**20**
D	D	D	A	C	D	C	C	D	D
21	**22**	**23**	**24**	**25**	**26**	**27**	**28**	**29**	**30**
B	A	C	D	A	B	A	B	A	B

EXPLANATORY ANSWERS

1. (A + B)'s 1 day's work = $\frac{1}{15}$

B's 1 day's work = $\frac{1}{20}$

A's 1 day's work = $\frac{1}{15} - \frac{1}{20} = \frac{4-3}{60} = \frac{1}{60}$

$\therefore$ A can do this work alone in 60 days.

5. Work to be done by C = $\left(1-\frac{7}{11}\right) = \frac{4}{11}$

$\therefore$ (A + B) : C = $\frac{7}{11}:\frac{4}{11} = 7:4$

$\therefore$ C's share = ₹ $\frac{4}{11}\times 550$ = ₹ 200

10. Ratio of time taken by A and B = 6 : 5
Ratio of work done in same time = 5 : 6
So, the money is to be divided among A and B in the ratio 5 : 6.

$\therefore$ B's share = ₹ $\frac{6}{11}\times 220$ = ₹ 120

11. 2 children = 1 man
$\therefore$ 8 children + 12 men = 4 + 12 = 16 men
Now, less men, more days
$12 : 16 :: 9 : x \Rightarrow \frac{12}{16} = \frac{9}{x} \Rightarrow x = 12$ days

12. B's daily earning = ₹ (150 – 94) = ₹ 56
A's daily earning = ₹ (150 – 76) = ₹ 74
C's daily earning = ₹ [150 – (56 + 74)] = ₹ 20

17. 10 men = 12 women $\Rightarrow$ 1 man = $\frac{6}{5}$ women

$\therefore$ 15 men + 6 women = $15\times\frac{6}{5}+6$
= 18 + 6 = 24 women
12 women can do the work in 10 days

24 women can do the same work in $\frac{10\times 12}{24}$ = 5 days

20. (B + C)'s 2 day's work = $2\left(\frac{1}{10}+\frac{1}{15}\right) = \frac{1}{3}$

Remaining work = $1-\frac{1}{3} = \frac{2}{3}$

Now, $\frac{1}{9}$ work is done by A in 1 day

$\therefore$ $\frac{2}{3}$ work will be done by A in $9\times\frac{2}{3}$ = 6 days

21. $\because$ 12 boys can do a piece of work in 16 days.

$\therefore$ 1 boy will do the same piece of work in 16 × 12 days.

$\therefore$ 6 boys will do the same piece of work in $\frac{16 \times 12}{6}$ days = 32 days.

23. A's 1 day's work $= \frac{1}{4}$; Hence, B's 1 day's work $= \frac{150}{100} \times \frac{1}{4} = \frac{3}{8}$

So, B will do the whole work in $\frac{8}{3} = 2\frac{2}{3}$ days.

25. Let number of children be x;

Now x children can do the work in 18 days.

Hence, $2x$ children will do $\frac{1}{2}$ of the work in $\frac{18 \times x}{2x \times 2} = \frac{9}{2}$ days $= 4\frac{1}{2}$ days.

27. A's 5 days' work $= 5 \times \frac{1}{40} = \frac{1}{8}$

Remaining work $= 1 - \frac{1}{8} = \frac{7}{8}$, which is done by B in 21 days.

Hence, B's 1 day's work $= \frac{7}{8 \times 21} = \frac{1}{24}$

Now, (A + B)'s 1 day's work $= \frac{1}{40} + \frac{1}{24} = \frac{8}{120} = \frac{1}{15}$

Hence, (A + B) will complete the work in 15 days.

28. In 2 hours the part of work $= \frac{1}{8} + \frac{1}{16} = \frac{3}{16}$ will be completed.

Hence, in 5 pairs of hours the part of work

$= 5 \times \frac{3}{16} = \frac{15}{16}$ will be completed

Remaining work $= 1 - \frac{15}{16} = \frac{1}{16}$ which will be done by A.

Time taken by A to complete the $\frac{1}{16}$ work $= \frac{1/16}{1/8} = \frac{1}{2}$ hour.

Hence, required number of hours $= 10 + \frac{1}{2} = 10\frac{1}{2}$ hours.

❖ ❖ ❖

11

Time & Distance

Important Formulae:

1. Speed = Distance ÷ Time
2. Distance = Time × Speed
3. Time = Distance ÷ Speed
4. x km/hr = $\left(x \times \frac{5}{18}\right)$ m/sec
5. x metres/sec = $\left(x \times \frac{18}{5}\right)$ km/hr.
6. If the speed of a body is changed in the ratio $m : n$, then the ratio of the time taken changes in the ratio $n : m$.
7. When a man covers a certain distance with a speed of x km/h and another equal distance at the rate of y km/h, then for the whole journey, the average speed is given by Average speed = $\frac{2xy}{x+y}$ km/h.

Example : A boy goes to school at a speed of 4 km/h and returns to the house at a speed of 3 km/h. If he takes 5 hrs. in all, what is the distance between the house and the school?

Solution: Let the distance between house and the school be x km.

$$\frac{x}{4}+\frac{x}{3}=5 \qquad \Rightarrow \qquad \frac{7x}{12}=5 \qquad \therefore \quad x=\frac{60}{7} \text{ km}$$

MULTIPLE CHOICE QUESTIONS

1. A car moving at 48 km/hr completes a journey in 10 hours. By how much the speed of this car should be increased so as to do this journey in 8 hours?
   A. 8 km/hr. B. 12 km/hr C. 10 km/hr D. 15 km/hr
2. Starting from a point at a speed of 4 km/hr a man reaches at a cerain place and returns back to the point from where he had started journey on bicycle at the speed of 16 km/hr. His average speed during the entire journey will be :
   A. 6.4 km/h B. 8.4 km/h C. 5.4 km/h D. 10 km/h
3. A motorist covers a certain distance at a average speed of 48 km/h in 45 minutes. What speed in km/h he must maintain to cover the same distance in 30 minutes?
   A. 66 km/h B. 79 km/h C. 80 km/h D. 72 km/h

4. Two points A and B are 150 km apart. A man completes his onward journey from A to B in 3 hours 20 minutes and return journey from B to A in 4 hours 10 minutes. His average speed during the entire journey will be less than his average speed during the journey from A to B by :
A. 5 km/h B. 7.5 km/h C. 9 km/h D. 3 km/h

5. A policeman saw a thief at a distance of 200 m. The policeman and the thief started running at the same time. If the policeman runs at a speed of $4\frac{1}{6}$ m per second and the thief at a speed of $3\frac{1}{3}$m per second, after what time the policeman will catch the thief?
A. 12 min B. 10 min C. 9 min D. 4 min

6. Kanchan walks from her home at 4 kms per hour and reaches her school 5 minutes late. If she walks at 5 kms per hour, she reaches the school 2½ minutes earlier. How far is the school from her home?
A. 3.5 kms B. 2.5 kms C. 2.75 kms D. 3.2 kms

7. A monkey wants to climb up a glazed pole. He climbs 12 metres in 1 minute and then he slips back 3 metres in the next minute. If the pole is 63 metre high, how long does he take to climb at the top of the pole?
A. $11\frac{1}{4}$min B. $12\frac{1}{2}$min C. $12\frac{3}{4}$min D. $14\frac{3}{4}$min

8. A and B start walking at the same time on a circular path with circumference 35 metre. If they walk in the same direction at 4 km/hr and 5 km/hr respectively, after what time will they meet together?
A. 35 hours B. 27 hours C. 24 hours D. 40 hours

9. While walking at $\frac{3}{5}$ of his usual speed Kamalkant reaches at his destination late by 30 minutes. His usual time consumed in reaching to his destination is:
A. 32 min B. 40 min C. 45 min D. 42 min

10. The distance between two stations A and B is 300 km. A train leaves the station A with a speed of 40 km/hr. At the same time another train departs from the station B with a speed of 50 km/hr. How much time will these two trains take to cross each other?
A. 3 hrs 40 min B. 3 hrs 20 min C. 2 hrs 20 min D. 3 hrs 45 min

11. Gulshan starts from a place P at 2 p.m. and walks to Q at 5 km per hour. Tarun starts from P at 3 p.m. and follows Gulshan on bicycle at 10 km per hour. By when Tarun will catch Gulshan?
A. At 5.30 p.m. B. At 4.00 p.m. C. At 4.30 p.m. D. At 6.00 p.m.

12. Nilesh goes to school from his village at the speed of 4 km/hr and returns from school to village at the speed of 2 km/hr. If he takes 6 hours in all, then what is the distance between the village and the school?
A. 8 km B. 6 km C. 5 km D. 4 km

13. A school bus covers a distance from a village to school at the speed of 12 km/hr and reaches the school 8 minute late. The next day the bus covers the same distance at the speed of 20 km/hr and reaches the school 10 minutes early. What is the distance between village and the school?
A. 6 km B. 9 km C. 12 km D. 15 km

14. By increasing the speed of the bus by 10 km/hr the time of journey for 72 km is reduced by 36 minutes. What was the original speed of the bus?
A. 30 km/hr B. 35 km/hr C. 40 km/hr D. 45 km/hr

15. A car completes a fixed journey in 8 hours. It covers half distance at the speed of 40 km/hr and rest at the 60 km/hr, the distance of the journeyTis:
A. 400 km B. 420 km C. 384 km D. 350 km

16. A car covers four consecutive extensions of 3 km each at the speeds of 10 km/hr, 20 km/hr, 30 km/hr and 60 km/hr. Its average speed of journey is:
A. 30 km/hr B. 25 km/hr C. 20 km/hr D. 10 km/hr

17. A girl rides her bicycle 10 km at an average speed of 12 km/hr and another 12 km at an average speed of 10 km/hr. Her average speed for the entire journey is approximately:
A. 12.2 km/hr B. 11.2 km/hr C. 10.8 km/hr D. 10.4 km/hr

18. Raman drove from home to a neighbouring town at the speed of 50 km/hr and on his returning journey, he drove at the speed of 45 km/hr and also took an hour longer to reach home. What distance did he cover each way?
A. 900 km B. 500 km C. 450 km D. 225 km

19. A man takes 6 hours 35 minutes in walking to a certain place and riding back. He would have taken 2 hours less by riding both ways. What would be the time he would take to walk both ways?
A. 10 hours B. 8 hours 35 minutes
C. 8 hours 25 minutes D. 8 hrs

20. A man covers a distance of 6 km at the rate of 4 km/hr and other 4 km at 3 km/hr this average speed is

A. $3\frac{5}{9}$ km/hr B. $3\frac{9}{17}$ km/hr C. $5\frac{9}{17}$ km/hr D. $9\frac{3}{17}$ km/hr

21. A cyclist rides 24 km at 16 km/h and further 36 km at 15 km/hr. Find his average speed for the journey.
A. 15.38 km/hr B. 15.5 km/hr C. 16 km/hr D. 16.5 km/hr

22. A car is running at a speed of 108 km/hr. Find the distance covered by it in 15 seconds.
A. 450 m B. 475 m C. 500 m D. 550 m

23. How long will a boy take to run round a square field of side 35 meters, If he runs at the rate of 9 km/hr?
A. 56 sec. B. 54 sec. C. 52 sec. D. 50 sec.

24. A person crosses a 600 m long street in 5 minutes. Find his speed in km/hr.
A. 10 B. 8.4 C. 7.2 D. 3.6

25. A man walking at the rate of 5 km/hr crosses a bridge in 15 minutes. What is the length of the bridge in meters?
A. 1250 B. 1000 C. 750 D. 600

26. A truck covers a distance of 550 m in 1 minute whereas a bus covers a distance of 33 km in 45 minutes. The ratio of their speeds is:
A. 50 : 3 B. 3 : 5 C. 4 : 3 D. 3 : 4

27. A train travels at an average of 50 miles/hr for $2\frac{1}{2}$ hrs and then travels at a speed of 70 miles/hr for $1\frac{1}{2}$ hrs. Find the distance travelled by the train in entire 4 hrs.
A. 230 miles B. 200 miles C. 150 miles D. 120 miles

28. Sound is said to travel in air at about 1100 feet/sec. A man hears the axe striking the tree $\frac{11}{5}$ seconds after he sees it strike the tree. Find the distance between the man and the wood chopper.
A. 2629 ft. B. 2500 ft. C. 2420 ft. D. 2197 ft.

29. A motor car starts with the speed of 70 km/hr with its speed increasing every two hours by 10 km/hr. What is the time taken (in hours) in covering 345 km by it?
A. 5 hrs. B. $4\frac{1}{2}$ hrs. C. 4 hrs 5 min. D. 4 hrs

30. A person has to cover a distance of 6 km in 45 minutes. If he covers one-half of the distance in two-thirds of the total time. Find his speed (in km/hr) to cover the remaining distance in remaining time.
A. 15 B. 12 C. 8 D. 6

ANSWERS

1	2	3	4	5	6	7	8	9	10
B	A	D	A	D	B	C	A	C	B
11	**12**	**13**	**14**	**15**	**16**	**17**	**18**	**19**	**20**
B	A	B	A	C	C	C	C	B	B
21	**22**	**23**	**24**	**25**	**26**	**27**	**28**	**29**	**30**
A	A	A	C	A	D	A	C	B	B

EXPLANATORY ANSWERS

2. Average speed during the entire journey

$$= \frac{2xy}{x+y} = \frac{2\times4\times16}{4+16} = \frac{8\times16}{20} = 6.4 \text{ km/hr.}$$

3. Let required speed be x km/hr; then

$$x \times \frac{1}{2} = 48 \times \frac{3}{4} \qquad \therefore\ x = 48 \times \frac{3}{4} \times 2 = 72 \text{ km/hr}$$

5. Suppose the policeman will catch the thief after t seconds

then, $\left(\frac{25}{6}-\frac{10}{3}\right)t = 200 \Rightarrow \frac{5}{6}t = 200 \quad \therefore t = \frac{200\times6}{5} = 240$ sec = 4 min.

11. Let Tarun will catch Gulshan after t hours the starting of Tarun; then,
$10t = 5(t+1) \Rightarrow 5t = 5 \therefore t = 1$ hr
Hence, required time = 3 p.m. + 1 hr. = 4 p.m.

21. Required average speed $= \dfrac{24+36}{\frac{24}{16}+\frac{36}{15}} = \dfrac{60}{\frac{3}{2}+\frac{12}{5}} = \dfrac{60\times10}{39} = 15.38$ km/hr

22. Required distance $= 108 \times \dfrac{15}{60\times60}$ km $= \dfrac{9}{20}$ km $= \dfrac{9}{20}\times1000 = 450$ m

23. 9 km/hr $= 9 \times \dfrac{5}{18} = \dfrac{5}{2}$ m/s

Time taken $= \dfrac{4\times35}{5/2} = 4 \times 7 \times 2 = 56$ sec.

24. Speed $= \dfrac{600\text{m}}{5\times60\text{ s}} = 2\text{m}/s = 2 \times \dfrac{18}{5}$ km/hr $= \dfrac{36}{5} = 7.2$ km/hr.

❖ ❖ ❖

12 Mensuration

Perimeter

Perimeter of a geometrical figure is the total length of the sides enclosing the figure.

Triangle

A triangle is a plane figure bounded by three sides. It includes three angles. It is denoted by the symbol Δ. The sum of angles of a triangle is 180°.

(*i*) **Equilateral Triangle:** A triangle in which all sides are equal is called an equilateral triangle.

(*ii*) **Isosceles Triangle:** A triangle in which two sides are equal is called an isosceles triangle.

(*iii*) **Scalene Triangle:** A triangle in which all sides are different or unequal is called scalene triangle.

(*iv*) **Right Angled Triangle:** A triangle having one of the angles equal to 90° is called a right angled triangle. The side opposite to the right angle of a triangle is called its hypotenuse.

Quadrilateral

A plane figure bounded by four straight lines is called a quadrilateral.

Various Types of Quadrilaterals:

(*i*) **Rectangle:** A quadrilateral whose opposite sides are equal and all angles are at right angles. The diagonals of a rectangle are equal.

(*ii*) **Square:** A rectangle having all sides are equal is called a square.

(*iii*) **Parallelogram:** A quadrilateral whose opposite sides are equal and parallel is called parallelogram.

(*iv*) **Rhombus:** A parallelogram having all the sides equal is called a rhombus. Diagonals of a rhombus are not equal and they bisect each other at right angles.

(*v*) **Trapezium:** A quadrilateral having one pair of opposite sides parallel, is called a trapezium.

Circle

The path traced by a point which moves in such a way that its distance from a fixed point is always same, is called a circle. The fixed point is called its centre and fixed distance is called its radius.

(*i*) **Arc:** Any part of the circumference of a circle is called an arc.

(*ii*) **Chord:** The straight line joining the ends of an arc of a circle is called a chord.

(*iii*) **Diameter:** The chord passing through the centre of a circle is called its diameter.

(*iv*) **Segment:** The area enclosed by an arc and a chord is called a segment.

(*v*) **Sector:** The area bounded by an arc and two radii is called a sector.

Formulae for Area of Various Figures:

(*i*) **Rectangle:**

Area of rectangle = $l \times b$ Perimeter of rectangle = $2\,(l + b)$.

(*ii*) **Square:**

Area of square = $(\text{side})^2$ Perimeter of square = $4 \times$ side

Area of room = $l \times b$

Area of 4 walls of a room = $2(l + b) \times h$

(*iii*) **Parallelogram:**

Area of Parallelogram = $b \times h$ Area of rhombus = $\frac{1}{2} \times d_1 \times d_2$.

(*iv*) **Trapezium:**

Area of trapezium = $\frac{1}{2}$(sum of parallel sides) × (distance between them)

(*v*) **Triangle:**

(*a*) Area of right triangle = $\frac{1}{2} \times b \times h$

(*b*) Area of equilateral triangle = $\frac{\sqrt{3}}{4} \times (\text{side})^2$

(*c*) Area of scalene triangle = $\sqrt{s(s-a)(s-b)(s-c)}$ where, $s = \frac{a+b+c}{2}$

(*vi*) **Circle:**

(*a*) Area of circle = πr^2 (*b*) Circumference of a circle = $2\pi r$

(*c*) Length of arc = $\frac{\theta}{360} \times 2\pi r$ (*d*) Area of sector = $\frac{\theta}{360} \times \pi r^2$

Polygon

A polygon is plane figure bounded by multiple number of sides. Normally, it is used for figures enclosed by more than four sides: *e.g.*, pentagon, hexagon, octagon etc.

Regular Polygon

It is a polygon whose all sides are equal. For a regular polygon of n equal sides, its vertex angle θ is given by $\theta = \left(\frac{n-2}{n}\right) \times 180°$

EXAMPLE: Find the area and perimeter of a rectangle whose length is 25 m and breadth is 15 m.

SOLUTION: Area of rectangle = $l \times b = 25 \times 15 = 375$ m^2

Perimeter of rectangle = $2(l + b) = 2(25 + 15) = 80$ m

EXAMPLE: Find the area of a parallelogram whose base is 35 m and altitude 18 m.

SOLUTION: Area of parallelogram = $b \times h = 35 \times 18 = 630$ m^2

EXAMPLE: Find the circumference and the area of a circle of radius 3.5 cm.

SOLUTION: Circumference = $2\pi r = 2 \times \frac{22}{7} \times 3.5 = 22$ cm

Area of circle = $\pi r^2 = \frac{22}{7} \times 3.5 \times 3.5 = 38.5$ cm^2

Volume and Surface Area

Cuboid:

Volume of cuboid = $l \times b \times h$ cubic units

Whole surface area = $2(lb + bh + hl)$ square units

Diagonal of cuboid = $\sqrt{l^2 + b^2 + h^2}$ units

Area of 4 walls of a room = $2(l + b) \times h$ square units

Cube:

Volume of cube = a^3 cubic units

Side of cube = $\sqrt[3]{\text{Volume}}$

Lateral surface area = $4a^2$ square units

Total surface area = $6a^2$ square units

Diagonal of the cube = $\left(\sqrt{3}\,a\right)$ units

Cylinder:

Volume of cylinder = $\pi r^2 h$ cubic units

Lateral surface area = $2\pi rh$ square units

Total surface area = $2\pi r(h + r)$ square units

Cone:

Volume of cone = $\frac{1}{3}\pi r^2 h$ cubic units

Lateral surface area = πrl square units

Total surface area = $\pi r(l + r)$ square units

Slant height (l) = $\sqrt{r^2 + h^2}$

Sphere:

Volume of sphere = $\frac{4}{3}\pi r^3$ cubic units

Surface area = $4\pi r^2$ square units

Hemisphere:

Volume = $\frac{2}{3}\pi r^3$ cubic units

Lateral surface area = $2\pi r^2$ square units

Total surface area = $3\pi r^2$ square units

Frustum:

Volume = $\frac{1}{3}\pi h(r_1^2 + r_1 r_2 + r_2^2)$ cubic units

Curved surface area = $\pi(r_1 + r_2) \times l$ square units

Total surface area = $\pi\left[r_1^2 + r_2^2 + (r_1 + r_2)l\right]$ square units

Pyramid: Volume = $\frac{1}{2} \times$ (area of base) $\times$ height cubic units

Example: Three cubes whose edges measure 3 cm, 4 cm and 5 cm respectively form a single cube. Find the total surface area of the new cube.

Solution: Let the edge of new cube = x cm

$x^3 = 3^3 + 4^3 + 5^3$

$= 27 + 64 + 125 = 216 \text{ cm}^3$

$\Rightarrow x^3 = 6 \times 6 \times 6 \Rightarrow x = 6$ cm

Total surface area of cube = $6(x)^2 = 6 \times 6 \times 6 = 216 \text{ cm}^2$

Hence, total surface area of new cube = 216 cm^2.

MULTIPLE CHOICE QUESTIONS

1. The length of a plot is four times its breadth. A playground measuring 1200 square metres occupies a third of the total area of the plot. What is the length of the plot, in metres?

A. 20 B. 30 C. 60 D. None of these

2. The width of a rectangular hall is $\frac{3}{4}$ of its length. If the area of the hall is 300 m^2, then the difference between its length and width is:

A. 3 m B. 4 m C. 5 m D. 15 m

3. The length and breadth of a rectangular piece of land are in ratio of 5 : 3. The owner spent ₹ 3000 for surrounding it from all the sides at ₹ 7.50 per metre. The difference between its length and breadth is:
A. 50 m B. 100 m C. 150 m D. 200 m

4. A room 8 m × 6 m is to be carpeted by a carpet 2 m wide. The length of carpet required is:
A. 12 m B. 36 m C. 24 m D. 48 m

5. The length of a rectangle is increased by 60%. By what per cent would the width have to be decreased to maintain the same area?
A. $37\frac{1}{2}\%$ B. 60% C. 75% D. 120%

6. A man walked 20 m to cross a rectangular field diagonally. If the length of the field is 16 m, the breadth of the rectangle is:
A. 4 m B. 16 m
C. 12 m D. Cannot be determined

7. If the ratio of the areas of two squares is 9 : 1, the ratio of their perimeters is:
A. 9 : 1 B. 3 : 1 C. 3 : 4 D. 1 : 3

8. The perimeter of both, a square and a rectangle are each equal to 48 m and the difference between their areas is 4 m^2. The breadth of the rectangle is:
A. 10 m B. 12 m C. 14 m D. None of these

9. Area of a square with side x is equal to the area of a triangle with base x. The altitude of the triangle is:
A. $\frac{x}{2}$ B. x C. $2x$ D. $4x$

10. If only the length of the rectangular plot is reduced to $\frac{2}{3}$rd of its original length, the ratio of original area to reduced area is:
A. 2 : 3 B. 3 : 2 C. 1 : 2 D. None of these

11. If the radius of a circle be reduced by 50%, its area is reduced by:
A. 25% B. 50% C. 75% D. 100%

12. The perimeter of a rhombus is 52 m while its longer diagonal is 24 m. Its other diagonal is:
A. 5 m B. 10 m C. 20 m D. 28 m

13. The circumference of a circle is 352 m, then its area in m^2 is:
A. 9856 B. 8956 C. 6589 D. 5986

14. A wheel makes 100 revolutions in covering a distance of 88 km. The diameter of the wheel is:

A. 240 m B. 400 m C. 280 m D. 140 m

15. If the diameter of a circle is increased by 100%, its area is increased by:

A. 100% B. 200% C. 300% D. 400%

16. The area of a sector of a circle of radius 5 cm formed by an arc of length 3.5 cm, is:

A. 35 cm^2 B. 17.5 cm^2 C. 8.75 cm^2 D. 55 cm^2

17. A circular wire of radius 42 cm is cut and bent in the form of a rectangle whose sides are in the ratio 6 : 5. The smaller side of the rectangle is:

A. 30 cm B. 60 cm C. 72 cm D. 132 cm

18. The length of a minute hand on a wall clock is 7 cm. The area swept by the minute hand in 30 minutes is:

A. 147 cm^2 B. 210 cm^2 C. 154 cm^2 D. 77 cm^2

19. A circle and a square have same area. The ratio of the side of the square and the radius of the circle is:

A. $\sqrt{\pi} : 1$ B. $1 : \sqrt{\pi}$ C. $1 : \pi$ D. $\pi : 1$

20. The dimensions of the floor of a rectangular hall are 4 m × 3 m. The floor of the hall is to be tiled fully with 8 cm × 6 cm rectangular tiles without breaking tiles to smaller sizes. The number of tiles required is:

A. 4800 B. 2600 C. 2500 D. 2400

21. The surface area of a cube is 726 m^2. The volume of cube is:

A. 1300 m^3 B. 1331 m^3 C. 1452 m^3 D. 1542 m^3

22. Sum of the length, width and depth of a cuboid is s and its diagonal is d. Its surface area is:

A. s^2 B. d^2 C. $s^2 - d^2$ D. $s^2 + d^2$

23. A wooden box of dimensions 8 m × 7 m × 6 m is to carry rectangular boxes of dimensions 8 cm × 7 cm × 6 cm. The maximum number of boxes that can be carried in 1 wooden box is:

A. 1200000 B. 1000000 C. 9800000 D. 7500000

24. The length of the longest rod that can be placed in a room 30 m long, 24 m broad and 18 m high is:

A. 30 m B. $15\sqrt{2}$ m C. 60 m D. $30\sqrt{2}$ m

25. If the volume of two cubes are in the ratio 8 : 1, the ratio of their edges is:

A. 8 : 1 B. $2\sqrt{2} : 1$ C. 2 : 1 D. None of these

26. A metal sheet 27 cm long 8 cm broad and 1 cm thick is melted into a cube. The difference between the surface areas of two solids will be:
A. 284 cm^2 B. 296 cm^2 C. 286 cm^2 D. 300 cm^2

27. If each edge of a cube is increased by 50%, the percentage increase in surface area is:
A. 50% B. 75% C. 100% D. 125%

28. If a right circular cone of vertical height 24 cm has a volume of 1232 cm^3, then the area of its curved surface in cm^2 is:
A. 1254 B. 704 C. 550 D. 154

29. Two cubes have volumes in the ratio 1 : 27. The ratio of their surface areas is:
A. 1 : 3 B. 1 : 8 C. 1 : 9 D. 1 : 18

30. If the volumes of two cones are in the ratio 1 : 4 and their diameters are in the ratio 4 : 5, then the ratio of their heights is:
A. 1 : 5 B. 5 : 4 C. 5 : 16 D. 25 : 64

31. The radius of a wire is decreased to one-third. If volumes remains the same, length will increase:
A. 1 time B. 3 times C. 6 times D. 9 times

32. A cylindrical piece of metal of radius 2 cm and height 6 cm is shaped into a cone of same radius. The height of cone is:
A. 18 cm B. 14 cm C. 12 cm D. 8 cm

33. If 1 cubic cm of cast iron weight 21 g then the weight of a cast iron pipe of length 1 m with a bore of 3 cm and in which the thickness of the metal is 1 cm, is:
A. 21 kg B. 24.2 kg C. 26.4 kg D. 18.6 kg

34. The number of solid spheres, each of diameter 6 cm, that could be moulded to form a solid metal cylinder of height 45 cm and diameter 4 cms, is:
A. 3 B. 4 C. 5 D. 6

35. A right cylinder and a right circular cone have the same radius and the same volume. The ratio of the height of the cylinder to that of the cone is:
A. 3 : 5 B. 2 : 5 C. 3 : 1 D. 1 : 3

36. If a solid sphere of radius 10 cm is moulded into 8 spherical solid balls of equal radius, then surface area of each ball (in cm^2) is:
A. 100π B. 75π C. 60π D. 50π

37. The radii of two spheres are in the ratio 1 : 2. The ratio of their surface areas, is:
A. 1 : 2 B. 1 : 4 C. $1:\sqrt{2}$ D. 3 : 8

38. The radii of two cylinders are in the ratio 2 : 3 and their heights are in the ratio 5 : 3, then their volumes will be in ratio:
A. 4 : 9 B. 27 : 20 C. 20 : 27 D. 9 : 4

39. The volume of a hemisphere is 19404 cm^3. The total surface area is:
A. 2772 cm^2 B. 4158 cm^2 C. 5544 cm^2 D. 1386 cm^2

40. If the volume and surface area of a sphere are numerically the same, then its radius is:
A. 1 unit B. 2 units C. 3 units D. 4 units

41. A rectangle measures 50 cm × 25 cm. Its area is
A. 1150 sq. cm. B. 1250 sq. cm. C. 1275 sq. cm. D. 1280 sq. cm.

42. A field is in the form of a square whose perimeter is 580 m. Area of this field is
A. 21025 sq. m. B. 20225 sq. m.
C. 30025 sq. m. D. 19975 sq. m.

43. Find the area of the square whose each side measures 20 cm.
A. 300 sq. cm. B. 380 sq. cm.
C. 360 sq. cm. D. 400 sq. m.

44. Area of a circle is 154 sq. cm. Its circumference will be
A. 44 cm B. 48 cm C. 54 cm D. 68 cm

45. The base and the height of a triangle is 8 cm and 10 cm respectively. Its area will be
A. 40 sq. cm. B. 20 sq. cm. C. 49 sq. cm. D. 64 sq. cm.

46. A solid in the form of a cuboid is 4 cm × 3 cm × 2 cm. Its volume will be
A. 20 cu cm B. 22 cu cm C. 28 cu cm D. 24 cu cm

47. A reservoir is 3 m long, 2 m wide and 1 m deep. Its capacity in litres is
A. 8000 litres B. 10000 litres
C. 6500 litres D. 6000 litres

48. Surface area of a cube is 1014 sq. cm. Its volume will be
A. 2197 cu cm B. 2297 cu cm
C. 2179 cu cm D. 2117 cu cm

49. If the volumes of two cubical blocks are in the ratio of 8 : 1, what will be the ratio of their edges?
A. 1 : 2 B. 2 : 1 C. 4 : 1 D. 2 : 3

50. Two spheres have their surface areas in the ratio 9 : 16. Their volumes are in the ratio of
A. 64 : 27 B. 27 : 64 C. 16 : 27 D. 11 : 27

ANSWERS

1	2	3	4	5	6	7	8	9	10
D	C	A	C	A	C	B	A	C	B
11	**12**	**13**	**14**	**15**	**16**	**17**	**18**	**19**	**20**
C	B	A	C	C	C	B	D	A	C
21	**22**	**23**	**24**	**25**	**26**	**27**	**28**	**29**	**30**
B	C	B	D	C	C	D	C	C	D
31	**32**	**33**	**34**	**35**	**36**	**37**	**38**	**39**	**40**
D	A	C	C	D	A	B	C	B	C
41	**42**	**43**	**44**	**45**	**46**	**47**	**48**	**49**	**50**
B	A	D	A	A	D	D	A	B	B

EXPLANATORY ANSWERS

1. Area of the plot = $3 \times 1200 = 3600$ m^2
Let breadth be x m. Then length = $4x$ m
According to the question,
$4x \times x = 3600 \Rightarrow x^2 = 900 \Rightarrow x = 30$
Hence, length of the plot = $4 \times 30 = 120$ m.

4. Length of the carpet = $\dfrac{8 \times 6}{2} = 24$ m.

6. Breadth $= \sqrt{(20)^2 - (16)^2}$

$= \sqrt{400 - 256} = \sqrt{144} = 12$ m.

12. Side of rhombus = $\dfrac{52}{4} = 13$ m

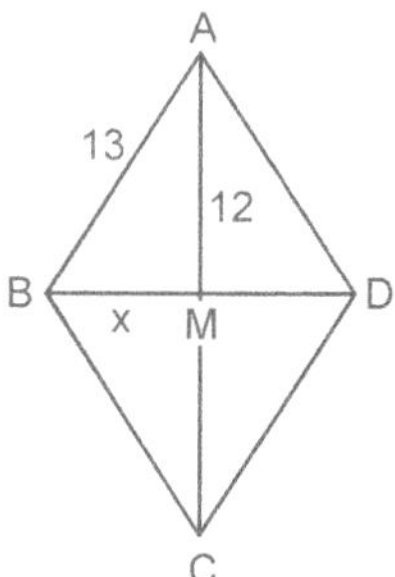

In ΔABM,

$x^2 = (13)^2 - (12)^2$
$x^2 = 169 - 144$
$x^2 = 25$
$\Rightarrow$ $x = 5$ m
$\therefore$ Another diagonal = $2 \times 5 = 10$ m

16. Area of sector = $\left(\dfrac{1}{2} \times r^2 \times \dfrac{\text{arc}}{r}\right)$

$= \dfrac{1}{2} \times 5 \times 3.5 = 8.75$ cm^2

21. Surface area of cube = $6a^2$

$6a^2 = 726 \Rightarrow a^2 = \dfrac{726}{6} = 121 \Rightarrow a = 11$ m

Volume of cube = $a^3 = 11 \times 11 \times 11 = 1331$ m^3

23. Number of boxes = $\dfrac{800 \times 700 \times 600}{8 \times 7 \times 6} = 1000000$

25. Let their volumes be $8x^3$ and x^3.
Then, their sides are $2x$ and x
$\therefore$ Ratio of their edges = 2 : 1

38. Let the radii of cylinders are $2r$ and $3r$ and heights are $5x$ and $3x$

Ratio of their volumes = $\dfrac{\pi(2r)^2 \times 5x}{\pi(3r)^2 \times 3x} = \dfrac{4r^2 \times 5}{9r^2 \times 3} = \dfrac{20}{27}$

39. Volume of hemisphere = 19404

$\Rightarrow \quad \dfrac{2}{3}\pi r^3 = 19404 \Rightarrow \dfrac{2}{3} \times \dfrac{22}{7} r^3 = 19404$

$\Rightarrow \quad r^3 = \dfrac{3 \times 19404 \times 7}{2 \times 22} = 9261$

$\Rightarrow \quad r = 21$ cm

Surface area = $3\pi r^2 = 3 \times \dfrac{22}{7} \times 21 \times 21 = 4158$ cm^2

40. $\dfrac{4}{3}\pi r^3 = 4\pi r^2$

$\Rightarrow \dfrac{r}{3} = 1 \Rightarrow r = 3$ units

41. Area of the rectangle = $l \times b = 50 \times 25 = 1250$ sq. cm

42. Here, $4 \times$ side = 580 $\Rightarrow$ side = $\dfrac{580}{4} = 145$ m

$\therefore$ Area = (side)^2 = (145)^2 = 21025 sq. m.

43. Area of the square = (side)^2 = (20)^2 = 400 sq. cm.

44. Area of the circle = $\pi r^2 \Rightarrow \pi r^2 = 154 \Rightarrow r^2 = \dfrac{154 \times 7}{22} \Rightarrow r = 7$ cm

$\therefore$ Circumference of the circle = $2\pi r = 2 \times \dfrac{22}{7} \times 7 = 44$ cm.

45. Area of the triangle $= \frac{1}{2} \times 8 \times 10 = 40$ sq. cm.

46. Volume of the cuboid $= l \times b \times h = 4 \times 3 \times 2 = 24$ cu. cm.

47. Volume of the reservoir $= l \times b \times h = 3 \times 2 \times 1 = 6$ cu. m
($\because$ 1 cu m = 1000 litre)
$\therefore$ Capacity of the reservoir $= 6 \times 1000 = 6000$ litre.

48. Here, $6 \times (\text{side})^2 = 1014 \Rightarrow (\text{side})^2 = \frac{1014}{6} = 169$

$\therefore$ side $= \sqrt{169} = 13$ cm

Hence, Volume of the cube $= (\text{side})^3 = (13)^3 = 2197$ cu cm.

49. Here, $a_1^3 : a_2^3 = 8 : 1$

$$\therefore \left(\frac{a_1}{a_2}\right)^3 = \left(\frac{2}{1}\right)^3 \Rightarrow a_1 : a_2 = 2 : 1$$

Therefore, ratio of their edges = 2 : 1.

50. Here, $4\pi r_1^2 : 4\pi r_2^2 = 9 : 16 \Rightarrow r_1^2 : r_2^2 = 9 : 16$

$$\Rightarrow \left(\frac{r_1}{r_2}\right)^2 = \left(\frac{3}{4}\right)^2 \Rightarrow r_1 : r_2 = 3 : 4$$

$$\Rightarrow \frac{r_1^3}{r_2^3} = \frac{27}{64}$$

$$\Rightarrow r_1^3 : r_2^3 = 27 : 64.$$

Therefore, ratio of their volumes $= \frac{4}{3}\pi r_1^3 : \frac{4}{3}\pi r_2^3 = r_1^3 : r_2^3$

$= 27 : 64$

ALGEBRA

13 Set Theory

Set : It is a well defined collection of objects. The objects which belong to a set are called its member or elements.

Method of Representing a Set

(a) Tabular Form or the Roster Form

(b) Set Builder Form or Rule Method

Tabular Form : In this form all the elements of the set are separated by commas and enclosed between brackets { }, *e.g.,* : N = {1, 2, 3, 4, ...}.

Rule Method : In this form, the elements of the set are represented in terms of one or several characteristic properties, *e.g.,* $N = \{x \mid x \in N\}$

Empty or Null Set : The set which contains no element is called the empty set. The symbols for the empty set is ϕ, *e.g.,* $\phi = \{\ \}$.

The set of odd numbers is divisible by 2.

Singleton : A set containing only one element is called a singleton, *e.g.,* {1}, {*a*} etc.

Equal Sets : Two sets A ana B are said to be equal if both have the same elements. e.g., $A = \{a, b, c, d\}$ and $B = \{b, c, a, d\}$, Then A = B.

Equivalent Sets : Two sets A and B are said to be equivalent if we can find a one-to-one correspondence between the element of the two sets.

e.g., A = {1, 2, 3, 4} and $\{b, c, a, d\}$, Then $A \sim B$ but $A \neq B$.

Note : Equal sets are always equivalent but vice-versa is not true.

Finite and Infinite Set : The set which contains a definite number of element is called a finite set. *e.g.,* The set of days in a week. The set which contains an infinite number of element is called an infinite set. *e.g.,* The set of natural numbers.

Disjoint Sets : Two sets A and B are said to be disjoint if they do not have any elements in common. *e.g.,* A = {1, 2, 3}, B = {4, 5, 6} are disjoint set.

Subsets : If every member of set A is also in set B then A is said to be a subset of B and B is called a super set A. e.g., : A = {1, 2, 3}, B = {1, 2, 3, 4, 5, 6} $\therefore A \subset B$.

Power Set : The set of all the subset of a set is called the power set. If *n* is the number of element of a set A then the number of subset of A, *i.e.*, the no. of elements of P(A) = 2^n. A = {1, 2, 3} ∴ P(A) = 2^3 = 8.

Universal Set : The largest set containing every set is called universal set. It is denoted by U.

Union of Sets : The union of two sets A and B is the set of all elements of A with all the elements of B. It is denoted by A ∪ B.

e.g., A = {1, 2, 3}, B = {1, 3, 4}, ∴ A ∪ B = {1, 2, 3, 4}

Intersection of Sets : The intersection of two sets is the set of all elements which are in A and also in B. It is written as A ∩ B.

e.g., A = {1, 2, 3}, B = {2, 3, 4}, ∴ A ∩ B = {2, 3}.

Complement of a Set : The set of three elements of universal set (U) which are not the element of A is called the complement of A and is denoted by A^1 of A^c. e.g., If U = {1, 2, 3, 4, 5, 6} and A = {1, 3, 5}, A^1 = {2, 4, 6}.

Complement of a Union and Intersection of Two Sets :

(*a*) $(A \cup B)^1 = A^1 \cap B^1$ (*b*) $(A \cap B)^1 = A^1 \cup B^1$.

Important Result

(*a*) $n(A \cup B) = n(A) + n(B)$, If A and B are disjoint set.

(*b*) $n(A \cup B) = n(A) + n(B) - n(A \cap B)$.

MULTIPLE CHOICE QUESTIONS

1. Let a = {x : x is a multiple of 3} and B = {x : x is a multiple of 5}. Then A ∩ B is given by

A. {3, 6, 9, ...} B. {5, 10, 15, 20, ...}
C. {15, 30, 45, ...} D. None of these

2. If X and Y are two sets, then X ∪ (Y ∩ X)' equals

A. X B. Y C. ϕ D. None of these

3. Let A = {1, 2, 3, 4, 5}, B = 2, 3, 6, 7}. Then the number of elements in (A × B) ∩ (B × A) is

A. 18 B. 6 C. 4 D. 0

4. In a group of 52 persons, 16 drink tea but not coffee and 33 drink tea. It is assumed that every person takes tea or coffee. Then the number of persons who take coffee but not tea is given by

A. 19 B. 36
C. Cannot be found by the given data D. None of these

5. A survey of 100 Indians shows that 60 like cheese whereas 70 like apples. let n be the number of persons who like both cheese and apple. Then

A. n = 30 B. n = 60 C. n = 10 D. None of these

6. Let n (U) = 700, n(A) = 200, n(B) = 300, $n(A \cap B)$ = 100. Then $n(A' \cap B')$ =

A. 400 B. 600 C. 300 D. None of these

7. Two finite sets have m and n elements. The total number of subsets of the first set is 56 more than the total number of subsets of the second set. The values of m and n are

A. 7, 6 B. 6, 3 C. 5, 1 D. 8, 7

8. Let A = {1, 2, 3}, B = {1, 3, 5}. A relation R : A $\rightarrow$ B is defined by R = {(1, 3), (1, 5), (2, 1)}. Then R^{-1} is defined by

A. {(1, 2), (3, 1), (1, 3), (1, 5)} B. {(1, 2), (3, 1), (2, 1)}
C. {(1, 2), (5, 1), (3, 1)} D. None of these

9. The relation R is defined on the set of natural numbers as {(a, b): $a = 2b$}. Then R^{-1} is given by

A. {(2, 1), (4, 2), (6, 3)...} B. {(1, 2), (2, 4), (3, 6)...}
C. R^{-1} is not defined D. None of these

10. The relation R defined on the set of natural numbers as {(a, b) : a differs from b by 3}, is given by

A. {(1, 4), (2, 5), (3, 6), ...} B. {(4, 1), (5, 2), (6, 3), ...}
C. {(1, 3), (2, 6), (3, 9), ...} D. None of these

11. A relation R defined on the set of integers by R = {(a, b): a divides b}. Then R is

A. reflexive B. symmetric C. transitive D. equivalence

12. Given two finite sets A and B such that n(A) = 2, n(B) = 3. Then total number of relations from A to B is

A. 4 B. 8 C. 64 D. None of these

13. The solution set of $8x \equiv 6 \pmod{14}$, $x \in Z$, are

A. [8] $\cup$ [6] B. [8] $\cup$ [14]
C. [6] $\cup$ [13] D. [8] $\cup$ [6] $\cup$ [13]

14. Let n(A) = n. Then the number of all relations on A is

A. 2^n B. $2^{(n)!}$ C. 2^{n^2} D. None of these

15. If A and B be two subsets of a set U, then which of the following is false?

A. A $\cap$ B = A B. A $\cap$ U = A C. A $\cap$ B $\in$ A D. B $\cup$ A $\cap$ B

16. It is given that n (P(S)) = 64, where P (S) is power set of S, then n (S) is:

A. 2 B. 4 C. 8 D. 6

17. If A and B are two sets, then A $\cup$ (A $\cap$ B) is:

A. A $\cap$ B B. A C. B D. none of these

18. If A and B are two subsets of universal set U, then A – B is equal to:

A. A $\cap$ B B. A $\cap$ B' C. A' $\cap$ B D. A' $\cap$ B'

19. If P, Q $\subset$ U, then P $\cap$ (P $\cup$ Q); is equal to:

A. P B. Q C. f D. none of these

20. In a town of 840 persons, 450 persons read Hindi, 300 read English and 200 read both. The number of persons who read neither, is:

A. 210 B. 290 C. 180 D. 260

21. Let A and B have 2 and 5 elements respectively. What can be the maximum and minimum number of elements in $A \cap B$?

A. 5 and 2 B. 5 and 0 C. 25 and 4 D. 2 and 0

22. If $A = \{a, c, d, g\}$ and $B = \{b, d, j, k\}$, then which of the following is true?

A. $A \cap B$ is a null set
B. A and B are disjoint sets
C. $A \cap B$ is a singleton set
D. All of the above are true

23. If A and B are subsets of a set X, then $[A \cap (X - B)] \cup B$ is equal to:

A. $A \cup B$ B. $A \cap B$ C. A D. B

24. If $A = \{1, 2\}$, $B = \{2, 5\}$, $C = \{5, 7\}$ then $(A \times B) \cap (A \times C)$ is equal to:

A. $\{(2, 5), (1, 5)\}$
B. $\{(2, 2), (5, 5)\}$
C. $\{(2, 7), (1, 5)\}$
D. none of these

25. Let $A = \{a, b, c, d, \}$, which one of the following subsets of $A \times A$ is not a function on A?

A. $\{(a, d), (d, a), (a, b), (d, c)\}$
B. $\{(d, a), (a, b), (b, c), (c, d)\}$
C. $\{(a, d), (b, a), (c, b), (d, c)\}$
D. $\{(d, a), (a, d), (b, a), (c, c)\}$

ANSWERS

1	2	3	4	5	6	7	8	9	10
C	C	C	A	A	C	B	C	B	D
11	**12**	**13**	**14**	**15**	**16**	**17**	**18**	**19**	**20**
C	C	C	C	A	D	B	B	C	B
21	**22**	**23**	**24**	**25**					
D	C	A	A	A					

EXPLANATORY ANSWERS

2. $X \cap (Y \cup X)' = X \cap (Y' \cap X')$
$= (X \cap X') \cap Y'$
$= \phi \cap X' = \phi$

5. Let A = Apples, $C \equiv$ Cheese

Then $n(A \cap C) \leq n(A)$

$n(A \cap C) \leq n(C)$

$\Rightarrow n(A \cap C) \leq 60$

Also $n(A \cap C) = n(A) + n(C) - n(A \cup C)$

$\geq 70 + 60 - 100 = 30$

$\therefore\ 30 \leq n(A \cap C) \leq 60$

6. $n(A' \cap B') = n(A \cup B)'$

$= 700 - n(A \cup B)$

$= 700 - [200 + 300 - 100]$

$= 300$

7. $2^m = 2^n + 56$

which is satisfied when $m = 6$, $n = 3$.

8. $(x, y) \in R \Leftrightarrow (y, x) \in R^{-1}$,

$\therefore\ R^{-1} = \{(3, 1), (5, 1), (1, 2)\}$

9. $R = \{(2, 1), (4, 2), (6, 3), ...\}$

so $R^{-1} = \{(1, 2), (2, 4), (3, 6), ...\}$

10. $R = \{(a, b): a, b \in N, A \sim b = 3\}$

$= \{(n, n + 3), (n + 3, n) : n \in N\}$

$= \{(1, 4), (4, 1), (2, 5), (5, 2), ...\}$

23. See the figures

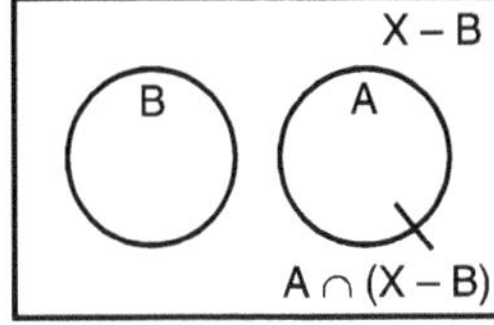

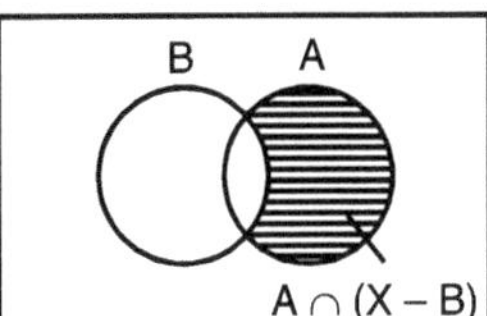

In both cases

24. $A \times B = \{(1, 2) (1, 5), (2, 2), (2, 5)\}$

$A \times C = \{(1, 5), (1, 7), (2, 5), (2, 7)\}$

$\therefore\ (A \times B) \cap (A \times C) = \{(1, 5), (2, 5)\}$

14

Simplification & Factorization

A function $p(x)$ defined by $p(x) = a_0 + a_1x + a_2\,x^2 + ... + a_nx^n$ is called a polynomial function in x.

Where, $a_0, a_1 ... a_n$ are real numbers and called co-efficient of the polynomial.

Factor Theorem: If $f(x)$ is completely divisible by $(x - a)$, then $f(a) = 0$

Thus, $(x - a)$ is a factor of $f(x)$.

Some Important Formulae

1. $(a + b)^2 = a^2 + 2ab + b^2$

2. $(a - b)^2 = a^2 - 2ab + b^2$

3. $a^2 - b^2 = (a + b)\,(a - b)$

4. $a^2 + b^2 = (a + b)^2 - 2ab$

5. $(a + b + c)^2 = a^2 + b^2 + c^2 + 2ab + 2bc + 2ca$

6. $(a + b)^3 = a^3 + 3a^2b + 3ab^2 + b^3$

$= a^3 + b^3 + 3ab\,(a + b)$

7. $(a - b)^3 = a^3 - 3a^2b + 3ab^2 - b^3$

$= a^3 - b^3 - 3ab\,(a - b)$

8. $a^3 + b^3 = (a + b)\,(a^2 - ab + b^2)$ [for factorisation]

$a^3 + b^3 = (a + b)^3 - 3ab\,(a + b)$ [for evaluation when $a+b$ and ab are given]

9. $a^3 - b^3 = (a - b)(a^2 + ab + b^2)$ [for factorisation]

$a^3 - b^3 = (a - b)^3 + 3ab\,(a - b)$ [for evaluation]

10. If $a + b + c = 0$, then $a^3 + b^3 + c^3 = 3abc$

MULTIPLE CHOICE QUESTIONS

1. If $\left(x+\frac{1}{x}\right)=5$, then $\left(x^2+\frac{1}{x^2}\right)$ is equal to:

A. 20 B. 24 C. 27 D. 23

2. If $\left(x+\frac{1}{x}\right)=4$, then $\left(x^4+\frac{1}{x^4}\right)$ is equal to:

A. 190 B. 180 C. 193 D. 194

3. If $\left(x^2+\frac{1}{x^2}\right)=66$, then $\left(x-\frac{1}{x}\right)$ is equal to:

A. 6 B. 12 C. 8 D. 9

4. If $a + b = 8$, $a - b = 4$, then $a^2 + b^2$ is equal to:

A. 20 B. 40 C. 10 D. 30

5. If $x^2 + 5x - 2k$, is exactly divisible by $(x - 1)$, then the value of k is:

A. 1 B. 2 C. 3 D. 4

6. If $(x - 2)$, is a factor of $x^2 + 4x - 2k$, then the value of k is:

A. 1 B. 3 C. 4 D. 6

7. If $x^{100} + 2x^{99} + k$, is divisible by $(x + 1)$, then the value of k is:

A. 1 B. 4 C. 3 D. 0

8. Value of k for which $(x - 2)$ is a factor of $(x^2 - kx + 2)$ is:

A. 2 B. 3 C. 4 D. 5

9. If $x-\frac{1}{x}=3$. The value of $x^2+\frac{1}{x^2}$ is :

A. 2 B. 12 C. 10 D. 11

10. If $x-\frac{1}{x}=2$, then $x^3-\frac{1}{x^3}$ is :

A. 14 B. 16 C. 15 D. 12

11. If $x - 2$ is a factor of $x^2 + 3ax - 2a$, then a is equal to

A. 2 B. –2 C. 1 D. –1

12. The value of k for which $x - 1$ is a factor of $4x^3 + 3x^2 - 4x + k$, is :

A. 3 B. 1 C. –2 D. –3

13. If $x - a$ is a factor of $x^3 - 3x^2a + 2a^2x + b$, then the value of b is :

A. 0 B. 2 C. 1 D. 3

14. If $x^{140} + 2x^{151} + k$ is divisible by $x + 1$, then the value of k is :

A. 1 B. –3 C. 2 D. –2

15. If $x + 2$ and $x - 1$ are the factors of $x^3 + 10x^2 + mx + n$, then the values of m and n are respectively :

A. 5 and –3 B. 17 and –8 C. 7 and –18 D. 23 and –19

16. Let $f(x)$ be a polynomial such that $f\left(-\frac{1}{2}\right)=0$, then a factor of $f(x)$ is :

A. $2x - 1$ B. $2x + 1$ C. $x - 1$ D. $x + 1$

17. When $x^3 - 2x^2 + ax - b$ is divided by $x^2 - 2x - 3$, the remainder is $x - 6$. The values of a and b are respectively :

A. –2, –6 B. 2 and –6 C. –2 and 6 D. 2 and 6

18. One factor of $x^4 + x^2 - 20$ is $x^2 + 5$. The other factor is :

A. $x^2 - 4$ B. $x - 4$ C. $x^2 - 5$ D. $x + 2$

19. If $(x - 1)$ is a factor of polynomial $f(x)$ but not of $g(x)$, then it must be a factor of :

A. $f(x)\, g(x)$ B. $-f(x) + g(x)$
C. $f(x) - g(x)$ D. $\{f(x) + g(x)\}\, g(x)$

20. $(x + 1)$ is a factor of $x^n + 1$ only if :

A. n is an odd integer B. n is an even integer
C. n is a negative integer D. n is a positive integer

21. If $x^2 + \frac{1}{x^2} = 7$, then the values of $x + \frac{1}{x}$ is :

A. 2 B. 3 C. 5 D. 6

22. If $x + \frac{1}{x} = 4$, then the value of $x^3 + \frac{1}{x^3}$ is :

A. 52 B. 64 C. 68 D. 76

23. The factors of $x^8 + x^4 + 1$ are :

A. $\left(x^4 + 1 - x^2\right), \left(x^2 + 1 + x\right), \left(x^2 + 1 - x\right)$

B. $\left(x^4 + 1 - x^2\right), \left(x^2 - 1 + x\right), \left(x^2 + 1 + x\right)$

C. $\left(x^4 - 1 + x^2\right), \left(x^2 - 1 + x\right), \left(x^2 + 1 + x\right)$

D. $\left(x^4 - 1 + x^2\right), \left(x^2 + 1 - x\right), \left(x^2 + 1 + x\right)$

24. The expression $10xy^4 - 10x^4y$ can be expressed in factors as :

A. $10xy(x - y)\left(x^2 + xy + y^2\right)$ B. $10xy(y - x)\left(x^2 - xy + y^2\right)$

C. $10xy(y - x)\left(x^2 + xy + y^2\right)$ D. None of these

25. The algebraic expression $4x^2 + 9y^2 + 25z^2 + 12xy - 30yz - 20zx$ can be factorised as :

A. $(2x + 3y + 5z)^2$ B. $(2x + 3y - 5z)^2$

C. $(2x - 3y + 5z)^2$ D. None of these

26. One of the factors of the expressions $x^2+5x+25$ is :

A. $x+5$ B. $x-5$

C. $x+\sqrt{5}$ D. Cannot be factorised

27. If $x+y=8$ and $xy=7$ then the value of x^3+y^3 is :

A. 344 B. 342 C. 345 D. 340

28. The expression $49x^2+64$ when expressed as factors is :

A. $(7x+8)^2$ B. $(7x+8)(7x-8)$

C. $(7x-8)^2$ D. Cannot be factorised

29. $(4x+3y)^2+(4x-3y)^2$ is equal to :

A. $16x^2-9y^2$ B. $32x^2+18y^2$ C. $16x^2+9y^2$ D. $32x^2+9y^2$

30. The expression $32x^3+108y^3$ can be expressed in factors as :

A. $(4x+3y)(4x^2-6xy+9y^2)$ B. $(4x-3y)(4x^2+6xy+9y^2)$

C. $(4x+3y)(4x^2+6xy+9y^2)$ D. None of these

ANSWERS

1	2	3	4	5	6	7	8	9	10
D	D	C	B	C	D	A	B	D	A
11	**12**	**13**	**14**	**15**	**16**	**17**	**18**	**19**	**20**
D	D	A	A	C	B	C	A	A	A
21	**22**	**23**	**24**	**25**	**26**	**27**	**28**	**29**	**30**
B	A	A	C	B	D	A	D	B	D

EXPLANATORY ANSWERS

1. $\because \left(x+\frac{1}{x}\right)=5$

$$\therefore\ x^2+\frac{1}{x^2} = \left(x+\frac{1}{x}\right)^2-2 = 25-2 = 23$$

4. $\because \quad (a+b)^2 + (a-b)^2 = 2a^2 + 2b^2 = 2(a^2+b^2)$

$\Rightarrow \quad (8)^2 + (4)^2 = 2(a^2+b^2)$

$64 + 16 = 2(a^2+b^2)$

$\Rightarrow \quad 80 = 2(a^2+b^2)$

$\therefore \quad a^2 + b^2 = 40$

8. $\because x - 2 = 0 \Rightarrow x = 2$

$x^2 - kx + 2 = 0 \Rightarrow 4 - k(2) + 2 = 0$

$6 - 2k = 0 \Rightarrow 2k = 6$

$k = 3.$

10. $\because \quad x - \frac{1}{x} = 2$

$$\therefore \quad x^3 - \frac{1}{x^3} = \left(x - \frac{1}{x}\right)^3 + 3x \cdot \frac{1}{x}\left(x - \frac{1}{x}\right)$$

$$= (2)^3 + 3(2) = 8 + 6 = 14.$$

18. $\because$ One factor of $x^4 + x^2 - 20$ is $x^2 + 5$

$(x^2+5)(x^2-4) = x^4 + x^2 - 20$

$\therefore$ Other factor $= x^2 - 4$.

22. $\because \quad x + \frac{1}{x} = 4$

$$\therefore \quad x^3 + \frac{1}{x^3} = \left(x + \frac{1}{x}\right)^3 - 3 \cdot x \cdot \frac{1}{x}\left(x + \frac{1}{x}\right)$$

$$= (4)^3 - 3(4)$$

$$= 64 - 12 = 52$$

27. $\because x + y = 8$ and $xy = 7$

$\therefore \quad x^3 + y^3 = (x+y)^3 - 3xy(x+y)$

$= (8)^3 - 3(7)(8)$

$= 512 - 168 = 344.$

29. $(4x+3y)^2 + (4x-3y)^2 = 2(4x)^2 + 2(3y)^2$

$= 32x^2 + 18y^2$

[$\because (a+b)^2 + (a-b)^2 = 2a^2 + 2b^2$].

15

Linear equation & Quadratic Equation

The System of Equations

$a_1x + b_1y + c_1 = 0$ and $a_2x + b_2y + c_2 = 0$ may be either unique solution or no solution or infinitely many solutions.

Unique solution is known as consistent or not parallel. No solution is known as inconsistent or parallel, while many solutions are known as coincident or dependent.

(*a*) **For unique solution:** $\frac{a_1}{a_2} \neq \frac{b_1}{b_2}$

(*b*) **For no solution:** $\frac{a_1}{a_2} = \frac{b_1}{b_2} \neq \frac{c_1}{c_2}$

(*c*) **For many solutions:** $\frac{a_1}{a_2} = \frac{b_1}{b_2} = \frac{c_1}{c_2}$

Algebraic Methods of Solving Simultaneous Linear Equations in Two Variables

(*a*) Substitution Method
(*b*) Elimination Method
(*c*) Cross Multiplication Method

Quadratic Equation

Definition : A polynomial equation in which the highest power of the unknown variable is two. The general form of a quadratic equation in the variable x is

$$ax^2 + bx + c = 0$$

where, a, b and c are constant.

Solution of a Quadratic Equation

$$x = \frac{-b \pm \sqrt{b^2 - 4ac}}{2a}$$

$b^2 - 4ac = \text{D}$ is called discriminant.

(*a*) If D > 0 then there are real and distinct roots given by

$$\alpha = \frac{-b+\sqrt{b^2-4ac}}{2a}, \ \beta = \frac{-b-\sqrt{b^2-4ac}}{2a}$$

(*b*) If D = 0, there are real and equal roots

$$\alpha = \beta = \frac{-b}{2a}$$

(*c*) If D < 0, there are no real roots.

Sum of the roots

$$\alpha + \beta = \frac{-b}{a}$$

Product of the roots

$$\alpha\beta = \frac{c}{a}$$

Ex. 1 : The roots of the equation $6x^2 - 5x - 21 = 0$ are

Sol. $6x^2 - 14x + 9x - 21 = 0$

$\Rightarrow$ $2x(3x - 7) + 3(3x - 7) = 0$

$\Rightarrow$ $(3x - 7)(2x + 3) = 0$

$\Rightarrow$ $x = \frac{7}{3}, \ x = -\frac{3}{2}$

Ex. 2 : If α and β are the roots of the quadratic equation $3x^2 + 3x + 2 = 0$ then $\alpha^3 + \beta^3 = ...$

Sol. $a = 3, b = 3, c = 2$

$\Rightarrow$ $\alpha + \beta = -1, \ \alpha\beta = \frac{2}{3}$

$$\alpha^3 + \beta^3 = (-1)^3 - 3 \times \frac{2}{3} \times (-1)$$

$$= -1 + 2 = 1$$

MULTIPLE CHOICE QUESTIONS

1. The system of linear equations $2x + 3y = 7$ and $4x + 6y = 10$ has :

   A. no solution   B. unique solution

   C. infinite solution   D. no conclusion can be drawn

2. The value of k for which the system of equations $x + 2y + 7 = 0$ and $2x + ky + 14 = 0$ will have infinitely many solutions is :

   A. 2   B. 4   C. 6   D. 8

3. For what value of α, the system of equations $\alpha x + 3y = \alpha - 3$ and $12x + \alpha y = \alpha$ will have a unique solution?
A. $\alpha \neq \pm 6$ B. $\alpha \neq \pm 3$ C. $\alpha \neq \mp 6$ D. None of these

4. For what value of k, the system of equations will represent the coincident lines $x + 5y - 7 = 0$ and $4x + 20y + k = 0$?
A. 28 B. –28 C. –26 D. None of these

5. A lady has 50 paise and ₹ 1 coins in her purse. If in all, she has 40 coins totally ₹ 25.50 how many of each type of coins does she have?
A. 26, 11 B. 11, 29 C. 29, 11 D. None of these

6. A father is three times as old as his son. After twelve years his age will be twice as the age of his son. Find their present ages in years.
A. 12, 26 B. 24, 36 C. 36, 12 D. None of these

7. Ten years ago, father was twelve times as old as his son. Ten years after, he will be twice as old as his son will be. Find their present ages in years.
A. 12, 36 B. 12, 24 C. 12, 34 D. None of these

8. The present age of a father is 3 years more than three times the age of son. Three years hence father's age will be 10 years more than twice the age of son. Determine their present ages in years.
A. 10, 33 B. 33, 10 C. 10, 30 D. None of these

9. In a triangle ABC, $\angle C = 3\angle B = 2(\angle A + \angle B)$.
Find three angles in degrees.
A. 20°, 50°, 120° B. 30°, 40°, 120°
C. 20°, 40°, 120° D. None of these

10. The fraction becomes 2 when 1 is added to both the numerator and the denominator, and it becomes 3 when 1 is subtracted from both the numerator and denominator. The given fraction is :
A. $\frac{7}{3}$ B. $\frac{4}{7}$ C. $\frac{3}{7}$ D. $\frac{7}{4}$

11. In the system of equations $x + y = 13$ and $2x + 3y = 32$, the values of x and y are:
A. 5 and 6 B. 7 and 8 C. 7 and 6 D. 6 and 7

12. If $y = 4$, find the value of x in the equation $3x + 4y = 25$.
A. 3 B. 8 C. 5 D. 4

13. The equation whose roots are 5, 9 is :
A. $x^2 - 5x + 14 = 0$ B. $x^2 - 14x + 14 = 0$
C. $x^2 - 45x + 14 = 0$ D. $x^2 - 14x + 45 = 0$

14. If α, β be the values of x satisfying the equation $x^2 - px + q = 0$, the value of $\frac{1}{\alpha}+\frac{1}{\beta}$ is :

A. $\frac{q}{p}$ B. $-\frac{p}{q}$ C. $\frac{p}{q}$ D. $\frac{1}{q}$

15. If one of the roots of the equation is $2+\sqrt{3}$, the other has to be :

A. $\sqrt{3}-2$ B. 2 C. $2-\sqrt{3}$ D. $\sqrt{3}$

16. If α, β are the roots of $2x^2 - x + 1 = 0$, the value of $\alpha^2 + \beta^2$ is :

A. 1 B. 0 C. 5/4 D. –3/4

17. Find the values of 'p' for which the quadratic equation $px^2 + 4x + 1 = 0$ has real roots.

A. $p \leq 4$ B. $p \geq 6$ C. $p \geq 4$ D. None of these

18. Determine 'k' such that the quadratic equation $x^2 + 7(3 + 2k) - 2x(1 + 3k) = 0$ has equal roots.

A. 2, –10/9 B. 3, –10/9 C. 2, 10/9 D. None of these

19. For what value of 'k' the equation $(k + 3)x^2 - (5 - k)x + 1 = 0$ has coincident roots?

A. 1, 13 B. 1, 12 C. 3, 13 D. None of these

20. Find the value of 'k' so that the sum of the roots of equation $3x^2 + (2x + 1)x - k + 5 = 0$ is equal to the product of roots.

A. 4 B. 2 C. 3 D. –6

21. Find the value of 'p' so that equation $4x^2 - 8px + 9 = 0$ has roots whose difference is 4.

A. ±3 B. ±2/5 C. ±5/2 D. None of these

22. Find the value of 'm' so that the equation $9x^2 - 8mx - 9 = 0$ has one root as the negative of the other.

A. 0 B. 1 C. 2 D. None of these

23. If α and β are the roots of $x^2 - 2x - 1 = 0$, find the value of $\alpha^2\beta + \beta^2\alpha$.

A. –3 B. –2 C. 2 D. None of these

24. If a and b are the roots of the equation $x^2 - 5x + 6 = 0$, find the value of $(a^2 - b^2)$.

A. ±3 B. ±5 C. ±4 D. None of these

25. For what values of 'p' for which the quadratic equation $px^2 - 4x + p$ has real linear factors?

A. $-2 \leq p < 3$ B. $-2 \leq p \leq 2$ C. $-2 \geq p \leq 2$ D. None of these

26. The numerical difference of the roots of $x^2 - 6x + 6 = 0$ is
A. 0 B. $\sqrt{6}$ C. $\sqrt{(12)}$ D. $\sqrt{(18)}$

27. If one root of $5x^2 + 13x + k = 0$ is reciprocal of the other, then k is equal to
A. 0 B. 5 C. 1/6 D. 6

28. If one root of the equation
$x^2 + px + 12 = 0$ is 4, while the equation
$x^2 + px + q = 0$ has equal roots, the value of q is
A. 49/4 B. 4/49 C. 4 D. None of these

29. If α and β are the roots of the equation
$ax^2 + bx + c = 0$, then $(1 + \alpha + \alpha^2)(1 + \beta + \beta^2) =$
A. 0 B. positive C. negative D. None of these

30. If the roots of $ax^2 + bx + c = 0$ are α, β and the roots of $Ax^2 + bx + C = 0$ are $\alpha - k, \beta - k$ then $(B^2 - 4AC)/(b^2 - 4ac)$ is equal to
A. 0 B. 1 C. $(A/a)^2$ D. $(a/A)^2$

ANSWERS

1	2	3	4	5	6	7	8	9	10
A	B	A	B	C	A	C	A	C	A
11	**12**	**13**	**14**	**15**	**16**	**17**	**18**	**19**	**20**
C	A	D	C	C	D	A	A	A	D
21	**22**	**23**	**24**	**25**	**26**	**27**	**28**	**29**	**30**
C	A	B	B	B	C	B	A	B	C

EXPLANATORY ANSWERS

3. Since, the given equations have unique solution.

$$\therefore \frac{a_1}{a_2} \neq \frac{b_1}{b_2}$$

$$\frac{\alpha}{12} \neq \frac{3}{\alpha} \Rightarrow \alpha^2 \neq 36 \Rightarrow \alpha \neq \pm 6$$

4. Since, the given set of equations represent coincident lines.

then, $\frac{1}{4} = \frac{5}{20} = \frac{-7}{K} \Rightarrow K = -28$

12. $3x + 4y = 25$
$\Rightarrow \quad 3x + 4 \times 4 = 25 \quad (\because y = 4)$

or $3x + 16 = 25 \Rightarrow 3x = 25 - 16$

$\Rightarrow 3x = 9 \Rightarrow x = 9/3 = 3$

13. Roots are 5 and 9
Sum of the roots = $5 + 9 = 14$
Product of roots = $5 \times 9 = 45$
$\therefore x^2 -$ Sum of roots (x) + Product of roots = 0
$\Rightarrow x^2 - 14x + 45 = 0$

14. $\alpha + \beta = p, \quad \alpha\beta = q$

$$\therefore \frac{1}{\alpha} + \frac{1}{\beta} = \frac{\alpha+\beta}{\alpha\beta} = \frac{p}{q}$$

17. For real roots $D \geq 0$

$\Rightarrow (4)^2 - 4.p.1 \geq 0 \qquad \Rightarrow 16 \geq 4p$

$\Rightarrow 4p \leq 16 \qquad \Rightarrow p \leq 4$

20. $\alpha + \beta = \alpha\beta$

$$\frac{-(2k+1)}{3} = \frac{-k+5}{3}$$

$-2k - 1 = -k + 5 \qquad k = -6$

23. Here, $\alpha + \beta = 2, \alpha\beta = -1$
Now, $\alpha^2\beta + \alpha\beta^2 = \alpha\beta(\alpha + \beta)$
$= -1(2) = -2$

26. $\alpha + \beta = 6, \alpha\beta = 6$
$\therefore \alpha - \beta = \sqrt{[(\alpha + \beta)^2 - 4\alpha\beta]} = \sqrt{(12)}$

27. Let α and $1/\alpha$ be the roots.
$\therefore$ Product of roots $= \alpha(1/\alpha) = 1$
$= k/5 \Rightarrow k = 5$

28. $\because$ One root of equation
$x^2 + px + 12 = 0$ is 4
$\therefore 16 + 4p + 12 = 0 \Rightarrow p = -7$
If equation $x^2 + px + q = 0$ has equal roots,
then $p^2 - 4q = 0 \Rightarrow q = p^2/4 = 49/4$

16

Logarithm

Definition

The logarithm of any number to a given base is the index of the power to which the base must be raised in order to equal the given number.

If b be any number and p and N two other numbers such that $b^p = N$, then p is called the logarithm of N to the base b and is written as $\log_b N$. Thus the exponential identity $b^p = N$ is equivalent to logarithmic identity $\log_b N = p$.

Exponential	*Logarithmic*
$b^p = n$	$\log_b N = p$
$3^2 = 9$	$\log_3 9 = 2$
$4^{-2} = \frac{1}{16}$	$\log_4\left(\frac{1}{16}\right) = -2$
$4^{-2} = 0.0625$	$\log_4 (0.0625) = -2$
$64^{1/3} = 4$	$\log_{64}(4) = \frac{1}{3}$

Properties of Logarithms:

(i) $a^{\log_a^x} = x;\ a \neq 0, \pm 1, x > 0.$

(ii) $a^{\log_b^x} = x^{\log_b^a};\ a > 0, b > 0, \neq 1, x > 0.$

(iii) $\log_a a = 1, \log_a 1 = 0;\ a > 0, \neq 1.$

(iv) $\log_a x = \dfrac{1}{\log_x a};\ x, a > 0, \neq 1.$

(v) $\log_a x = \log_b x . \log_a b = \dfrac{\log_b x}{\log_b a};\ a, b > 0, \neq 1, x > 0.$

(vi) For $x, y > 0, a > 0, \neq 1$

(a) $\log_a (x.y) = \log_a x + \log_a y$

(b) $\log_a (x/y) = \log_a x - \log_a y$

(c) $\log_a (x^n) = n \log_a x.$

Example : Compute $\log_{30} 8$ if $\log_{30} 3 = a$ and $\log_{30} 5 = b$.

Solution : $\log_{30} 8 = 3 \log_{30} 2 = 3\log_{30} \frac{30}{15} = 3[1 - \log_{30} 3 - \log_{30} 5]$

$= 3\ (1 - a - b)$

MULTIPLE CHOICE QUESTIONS

1. $\log_5 5 \log_4 9 \log_3 2$ simplifies to:
A. 2 B. 1 C. 5 D. None of these

2. $\log_3 11.\log_{11} 13.\log_{13} 15.\log_{15} 27 = ?$
A. 1 B. 2 C. 3 D. None of these

3. $\log_{2\sqrt{2}} 512 = ?$
A. 4 B. 5 C. 6 D. 7

4. If $A = \log_2 \log_2 \log_4 256 + 2\log_{\sqrt{2}} 2$, then A equals:
A. 2 B. 3 C. 5 D. 7

5. $25^{\left(1/2+\log_{1/5} 27+\log_{125} 81\right)} = ?$
A. 0 B. 1 C. 10/81 D. $5\sqrt[3]{9/81}$

6. The domain of the function $\sqrt{(\log_{0.5} x)}$ is:
A. $(1, \infty)$ B. $(0, \infty)$ C. $(0, 1)$ D. $(0.5, 1)$

7. If $\log_{10} 3 = 0.477$, the no. of digits in 3^{40} is:
A. 18 B. 19 C. 20 D. 21

8. If $a^x = b$, $b^y = c$, $c^z = a$, then value of xyz is:
A. 0 B. 1 C. 2 D. 3

9. $7 \log (16/15) + 5 \log (25/24) + 3 \log (81/80) = ?$
A. 0 B. 1 C. log 2 D. log 3

10. If $\log_{16} x + \log_4 x + \log_2 x = 14$, then $x = ?$
A. 16 B. 32 C. 64 D. None of these

11. If $N = m!$ (m is a fixed positive integer > 2), then

$$\frac{1}{\log_2 N}+\frac{1}{\log_3 N}+\dots\dots\dots+\frac{1}{\log_m N}$$ is equal to:

A. – 1 B. 0 C. 1 D. 2

12. $\log (\log_{ab} a + 1/\log_b ab) = ?$
A. 0 B. 1 C. $\log ab$ D. None of these

13. The value of $\sqrt{(\log^2_{0.5} 4)}$ is:
A. – 2 B. $\sqrt{(-4)}$ C. 2 D. None of these

14. If $\dfrac{\log_8 17}{\log_9 23}-\dfrac{\log_{2\sqrt{2}} 17}{\log_3 23} = ?$
A. 0 B. 1 C. 17/8 D. 23/17

15. $\frac{1}{\log_{xy} xyz}+\frac{1}{\log_{yz} xyz}+\frac{1}{\log_{zx} xyz} = ?$

A. 0 B. 1 C. 2 D. $\log_x xyz$

16. The equation $\log_e x + \log_e (1 + x) = 0$ can be written as:

A. $x^2 + x - 1 = 0$ B. $x^2 + x + 1 = 0$
C. $x^2 + x - e = 0$ D. $x^2 + x + e = 0$

17. If $2 \log_{16} (x^2 + x) - \log_4 (x + 1) = 2$, then $x = ?$

A. – 1 B. 16 C. 2 D. None of these

18. If $\frac{1}{\log_a x}+\frac{1}{\log_c x}=\frac{2}{\log_b x}$, then a, b, c are in:

A. A.P. B. G.P. C. H.P. D. None of these

19. $\log_{10} \tan 1° + \log_{10} \tan 2° + ... + \log_{10} \tan 89° = ?$

A. 0 B. 1 C. 2 D. 3

20. The number $\log_2 7$ is:

A. an integer B. a rational number
C. an irrational number D. a prime number

21. If $\log_{10}{}^{3} = 0.477$, the number of digits in 3^{50} is:

A. 23 B. 24 C. 50 D. 150

22. If $\log_8 m + \log_8{}^{1/6} = \frac{2}{3}$; then m is equal to:

A. 4 B. 12 C. 18 D. 24

23. If the logarithm of a number of the base $\sqrt{8}$ is 6, then the number is:

A. $\sqrt{48}$ B. $\frac{\sqrt{8}}{6}$ C. $6\sqrt{8}$ D. 512

24. If log 2 = 0.3010 and log 3 = 0.4771, then the value of log 48 is

A. 1.6731 B. 1.6811 C. 1.6911 D. 1.8611

25. If $\log_4{}^{7} = x$, then $\log_7{}^{16}$ is equal to:

A. $2/x$ B. x C. $2x$ D. x^2

26. The value of the real number x satisfying $\log_9{}^{x} - \log_9\left(\frac{x}{10}+\frac{1}{9}\right) = 1$ is:

A. 2 B. 4 C. 9 D. 10

27. The value of $\log_2 \log_2 \log_3 \log_3 27^3$ is

A. 0 B. 1 C. 2 D. 3

28. $\log_{10}{}^{10} + \log_{10}{}^{100} + ... + \log_{10} 1\underbrace{0000...0}_{n}$ is equal to:

A. n B. $(n+1)$ C. (n^2+n+1) D. $\frac{n(n+1)}{2}$

29. If $\log_{10}(x+5) + \log_{10}{}^{10} = 4$, then the value of x is:

A. 795 B. 890 C. 995 D. 1000

30. If $\log_4{}^{x^2(x-1)^2} - \log_2{}^{(x-1)} = 1$, then the value of x will be:

A. 1 B. 2 C. 3 D. 4

ANSWERS

1	2	3	4	5	6	7	8	9	10
B	C	C	C	D	C	C	B	C	D
11	**12**	**13**	**14**	**15**	**16**	**17**	**18**	**19**	**20**
C	A	C	A	C	A	B	B	A	C
21	**22**	**23**	**24**	**25**	**26**	**27**	**28**	**29**	**30**
B	D	D	B	A	D	A	D	C	B

EXPLANATORY ANSWERS

1. Given expression $= 1.\log_{2^2} 3^2.\log_3 2$

$$= \frac{2}{2}\log_2 3.1/(\log_2 3) = 1.$$

2. Given expression $= \log_3 27 = \log_3 3^3 = 3\log_3 3 = 3.$

3. $\log_{2\sqrt{2}} 512 = \log_{2^{3/2}} 2^9 = \{9/(3/2)\}\log_2 2 = 6.$

8. $a = c^z = (b^y)^z = b^{yz} = (a^x)^{yz}$

$= a^{xyz} \Rightarrow xyz = 1.$

21. Let $x = 3^{50}$

$\Rightarrow \log x = 50 \log 3 = 50 \times 0.477 = 23.850$

Hence, requried number of digits = 23 + 1 = 24

22. $\log_8{}^m + \log_8{}^{1/6} = \frac{2}{3} \Rightarrow \log_8{}^{\left(m\times\frac{1}{6}\right)} = \frac{2}{3}$

$\Rightarrow m\times\frac{1}{6} = 8^{2/3} \quad \Rightarrow \frac{m}{6} = \left(2^3\right)^{2/3}$

$\Rightarrow \frac{m}{6} = 4 \quad \therefore m = 24$

23. $\log_{\sqrt{8}}{}^{x} = 6 \quad \Rightarrow x = \left(\sqrt{8}\right)^6 = \left(2^{3/2}\right)^6$

$\therefore x = 2^9 = 512$

24. $\log 48 = \log (2^4 \times 3) = 4 \log 2 + \log 3$

$= 4 \times 0.3010 + 0.4771 = 1.6811$

25. $\log_4 7 = x \quad \Rightarrow \log_7{}^{4} = \frac{1}{x} \quad \Rightarrow 2\log_7{}^{4} = \frac{2}{x}$

$\Rightarrow \log_7{}^{4^2} \quad \Rightarrow \log_7{}^{16} = \frac{2}{x}$

26. $\log_9 x - \log_9\left(\frac{x}{10}+\frac{1}{9}\right) = 1 \quad \Rightarrow \log_9 x - \log_9\left(\frac{x}{10}+\frac{1}{9}\right) = \log_9{}^{9}$

$\Rightarrow \log_9{}^{x/\left(\frac{x}{10}+\frac{1}{9}\right)} = \log_9{}^{9} \quad \Rightarrow \log_9\left(\frac{90x}{9x+10}\right) = \log_9{}^{9}$

$\Rightarrow \frac{90x}{9x+10} = 9 \quad \Rightarrow 90x = 81x + 90 \quad \Rightarrow 9x = 90 \quad \Rightarrow x = 10$

27. $\log_2 \log_2 \log_3 \log_3{}^{27^3} = \log_2 \log_2 \log_3 \log_3\left(3^3\right)^3 = \log_2 \log_2 \log_3 9 \log_3{}^{3}$

$= \log_2 \log_2 \log_3{}^{3^2} \times 1 = \log_2 \log_2{}^{2} \log_3{}^{3} = \log_2 \log_2{}^{2} \times 1$

$= \log_2 \times 1 = \log_2{}^{1} = 0$

28. $\log_{10} 10 + \log_{10} 100 + \ldots.. + \log_{10} 1\underbrace{00000\ldots0}_{n}$

$= \log_{10}{}^{10} + \log_{10}{}^{10^2} + \ldots\ldots + \log_{10}{}^{10^n}$

$= \log_{10}{}^{10} + 2\log_{10}{}^{10} + \ldots\ldots + n\log_{10}{}^{10}$

$= 1 + 2 + \ldots\ldots + n = \frac{n(n+1)}{2}$

29. $\log_{10}{}^{(x+5)} + \log_{10}{}^{10} = 4 \quad \Rightarrow \log_{10}{}^{(x+5)} + 1 = 4$

$\Rightarrow \log_{10}{}^{(x+5)} = 3 \quad \Rightarrow x + 5 = 10^3 \quad \therefore x = 1000 - 5 = 995$

30. $\log_4{}^{x^2(x-1)^2} - \log_2{}^{(x-1)} = 1 \quad \Rightarrow \log_{2^2}{}^{[x(x-1)]^2} - \log_2{}^{(x-1)} = 1$

$\Rightarrow \frac{2}{2}\log_2{}^{x(x-1)} - \log_2{}^{(x-1)} = 1 \Rightarrow \log_2{}^{\frac{x(x-1)}{x-1}} = 1$

$\Rightarrow \log_2 x = 1 \quad \therefore x = 2^1 = 2$

17

Geometry

Important Definations and facts

Line : To connect two points on a plane is called a line. It may be straight line, a curved line (a line has only length, it has no breadth).

Point : On a given point there passes infinitely many lines.

Parrallel straight lines : Two lines on a plane which never intersect each other are called parrallel lines.

Angle : An angle is the union of two non-collinear rays with a common initial point.

1. **Right angle :** An angle whose measure is 90° is called a right angle.
2. **Actute angle :** An angle whose measure is less than 90° is called an actue angle.
3. **Obtuse angle :** An angle whose measure is more than 90° less than 180° is called an obtuse angle.
4. **Reflex angle :** An angle having measure more than 180° and less than 360° is called a reflex angle.
5. **Supplementary angle :** Two angles, the sum of whose measures is 180° are called supplementary angle.
6. **Complementary angle :** Two angles, the sum of whose measure is 90° are called complementary angles.
   For example : 70 and 110 are a pair of summple- mentary angles while 50 and 40 are a pair of complementary angles.
7. **Adjacent angle :** Two angles are called adjacent angle if they have the same vertex, they have a common arm and uncommon arms are on either side of the common arm.

Triangle

Triangle : Figure on a plane formed by three lines.

Types of Triangles

(*a*) Types of triangle on the basis of sides.

(*i*) Equilateral Triangle : All three sides are equal.

(*ii*) Isosceles Triangle : Two sides are equql.

(*iii*) Scalence Triangle : Non of side is equal (unequal)

(*b*) Types of triangle on the bases of angle :

(*i*) Right angle triangle : One angle is of a right angle (90°)

(*ii*) Obtuse angle triangle : Triangle with one angle an obtuse angle.

Note : The sum of the three angles of a triangle is 180°.

Quadrilateral

Quadrilateral : Figure on a plane formed by four lines. The sum is interior angles is 360°

The Types of Triangles Quadrilateral

(*i*) **Square :** All the four sides are equal and each angle is of 90°. The diagnonals are equal and intersect at 90°.

(*ii*) **Rhombus :** All the four sides are equal and angles are not necessary to be right angle. In a rhombus. (a) Diagonals intersect at 90° to each other. (b) Diagonals bisect each other.

(*iii*) **Rectangle :** It is a parallelogram having all the angles of 90° but the length and breadth are unequal.

(*iv*) **Parallelogram :** A quadrilateral which has both pairs of opposite sides parallel.

In a parallelogram : (a) Each pair of opposite side are equal. (b) Each pair of opposite angles are equal.

(*v*) **Trapezium :** A qudrilateral which has one pair of opposite sides parallel.

Interior Angles of a Polygon:

1. Sum of the exterior angles of any polygon is 360°.
2. Sum of the interior angles of any polygon is $(2n - 4)$ 90, here n stands for number of sides.

For example :

(*i*) Find the sum of the interior angles of a hexagon (figure with six angles).

Sol. $(2 \times 6 - 4)\ 90 = 8 \times 90 = 720°$.

(*ii*) Find the sum of the interior angles of a pentagon (figure with five angle).

Sol. $(2 \times 5 - 4)\ 90 = 6 \times 90 = 540°$.

(*iii*) Each angle of a regular polygon = $\dfrac{2(n-4)90}{n}$

For example :

(*iv*) Find the value of each angle of a regular hexagon.

Sol. $\dfrac{(2\times 6-4)90}{6}$ or $\dfrac{8\times 90}{6} = 120°$

MULTIPLE CHOICE QUESTIONS

1. A tangent to a circle is a line that intersect the circle in only:
A. two points B. three points C. four points D. one point

2. A line intersecting a circle in two points is called:
A. tangent B. secant
C. point of contact D. None of these

3. The longest chord of a circle is called its:
A. radius B. secant C. diameter D. tangent

4. A tangent PQ at a point P of a circle of radius 5 cm meets a line through the centre O at a point Q, so that OQ = 12 cm. Length PQ is:
A. $\sqrt{119}$ cm B. 13 cm C. 10 cm D. 12 cm

5. In a right angled triangle hypotenuse is:
A. Any side of the triangle B. Side opposite to right angle
C. Side opposite to acute angle D. None of these

6. If the perimeter and area of a circle are numerically equal, then the radius of the circle is :
A. 6 units B. π units C. 4 units D. 2 units

7. The area of a circle is 301.84 cm^2. Then its radius is :
A. 9.2 cm B. 9.3 cm C. 9.8 cm D. 9.6 cm

8. If three altitudes of a triangle are equal then the triangle is :
A. Right angled B. Equilateral C. Isosceles D. Scalene

9. The height of an equilateral triangle is :
A. $\frac{\sqrt{3}}{4}\times\text{Side}$ B. $\frac{\sqrt{3}}{2}\times\text{Side}$ C. $\frac{\sqrt{3}}{4}\times\text{Side}^2$ D. None of these

10. ABC is an isosceles right triangle. If $AB^2 = 2AC^2$ then right angle is at:
A. C B. A C. B D. None of these

11. The length of an altitude of an equilateral triangle of side $2a$ is :
A. $\sqrt{2}a$ cm B. $\sqrt{3}a$ cm C. 2 cm D. 1 cm

12. If $\angle A = 100°$, AB = AC, CD bisects $\angle ACB$ and BD bisects $\angle ABC$. The values of x and y are:
A. 15° and 70° B. 20° and 140°
C. 10° and 160° D. 20° and 125°

13. A perpendicular at the end of the radius of a circle is :
A. diameter B. tangent C. chord D. anyline

14. ABC and BDF are two equilateral triangles such that D is the mid-point of BC. The ratio of the areas of triangles ABC and BDF is :

A. 2 : 1 B. 1 : 2 C. 4 : 1 D. 1 : 4

15. The exterior angle of a quadrilateral are $x°$, $(x + 5)°$, $(x + 10)°$ and $(x + 25)°$, then value of x is :

A. 50° B. 80° C. 60° D. 70°

16. The point equidistant from the three sides of a triangle is :

A. circumference B. centroid C. incentre D. orthocentre

17. In ΔABC, AB = $6\sqrt{3}$ cm AC = 12 cm and BC = 6 cm. The ∠CAB and ∠ABC are:

A. 90° and 60° B. 30° and 90°
C. 60° and 90° D. 90° and 30°

18. Chords AC and BD of a circle intersect each other, than the figure ABCD formed will be :

A. square B. rectangle
C. parallelogram D. quadrilateral

19. Sides of two similar triangles are in the ratio of 4 : 9 then area of these triangles are in the ratio :

A. 2 : 3 B. 4 : 9 C. 81 : 16 D. 16 : 81

20. In the given figure ∠AOB = 80°. The value of x is :

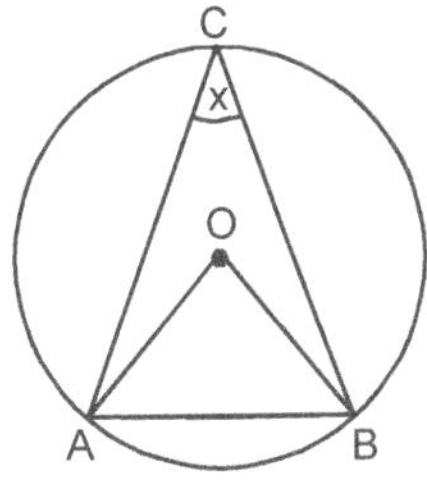

A. 10° B. 25° C. 40° D. 160°

ANSWERS

1	2	3	4	5	6	7	8	9	10
D	B	C	A	B	D	C	B	B	A
11	**12**	**13**	**14**	**15**	**16**	**17**	**18**	**19**	**20**
B	B	D	C	B	C	B	B	D	C

EXPLANATORY ANSWERS

1. A line meeting a circle in one point is called a tangent to the circle.

2. A line, which intersects a cirlce in two distinct points is called secant of the circle.

5.

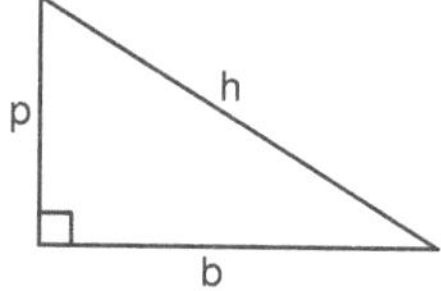

In any right-angled triangle hypotenuse is opposite to right angle.

6. From question,

circumference of circle = Area of circle

$$2\pi r = \pi r^2$$

$$\Rightarrow \quad r = 2$$

$$\therefore \quad \text{Radius} = 2 \text{ units.}$$

7. Area of the circle = πr^2

According to the question,

$$\pi r^2 = 301.84$$

$$\Rightarrow \quad \frac{22}{7} r^2 = 301.84$$

$$r^2 = \frac{7 \times 301.84}{22} = 96.04$$

$$\therefore \quad r = \sqrt{96.04} = 9.8 \text{ cm.}$$

8. If the altitudes of a triangle are equal then it is equilateral.

10. Let $\angle C = 90°$

In ΔACB,

$$(AB)^2 = (AC)^2 + (BC)^2$$

$$(AB)^2 = (AC)^2 + (AC)^2$$

$$AB^2 = 2AC^2$$

$$\therefore \quad \angle C = 90°.$$

13. A tangent to a circle is at right angle to the radius.

15. We have,

$$x° + (x + 5)° + (x + 10)° + (x + 25)° = 360°$$

$$4x + 40° = 360°$$

$$4x = 320°$$
$$x = 80°.$$

16. Point of concurrence of the bisector of the angles of a triangle is called incentre.

17. In ΔABC

$$(12)^2 = (6)^2 + \left(6\sqrt{3}\right)^2$$
$$144 = 36 + 108 = 144$$

∴ ΔABC is right-angled triangle

∴ $$\angle B = 90°$$

$$\sin A = \frac{BC}{AC} = \frac{6}{12} = \frac{1}{2}$$

⇒ $$\sin A = \sin 30°$$
$$A = 30°$$

∴ The angles ∠CAB and ∠ABC are 30° and 90° respectively.

18. Chords AC and BD must pass through the centre of the circle and will intersect at the centre,

∴ □ABCD is a rectangle.

19. ∵ ΔABC ~ ΔDEF

∴ $$\frac{ar\Delta ABC}{ar\Delta DEF} = \frac{(4)^2}{(9)^2} = \frac{16}{81} = 16 : 81.$$

20. We have,

$$\angle AOB = 2\angle ACB$$

[Angle of the centre is twice at the angle of circumference]

$$80° = 2x$$

∴ $$x = \frac{80}{2} = 40°.$$

18 Trigonometry

The word 'trigonometry' literally means the science which deals with the measurement of triangles.

Angle

An angle is a figure formed by two rays (called the arms) with the common initial point (called the vertex).

It is determined by rotating a ray about its end point.

Positive and Negative Angles

Angles determined by a **counter clockwise** rotation are said to be **positive** and angles determined by **clockwise** rotation are said to be **negative**.

The six trigonometric ratios of the acute angle θ are defined as follows :

$$\sin\theta = \frac{p}{h} = \frac{AB}{AC} \qquad \cos\theta = \frac{b}{h} = \frac{BC}{AC}$$

$$\tan\theta = \frac{p}{b} = \frac{AB}{BC} \qquad \cot\theta = \frac{b}{p} = \frac{BC}{AB}$$

$$\sec\theta = \frac{h}{b} = \frac{AC}{BC} \qquad \text{cosec}\,\theta = \frac{h}{p} = \frac{AC}{AB}$$

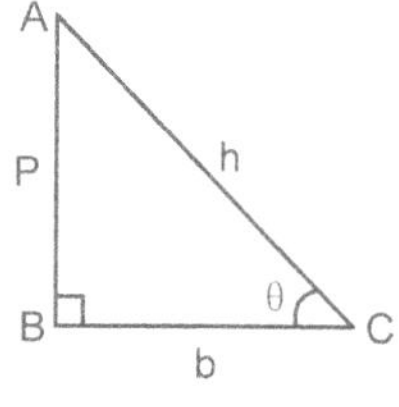

[p = perpendicular or opposite
b = base or adjacent
h = hypotenuse]

IMPORTANT FORMULAE

A. (*i*) $\tan\theta = \frac{\sin\theta}{\cos\theta} = \frac{1}{\cot\theta}$ (*ii*) $\cot\theta = \frac{\cos\theta}{\sin\theta} = \frac{1}{\tan\theta}$

(*iii*) $\sec\theta = \frac{1}{\cos\theta}$ (*iv*) $\text{cosec}\,\theta = \frac{1}{\sin\theta}$

B. (*i*) $\sin^2\theta + \cos^2\theta = 1$

$\sin^2\theta = 1 - \cos^2\theta \Rightarrow \sin\theta = \sqrt{1-\cos^2\theta}$

$\cos^2\theta = 1 - \sin^2\theta \Rightarrow \cos\theta = \sqrt{1-\sin^2\theta}$

(*ii*) $1 + \tan^2\theta = \sec^2\theta$

$\sec^2\theta - \tan^2\theta = 1$

$\sec^2\theta - 1 = \tan^2\theta$

(*iii*) $1 + \cot^2\theta = \text{cosec}^2\theta$

$\text{cosec}^2\theta - \cot^2\theta = 1$

$\text{cosec}^2\theta - 1 = \cot^2\theta$

(*iv*) $\tan^2\theta = \dfrac{\sin^2\theta}{\cos^2\theta}$

(*v*) $\cot^2\theta = \dfrac{\cos^2\theta}{\sin^2\theta}$

(*vi*) $\sec^2\theta = \dfrac{1}{\cos^2\theta}$

(*vii*) $\text{cosec}^2\theta = \dfrac{1}{\sin^2\theta}$

C. (*i*) $\sin(90 - \theta) = \cos\theta$ (*ii*) $\cos(90 - \theta) = \sin\theta$

(*iii*) $\tan(90 - \theta) = \cot\theta$ (*iv*) $\cot(90 - \theta) = \tan\theta$

(*v*) $\sec(90 - \theta) = \text{cosec}\theta$ (*vi*) $\text{cosec}(90 - \theta) = \sec\theta$

D. (*i*) $\sin(A \pm B) = \sin A \times \cos B \pm \cos A \times \sin B$

(*ii*) $\cos(A \pm B) = \cos A \times \cos B \mp \sin A \times \sin B$

E. (*i*) $\sin 2\theta = 2\sin\theta \cdot \cos\theta$

(*ii*) $\cos 2\theta = \cos^2\theta - \sin^2\theta = 1 - 2\sin^2\theta = 2\cos^2\theta - 1$

(*iii*) $\tan 2\theta = \dfrac{2\tan\theta}{1-\tan^2\theta}$

F. (*i*) $\sin 3\theta = 3\sin\theta - 4\sin^3\theta$ (*ii*) $\cos 3\theta = 4\cos^3\theta - 3\cos\theta$

T-Ratios of Standard Angles

θ	0°	30°	45°	60°	90°
$\sin\theta$	0	$\frac{1}{2}$	$\frac{1}{\sqrt{2}}$	$\frac{\sqrt{3}}{2}$	1
$\cos\theta$	1	$\frac{\sqrt{3}}{2}$	$\frac{1}{\sqrt{2}}$	$\frac{1}{2}$	0
$\tan\theta$	0	$\frac{1}{\sqrt{3}}$	1	$\sqrt{3}$	∞
$\cot\theta$	∞	$\sqrt{3}$	1	$\frac{1}{\sqrt{3}}$	0
$\sec\theta$	1	$\frac{2}{\sqrt{3}}$	$\sqrt{2}$	2	∞
$\text{cosec}\theta$	∞	2	$\sqrt{2}$	$\frac{2}{\sqrt{3}}$	1

MULTIPLE CHOICE QUESTIONS

1. If $\cos\theta = \frac{1}{2}$, find the value of $\frac{2\sec\theta}{1+\tan^2\theta}$

A. 1 B. 2 C. 3 D. 4

2. If $\sin\theta = \frac{5}{13}$ and $0 < \theta < 90°$, find out the value of $\cos\theta$.

A. $\frac{5}{12}$ B. $\frac{12}{13}$ C. $\frac{13}{12}$ D. $\frac{12}{5}$

3. If $5\tan\theta = 4$, find the value of $\frac{5\sin\theta - 3\cos\theta}{5\sin\theta + 2\cos\theta}$

A. 2 B. $\frac{3}{2}$ C. $\frac{1}{6}$ D. $\frac{2}{3}$

4. If $3\cot\theta = 2$, find the value of $\frac{4\sin\theta - 3\cos\theta}{2\sin\theta + 6\cos\theta}$

A. $\frac{2}{3}$ B. $\frac{3}{2}$ C. $\frac{1}{3}$ D. 3

5. If $3\tan\theta = 2$, find the value of $\frac{4\sin\theta - \cos\theta}{2\sin\theta + \cos\theta}$

A. $\frac{3}{2}$ B. $\frac{5}{7}$ C. $\frac{3}{7}$ D. 1

6. If $3\cot\theta = 4$, find the value of $\frac{5\sin\theta - 3\cos\theta}{5\sin\theta + 3\cos\theta}$

A. $\frac{1}{9}$ B. $\frac{2}{7}$ C. 3 D. 4

7. If $\tan\theta = \frac{3}{4}$, find the value of $\frac{4\sin\theta - 2\cos\theta}{4\sin\theta + 3\cos\theta}$

A. $\frac{2}{3}$ B. $\frac{4}{3}$ C. $\frac{1}{6}$ D. $\frac{5}{6}$

8. If $\tan A = \frac{5}{12}$, find the value of $\sin A + \cos A$, where A is an acute angle.

A. $\frac{13}{17}$ B. $\frac{17}{13}$ C. $\frac{12}{5}$ D. $\frac{5}{17}$

9. If $\tan\theta = \frac{2}{3}(0° < \theta < 90°)$, then find the value of $\sin\theta$

A. $\frac{2}{\sqrt{13}}$ B. $\frac{3}{\sqrt{12}}$ C. 1 D. 0

10. If $2\tan\theta = 1$, find the value of $\frac{3\cos\theta + 2\sin\theta}{2\cos\theta - \sin\theta}$

A. $\frac{8}{3}$ B. $\frac{5}{3}$ C. $\frac{2}{3}$ D. 2

11. Evaluate : $(\operatorname{cosec}\theta - \sin\theta)(\sec\theta - \cos\theta)(\tan\theta + \cot\theta)$

A. 1 B. 2 C. 3 D. 0

12. Evaluate : $(\sin A + \cos A)(\tan A + \cot A)$

A. $\sin A + \cos A$ B. $\sec A + \operatorname{cosec} A$

C. $\sin A$ D. $\cos A$

13. Evaluate $\frac{\sin\theta}{1+\cos\theta} + \frac{1+\cos\theta}{\sin\theta}$

A. $2\sin A$ B. $2\operatorname{cosec} A$ C. $2\tan A$ D. $2\cos A$

14. Evaluate $\frac{\tan A + \sec A - 1}{\tan A - \sec A + 1}$

A. $\sec A + \tan A$ B. $\sin A$ C. 1 D. 0

15. If $\sin x + \sin^2 x = 1$, then $\cos^2 x + \cos^4 x$ is :

A. 1 B. 2 C. 3 D. 4

16. If $\cos\theta - \sin\theta = \sqrt{2}\sin\theta$, then $\cos\theta + \sin\theta$ is:

A. $\sqrt{2}\sin\theta$ B. $\sqrt{2}\cos\theta$ C. $\sin\theta$ D. $\cos\theta$

17. Find the value of
$4(\sin^4 30° + \cos^4 60°) - 3(\sin^2 45° - 2\cos^2 45°)$.

A. 1 B. 2 C. 0 D. 3

18. Express $\cos 79° + \sec 79°$ in terms of angles between 0° and 45°

A. 1 B. 2

C. $\sin 11° + \operatorname{cosec} 11°$ D. $\cos 11° + \sec 11°$

19. Using the formula
$\cos(A - B) = \cos A\cos B + \sin A\sin B$, find the value of $\cos 15°$.

A. $\frac{\sqrt{3}-1}{2\sqrt{2}}$ B. $\sqrt{3}-1$ C. $\frac{\sqrt{3}+1}{2\sqrt{2}}$ D. $\sqrt{3}+1$

20. Using the formula
sin (A – B) = sin A cos B – cos A sin B, find the value of sin 15°

A. $\sqrt{3}$ B. $\sqrt{3}+1$ C. $\frac{\sqrt{3}-1}{2\sqrt{2}}$ D. $\frac{\sqrt{3}+1}{2\sqrt{2}}$

21. $\sin\theta\cos(90^\circ-\theta)+\cos\theta\sin(90^\circ-\theta)$ equal to :
A. 0 B. 1 C. –1 D. 2

22. $\cos^2 72^\circ + \cos^2 18^\circ$ = ?
A. 0 B. 1 C. –1 D. 2

23. $3\tan^2 30^\circ + \sec^4 45^\circ - \tan^2 60^\circ$ is equal to :
A. 0 B. 1 C. 2 D. 3

24. The value of sin 79° cos 11° + cos 79° sin 11°.
A. 1 B. 0 C. 2 D. –2

25. $(\sin\theta+\cos\theta)(1-\sin\theta\cos\theta)$ can be written as :
A. $\sin\theta+\cos\theta$ B. $\sin^3\theta-\cos^3\theta$
C. $\sin^3\theta+\cos^3\theta$ D. $\sin\theta-\cos\theta$

26. If $\cot^2\theta=\frac{7}{8}$ and $0<\theta<90^\circ$, then the value of $\frac{(1+\sin\theta)(1-\sin\theta)}{(1+\cos\theta)(1-\cos\theta)}$ is equal to :

A. $\frac{7}{8}$ B. $\frac{7}{6}$ C. $\frac{7}{5}$ D. $\frac{7}{4}$

27. $\sin 40^\circ.\sec 50^\circ-\frac{\tan 40^\circ}{\cot 50^\circ}+1$ =
A. 0 B. 1 C. –1 D. 2

28. The value of sin 20° – cos 70° is :
A. 1 B. 2 C. 3 D. 0

29. The value of $\text{cosec}^2(90^\circ-\theta)-\tan^2\theta$ is
A. 2 B. 3 C. 0 D. 1

30. If θ = 45 then $\frac{2\tan\theta}{1+\tan^2\theta}$ is :

A. 1 B. 0 C. 2 D. 3

31. The value of cos 1° cos 2° ... cos 100° is
A. 1 B. – 1 C. 0 D. None of these

32. cos 24° + cos 5° + cos 175° + cos 204° + cos 300° =
A. 1/2 B. – 1/2 C. $\sqrt{(3/2)}$ D. None of these

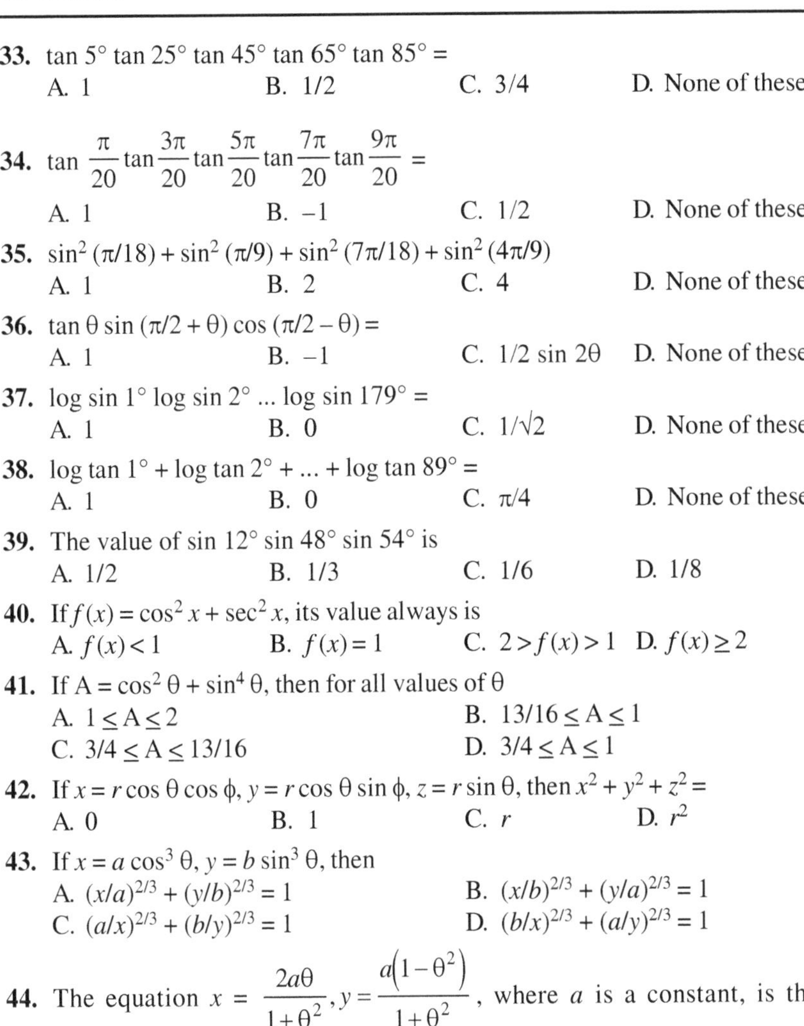

33. tan 5° tan 25° tan 45° tan 65° tan 85° =
A. 1 B. 1/2 C. 3/4 D. None of these

34. $\tan\frac{\pi}{20}\tan\frac{3\pi}{20}\tan\frac{5\pi}{20}\tan\frac{7\pi}{20}\tan\frac{9\pi}{20} =$
A. 1 B. −1 C. 1/2 D. None of these

35. $\sin^2(\pi/18) + \sin^2(\pi/9) + \sin^2(7\pi/18) + \sin^2(4\pi/9)$
A. 1 B. 2 C. 4 D. None of these

36. $\tan\theta \sin(\pi/2 + \theta)\cos(\pi/2 - \theta) =$
A. 1 B. −1 C. $1/2 \sin 2\theta$ D. None of these

37. log sin 1° log sin 2° ... log sin 179° =
A. 1 B. 0 C. $1/\sqrt{2}$ D. None of these

38. log tan 1° + log tan 2° + ... + log tan 89° =
A. 1 B. 0 C. $\pi/4$ D. None of these

39. The value of sin 12° sin 48° sin 54° is
A. 1/2 B. 1/3 C. 1/6 D. 1/8

40. If $f(x) = \cos^2 x + \sec^2 x$, its value always is
A. $f(x) < 1$ B. $f(x) = 1$ C. $2 > f(x) > 1$ D. $f(x) \geq 2$

41. If $A = \cos^2\theta + \sin^4\theta$, then for all values of θ
A. $1 \leq A \leq 2$ B. $13/16 \leq A \leq 1$
C. $3/4 \leq A \leq 13/16$ D. $3/4 \leq A \leq 1$

42. If $x = r\cos\theta\cos\phi$, $y = r\cos\theta\sin\phi$, $z = r\sin\theta$, then $x^2 + y^2 + z^2 =$
A. 0 B. 1 C. r D. r^2

43. If $x = a\cos^3\theta$, $y = b\sin^3\theta$, then
A. $(x/a)^{2/3} + (y/b)^{2/3} = 1$ B. $(x/b)^{2/3} + (y/a)^{2/3} = 1$
C. $(a/x)^{2/3} + (b/y)^{2/3} = 1$ D. $(b/x)^{2/3} + (a/y)^{2/3} = 1$

44. The equation $x = \frac{2a\theta}{1+\theta^2}, y = \frac{a(1-\theta^2)}{1+\theta^2}$, where a is a constant, is the parametric equation of the curve:
A. $x - y^2 = a^2$ B. $x^2 + y^2 = a^2$ C. $x^2 + 4y^2 = 4a^2$ D. $x = 2y$

45. The expression

$$3\left[\sin^4\left\{\frac{3}{2}\pi - \alpha\right\} + \sin^4(3\pi + \alpha)\right] - 2\left[\sin^6\left(\frac{1}{2}\pi + \alpha\right) + \sin^6(5\pi - \alpha)\right]$$ is

equal to

A. 0 B. 1 C. 3 D. $\sin 4\alpha + \cos 6\alpha$

46. $\frac{1}{\sin 10°} - \frac{\sqrt{3}}{\cos\ 10°}$ is equal to

A. 2 B. 4 C. 3 D. None of these

47. $\sqrt{3}$ cosec 20° – sec 20° is equal to

A. 2 B. 2 sin 20°/sin 40°
C. 4 D. 4 sin 20°/sin 40°

48. If tan A = $\frac{a}{a+1}$ and tan B = $\frac{1}{2a+1}$, then the value of A + B is

A. 0 B. $\pi/2$ C. $\pi/3$ D. $\pi/4$

49. In a triangle PQR, ∠ R = $\pi/2$. If tan (P/2) and tan (Q/2) are the roots of the equation $ax^2 + bx + c = 0$, then

A. $a + b = c$ B. $b + c = a$ C. $a + c = b$ D. $b = c$

50. $\sqrt{(\log_3 \tan x)}$ is real for

A. $n\pi + \pi/4 \le x < n\pi + \pi/2$ B. $n\pi < x < n\pi + \pi/2$
C. $n\pi \pm \pi/4 \le x < n\pi \pm \pi/2$ D. None of these

ANSWERS

1	2	3	4	5	6	7	8	9	10
A	B	C	C	B	A	C	B	A	A
11	**12**	**13**	**14**	**15**	**16**	**17**	**18**	**19**	**20**
A	B	B	A	A	B	B	C	C	C
21	**22**	**23**	**24**	**25**	**26**	**27**	**28**	**29**	**30**
B	B	C	A	C	A	B	D	D	A
31	**32**	**33**	**34**	**35**	**36**	**37**	**38**	**39**	**40**
C	A	A	A	B	D	B	B	D	D
41	**42**	**43**	**44**	**45**	**46**	**47**	**48**	**49**	**50**
D	D	A	B	B	B	C	D	A	A

EXPLANATORY ANSWERS

18. cos 79° + sec 79°
= cos (90° – 11°) + sec (90° – 11°)
= sin 11° + cosec 11°.

28. sin 20° – cos(90° – 20°) = sin 20° – sin 20° = 0.

29. $\sec^2\theta - \tan^2\theta = \dfrac{1}{\cos^2\theta} - \dfrac{\sin^2\theta}{\cos^2\theta} = \dfrac{1-\sin^2\theta}{\cos^2\theta} = \dfrac{\cos^2\theta}{\cos^2\theta} = 1.$

30. $\dfrac{2\tan 45°}{1+\tan^2 45°} = \dfrac{2\times 1}{1+1} = \dfrac{2}{2} = 1.$

31. $\because \cos 90° = 0$
$\therefore$ Given expression
$= \cos 1° \cos 2° \ldots \cos 89°.0 \cos 91° \ldots \cos 100° = 0.$

32. Given expression
$= \cos 24° + \cos 5° + \cos (180° - 5°) + \cos (180° + 24°) + \cos (360° - 60°)$
$= \cos 24° + \cos 5° - \cos 5° - \cos 24° + \cos 60° = 1/2.$

33. Given expression
$= \tan 5° \tan 25°.1 \tan (90° - 25°) \times \tan(90° - 5°)$
$= \tan 5° \tan 25° \cot 25° \cot 5° = 1.$

37. $\because \log \sin 90° = \log 1 = 0$
$\therefore$ Given expression $= 0$.

38. Given expression
$= \log (\tan 1°.\tan 2° \ldots \tan 44°. \tan 45°.\cot 44°.\cot 43° \ldots \cot 1°)$
$= \log 1 = 0.$

39. $\sin 12° \sin 48°. \sin 54°$

$= \dfrac{1}{2} (\cos 36° - \cos 60°) \cos 36°$

$= \dfrac{1}{4} (2 \cos^2 36° - \cos 36°)$

$= \dfrac{1}{4} (1 + \cos 72° - \cos 36°)$

$= \dfrac{1}{4} (1 + \sin 18° - \cos 36°) = \dfrac{1}{4}.\left(\dfrac{1}{2}\right) = \dfrac{1}{8}.$

40. $f(x) = (\cos x - \sec x)^2 + 2 \Rightarrow f(x) \geq 2$

47. Given expression

$= \dfrac{\sqrt{3}\cos 20° - \sin 20°}{\cos 20° \sin 20°}$

$$= \frac{2\left[\left(\frac{1}{2}\sqrt{3}\right)\cos 20° - \frac{1}{2}\sin 20°\right]}{\frac{1}{2}\sin 40°}$$

$$= \frac{4\sin(60°-20°)}{\sin 40°} = 4.$$

48. $\tan(\theta + \phi) = (\tan\theta + \tan\phi)/(1 - \tan\theta\tan\phi)$
$= 1 \Rightarrow \theta + \phi = \pi/4.$

49. $\tan(P/2) + \tan(Q/2) = -b/a,$
$\tan(P/2).\tan(Q/2) = c/a$
$\angle P + \angle Q = \pi/2$

$$\tan\left(\frac{1}{2}P + \frac{1}{2}Q\right) = 1$$

$$= \frac{\tan(P/2) + \tan(Q/2)}{1 - \tan(P/2)\tan(Q/2)}$$

$$= \frac{-b/a}{1 - c/a} = \frac{-b}{a-c}$$

$\Rightarrow a + b = c.$

50. $\sqrt{(\log_3 \tan x)}$ is real if $\log_3 \tan x \geq 0$
i.e., $\tan x \geq 1$ (as base = 3 > 1)
$\therefore \pi/4 \leq x < \pi/2$. General values are given by
$n\pi + \pi/4 \leq x < n\pi + \pi/2.$

SCIENCE

PHYSICS

PHYSICAL WORLD AND MEASUREMENT

Physics: Physics is branch of physical science in which the matter and energy mutually interact to each other. It is the study of nature & its laws.

Measurement

Physical quantity: Quantities expressed in the terms of laws of physics are called physical quantities. *Example:* Mass of an object, length, force, speed, distance, displacement, momentum, electric current etc. These physical quantities are of two types : (i) Scalars (ii) Vectors.

(*i*) **Scalars:** Those physical quantities which have magnitude only and sense or direction is not to be taken under the consideration are called *scalars. Example:* Mass, temperature, density, volume, electric current, work etc.

(*ii*) **Vectors:** Those physical quantities which have both magnitude and direction and which are represented by the directed line segment (®) obeying the triangle law of vectors or parallelogram law of vectors are called *vectors.*

Units of Measurement: To measure any quantity, a definite and a substantial amount of that quantity is assumed to be standard which is called the *unit* of the quantity. There are usually two types of units :

(*i*) Fundamental Units (*ii*) Derived Units.

(*i*) **Fundamental Units:** If the physical quantity be expressed in the terms of those units which are used as standards and these standards are independent to each other, then these units are called *Fundamental Units.*

(*ii*) **Derived Units:** If a physical quantity be expressed in terms of two or more fundamental units then these units are called *Derived Units* and these units have no independent existence like Fundamental units. The unit of force, momentum, work, potential and kinetic energy, density etc. are Derived Units.

Dimensions of Physical Quantities

In Physics Length, Mass, Time, Temperature, Electric current etc. which are symbolically represented by L, M, T, O, A have vital and significant role. All the physical quantities are expressed in terms of power (exponents) of these symbols called *dimension. Example:* Area = L × L = L^2,

$$\text{Density} = \frac{\text{Mass}}{\text{Volume}} = \frac{M}{L^3} = ML^{-3}$$

$$\text{Force} = \text{mass} \times \text{acceleration} = M \times LT^{-2} = MLT^{-2}$$

Limitations of the theory of dimensions

1. If a physical quantity is given, its dimensions are unique but converse may or may not be true i.e. if dimensions are given, physical quantity may or may not be unique as many physical quantities has same dimensions. e.g. physical quantity work has got the unique dimensions as $[ML^2T^{-2}]$ but if the dimensions $[ML^2T^{-2}]$ are give to us then they may represent the physical quantities like Work, Energy and Torque, i.e., physical quantity is not unique.
2. Theory of dimensions does not give any information about dimensionsless constant *K*.
3. Theory of dimensions cannot be applied to formulae containing trigonometrical, exponential etc functions e.g. $y = a\sin wt$ and $N = N_0e^{-lt}$.
4. Theory of dimensions cannot be applied to derive formula containing more than three physical quantities, however, it can be used to check the formula. If a physical quantity depends upon more than three factors, then relation among them cannot be established because we can have only three equations by equating the powers of M, L and T and only the values of three powers can be calculated.

Units and Dimensions of Physical Quantities

Quantity	*Common Symbol*	*SI Unit*	*Dimension*
Displacement	s	METRE (m)	L
Mass	m, M	KILOGRAM (kg)	M
Time	t	Second (s)	T
Area	A	m^2	L^2
Volume	V	m^3	L^3
Density	p	kg m^{-3}	M L^{-3}

Velocity	v, u	m s^{-1}	L T^{-1}
Acceleration	a	m s^{-2}	LT^{-2}
Force	F	newton (N)	ML T^{-2}
Work	W	joule (J)(=N–m)	ML^2 T^{-2}
Energy	E, U, K	joule (J)	ML^2 T^{-2}
Power	P	watt (W) (=J s^{-1})	ML^2 T^3
Momentum	p	kg–m s^{-1}	MLT^{-1}
Gravitational constant	G	N–m^2kg^{-2}	L^3 $M^{-1}T^{-2}$
Plane angle	θ, φ	radian(rad)	
Angular velocity	ω	rad s^{-1}	T^{-1}
Angular acceleration	α	rad s^{-2}	T^{-2}
Angular momentum	L	kg–m^2 s^{-1}	ML^2 T^{-1}
Moment of inertia	I	kg–m^2	ML^2
Torque	τ	N–m	ML^2 T^{-2}
Angular frequency	ω	rad s^{-1}	T^{-1}
Frequency	v	hertz (Hz)	T^{-1}
Period	T	s	T
Young's modulus	Y	N m^{-2}	M L^{-1} T^{-2}
Bulk modulus	B	N m^{-2}	M $L^{-1}T^{-2}$
Shear modulus	η	N m^{-2}	MLT^{-2}
Surface tension	S	N m^{-1}	M T^{-2}
Coefficient of viscosity	η	N–s m^{-2}	M L^{-1} T^{-1}
Pressure	P, p	N m–2, Pa	M $L^{-1}T^{-2}$
Wavelength	λ	m	L
Intensity of wave	I	W m^{-2}	M T^{-3}
Temperature	T	KELVIN (K)	⊖
Specific heat capacity	c	J kg^{-1}–K^{-1}	$L2T^{-2}K^{-1}$
Stefan's constant	σ	W m^{-2} –K^{-4}	M T^{-3} K^{-4}
Heat	Q	J	ML^2T^{-2}
Thermal conductivity	K	W m^{-1}–K^{-1}	MLT^{-3} K^{-1}
Current	I	AMPERE(A)	I
Electromotive force	E	volt (V)	$ML^2I^{-1}T^{-3}$
Dielectric constant	k		
Electric dipole moment	p	C–m	LIT
Electric field	E	V m^{-1} (=N C^{-1})	ML $I^{-1}T^{-3}$
Potential (voltage)	V	volt (V)(=J C^{-1})	ML^2 I^{-1} T^{-3}
Electric flux	Φ	V–m	ML^3 I^{-1} T^{-3}

Capacitance	C	farad (F)	$I^2T^4\ M^{-1}L^{-3}$
Permittivity of space	ε0	$C2N^{-1}–m^{-2}$ (=F m^{-1})	$I^2T^4\ M^{-1}L^{-3}$
Permeability of space	μ0	N A^{-2}	ML $I^{-2}T^{-2}$
Magnetic field	B	tesla (T) (=Wb m^{-2})	M $I^{-1}T^{-2}$
Magnetic fulx	Φ_B	weber (Wb)	$ML^2I^{-1}T^{-2}$
Magnetic dipole moment	μ	N–m T^{-1}	IL^2
Inductance	L	henry (H)	$ML^2I^{-2}T^{-2}$
Amount of substance	n	MOLE (mol)	N
Luminous intensity	I	CANDELA (cd)	J
Solid angle	ω	steradian (sr)	

MOTION

If the position of a material system as measured by a particular observer changes with respect to time, that system is said to be in motion with respect to the observer. Absolute motion, has no significance, and only relative motion may be defined. There are various kinds of motion—one dimensional, two-dimensional and three-dimensional.

(i) **Motion in One Dimension :** If only one of the three coordinates specifying the position of the object, change with respect to time, then the motion is called one dimensional motion. In this type of motion, the path followed by the body is a straight line, e.g., the motion of a man on a level road, motion of train on horizontal rails, motion under gravity etc.

(ii) **Motion in Two Dimensions :** If any two of the three coordinates specifying the position of the object change with respect to time, then the motion is called two dimensional motion. In this type of motion the body moves in a plane, e.g., circular motion and projectile motion.

(iii) **Motion in Three Dimensions :** If all the three coordinates of the position of the body change with respect to time, then the motion is called three dimensional motion. Examples of this type of motion are the motion of a bird, aeroplane, or a kite in sky.

Distance

The actual length of path travelled by a body is called the distance (S) travelled or covered by the body. It is a scalar quantity and is measured in metres in SI units.

Displacement

The shortest distance from the initial to the final position of a body is called displacement of the body.

Speed

Speed is the time rate of change of position. It is measured in metre per second, centimetre per second, kilometre per hour etc. Average speed is the total distance travelled divided by the time taken.

$$\text{Speed} = \frac{\text{distance travelled}}{\text{time taken}} = \frac{s}{t} = \text{m/s}$$

Velocity

The time rate of displacement (change of position vector) of the particle is called velocity. Thus,

$$\text{Velocity} = \vec{v} = \frac{d\vec{S}}{dt}, \text{ where } \vec{S} = \text{displacement.}$$

Acceleration

The rate of change of velocity is called acceleration.

Thus acceleration $\vec{a} = \dfrac{d\vec{v}}{dt}$. It is a vector quantity. Its unit is m/s^2.

Acceleration Due to Gravity

The acceleration with which a freely falling body moves towards the earth is called *acceleration due to gravity.* If a feather and an iron piece are released from the same height in vacuum, both will reach the ground simultaneously.

Uniform motion and uniform velocity

A body is said to be moving with uniform velocity if it covers equal displacement in equal interval of time. There is no acceleration in this type of motion and its v–t graph is a straight line parallel to time axis.

The area bounded between v–t curve and time axis in a particular time interval gives the displacement of the body during that time interval.

Variable or non-uniform motion

The velocity of the body is variable in this type of motion and the body covers unequal displacement in equal interval of time. If the direction or magnitude (or both) of velocity change with respect to time, then the motion is said to be variable or non-uniform.

Instantaneous Velocity and Instantaneous Acceleration

If the displacement and velocity graphs are curves instead of straight line then the velocity and acceleration at any instant can be calculated by drawing a tangent at that point and finding its slope. These values of velocities and acceleration are called instantaneous velocity and instantaneous acceleration respectively.

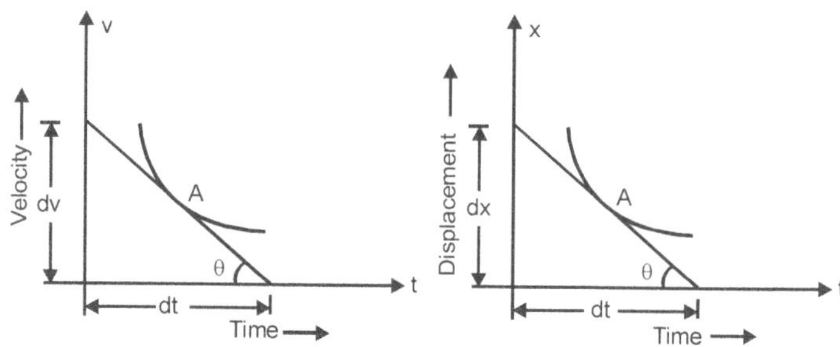

from x–t graph, Instantaneous Velocity at $A = \dfrac{dx}{dt} = \tan\theta$

from v–t graph, Instantaneous Acceleration at

$$A = \frac{dV}{dt} = \tan\theta$$

Equations of motion

The equations of motion are as follows :

(i) $v = u + at$ (ii) $s = ut + (1/2)\,at^2$ (iii) $v^2 = u^2 + 2as$

where u = initial velocity, v = final velocity after t seconds, a = acceleration, s = distance travelled in t seconds.

Note : The distance travelled in nth second is given by

$$S_n = u + (2n - 1)\,a/2$$

Motion under gravity

(a) Downward Motion (↓)

(i) $v = u + gt$ (ii) $h = ut + \frac{1}{2}gt^2$ (iii) $v^2 = u^2 + 2gh$

(b) Upward Motion (↑)

(i) $v = u - gt$ (ii) $h = ut - \frac{1}{2}gt^2$ (iii) $v^2 = u^2 - 2gh$

Relative Velocity

If the distance between the two bodies is changing either in magnitude or direction or both then each is said to have a relative velocity with respect to other.

The relative velocity of first body with respect to the second body is obtained by the vector addition of the negative velocity (velocity in opposite direction) of second body to the velocity of first body.

Scalar and vector quantities

The physical quantities are of two types: Scalars and Vectors.

(a) Scalar Quantities: There are many physical quantities which are completely described by their magnitude only (i.e. by a numerical value with appropriate unit) and are added according to the ordinary rules of algebra.

(b) Vector Quantities:

(*i*) There are certain physical quantities whose complete description not only requires their magnitude (i.e., a numerical value with appropriate unit) but also their direction in space, e.g. velocity of a train.

(*ii*) **Thus, the physical quantities which have magnitude and direction and which can be added according to the triangle rule, are called Vector quantities.** Other examples of Vector quantities are displacement, acceleration, force, momentum, electric field, etc.

(c) Types of Vectors

(*i*) **Like Vectors :** Two vectors are said to be like vectors if they have same direction but different magnitude.

(*ii*) **Equal Vectors:** Two vectors are equal, if they have the same magnitude and same or parallel directions.

(*iii*) **Unlike Vectors:** The vectors having opposite direction and different magnitude, are called unlike vectors.

(*iv*) **Opposite Vectors:** The vectors having same magnitude but opposite direction, are called opposite vectors.

(*v*) **Unit Vectors:** A vector divided by its magnitude is called a unit vector along the direction of the vector.

(*vi*) **Null Vector:** It is defined as a vector having zero magnitude. It has a direction which is indeterminate as its magnitude is zero.

Scalar product of two vectors

The scalar product of two vectors is defined as a scalar quantity having magnitude equal to the product of the magnitudes of two vectors and the cosine of the smaller angle between them.

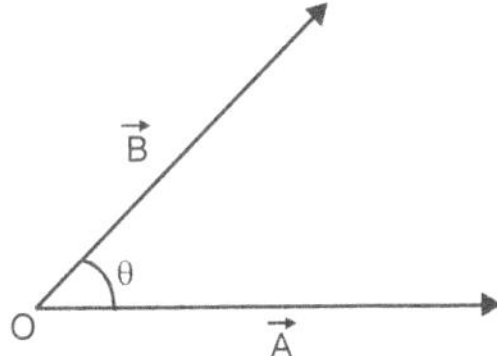

Mathematically, if θ is the angle between vectors $\vec{A}$ and $\vec{B}$, then

$$\vec{A}.\vec{B} = AB\cos\theta$$

Vector product of two vectors

The vector product of two vectors is defined as a vector having magnitude equal to the product of the magnitudes of two vectors with the sine of angle between them and direction ⊥ to the plane containing the two vectors in accordance with right handed screw rule or right hand thumb rule.

Mathematically, if θ is the angle between vectors $\vec{A}$ and $\vec{B}$, then

$$\vec{A} \times \vec{B} = AB \sin\theta\, \hat{n}$$

The direction of vector $\vec{A} \times \vec{B}$ is the same as that of unit vector $\hat{n}$.

Projectile Motion

Projectile fired at an Angle with Horizontal : An object thrown into space and under the action of earth's gravity is called a projectile. When an object is thrown upward in a direction different from the vertical then its is acted upon by acceleration due to gravity acting vertically downwards and moves along a curved path in a vertical plane. This motion is called the projectile motion and its path is called trajectory. e.g. the motion of a bomb dropped from an aeroplane, the motion of a cricket ball or football after being hit.

Equation of trajectory: $y = x \tan\theta - \frac{1}{2}\frac{g}{u^2 \cos^2\theta} x^2$

This equation is quadratic in x and linear in y. Therefore, it represents a parabola i.e. **a projectile fired at some angle with the horizontal moves along a parabolic path.**

Time of flight: $T = \dfrac{2u \sin\theta}{g}$

Maximum height attained: $H = \dfrac{u^2 \sin^2\theta}{2g}$

Horizontal Range: $R = \dfrac{u^2 \sin 2\theta}{g}$

Centripetal force (*h*)

An object moving on a circular path with uniform speed is always acted upon by a force, directed towards the centre of the circle. This force is known as centripetal force. If this force is absent, the circular motion will not be possible.

Types of Motion

Translatory Motion : A body has translatory motion, if all the particles move with the same velocity and their paths are parallel. There are two types of translatory motion—(a) Rectilinear Motion, (b) Curvilinear Motion.

Rotatory Motion : When a body rotates about a fixed axis, the motion is said to be rotatory. All the particles do not move with the same linear velocity. The particles nearer the axis move with less speed and the particles away from the axis move with more speed.

Circular Motion : Circular motion is a form of periodic (or cyclic) motion. There are many familiar examples of an object moving in a circle at constant speed, such as the moon around the earth, a satellite in circular oribit around the earth, a cyclist on a circular track at constant speed, and so on.

Uniform Circular Motion: An object is undergoing uniform circular motion if it is travelling at a constant speed while moving in a circle. Its main requirement is constant speed and motion in a circle.

FORCE

Force is any influence that tends to change the state of rest or the uniform motion in a straight line of a body. Force is a vector quantity, possessing both magnitude and direction; its SI unit is newton.

Force and Inertia

The property of a body to continue in its state of rest or that of uniform motion in a straight line in the absence of external force is called inertia. ***Newton's first law of motion is the law of inertia.***

Newton's First Law of Motion

Every body continues in its state of rest or of uniform motion in a straight line unless compelled by some external force to act otherwise. Newton's First law of motion gives ideas about :

(*i*) inertia, and

(*ii*) definition of force.

Newton's first law of motion can be divided into two parts. The first part is concerned with a basic property of matter, called **Inertia.** It is that property of the body by virtue of which the body is unable to change its state by itself in the absence of external forces, *e.g.*, if a chair is at rest then it will remain at rest unless a force is applied on it. It can be set into motion only by applying a force on it. **The inherent property of the bodies that they do not change their state unless acted upon by an external force, is called inertia.**

The second part of the first law of motion gives a definition for force. It is a push or pull which either changes or tends to change the state of rest or uniform motion of a body.

Momentum

The product of mass (M) of a body and its velocity ($\vec{v}$) is called momentum ($\vec{p}$). Thus $\vec{p} = M\vec{v}$. Its unit is kg m/s. The momentum of an object can be defined as follows: momentum = mass × velocity

Newton's Second Law of Motion

The rate of change of momentum of an object is directly proportional to the force acting, on it and takes place in the direction in which the force acts. The unit of force is Newton. Newton's second law of motion gives : (*i*) expression of force, and (*ii*) the direction of force.

A body of mass m moving with a velocity $\vec{v}$ has got a momentum $\vec{p} = m\vec{v}$.

$$\text{Hence } \vec{F} = \frac{d}{dt}(m\vec{v}) = m\frac{d\vec{v}}{dt} = m\vec{a}$$

where $\vec{a} = (d\vec{v}/dt)$, is the acceleration produced in the motion of the body.

Newton's Third Law of Motion

To every action there is always an equal and opposite reaction.

In general, if a body A exerts force $\vec{F}_{AB}$ (which may be gravitational, electrical or magnetic etc.) on a body B, then the body B will exert a force $\vec{F}_{BA}$ on body A, such that $\vec{F}_{AB} = -\vec{F}_{BA}$

Motion of a Man in a Lift

We consider the following cases:

Case (i): When the lift is accelerated upwards: Suppose R be the upward thrust of the floor on the man (normal Reaction) and mg is the weight of the man acting downwards.

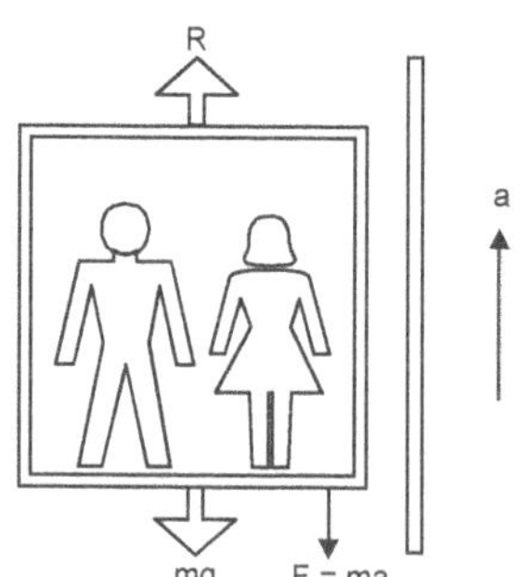

Hence,

unbalanced force = mass × acceleration

or $R - mg = ma$

or $R = mg + ma = m(g + a)$

Thus, if the man is standing on weighing machine, it will show a larger weight than mg.

Case (ii): When the lift is accelerated downward:

In this case, inertial force $F = ma$, is to be applied vertically upward (Fig. 3.4). Now

$$R + F = mg$$

or $$R + ma = mg$$

or $$R = m\,(g - a)$$

Now the weighing machine will show a weight smaller than mg.

Case (iii): When the lift moves with uniform velocity (or is at rest)

In this case $a = 0$ and R = mg.

In the case of free fall of the lift,

$a = g$, then $R = m\,(g - g) = 0$, i.e., the man will feel weightlessness.

Types of Forces

The Gravitational Force : All objects fall because of the gravitational force of attraction exerted on them by the earth. The acceleration due to gravity 'g' is independent of the mass of the object. The force acting is given by F = mg and is the weight of the object. The value of 'g' which is about 9.8m/s^2 also shows minor geographical variations. The weight of the body varies accordingly, but its mass remains the same.

The Electrostatic Force : Between any two electric charges there always exists a force called electrostatic force.

The Magnetic Force : The magnetic property of lodestone has been known since ancient times. Similarly, the use of a magnetic compass has been in vogue for a very long time.

Mechanical Force : These are the forces that are exerted by active or living objects, e.g. humans, animals, engines, moving objects, springs, etc.

Centripetal Force : When a body moves along a circular path with uniform speed, the magnitude of the velocity remains the same but its direction changes at every point. It means that there is change in velocity. Whenever there is change in velocity, there must be some acceleration. As a body has mass also, a force must act upon the body. This force must act along such a direction that the magnitude of the velocity does not change, this force is called centripetal force.

Centrifugal Force : Centrifugal Force is a fictitious or pseudo outward force on a particle rotating about an axis which by Newton's third law is equal and opposite to the centripetal force.

Kepler's law

Early in the seventeenth century, the German astronomer and natural philosopher Johannes Kepler deduced three laws that first described the-motions of the planets about the sun: (1) the planets orbit the sun in elliptical paths, with the sun at one focus of the ellipse (2) The second law states that the areas described in a planetary orbit by the straight line joining the centre of the planet and the centre of the sun are equal for equal time intervals; (3) Kepler's third law states that the ratio of the cube of a planet's mean distance, d, from the sun to the square of its orbital period, t, is a constant; that is, d^3/t^2.

Weightlessness

Weightlessness is the state of not experiencing the effects of gravity. Since weight is a force, weightlessness implies the absence of this force.

FRICTION

Friction is the force that tries to stop materials sliding over each other. Friction is caused in two ways. First, rougher surfaces have ridges and bumps which catch in each other. Second, all materials are made up of tiny particles called molecules, and these have a tendency to stick to each other when materials are pressed together.

Angle of Repose (α)

Angle of repose is relevant to the motion of a body on a rough inclined plane. If a body placed on such an inclined plane, is just on the point of sliding down because of its own weight, then the angle of inclination of the plane with the horizontal is called the angle of repose (α) for the two surfaces in contact.

From fig.

$$F = mg \sin \alpha$$

and $$R = mg \cos \alpha$$

$$\therefore \quad \frac{F}{R} = \tan \alpha = \mu \qquad \ldots(1)$$

Again $$\mu = \tan \lambda \qquad \ldots(2)$$

Hence $$\alpha = \lambda$$

Angle of Repose = Angle of limiting friction

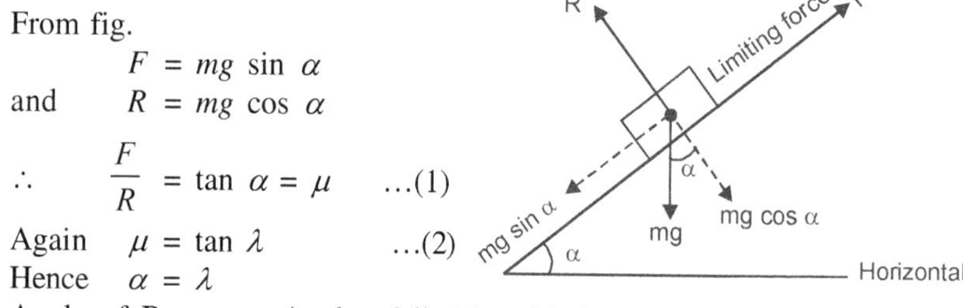

Laws of Friction

(*i*) The force of friction at the point of contact of two bodies is in the direction opposite to that in which the point of contacts starts moving.

(*ii*) When the body is just on the point of moving, the force of friction is limiting. The ratio of limiting friction to normal reaction bears a constant ratio and is denoted by m. The limiting friction is $m R$.

(*iii*) The limiting friction is independent of areas in contact provided the normal reaction is unaltered.

(*iv*) When the body starts moving, the above law of limiting friction still holds good and is independent of the velocity.

Linear Momentum and its Conservation Principle

The linear momentum of a particle of mass m moving with velocity v is defined as $\vec{p} = m\vec{v}$. **If no external force acts upon a system of two or more bodies, then the total momentum of the system remains constant.** This is known as the principle of conservation of momentum.

Applications of The Principle of Conservation of Linear Momentum

When a bullet is fired from a gun, the gun recalls or gives a kick in backward direction.

Suppose M be the mass of gun and m the mass of bullet. Initially, both the gun and bullet are at rest. Suppose, the bullet moves with a velocity $\vec{v}$, when gun is fired and the gun moves with velocity $\vec{V}$.

According to the principle of conservation of linear momentum.

Total momentum of the gun and bullet before firing = total momentum of the gun and bullet after firing

i.e. $0 = M\vec{V} + m\vec{v}$ or $\vec{V} = -(m/M)\vec{v}$

(a) The negative sign shows that $\vec{V}$ and $\vec{v}$ are in opposite direction. i.e. if bullet moves forward, the gun will move in backward direction. The backward motion of the gun is called recoil of the gun.

(b) When bullet is fired from a gun, the bullet also exerts a reactionary-force on the gun which is pushed back and acquires an equal momentum in the backward direction. It is due to this reason that gunner feels a push in the backward direction.

(c) Since the mass of the gun (M) is much greater than the mass of the bullet (m), the velocity of recede of the gun is much less than the velocity of proceed of the bullet.

(d) If a bullet be fired by a light gun and another similar bullet by a heavy gun that the light gun will recede with a larger velocity and is likely to hurt the shoulder of the gunner more severely.

When a man jumps from a boat to the shore, the boat slightly moves away from the shore

Initially, the total momentum of the boat and the man is zero. When a man jumps from the boat, total momentum can be zero, only if the boat moves in a direction opposite to the direction of jumping of man.

Rocket Launching : As the fuel in rocket undergoes combustion, the gases so produced leave the body of the rocket with large velocity and give upthrust to the rocket. If we assume that the fuel is burnt at a constant rate, then the rate of change of momentum of the rocket will be constant. As more and more fuel gets burnt, the mass of the rocket goes on decreasing and it leads to increase of the velocity of rocket more and more rapidly.

Types of Friction

Friction is classified into three types:

- **Static Friction:** The opposing force that comes into play when one body tends to move over the surface of another but the body remains at rest, is known as static friction.
- **Limiting Friction:** This is the maximum static friction that comes into play when one body is at the verge of motion over another body.
- **Dynamic/Kinetic Friction:** This is the force of friction that comes into play when one body is moving over another body.

Limiting friction is greatest of all frictions. Kinetic friction is of two types. *i.e.* sliding friction and rolling friction.

HEAT

Heat is a type of energy by which mechanical work can be done. In otherwords the thermal energy due to which the existance of the temperature in the body appears is called heat.

It is measured in calories or joules or kilocalories.

1 kcal. = 1000 cal. 1 cal. = 4.18 joules.

1 calorie is the quantity of heat which raises the temperature of 1 gm of water by 1°C.

Temperature

It is the degree of hotness or coldness of an object. It is measured by an instrument called thermometer. Temperature is measured in °C or °F.

There are two fixed temperature scales:

1. Lower Fixed Scale, *i.e.,* melting point of ice (0°C)
2. Upper Fixed Scale, *i.e.,* boiling point of water (100°C)

Normal human body temperature is 37°C or 98.6°F.

Specific Heat

The specific heat of a substance is the amount of heat needed to raise the temperature of 1 kg of it through 1°C.

It is measured in kcal/kg °C or cal/gm °C.

Amount of heat gained or lost by a substance depends on

(*i*) Rise or fall in temperature

(*ii*) The mass of the substance

(*iii*) Specific heat of the substance.

Thus, Heat gained or lost = mst, i.e., H = mst.

where m = mass of the substance

s = specific heat of the substance; t = temperature difference.

Thermal Capacity

The thermal capacity of a body is the amount of heat required to raise the temperature of the whole body by 1°C. Thermal capacity = mass × specific heat. Its unit is $\frac{\text{Cal}}{°\text{C}}$ or $\frac{\text{K Cal}}{°\text{C}}$.

Thermal Expansion

Most of the solids, liquids and gases expand on heating. This property of expansion of matter on heating is called thermal expansion.

Expansion of solids : Usually if any solid body be heated then body expands in length, breadth and thickness and if the expansion in length is only substantial then it is called linear expansion but if length and breadth both expands, substantially it is called superficial expansion and ultimately if the length, breadth and thickness expand then it is called volume expansion or cubical expansion.

Coefficient of linear expansion–It is defined as increase in per degree celsius temperature with unit length of the body.

Thus; coefficient of linear expansion

$$= \frac{\text{increase in length}}{\text{original length} \times \text{increase in temp.}} \Rightarrow \alpha = \frac{\Delta L}{L \times \Delta\theta}$$

Coefficient of linear expansion is represented by α and its unit is per degree celsius.

Coefficient of superficial expansion—It is defined as increase in per degree celsius temperature with increase in unit area of the body and it is represented by β. Thus; coefficient of superficial expansion

$$= \frac{\text{increase in area}}{\text{original volume} \times \text{increase in temp.}}, \quad \beta = \frac{\Delta V}{V \times \Delta\theta}$$

Coefficient of cubical expansion—It is defined as increase in per degree celsius temperature with increase in unit volume of the body and it is represented by γ.

Thus coefficient of cubical expansion

$$= \frac{\text{increase in volume}}{\text{original volume} \times \text{increase in temp.}}, \Rightarrow \gamma = \frac{\Delta V}{V \times \Delta\theta}$$

Here, it is observed that, $\beta = 2\alpha$ and $\gamma = 3\alpha$

Thus, $\alpha : \beta : \gamma = 1 : 2 : 3$

Application related to expansion of solids :

(i) The railway tracks are constructed from the steel iron and these are made adjustable to sustain tremendeous load and the thermal expansion and that's why some free space is left at the joints of two such tracks.

(ii) If we pour to keep the hot water inside the thick glass (jars) then, inside surface of the jar suffers thermal expansion while outer surface of the jar due to its thickness doesn't suffer for thermal expansion and unaffected that's why glass jars crack.

Expansion of liquids : As there is no shape of liquids like solids and liquids are always kept in any container or vessel. Thus linear expansion and superficial expansions in the liquids has no any relevancy and significance.

Anomalous expansion in water : Ordinarily the volume of most of the liquids increase with supply of heat or thermal energy while its density decreases. But the behaviour of the water is just opposite. If the water be heated which is already at 0°C. up to 4°C then its volume decreases and density increases. At 4°C the volume of the water is minimum and its density is maximum but on onwards heating water behaves like ordinary liquids. Thus when water of 4°C is heated further its volume increases and density decreases. It is called anomalous expansion of water.

Expansion of gases : Since the gases are the most active participant of the thermal expansions but due to heat supplied to the gas not only the temperature increases but also the pressure and volume changes under the suitable conditions and the Boyle's law, Charle's law etc. were derived.

Boyle's law - pV = a constant at constant temperature.

Charle's law - $\frac{V}{T}$ = a constant at constant pressure.

Boyle's and Charle's law combinedly provides gas eqn.

$\frac{pV}{T}$ = a constant, called gas constant (R)

= 8.31 joule/mole-kelvin.

Specific heat capacity at constant pressure (C_p) : The amount of heat required to raise the temperature of 1 kg of a gas through 1 K at constant pressure is called specific heat capacity of the gas at constant pressure (C_p)

Specific heat capacity at constant volume (C_v) : The amount of heat required to raise the temperature of 1 kg of a gas through 1 k at constant volume is called specific heat capacity of the gas at constant volume (C_v).

Molar heat capacity at constant pressure (C_p) : The amount of heat required to raise the temperature of 1 mole (gm-molecule) of a gas through 1K at constant pressure is called molar heat capacity at constant pressure (Cp).

Molar heat capacity at constant volume (C_v) : The amount of heat required to raise the temperature of 1 mole (gm-molecule) of a gas through 1K at constant volume is called molar heat capacity at constant volume (C_v).

Relation between C_p and C_v :

(i) C_p is greater than C_v and Mayer established a relation; $C_p - C_v = R$, called Mayer's relation.

Here R is called gas constant and its value = $1.99 \simeq 2$ cal/mole-K = 8.31 Joule/mole-K

(ii) $\frac{C_p}{C_v} = \gamma$ = ratio of specific heat capacities.

Stefan's law : It states that the total radiant energy (E) emitted per second from unit surface area of a black body is proportional to the fourth power of its absolute temperature (T)

Thus $E \propto T^4 \Rightarrow E = \sigma T^4$, Here σ is called stefan's constant.

Boltzmann established this law theoretically from thermodynamical consideration and hence extended form of Stefan's law is called Stefan Boltzmann's law.

If a black body at absolute temperature T surrounded by another black body at a absolute temperature T_0 will loose an amount of energy σT^4 per sec per unit area and gain from the surroundings an amount σT_0^4 per sec per unit area. Hence the net loss of energy per sec per unit area of the body will be $E = \sigma(T^4 - T_0^4)$ called Stefan–Boltzmann's law.

Newton's law of cooling : It states that the rate of loss of heat energy of any hot body by the process of thermal energy is proportional to the difference between the mean temperature and the surroundings.

Thus; the rate of heat energy lost $\left(\frac{Q}{t}\right) = k\left(\frac{\theta_1 + \theta_2}{2} - \theta_0\right)$

where; k = a proportionality constant
θ_1, θ_2 = two temperatures of small time interval
θ_0 = temperature of the surrounding, t = time.

Equilibrium Temperature

When a hot substance is mixed with a cold substance, then the temperature of a hot substance gradually decreases and that of cold substance gradually increases till both the substances attain the same temperature. This temperature is called equilibrium temperature.

Transfer of Heat

There are three different ways in which heat is transferred from a hot body to a cold one.

1. **Conduction:** It is the process by which heat passes from the heated end of a body to its cold end e.g. if we heat one end of metallic spoon then the other end also becomes hot in a few minutes.
2. **Convection:** Convection is the mode of transfer of heat in liquids and gases which takes place by the actual movement of their molecules. When the movement of heated matter is taking place, we say that convection currents have been set up in them.
3. **Radiation:** Radiations are the invisible rays given by a hot body which can even travel through vacuum. The heat of the sun reaches us by radiation.

Latent Heat

Latent heat (hidden heat) of a substance is the amount of heat absorbed or released by a unit mass of the substance to change its state without change of temperature. The unit of latent heat is calories/gram or joules/kg.

Kinetic theory of gases

The following assumptions were postulated as below–

(i) Each and every particles of gases have identical masses and volumes and these particles are called molecules.

(ii) The molecules are in random motion and obey Newton's laws of motion. The molecules move in all directions with all possible velocities from zero to infinity and collide constantly with each other and also on the wall of the container. Though the molecules are constantly having their velocities changed in magnitude and direction due to mutual collisions, yet a particular temperature their over-all distribution in volume element remains unaffected.

(iii) The volume of the molecules is a negligibly small with compared to the volume occupied by the gas.

(iv) The collisions are perfectly elastic and are of negligible duration. The collisions of the molecules with each other and with the wall of the container conserve momentum and kinetic energy. The time of collision is negligible in comparison to the time spent in traversing the paths between two collisions.

(v) The gas exerts pressure on the walls of the container. This pressure arises due to the collisions of the molecules with the walls. As a molecule collides, it suffers a change in momentum. The rate of change of momentum is equal to the force exerted on the wall (Newton's 2nd law of motion).

THERMODYNAMICS

The branch of science that deals with the relation between heat and mechanical energy is called thermodynamics. It is mainly concerned with the transformation of heat into mechanical work and vice versa. It is our daily experience that mechanical work can be converted into heat. For example, heat is generated when we rub our hands or two pieces of metal together. Heat can also be converted into mechanical work, as in the steam engine.

Thermodynamic system: A collection of extremely large number of particles having a certain value of pressure, volume and temperature is called a thermodynamic system. For example, a large collection of gas molecules is a thermodynamic system. A thermodynamic system can be in solid, liquid or gaseous state.

Thermal equilibrium: The two systems are said to be in thermal equilibrium with each other, if they have same temperature. Thus, the temperature is a property which determines, whether the two systems will be in thermal equilibrium or not.

Thermodynamic process: A thermodynamic process takes place, if the thermodynamic variables of the system change with time. Thermodynamic process are of following types:

(a) Isothermal process: A thermodynamic process that takes place at constant temperature is called isothermal process.

(b) Adiabatic process: A thermodynamic process in which system is not allowed to exchange heat with surroundings is called adiabatic process.

(c) **Isochoric process:** A thermodynamic process that takes place at constant volume is called isochoric process.

(d) **Isobaric process:** A thermodynamic process that takes place at constant pressure is called isobaric process.

(e) **Cyclic process:** A thermodynamic process in which state of the system remains unchanged is called cyclic process.

The internal energy of a gas is defined as the sum of kinetic energy and the intermolecular potential energy of the molecules of the gas. internal energy of an ideal gas is wholly kinetic in nature and is a function of temperature only.

First law of thermodynamics : The first law of thermodynamics is simply the principle of conservation of energy applied to the thermodynamical system. According to this law if a substantial amount of thermal energy be supplied to a thermodynamic system then it is partially utilised in increasing its internal energy (temperature dependent) and partially utilised in doing external work.

If dQ be the thermal energy supplied and dU and dW are increase in internal energy and external work done respectively then according to First law of thermodynamics.

$$dQ = dU + dW.$$

All are expressed in same unit and it is called differential form of First law of thermodynamics.

In thermal physics practically all mechanical works can be transformed into thermal energy or heat energy but its converse is not true. First law of thermodynamics simply explains it, as equivalency of both mechanical work and quantity of heat are extracted mutually and nothing more.

Second law of thermodynamics : To extract a certain quantity of heat from a body and to convert it completely into work is permitted by the First law of thermodynamics and there is no any violation. But in actual practice it is found to be impossible. If this was possible, we could drive ships across an ocean by extracting heat from the water of the ocean. Thus First law simply tells that if a process takes place, energy would remain conserve. It doesn't tell us whether the process is possible or not. Similarly, if a hot body and a cold body be brought in contact, First law is not violated whether the heat flows from hot to cold or cold to hot. But by the experience heat never flows from cold to hot body.

Second law of thermodynamics explains about the possibility of the thermodynamical process, its direction and its relevancy. In this regard two important statements are well known:

Third law of thermodynamics : The entropy of any system at absolute zero (lower most temperature) is a universal constant, which may be taken to be zero. This is called third law of thermodynamics or Nernst heat theorem. Here two important consequences are :

(i) Specific heat capacities of system vanish at absolute zero.

(ii) Coeff. of volume expansion of any substance vanishes at absolute zero.

An alternate statement of the third law of thermodynamics is the unattainability of absolute zero. A fundamental feature of all cooling process is that the lower the temperature achieved, it is difficult to go still lower. Thus Third law of thermodynamic can also be stated as it is impossible by any procedure, no matter how idealised, to reduce any system to the absolute zero of temperature in a finite number of operations.

Entropy : If a substances takes or gives up an amount of heat Q in a reversible process at constant temperature T then $\frac{Q}{T}$ is called the increase or decrease in entropy of the substance. Thus change in entropy is denoted by $\Delta S = \frac{Q}{T}$. Obviously its SI unit is Joule/kelvin and its C.G.S. unit is Cal/kelvin. But Second law of thermodynamics imposes the restriction in which only those processes are possible for a system in which the entropy of the system plus surroundings always increases. Thus on account of the processes occurring in nature the entropy of the universe is continuously increasing that's why entropy doesn't obey the law of conservation.

SOUND

We live in a world full of sound. Some of the sounds are pleasant while others are unpleasant. Unpleasant sounds are called "noise". Sound is a consequence of the vibrations of any object, vibrating in a material medium. Sound needs a material medium to travel, *i.e.*, it cannot travel through vacuum. It can travel through solids and liquids also. It travels fastest in solids than in liquids and gases. Speed of sound is nearly 330 m/sec through air. Through water, the speed of sound is 1500 m/sec while through steel, the speed of sound is as high as 5000 to 6000 m/sec.

Human ear is quite sensitive to the frequency of the vibrating body producing sound. A normal ear can only hear sounds of frequencies from 20 Hz to 20,000 Hz. This range of frequencies from 20 Hz to 20,000 Hz constitutes the audible range of the normal human ear. We call these sounds as 'sonics'. Sound of frequencies greater than 20,000 Hz are called *ultrasonics*. Sounds of frequencies less than 20 Hz are called *infrasonics* or *subsonics*. Some animals like dogs, leopards, deers, monkeys and bats can hear ultrasonics.

Utilities :

(i) In medical science ultrasonics are used in bloodless surgical operations, in tumor and cavity detection of teeth etc. By ultrasonic radiation various nuerological disease and artherites are being cured.

(ii) In western and developed countries milk is purified by passing contaminated milk through ultrasonics. Generally contaminated (impure) milk has bacterias which are destroyed on passing ultrasonics.

(iii) Ultrasonics coagulate the dust particles in winter season thus the mists and fogs from the airports are diminished and which facilitate the aircrafts (aeroplane) in landing.

(iv) Ultrasonics are also utilised in measuring the sea depth, some commodities spread inside the sea like great rocks, icebergs, bigger fishes etc. SONAR (Sound Navigation and Ranging) is a technique by which inside located objects of the sea are detected.

Variation in the speed of sound :

Effect of Pressure : At the same temperature the speed of sound in the gas doesn't vary with pressure.

Effect of temperature : The speed of sound is directly proportional to the square root of its absolute temperature i.e. $v \propto \sqrt{T}$.

More appropriately as at 0°C the speed of the sound is 532 m/sec and if at t°C speed be v_t then $v_t = 332 + 0.61t$. Obviously; for every 1°C increase in temperature the speed of the sound is increased by 0.61 m/sec.

Effect of humidity : The density of dry air is more than that of moist air. Thus in moist air the speed of sound is more than dry air. This is the reason why in rainy season the siren of the train are listened up to a far distances sharply then summer season.

Effect of the speed of the medium : If the medium has also the speed then the speed of sound increases in the same direction and decreases in opposite direction.

Characteristics of musical sound

Musical notes differ from each other in resect of atleast one the three properties, namely—Intensity, Pitch and Quality. These three are called characteristics of a musical sound. A musical sound is bound to differ from another musical sound in atleast one of these three and hence they provide a means to distinguish one musical note from another.

Intensity and Louldness : The intensity of a musical sound is defined as the rate of flow of energy per unit area of a plane perpendicular to the directions of wave propagation. SI unit of the intensity is Joule/sec-meter^2 or watt/meter^2 (Wm^{-2})

The intensity of a simple harmonic wave is given by

$I = 2\pi^2 \rho u^2 a^2 u^2 v.$

Where; a = amplitude of the wave

ρ = density of the medium

u = frequency of the wave

v = wave speed.

For a sound sleeping man, 50 db sound is sufficient to wake up. To remain in the noise of 80 db is harmful and 90 db sound has its maximum limit to dare and if the such noise be continued everyday 10 hours then the man would become deaf. World Health Organisation (WHO) has recommended 45 db sound good for human ears, the sound of more than 75 db is assumed to be dangerous and the sound of 150 db can make human being abnormal (mad).

Pitch and Frequency : The pitch of a musical note is that physical cause which distinguishes a shrill note from a grave note of the same intensity and coming from the same instrument. Thus the degree of shrillness of a musical note is its pitch. The pitch of a note emitted by source depends upon its frequency of vibration. The greater the frequency of vibration of a source, the higher the pitch of the note emitted and vice-versa. That's why the pitch of a note is expressed by its frequency.

Quality or Timber : Quality or timber is a third feature of a musical note which distinguishes between two notes of the same intensity and pitch but produces in two different musical instruments. The quality or timber of a note is due to presence of different harmonics. The presence of harmonics affects the form of the wave emitted by a musical instruments.

Echo

Echoes are due to reflection of sound. We can observe echoes in many open places like open fields, hills etc. But we cannot hear echo in our homes. This is because of the limitation of our ear. The effect of a given sound 'stays on' in our ear for about 1/15 second. If therefore, a reflected sound reaches our ears before this interval, it mingles with the direct sound and we are not able to distinguish between the two. To get a clear echo, the reflecting wall etc. should be 11 m away (but it should be open place, too many reflecting surface should not be there).

Forced vibrations : Resonance : If anybody of being capable to vibrate freely then due to resisting forces the natural frequency of the body starts to decay and thus an external periodic force is needed. A tussel starts between the frequency of the external force and the natural frequency of the body and ultimately the frequency of the external periodic force predominants and by this frequency the body vibrates which is called forced vibration.

But a situation arises when the frequency of the external periodic force becomes equal to the natural frequency of the body of the free vibration and it is called resonance. Thus at the resonance the natural frequency of the body is being equal to the frequency of the external periodic force.

Beats : When two sound waves of the same amplitude but slightly different frequencies (not more than 16 Hz) travel along the same line, the loudness of the resultant sound wave formed by their superposition, fluctuates (varies) periodically and alternately which gives rise to a peak value with waxing noise and then fading out with waning noise. This phenomenon of waxing and waning in the loudness of the resultant wave is known as *beats.*

Dopper's effect in sound

When there is a relative motion between an observer and a source then the pitch of the note emitted by the source appears to be changed to the observer. This apparent change in pitch due to relative motion between the observer and the source and also sometimes due to motion of the medium is called Doppler's effect in sound or acoustical Doppeler's effect.

Actually Doppler firstly observed this effect in light waves. Thus the optical Doppler's effect in fact firstly propounded the spectral lines of certain stars which were found to be shifted towards the red or voilet end of the spectrum from their normal position by a very small distance. For the red and voilet end stars recede from the earth and approach to the earth respectively. Doppler's effect is also the basic characteristics of the wave and it is to be found in all types of wave.

The acoustical (sound) Doppler's effect can be observed from a railway platform when a whistling locomotive engine passes past the platform at a very high speed. Before passing the platform the pitch of the whistling appears higher and after passing past the platform, its pitch appears lower.

The formula derived for Doppler's effect in sound is

Appreant pitch or frequency (n')

$$= \frac{\text{relative velocity of the observer with respect to velocity of the sound}}{\text{relative velocity of the source with respect to velocity of the sound}} \times \text{Actual pitch or frequency}.$$

Thus; $$n' = \frac{v \pm v_0}{v \pm v_s}$$

Where; n' = appreant pitch or frequency
n = actual pitch or frequency
v = velocity of the sound
v_o = velocity of the observer
v_s = velocity of the source.

ELECTROSTATES, MAGNATISM, ELECTROMAGNETIC WAVES

Electrostatics

Electrostatics is the branch of physics that deals with the phenomena and properties of stationary or slow-moving electric charges.

There are two types of charges : Positive and Negative. Like charges repel and opposite charges attract. In general a material is either a conductor or an insulator. A conductor allows electric charge to Travel through it easily; an insulator does not.

Electric field : If an isolated charge be kept anywhere then the region or space around it upto which if any other charged particle be brought then experiences a force. This region or space is called electric field. Theoretically (or ideally) this space is assumed to be infinite.

Electric lines of force : An electric field is sometimes visualised by drawing a set of lines, which are such that their direction of any point (i.e., the direction of the tangent), is the same as that of the electric field at that point. Such lines are called lines of force.

A Pictorial view of the electric field due to a positive point charge and pair of two equal and opposite, +ve and –ve charges has been shown.

Conductor : The bodies in which electric charge carries (free electrons) are mobile then electric current is generated and these bodies are called good conductor or conductor.

All metallic bodies, acids, human body etc. are good conductor of electricity. The best conductors are metallic bodies, like silver, copper, iron etc. The silver and copper are two metals which have the best electrical conductivity. In all metallic bodies only free electrons are charge carriers due to which electric current generate.

Bad conductor and Insulator : Those bodies which do not have mobile charge carriers are called bad conductor. Sometimes in bad conductor also immobile charge carriers are provoked to become free in zig-zag way but not regularly like in weted rod of wood, thus it acts like good conductor. But if in any condition or circumstances the charge carriers do not be activate or provoked then bad conductor is called insulator.

Wood, rubber, mica etc. are example of bad conductors but asbastoss, ebonite are examples of insulators.

Semi conductor : Those bodies whose electrical conductivity or resistivity lies between the conductor and insulator are called semi conductors. At 0 K all semi conductors are insulators. In semi conductors the charge carriers are electrons and holes (+ve ions) both.

Germenium, silcon, selenium etc. are example of semi conductors. On adding impurity in pure semiconductor its electrical conductivity increases too. If the temperature of good conductor be increased then its electrical resistance increases, consequently its electrical conductance decreases. But in semi-conductor with rise in temperature its resistance decreases and consequently its conductivity increases. That's why it is said that semiconductor has negative temperature coeff. of resistance while metallic conductor has positive temperature coeff. of resistance.

Surface charge density : The charge confined in unit area of any conductor is called surface charge density.

Thus, surface charge density $= \dfrac{\text{electric charge}}{\text{Area}}$

Coulomb's law or Electrostatical force : If two stationary point charges q_1 and q_2 are kept apart at a finite distance r there exist a force of attraction or repulsion due to both point charges and this force is directly propotional to the product of charges q_1, q_2 and inversely proportional to the square of the distance r. This is called Coulomb's law.

Thus; $F \propto q_1, q_2, \propto \dfrac{1}{r^2}$ $\Rightarrow F = \dfrac{1}{4\pi \in_0} \dfrac{q_1 q_2}{r^2}$ (In air or vacuum)

[where; $\dfrac{1}{4\pi \in_0}$ is called a constant $= 9 \times 10^9$ N.m^2 coul.$^{-2}$]

Here $\in_0$ is called the absolute permitivity of free space and its numerical value in air or vacuum is 8.85×10^{-12} coul. N^{-1} m^{-2}.

If q_1 and q_2 be the charges of like nature then there would be a force of repulsion but for unlike nature there would be a force of attraction.

Electric field Intensity or Electric field strength or Electric Intensity

If in the electric field of a charged particles (say q) any other unit positive test charge (say q_0) be placed at any point then this test charge experiences a force and it is called electric field intensity of that point and then it would be vector quantity and its direction would be as that of force (coulomb force)

Obviously; $F = \dfrac{1}{4\pi \in_0} \dfrac{q q_0}{r^2}$ Newton.

But the electric field intensity; $E = \frac{F}{q_0} \frac{1}{4\pi \in_0} \frac{q}{r^2}$ N / coul.

Thus SI unit of electric field intensity is Newton/coulomb. An another SI unit is volt/metre.

Electric field of a hollow conductor : The electric field inside the hollow conductor is zero.

Electric dipole and electric dipole moment : If two stationary point charges of equal magnitude but of opposite sign be kept a small (short) distance apart then this electrical configuration is called *electric dipole.*

The product of the magnitude and the distance between both charges is called electric dipole moment represented by $\vec{p}$ and it is a vector quantity directed from –ve to +ve charge, along the dipole axis.

Thus $\vec{p} = 2aq$ (electric dipole moment)

Electric dipole kept in an electric field

(*i*) **If the field be uniform :** If a dipole be placed or kept in a uniform external electric field $\vec{E}$ making and angle θ with the field. The charge $+q$ experiences a force $q\vec{E}$ in the direction of field, while the charge $-q$ experiences an equal force in the opposite direction. Thus there is no net force on the dipole. But these two equal and opposite forces form a couple thus apply a torque which tends to set the dipole in the direction of the field.

(*ii*) **If the field be Non-uniform :** In a non-uniform field, the forces on the two charges will not be equal and opposite and so there would be a net force on the dipole and this force will also generate a couple and so a torque.

Thus in non-uniform field any dipole experiences a net force and a torque both.

Electric flux : The electric flux is defined as the product of the electric field intensity and the outward normal area of any particular patch where electric field is confined.

It is represented by ϕ_E. Thus; $\phi_E = EA$. Its SI unit is N/coul.m^2 or volt-metre.

Gauss's law : Gauss's law states that the electric flux ϕ_E through any closed surface is equal to $\frac{1}{\in_0}$ times the net charge q enclosed by the surface.

Thus; $\phi_E = EA = \frac{q}{\in_0}$. $\Rightarrow E = \frac{q}{\in_0} \cdot \frac{1}{A} = \frac{q}{\in_0} \cdot \frac{1}{4\pi r^2} = \frac{1}{4\pi \in_0} \cdot \frac{q}{r^2}$

(for the spherical surface $A = 4\pi r^2$) where; E = electric field intensitfy

This law gives a relation between the electric flux through any closed hypothetical surface (called Gausian surface).

Gauss's law is the most fundamental law instead of coulomb's law due to certain conceptual advantages.

The first advantages is that Gauss's law starts with the concept of electric field, which is more fundamental than the interaction of charges with which coulomb's law deals. According to modern field theory approach, the interaction between two charges is through the electric field. The second advantage is that all those results which are given by coulomb's law after tedious calculations are given most elengently in much simpler way by Gauss's law.

Electric potential : The electric potential at any point is defined as the work done by an external agent in bringing the unit positive test charge from infinity to that point confined in an electric field.

Thus if W work be done in bringing unit positive test charge q_0 then electric potential at a point = $V = \frac{W}{q_0} \Rightarrow W = Vq_0$.

The S.I. unit of electric potential is Joule/coul. or volt.

Electrical capacity and capacitor or condenser : When a conductor is given a charge, its potential rises in proportion to the charge given. Thus; if a charge Q raises the potential of a conductor by V, then $Q \propto V$ i.e., $Q = CV$, where C is a constant depending upon the size and shape of the conductor, the surrounding medium and the presence of other conductors nearby. This constant C is called electrical capacity or capacitance of the conductor.

Thus; $C = \frac{Q}{V}$

The S.I. unit of the electrical capacitance is coul./volt and its special name is *farad.*

It is also observed that farad is a too large unit and so in practice smaller units like microfarad and picofarad are used.

Thus we use; 1 microfarad ($1\mu f$) = $10^{-6} f$.

1 picofarad ($1pf$) = 10^{-12}f.

Capacitor or Condensor : Such a pair of conductors which can store a good amount of charge is called a *capacitor* or *condensor.* The conductors are called the plates of the capacitor. The net charge on a capacitor means the magnitude of charge on either plate.

There are broadly three types of capacitors–

1. Parallel-plate capacitor $\left(C = \frac{\epsilon_0 A}{d}\right)$ Where, A = area

2. Spherical capacitor $\left(C = 4\pi \epsilon_0 \dfrac{ab}{b-a}\right)$ d = plate seperation, a, b = inner and outer spherical or cylinderical radii.

3. Cylindrical capacitor $\left(C = \dfrac{2\pi \epsilon_0 l}{\log_e \left(\dfrac{b}{a}\right)}\right)$ l = length of the cylinder.

Dielectric : A dielectric (or an insulator) is a material in which all the electrons are tightly bound to the nuclei of the atoms. Thus there are no free electrons to carry current. Hence the electrical conductivity of a dielectric is very low. The conductivity of an ideal dielectric is zero. Glass, mica-plastic, oil etc. are examples of dielectrics.

Dielectric constant : When a dielectric material is placed between the plates of a capacitor, the capacitance of the capacitor increases. The ratio of the capacitance of a given capacitor with the material (dielectric) filling the entire space between its plates to the capacitance of the same capacitor in vacuum is called the *dielectric constant* or *specific inductive capacity* of the material. Thus if C_d be the capacitance with dielectric material and C_o that in vacuum, then dielectric constant (k) = $\dfrac{C_d}{C_O}$.

The value of dielectric constant is independent from the shape and size of the capacitor, but its value varies widely for different materials.

For vacuum; k = 1 air; k = 1.006 glass; k = 6 etc.

Combination of Capacitors

Series Combination $\dfrac{1}{C} = \dfrac{1}{C_1} + \dfrac{1}{C_2} + \dfrac{1}{C_3}$

Parallel Combination $C = C_1 + C_2 + C_3$.

CELL

It is a device in which chemical energy is converted into electrical energy. A cell consist of three basic parts: (a) an electrolyte, (b) positive terminal, (c) negative terminal.

Cell is of two types

(a) ***Primary cell:*** In primary cell, electrical energy is converted by chemical action which is irreversible, *e.g.*, dry cell, Daniel cell, voltaic cell, etc.

(*b*) ***Secondary cell:*** In secondary cell, electrical energy is stored up as chemical energy by electrolysis which is reversible. *e.g.*, alkaline Edison cell, acid or lead accumulators etc.

Combinations of cells

As a cell is a source of electric current, a single cell cannot give a strong current, hence two or more cells are to be combined to get strong current. The combination of cells is called a 'battery'. Cells can be combined in three ways: (1) In series, (2) In parallel and (3) In mixed grouping.

1. In series

In series combination, the negative pole of the first cell is connected to the positive pole of the second cell, the negative pole of the second to the positive pole of the third, the negative pole of the third to the positive pole of the fourth. Suppose, n cells each of e.m.f E and internal resistance r are connected in series. These cells are sending current in an external resistance R, then,

Total e.m.f. of the cell = nE.

Total internal resistance = nr.

∴ Total resistance of the circuit = $(nr + R)$.

Let i be the current in the circuit then $i = \dfrac{nE}{nr + R}$ ...(*i*)

Two cases arise here :

(*i*) If $nr << R$, then from equation (i), $i = \dfrac{nE}{R}$

(*ii*) If $nr >> R$, then $i = \dfrac{nE}{nr} = \dfrac{E}{r}$

In Parallel

In parallel combination, the positive poles of all the cells are connected to one point, and the negative poles to another point. Suppose n cells, each of e.m.f E and internal resistance r, are connected in parallel and this battery of n cells is connected to an external resistance R. Since the cells are connected in parallel, the e.m.f. of the battery will also be E. Let the equivalent internal resistance of the cell be R, then

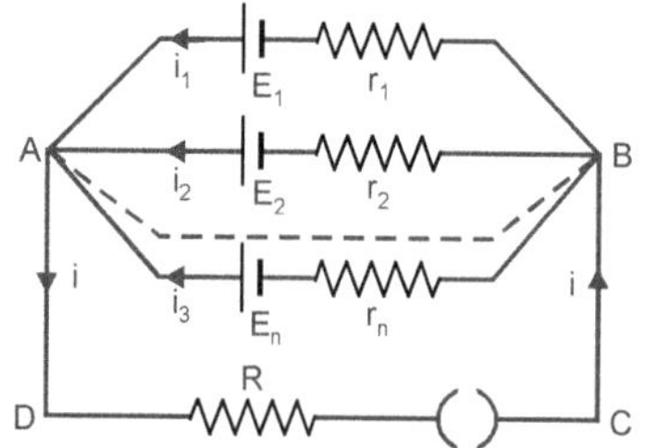

$$\frac{1}{R} = \frac{1}{r} + \frac{1}{r} + \ldots \text{ upto } n \text{ terms } = \frac{n}{r} \text{ or } R = \frac{r}{n}$$

∴ Total resistance of the circuit $= \left(\frac{r}{n} + R\right)$. If the current in the external circuit be i, then $i = \frac{E}{(r/n) + R} = \frac{nE}{r + nR}$

Two cases arise here

(i) If $\frac{r}{n} << R$, i.e. $i = \frac{E}{R}$ (approx), i.e. the total current will be equal to the current given by a single cell. Hence connecting the cells of small internal resistance in parallel has no advantage.

(ii) If $\frac{r}{n} >> R$, i.e. $i = n\frac{E}{r}$.

Mixed Grouping

In this combination, a certain number of cells are connected in various series, and all such series are then connected mutually in parallel.

Suppose n cells are connected in each series, and such m rows are connected in parallel. Let E be the e.m.f. of each cell and r be the internal resistance. This battery of cells is sending current in an external resistance R.

∴ Total resistance of the circuit = $\{(nr/m) + R\}$. Let the current in the external circuit be i, then

$$i = \frac{nE}{(nr/m) + R} = \frac{mnE}{nr + mR}.$$

Current Electricity: When the electric changes is in motion along wires is called current electricity.

Conductors and Non-conductors: Materials that allow electrons to pass freely through them are called conductors, *e.g.*, silver, copper, iron. Materials that do not allow electrons to pass through it freely are called non-conductors or insulator, *e.g.*, rubber, mica, glass etc.

Ohm's Law

It states that the ratio of potential difference across the ends of a conductor to the current is a constant quantity.

Mathematically, $\frac{V}{I}$ = constant or $\frac{V}{I} = R$

where, R is the proportionality constant and it is called resistance.

The unit of resistance is ohm.

Electrical Resistance of a Wire (R)

$$R = \rho . \frac{l}{A} \text{ ohm}$$

where, ρ = resistivity of the material of wire, l = length of the wire, A = cross-sectional area of the wire.

Conductivity: It is the reciprocal of resistivity and is measured in mho/metre. Mathematically, Conductivity = $\frac{1}{\rho}$

Combination of Resistances

In series: The combined resistance in series is equal to the sum of all individual resistance

e.g., $R = R_1 + R_2 + R_3 + ...$

In parallel: The reciprocal of the combined resistance is equal to the sum of the reciprocal of all individual resistance.

e.g., $\frac{1}{R} = \frac{1}{R_1} + \frac{1}{R_2} + \frac{1}{R_3} + ...$

Kirchoff's Laws

First Law: It states that the algebraic sum of all currents meeting at any point is zero, *i.e.,* $\Sigma i = 0$.

Second Law: It states that in any closed circuit the algebraic sum of *e.m.f.* is equal to the algebraic sum of the product of resistance of each part of the circuit and the current flowing through them, *i.e.,* $\Sigma E = \Sigma IR$.

Wheat-stones Bridge

It is a four arm bridge in which all the arms have resistance and is used to measure unknown resistance. For a balanced bridge the working condition is

$$\frac{P}{Q} = \frac{R}{S}$$

where, P, Q, R, S are the resistance of the wheat-stone's bridge.

Heating Effect of Current

It states that the amount of heat produced in a conductor by the steady current through it, is proportional to

(*a*) the square of the current

(*b*) the resistance of the conductor

(*c*) the time for which the current flow, Mathematically,

$$H = \frac{I^2 Rt}{4.2}$$ calories. It is also called Joule's law of heating.

Lighting Effect

It is produced by passing an electric current through a substance that either glow when current flows through it or causes another substance to glow, *e.g.*, incandescent filament lamp, the electric discharge lamp.

Magnetic Effect of Current

It states that whenever an electric current flows in conductor then the magnetic field is established around the conductor. There are some rules from which we know the direction of current and magnetic field.

(*a*) ***Ampere's Swimming Mass Rule:*** It states that if a person is assumed to swim above the conductor with his face downwards and in the direction of the current then the direction of thumb gives the direction of magnetic field.

(*b*) ***Right Hand Rule:*** If a conductor carrying current is held in the right-hand such that the thumb points in the direction of the current then the direction of curl of the rest of fingers give the direction of magnetic field. .

(*c*) ***Maxwell's Cork Screw Rule:*** If a right-handed cork screw is assumed to be rotated in such a direction that the tip of the screw advances in the direction of the current, then the direction of rotation of thumb gives the direction of magnetic field.

Galvanometer: It is an instrument for measuring small currents by the mechanical reaction between the magnetic field of the current and that of a magnet.

Ammeter: It is meter used to measure electric current. An ammeter can be made from a galvanometer by connecting a resistance parallel to the galvanometer.

Voltmeter: It is a meter used to measure electrical voltages. The galvanometer with a high resistance in series is a voltmeter.

Transformer: It is an electrical device that is used to increase or decrease the amount of voltage between two circuits. Power transformers are used to distribute power from generating station to home and workshop.

Measurement of Electrical Power

The watt (W) measure the power of the electric current and one watt is the power produced by a current of one ampere under the influence of one volt.

1 kWh unit is the unit of electrical energy which is consumed by consumer.

Magnetism

It is the natural force by which a magnet attracts pieces of iron; nickel, cobalt and some alloys containing these metal and these metal is called magnetic.

Natural Magnets: A naturally occurring mineral called magnetite or lode stone.

Artificial Magnets: These are the magnetic elements to which the properties of a magnet have been imparted by artificial means. A steel object is made artificial magnet easily.

Law of Magnetism

m_1 and m_2 are the pole strength and r is the separation between them. The amount of force exerted by the pole is given by

$$F = \frac{1}{\mu} \cdot \frac{m_1 . m_2}{r^2}$$

where, μ is a constant and called permeability of the medium.

Magnetic field: It is an effect of every magnet to produce a magnetic field in the space around it.

Intensity of Magnetic field: $E = \dfrac{m}{\mu r^2}$

Biot-Savart Law

In 1819 Biot and Savart on completely experimental observations, stated a formula for calculating the magnetic field at a point P due to current flowing in the conductor.

The magnetic field $\vec{dB}$ at the point P due to the small current element of length $\vec{dl}$ is $\vec{dB} = \dfrac{\mu_0}{4\pi} I . \dfrac{\vec{dl} \times \vec{r}}{r^3}$,

where μ_0 is a constant known as permeability of vacuum (or free space) and its value is $\mu_0 = 4\pi \times 10^{-7} \dfrac{\text{Wb}}{\text{amp} \times \text{metre}}$

or $\mu_0 = 4\pi \times 10^{-7}$ TmA^{-1}

Biot Savart law can also be written as

$$\vec{dB} = \frac{\mu_0}{4\pi} \cdot \frac{I \vec{dl} \times \vec{r}}{r^2}$$

where $\hat{r}$ is the unit vector directed from the element to the point P.

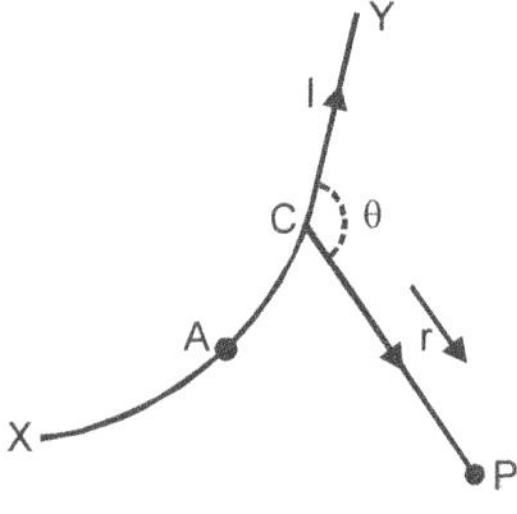

The magnitude of the field is given by $dB = \frac{\mu_0}{4\pi} \cdot \frac{I\, dl \sin\theta}{r^2}$

The direction of $\vec{dB}$ is the direction of the vector $\vec{dl} \times \vec{r}$. Therefore at the point P, the direction of $\vec{dB}$ is perpendicular to the plane of paper and is directed inwards.

Force on a moving charge in a magnitude field-Lorentz force

Let us consider a charge $+q$ moving in a uniform magnetic field of strength $\vec{B}$ directed along Y-axis. The charge $+q$ is moving in $X - Y$ plane making an angle θ with the direction of $\vec{B}$ as shown in the Fig. The charged particle experiences a force $\vec{F}$ along Z-axis i.e. perpendicular to the plane of $\vec{v}$ and $\vec{B}$ in outward direction, such that following rules are obeyed :

(i) The magnitude of force is directly proportional to the magnitude of charge, i.e. $F \propto q$

(ii) The magnitude of force is directly proportional to the component of velocity along a direction perpendicular to the direction of the magnetic field i.e., $F \propto v \sin\theta$

Combining the two factors, we have $F \propto q\, v \sin\theta$ or $F = B\, q\, v \sin\theta$ where the constant of proportionality $\vec{B}$ represents the strength of the magnetic field in which the charge is moving.

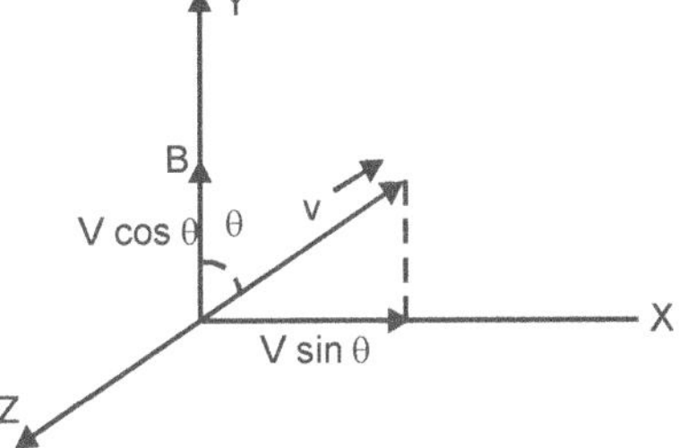

Vectorially the above expression can be written as $\vec{F} = q(\vec{v} \times \vec{B})$

It is clear by the property of cross product that $\vec{v}$ is perpendicular to the plane containing $\vec{F}$ and $\vec{B}$.

Ampere's Circuital Law

This law states that the line integral of magnetic flux density $(\vec{B})$ around any closed path or circuit is equal to μ_0 (permeability of free space) times the total current I enclosed by the closed circuit. Mathematically

$$\oint \vec{B}.\vec{dl} = \mu_0 I$$

Magnetic Dipole Moment

Suppose a magnetic dipole is placed at an angle θ with the direction of a uniform magnetic field B. The moment of the couple acting on the dipole is given by

$$\tau = MB \sin \theta$$

where M is the moment of the magnetic dipole. If the axis of the magnetic dipole be perpendicular to the magnetic field $B(\theta = 90°$ or $\sin \theta = 1)$, then the moment of the couple acting on it will be maximum. If it be τ_{max}, then

$$\tau_{max} = MB \quad \therefore \quad M = \tau_{max}/B$$

If $B = 1$, then $M = \tau_{max}$. Hence, the magnetic moment of a magnetic dipole is the moment of the couple which acts on the dipole when kept perpendicular to a uniform unit magnetic field.

Magnetic Moment

The product of pole strength (m) and effective length ($2l$) of the magnet is called the Magnetic Moment. Thus $M = 2ml$.

Its units are Ampere-m^2 and it is a vector quantity. Its direction is along the axis of the magnet from north pole of the magnet to the south pole.

Magnetic Field

The region around a pole in which magnetic effect can be experienced is called magnetic field.

Properties of magnetic lines of force

The properties of magnetic lines of force are as follows

(1) Magnetic lines of force travel from north pole to south pole outside the magnet and from south to north pole inside the magnet.
(2) Magnetic lines of force are closed curves.
(3) Magnetic lines of force emerge out normally from the magnetised surface.
(4) The tangent drawn at any point of the magnetic lines of force represent the direction of magnetic field at that point.
(5) Two lines of force never intersect each other.
(6) Magnetic lines of force try to contract in length and repel each other laterally.
(7) The lines of force of uniform field are parallel to each other.
(8) The field is strong at places where the lines of force are crowded while it is weak at places where they are farther apart.

Intensity of Magnetic field

The number of lines of force crossing unit area of the surface, normally is called intensity of magnetic field.

or

The force acting on unit pole placed in the magnetic field is called intensity of magnetic field.

i.e. $H = (\mu_0/4\pi) \cdot (m/r^2)$

Galvanometer : Galvanometers are electrical devices used for the detection or measurement of the electric currents. The action of these Galvanometers is facilitated by the torque experienced by a magnetic needle due to the magnetic field of a current loop.

Shunt : Shunt is an electrical system of configuration of the electric conductor or wire of small resistance. Sometimes it is not desirable to send heavy electric currents through a sensitive Galvanometer and thus in order to protect such Galvanometer a low resistance wire or conductor is added in parallel to its coil. Shunt decreases the effective resistance of the instrument. It increases the current measuring range but decreases the sensitiveness of the instrument.

Ammeter : Ammeter is a current measuring device and can measure high current. Basically it is a low resistance moving coil galvanometer. It is always connected in series in the electrical circuit in which the current is to be measured. An ideal ammeter should have zero resistance. In fact ammeter of low resistance is more accurate although it is less sensitive.

Voltmeter : Voltmeter is a potential difference (pd) measuring device and basically it is high resistance moving coil galvanometer. It is always connected in parallel to the resistance across which p.d. is to be measured. Its reading is not accurate because it draws current so the p.d. across the resistance decreases (since the current through it decreases). Hence a voltmeter of high resistance is more accurate.

Potentiometer : A potentiometer is a device to measure the *emf* of a cell or p.d. between the ends of current-carrying conductor without drawing any current from the circuit. It operates on the principle that an *emf* or p.d. can be balanced against another *emf* or p.d. and produce zero current.

Electromagnetic induction

"Whenever the magnetic lines of force linked with a closed circuit change an induced e.m.f. is always produced in the circuit and lasts only so long as the change lasts." The induced e.m.f. giving rise to such currents is called the induced electromotive force and the phenomenon is called **electromagnetic induction**.

Faraday's laws of electromagnetic induction

Whenever the number of lines of force i.*e*. magnetic flux linked with any closed circuit change, an induced current flows through the circuit which lasts only so long as the change lasts. An increase in the number of lines of force produces an inverse current, while a decrease of such lines produces a direct current.

The induced emf, e is equal to the negative rate of change of magnetic flux : If $\Delta\phi$ be the change in magnetic flux in a time interval Δt, then the induced emf in the circuit is $e = -\frac{\Delta\phi}{\Delta t}$

In the limit $\Delta t \to 0$, $e = -\frac{d\phi}{dt}$

The negative sign indicated that the induced e.m.f. opposes the change in magnetic flux (Lenz's law).

Induced current and induced charge

If the rate of change of magnetic flux in a coil of N turns is $\Delta\phi/\Delta t$, then the induced emf in the circuit is given by

$$e = -N(\Delta\phi/\Delta t).$$

Let the coil be closed and the total resistance of its circuit be R, then the induced current in the circuit will be

$$i = \frac{e}{R} = \frac{N}{R}\frac{\Delta\phi}{\Delta t}.$$

From this equation it is clear that the induced current in the circuit depends upon the resistance whereas the induced emf is independent of resistance. The charge flowing through the circuit in time-interval Δt will be given by

$$q = i \times \Delta t$$

$$= \frac{N}{R}\frac{\Delta\phi}{\Delta t} \times \Delta t = \frac{N}{R}\Delta\phi$$

$$= \frac{\text{number of turns} \times \text{change in magnetic flux}}{\text{resistance}}$$

From above equation it is clear that the induced charge does not depend upon the time-interval. The charge in the circuit will remain the same whether the change in magnetic flux be rapid or slow.

Lenz's Law

According to Lenz's Law the direction of the induced e.m.f. is always such as to oppose the change that cause it. This is in accordance with the principle of conservation of energy. Let the north pole of a magnet approach a coil (Fig.). Then the lines of force threading the coil will increase, which will induce an e.m.f. in the coil. The current in the coil should be anti-clockwise as seen from the side of the magnet, and so the face of the coil facing the north pole is also a north pole, and thus tending to repel the approaching magnet, due to which the current is induced.

Similarly, if the current in the circuit increases, the induced emf tries to decrease it while if the current in the circuit decreases, the induced emf tends to increase it.

Direction of induced current fleming's right-hand rule

If on stretch the right-hand thumb and two nearby fingers perpendicular to one another, the first finger points in the direction of magnetic field and the thumb in the direction of motion of the conductor, then the middle finger will point in the direction of the induced current (Fig.)

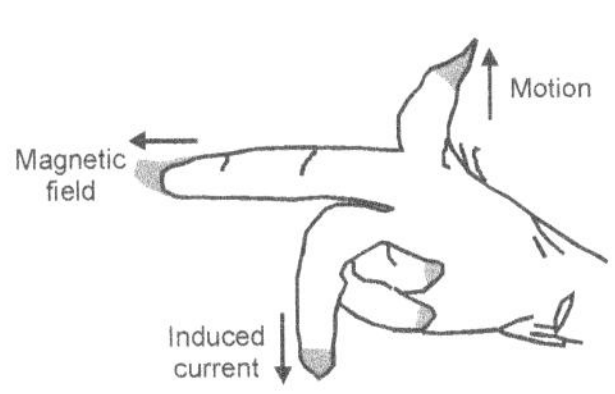

Faraday's Laws of electromagnetic induction :

Ist law : When the magnetic flux through a circuit is changing, an induced *emf* is setup whose magnitude at any instant is equal to the negative rate of change of magnetic flux. This is also called Neumann's law.

Thus; if ϕ_B be the magnetic flux linked with the circuit at any instant and ε the induced *emf*, then

$$\varepsilon = -\frac{d\phi_B}{dt} = -\frac{d(BA)}{dt} - Blv$$

Where, B = magnetic field

l = length of the conductor

v = velocity of induced charge

2nd law : The direction of the *induced emf* of current is such as to oppose the change that produced it. This is called *Lenz's law.*

The phenomenon of electromagnetic induction is frequently utilized in artificial pacemaker, Dynamo, transformer etc.

Self-induction : When a current flows through a coil, it produces a magnetic flux which is linked with the coil. If the current through the coil is changed, the flux linked with the coil also changes. An induced *emf E* is therefore set up in the coil. By Lenz's law the direction of the induced *emf* is such as to oppose the change of the current.

Thus the induced *emf* is against the current when the current is increasing and in the direction of the current when the current is decreasing. This phenomenon is called *self induction* and the *induced emf* is called *back emf.*

If ϕ_B be the magnetic flux (flux linkage) of the coil then current induced in the coil is directly proportional to it.

$\phi_B \propto i$, i.e., $\phi_B = L\, i$

Here; L is a constant called coeff. of self inductance

SI unit of self-inductance is henry. Also another unit of self inductance is volt-sec/amp.

Mutual Induction : Whenever the current passing through a coil changes, the magnetic flux due to the current, which may be linked also with a neighbouring coil, changes. Hence an induced *emf* is setup in the neighbouring coil. This phenomenon is called *mutual induction.* The coil in which the current changes is called the *primary* coil while the other in which the *emf* is setup is called the *secondary coil.*

Also for two given coils situated in a fixed relative position, the flux linkage through the secondary is proportional to the current i in the primary.

Thus; $N_s\, \phi_B \propto i$, i.e., $N_s\, \phi_B = Mi$

Here proportionality constant M is called coeff. of mutual induction. SI unit of mutual induction is also *henry*. Also another unit of mutual induction is volt-sec/amp.

Applications of electrolysis :

(*i*) Extraction of metals
(*ii*) Analysis by electrolysis
(*iii*) Electroplating
(*iv*) Electro-typing
(*v*) Electrolytic capacitor or condensor
(*vi*) Purification of metals

Diamagnetic: The magnetic lines of force of diamagnetic material cannot penetrate certain material as they can penetrate air or vaccum, *e.g.,* bismuth, antimony etc.

Paramagnetic: The magnetic lines of force of paramagnetic material can penetrate material easily, *e.g.,* iron, liquid oxygen etc.

Ferromagnetic: The material by which thunder is easily magnetised called ferromagnetic, *e.g.,* nickel, cobalt, iron, etc.

Earth's Magnetism

The earth is a huge magnet, other magnets will be influenced by it. It is a natural magnet with a North and South magnetic pole, a magnetic axis and a field of force that extends into space. The lines of force of the earth's field are parallel to the surface near the equator.

Magnetic Meridian: If a magnetic needle is hanged freely from its centre of gravity, then the vertical plane passing through the axis of the magnetic needle is known as the magnetic meridian.

Angle of Declination: The acute angle in between magnetic meridian and the geographical meridian is known as the angle of declination at any place.

Angle of Dip (θ): It is the angle at any place which is made in between the horizontal direction and the direction of earth's magnetic field in magnetic meridian.

X-ray: It is the electro-magnetic radiation of extremely short wavelength (0.1Å to 100Å) produced when high energy electrons lose kinetic energy in approaching or striking a target.

Use of X-rays

(*a*) In Surgery, (*b*) In Radiotherapy, (*c*) In Engineering and Industry, (*d*) In Research, (*e*) In Customs Department.

LIGHT

Light is a form of energy which produces in our eyes the sensation of sight. It has both particle nature as well as wave nature, *i.e.*, light may be considered to give out energy either as a stream of particles called photons (Particle nature) or as a continuous stream of energy along a ray or as wave motion in the medium (Wave nature).

The concept of light particles such as photon is useful in the study of interaction of light with matter *e.g.*, Photoelectric effect.

Reflection of Light

When a light falls on a smooth polished surface, it bounces back. This is called reflection of light. It is of two types:

(1) **Regular Reflection:** When a parallel beam of light falls on a smooth surface, the reflected rays are also parallel to each other.

(2) **Irregular Reflection:** When a parallel beam of light falls on rough surface, it gets reflected in different directions. This type of reflection enables us to see the various objects around us.

The reflection of light always obeys laws of reflection. An opaque surface like mirrors reflects light according to the laws of reflection which says that angle of incidence of a ray is equal to the angle of reflection.

Refraction

The phenomenon of change in the direction of a beam of light as it passes from one medium to another is called refraction of light, *e.g.*, pencil appears to be bent in water. When light enters rarer medium from a denser medium it goes away from normal. When light enters denser medium from a rarer medium it bends towards normal. When a ray of light enters from one medium to another, the ratio of its speeds of propagation in the two medium (measured in terms of refractive index μ) determines the extent of refraction and change in direction.

Convex Lens: The middle portion of these lenses is thicker than the edges. These are also called converging lenses, because they converge a parallel beam of light after refraction through them. They are used to correct hypermetropia.

Concave Lens: The middle portion of these lenses is thinner than the edges. These are also called diverging lens because they diverge the parallel beam of light. Concave lens is used to correct myopia.

Power of a Lens

It is defined as the reciprocal of its focal length in metres. Its unit is Dioptres (D). A convex lens has positive focal length, so the power of convex lens is positive. A concave lens has negative focal length, so the power of concave lens is negative.

Dispersion of Light

When a beam of white light passes through a prism, then it gets split up into its constituent colours. This is called dispersion of light. The image thus formed on a screen is called a spectrum.

The refractive index of the material of a prism is given by $\mu = \dfrac{\sin\left(\dfrac{A + D}{2}\right)}{\sin\dfrac{A}{2}}$

where A is the angle of the prism and D is the angle of minimum deviation.

Interference of Light

When two or more wave trains act simultaneously on any particle in a medium, the displacement of the particle at any instant is due to the superposition of all the wave trains. This phenomenon is called interference of light.

Diffraction : Bending of light round the edges of an obstacle within the geometrical shadow is called diffraction. That is why even if we are not able to see the source of the light, we can see the light.

ELECTRONIC DEVICES

Unipolar transistor or Field effect transistor (*FET*): A field-effect transistor (*FET*) is a semiconductor electronic device in which the current is controlled by the variation of an electric field and is carried by majority charge carriers only.

Cathode Ray oscilloscope (CRO) : Cathode ray oscilloscope (*CRO*) is one of the most widely used device having large number of applications. A cathode ray oscilloscope consists of the following main components- cathode ray tube, horizontal and vertical voltage amplifiers, power supply circuits etc.

The a.c. and d.c. both voltage can be measured by *CRO*, it is used in television receiver and Radar. It is also used for radio servicing and to locate the falts in various electronic equipments.

Television

Television is one through which sound wave and light wave (audio and video both) are transmitted by an electromagnetic wave by the means of resonance from any suitable place.

(*i*) **RADAR (Radio Detection and Ranging):** It is a device through which the actual location (position) and the configuration of the unwanted bodies are detected and measured by the electromagnetic wave of the flying aircraft at higher altitudes.

(*ii*) **LASER (Light Amplification by Stimulated Emission of Radiation):** Laser is a device that produces an intense, coherent and highly directional beam of the single frequency. It can be transmitted over a great distance without being spread. The light beam can be intense enough to vaporise the hardest and the most heat resistant materials.

Communication System

Diode valve: A device in which two electrodes, a cathode and an anode are inserted in a cylindrical glass valve which is fully evacuated. Here anode acts as a plate, while cathode acts as a filament and both are kept separate and attached through a pin.

Triode valve: A device which was similar to the diode valve along with which an another element called control grid is attached.

Semiconductor: A semiconductor is a solid material whose electrical resistivity is higher than that of a conductor and lower than that of an insulator. Typical values of the resistivity of a semiconductor lie between 10^{-12} to 1 ohm - meter at room temperature. The electrical resistance of a semiconductor decreases with increase in temperature over a particular temperature - range which is the specific characteristic of the semi-conductor.

(*i*) ***n*-type semiconductor:** A pentavalent element be doped or mixed in *Ge* and *Si*. Such semiconductors are called *n*-type.

(*ii*) ***p*-type semiconductor:** A trivalent element be doped or mixed in *Ge* and *Si*. Such semiconductors are called *p*-type semiconductor.

***pn-junction* or semiconductor diode:** Semiconductors pure or impure are bilateral and current flows in either direction with equal magnitude. Although if in a semiconductor there exists a *p-type* region on one side and *n-type* region on the other then the semiconductor becomes unilateral; current flows easily in only one direction.

Application of *pn-junction* : (*i*) As rectifier, (*ii*) Zener diode, (*iii*) Tunnel diode, (*iv*) Photo conductor, (*v*) Solar Cell.

MULTIPLE CHOICE QUESTIONS

1. The S.I. Unit of entropy is :
A. Joule/sec B. Joule/kelvin
C. J-kelvin D. Joule-sec

2. The unit of work is :
A. Joule B. Newton
C. Watt D. Dyne

3. The parsec is the unit of :
A. distance B. time
C. shining of light D. magnetic force

4. The light year is the unit of :
A. distance B. time
C. intensity of light D. mass

5. Which of the following is not the unit of time:
A. leap year B. lunar month
C. light year D. None of these

6. Which of the following is not matched :
A. Decibel—unit of the sound
B. Horse power—unit of the power
C. Nautical mile—unit of the distance
D. Celsius—unit of the heat

7. The unit of magnetic flux is :
A. weber B. weber/meter
C. weber-ampere D. weber-sec

8. The S.I. unit of the Young's modulus of the elasticity is :
A. dyne/cm. B. newton/meter
C. newton/meter^2 D. newton-sec

9. Which of the following is a vector quantity:
A. energy B. momentum
C. moment of inertia D. All of these

10. The electric current is a :
A. scalar quantity B. vector quantity
C. Both A and B D. None of these

11. The electric current density is a :
A. vector quantity B. scalar quantity
C. Both A and B D. None of these

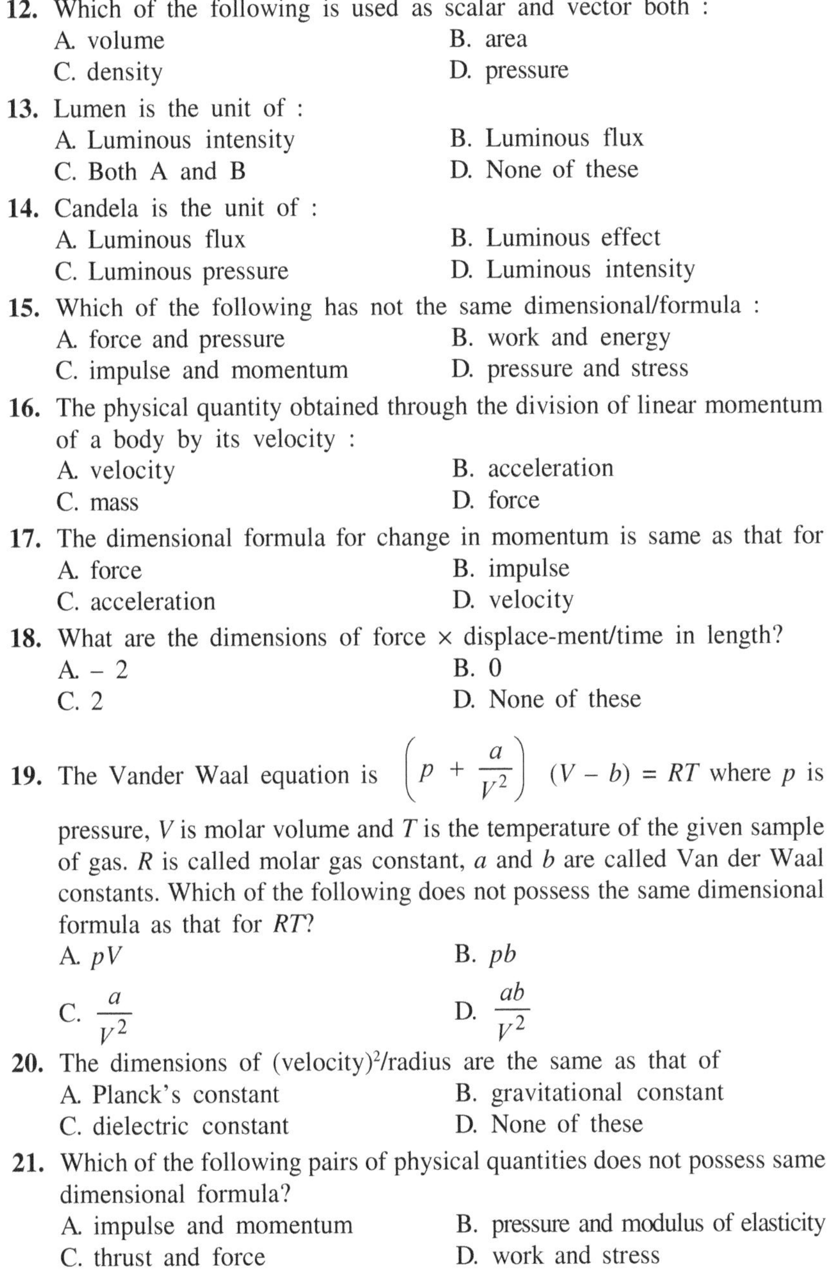

12. Which of the following is used as scalar and vector both :

A. volume
B. area
C. density
D. pressure

13. Lumen is the unit of :

A. Luminous intensity
B. Luminous flux
C. Both A and B
D. None of these

14. Candela is the unit of :

A. Luminous flux
B. Luminous effect
C. Luminous pressure
D. Luminous intensity

15. Which of the following has not the same dimensional/formula :

A. force and pressure
B. work and energy
C. impulse and momentum
D. pressure and stress

16. The physical quantity obtained through the division of linear momentum of a body by its velocity :

A. velocity
B. acceleration
C. mass
D. force

17. The dimensional formula for change in momentum is same as that for

A. force
B. impulse
C. acceleration
D. velocity

18. What are the dimensions of force × displace-ment/time in length?

A. – 2
B. 0
C. 2
D. None of these

19. The Vander Waal equation is $\left(p + \frac{a}{V^2}\right)(V - b) = RT$ where p is pressure, V is molar volume and T is the temperature of the given sample of gas. R is called molar gas constant, a and b are called Van der Waal constants. Which of the following does not possess the same dimensional formula as that for RT?

A. pV
B. pb
C. $\frac{a}{V^2}$
D. $\frac{ab}{V^2}$

20. The dimensions of $(\text{velocity})^2/\text{radius}$ are the same as that of

A. Planck's constant
B. gravitational constant
C. dielectric constant
D. None of these

21. Which of the following pairs of physical quantities does not possess same dimensional formula?

A. impulse and momentum
B. pressure and modulus of elasticity
C. thrust and force
D. work and stress

22. Which of the following pairs does not have the same dimensions?
A. frequency and angular frequency
B. angular velocity and velocity gradient
C. velocity gradient and angular frequency
D. angular frequency and potential gradient

23. Which of the following pair does not possess same dimensions?
A. impulse and momentum
B. angular frequency and velocity gradient
C. stress and strain
D. surface tension and surface energy

24. The equation which depicts the relation between the basic and derived units is called
A. defining equation
B. dimensional equation
C. homogeneity equation
D. None of these

25. Given that M is the mass suspended from a spring of force constant k. The dimensional formula for $[M/k]^{1/2}$ is same as that for
A. frequency
B. time period
C. velocity
D. wavelength

26. Given that $\tan\theta = v^2/rg$ gives the angle of banking of the cyclist going round the curve. Here v is the speed of cyclist, r is the radius of the curve and g is acceleration due to gravity. Which of the following statements about this relation is true?
A. it is both dimensionally as well as numerically correct
B. it is neither dimensionally correct nor numerically correct
C. it is dimensionally correct but not numerically
D. it is numerically correct but not dimensionally

27. Given that T stands for time period and l stands for length of simple pendulum. If g is the acceleration due to gravity, then which of the following statements about the relation $T^2 = l/g$ is correct?
A. it is correct both dimensionally as well as numerically
B. it is neither dimensionally correct nor numerically
C. it is dimensionally correct but not numerically
D. it is numerically correct but not dimensionally

28. A thermal physical quantity is measured in calorie per gram. Its dimensional formula will be
A. ML^0T^{-2}
B. $M^2L^2T^0$
C. M^2LT^{-2}
D. $M^0L^2T^{-2}$

29. Given that C denotes capacitance of a capacitor and V is the potential difference across its plates. Then the dimensions of CV^2 are same as that of

A. force
B. torque
C. momentum
D. power

30. The dimensions of $[\mu_0 \varepsilon_0]^{-1/2}$ are the same as that of

A. time period
B. wavelength
C. frequency
D. velocity

31. The range of a projectile is maximum. If the range is R, what is the maximum height?

A. 2 R
B. R
C. $R/2$
D. $R/4$

32. A ball is thrown horizontally from the top of a tower. What happens to the horizontal component of its velocity?

A. increases
B. decreases
C. remains unchanged
D. first decreases and then increases

33. A projectile is fired with a velocity of 10 ms^{-1} at an angle of 60° with the horizontal. Its velocity at the highest point is

A. zero
B. 5 ms^{-1}
C. 8.66 ms^{-1}
D. 10 ms^{-1}

34. A projectile can have the same range R for two angles of projection. If t_1 and t_2 be the times of flight in the two cases then what is the product of the two times of flight?

A. $t_1 t_2 \propto R^2$
B. $t_1 t_2 \propto R$
C. $t_1 t_2 \propto \frac{1}{R}$
D. $t_1 t_2 \propto \frac{1}{R^2}$

35. A ball is projected upwards from the top of tower with a velocity 50 ms^{-1} making angle 30° with the horizontal. The height of the tower is 70 m. After how many seconds from the instant of throwing will the ball reach the ground?

A. 2 s
B. 5 s
C. 7 s
D. 9 s

36. The distance travelled by a body dropped from the top of a tower is proportional to

A. mass of the body
B. weight of the body
C. height of tower
D. square of time

37. A heavy and a lighter body are dropped from the top of a tower. Which will reach the ground first?

A. lighter one
B. heavier one
C. both will reach simultaneously
D. cannot be predicted

38. A ball is thrown horizontally and another is just dropped from the top of tower. Which will reach the ground first?

A. first ball
B. second ball
C. both will reach simultaneously
D. depends upon the masses of the balls

39. A ball is projected from the top of a tower at an angle 60° with the vertical. What happens to the vertical component of its velocity?

A. increases continuously
B. decreases continuously
C. remains unchanged
D. first decreases and then increases

40. A ball is thrown at an angle θ with the horizontal. Its horizontal range is equal to its maximum height. This is possible when tan θ = ...

A. 0.5
B. 1
C. 2
D. 4

41. Two projectiles are fired at different angles with the same magnitude of velocity such that they have the same range. At what angles they might have been projected?

A. 10° and 50°
B. 25° and 65°
C. 35° and 75°
D. None of these

42. Four projectiles are fired with the same velocities at angles 25°, 40°, 55°, and 70° with the horizontal. The range of projectile will be largest for the one projected at angle

A. 25°
B. 40°
C. 55°
D. 70°

43. A bullet is fired horizontally with a velocity of 200 ms^{-1}. If acceleration due to gravity is 10 ms^{-2}, in the first second it will fall through a height of

A. 5 m
B. 10 m
C. 20 m
D. 200 m

44. A projectile is thrown at an angle of 40° with the horizontal and its range is R_1. Another projectile is thrown at an angle 40° with the vertical and its range is R_2. What is the relation between R_1 and R_2?

A. $R_1 = R_2$
B. $R_1 = 2\ R_2$
C. $R_2 = 2\ R_1$
D. $R_1 = 4\ R_2/5$

45. A ball thrown by one player reaches the other in 2 seconds. The maximum height attained by the ball above the point of projection will be about

A. 2.5 m B. 5 m

C. 7.5 m D. 10 m

46. The velocity time graph of a lift moving downwards is a straight line inclined to the time axis at 45°. If mass of the lift is M kg, what is the effective weight (in newton) of the lift? Take $g = 10$ ms^{-2}.

A. 10 M B. 9 M

C. M D. None of these

47. A monkey of mass 20 kg is holding a vertical rope. The rope can break when a mass of 25 kg is suspended from it. What is the maximum acceleration with which the monkey can climb up along the rope?

A. 2.5 ms^{-2} B. 5 ms^{-2}

C. 7 ms^{-2} D. 10 ms^{-2}

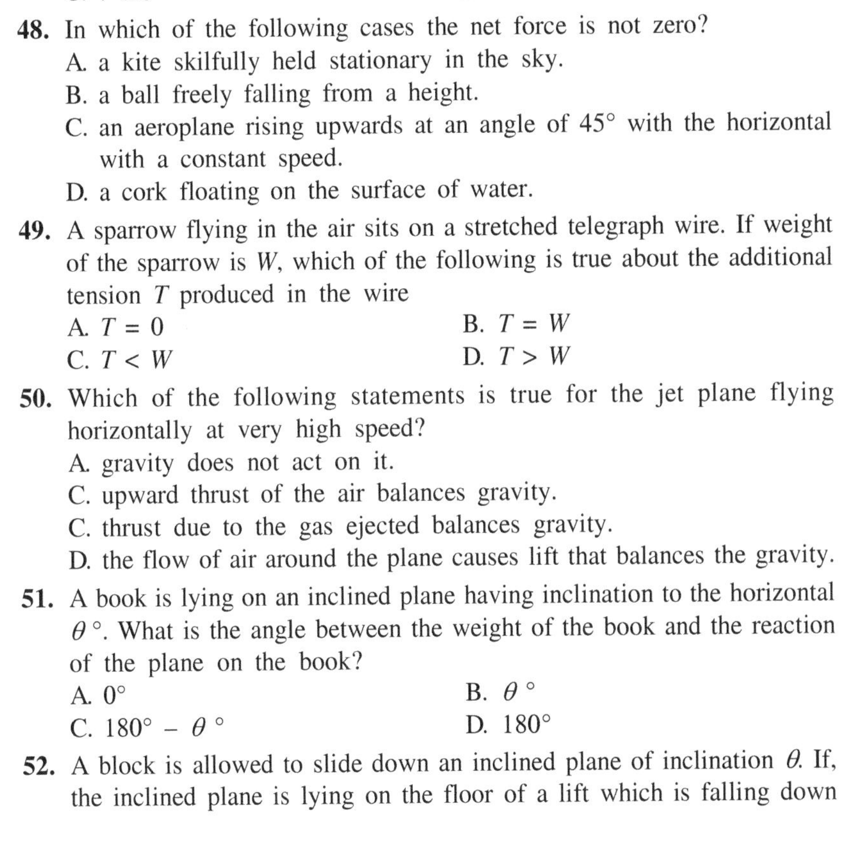

48. In which of the following cases the net force is not zero?

A. a kite skilfully held stationary in the sky.

B. a ball freely falling from a height.

C. an aeroplane rising upwards at an angle of 45° with the horizontal with a constant speed.

D. a cork floating on the surface of water.

49. A sparrow flying in the air sits on a stretched telegraph wire. If weight of the sparrow is W, which of the following is true about the additional tension T produced in the wire

A. $T = 0$ B. $T = W$

C. $T < W$ D. $T > W$

50. Which of the following statements is true for the jet plane flying horizontally at very high speed?

A. gravity does not act on it.

C. upward thrust of the air balances gravity.

C. thrust due to the gas ejected balances gravity.

D. the flow of air around the plane causes lift that balances the gravity.

51. A book is lying on an inclined plane having inclination to the horizontal θ°. What is the angle between the weight of the book and the reaction of the plane on the book?

A. 0° B. θ°

C. 180° − θ° D. 180°

52. A block is allowed to slide down an inclined plane of inclination θ. If, the inclined plane is lying on the floor of a lift which is falling down

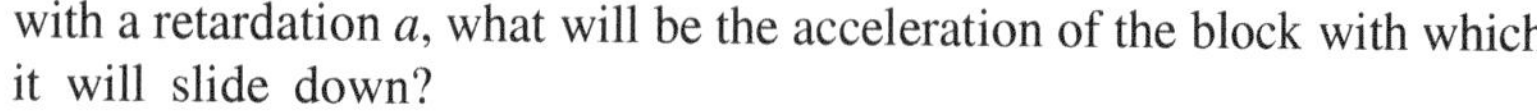
with a retardation a, what will be the acceleration of the block with which it will slide down?

A. $(g + a) \sin \theta$
B. $(g - a) \sin \theta$
C. $g \sin \theta + a$
D. $g \sin \theta - a$

53. A body is at rest on the surface of the earth. Which of the following statements is correct?

A. no force is acting on the body
B. only weight of the body acts on it
C. net downward force is equal to the net upward force
D. None of these

54. A fireman wants to slide down a rope. The breaking load for the rope is 3/4th of the weight of the man. With what minimum acceleration should the fireman slide down? Acceleration due to gravity is g.

A. $\frac{1}{4}g$
B. $\frac{1}{2}g$
C. $\frac{3}{4}g$
D. zero

55. A particle of mass 2 kg is moving along a circular path of radius 1 m. If its angular speed is 2π rad s^{-1}, the centripetal force on it is

A. 4π N
B. 8π N
C. $4\pi^4$ N
D. $8\pi^2$ N

56. The angle between frictional force and the instantaneous velocity of the body moving over a rough surface is

A. zero
B. $\pi / 2$
C. π
D. equal to the angle of friction

57. A body is placed on an inclined plane and has to be pushed down. The angle made by the normal reaction with the vertical will be

A. equal to the angle of repose
B. equal to the angle of friction
C. less than the angle of repose
D. more than the angle of friction

58. Brakes of very small contact area are not used although friction is independent of area, because friction

A. resists motion
B. causes wear and tear
C. depends upon nature of the materials
D. operating in this case is sliding friction

59. Why a horse need to pull harder during the first few steps in pulling the cart?

A. limiting friction is greater than dynamic friction.
B. sliding friction is greater than rolling friction.

C. no frictional force acts after the cart comes in motion.
D. air friction is greater during first law steps of motion.

60. A body is sliding down an inclined plane having angle of friction θ. If the coefficient of friction is μ, then the acceleration of the body down the inclined plane is

A. g (sin θ + μ cos θ)
B. g (sin θ − μ cos θ)
C. g (cos θ + μ sin θ)
D. g (cos θ − μ sin θ)

61. When a body is moving in a circular orbit, work done will be

A. positive
B. negative
C. zero
D. None of these

62. When a body moves with a constant speed along a circle

A. no acceleration is produced in the body
B. its velocity remains constant
C. no work is done on it
D. no force acts on the body

63. What is **F**. **ds**?

A. Torque
B. Impulse
C. Momentum
D. Work

64. A 60 kg weight is dragged on a horizontal surface by a rope. If coefficient of friction is μ = 0.5, the angle of rope with surface is 60° and g = 9.8 m/sec^2, then work done is

A. 294 joule
B. 15 joule
C. 588 joule
D. 197 joule

65. A uniform chain of mass M and length L is lying on a smooth table with half of its length hanging vertically down the edge of the table. The work done in pulling the hanging part of the chain over the table is

A. MgL / 2
B. MgL / 4
C. MgL / 8
D. MgL / 16

66. "A boy carrying a box on his head is walking on a level road from one place to another on a straight road is doing no work". This statement is

A. correct
B. incorrect
C. partly correct
D. insufficient data

67. A string of mass m is stretched by a length ℓ. What is the work done where g is the acceleration due to gravity?

A. 1/2 mgℓ
B. mgℓ
C. 1/4 mgℓ
D. 4 mgℓ

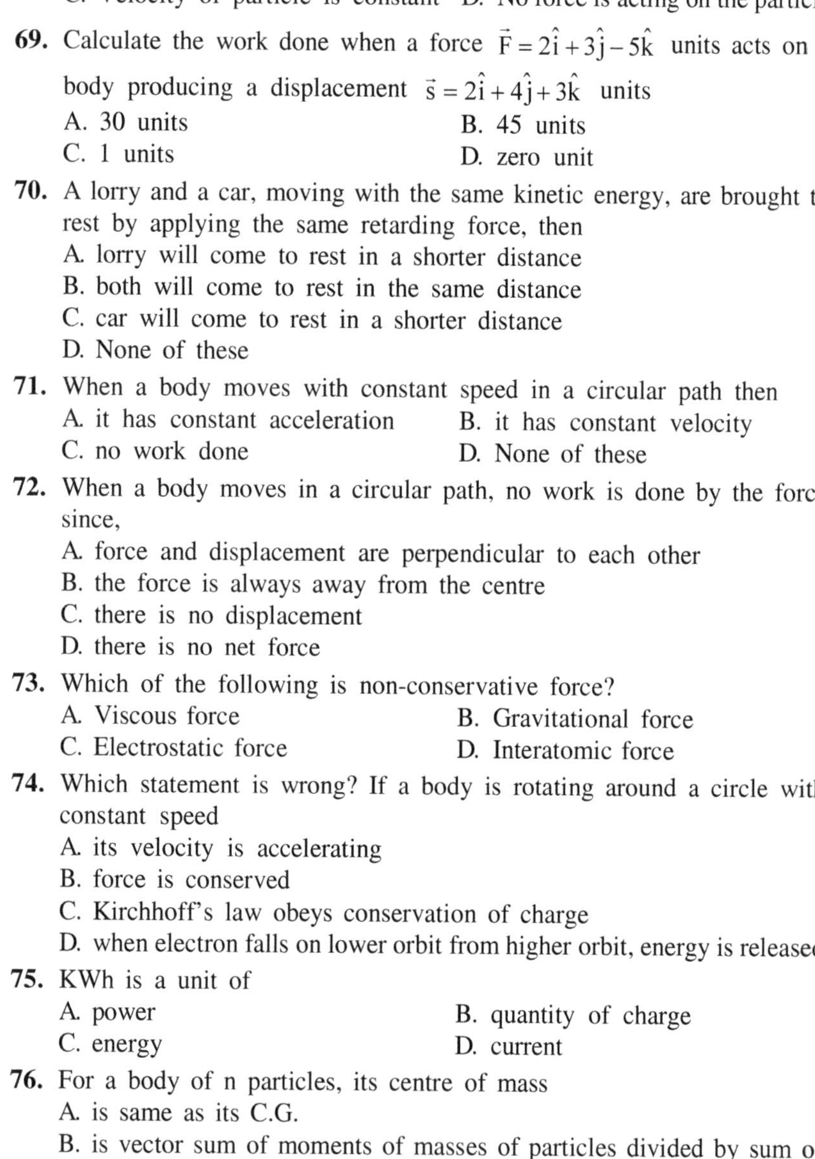

68. If a particle is rotating in a circle, which of the following is true?
A. No work is done
B. Particle has no acceleration
C. Velocity of particle is constant
D. No force is acting on the particle

69. Calculate the work done when a force $\vec{F} = 2\hat{i} + 3\hat{j} - 5\hat{k}$ units acts on a body producing a displacement $\vec{s} = 2\hat{i} + 4\hat{j} + 3\hat{k}$ units
A. 30 units
B. 45 units
C. 1 units
D. zero unit

70. A lorry and a car, moving with the same kinetic energy, are brought to rest by applying the same retarding force, then
A. lorry will come to rest in a shorter distance
B. both will come to rest in the same distance
C. car will come to rest in a shorter distance
D. None of these

71. When a body moves with constant speed in a circular path then
A. it has constant acceleration
B. it has constant velocity
C. no work done
D. None of these

72. When a body moves in a circular path, no work is done by the force since,
A. force and displacement are perpendicular to each other
B. the force is always away from the centre
C. there is no displacement
D. there is no net force

73. Which of the following is non-conservative force?
A. Viscous force
B. Gravitational force
C. Electrostatic force
D. Interatomic force

74. Which statement is wrong? If a body is rotating around a circle with constant speed
A. its velocity is accelerating
B. force is conserved
C. Kirchhoff's law obeys conservation of charge
D. when electron falls on lower orbit from higher orbit, energy is released

75. KWh is a unit of
A. power
B. quantity of charge
C. energy
D. current

76. For a body of n particles, its centre of mass
A. is same as its C.G.
B. is vector sum of moments of masses of particles divided by sum of masses

C. is vector sum of moments of weights of masses divided by sum of masses
D. is vector sum of torques divided by sum of masses

77. Two identical balls each of radius 10 cm are placed touching each other. The distance of their centre of mass from the point of contact is

A. zero
B. 5 cm
C. 10 cm
D. 15 cm

78. A piece of mass at rest splits into 2 parts of mass M and m and velocity of the small fragments of mass m is *v*, then the velocity of big fragment may be given as

A. $V = \frac{M}{(M-m)v}$
B. $V = \frac{(M-m)v}{M}$
C. $V = \frac{m}{M}v$
D. $V = \frac{M}{m}v$

79. A solid sphere of radius R is placed on smooth horizontal surface. A horizontal force F is applied at height h from the lowest point. For the maximum acceleration of centre of mass, which is correct?

A. h = R
B. h = 2R
C. h = 0
D. No relation between h and R

80. If a force acts on a body at a point away from the centre of mass, then

A. linear acceleration changes
B. angular acceleration changes
C. both change
D. none changes

81. The torque acting on a body is the rotational analogue of

A. mass of the body
B. linear kinetic energy of the body
C. linear velocity of the body
D. force in linear motion

82. If torque is zero then

A. angular momentum is conserved
B. linear momentum is converved
C. energy is conserved
D. angular momentum is not conserved

83. A particle is moving in the XY plane with constant velocity along a line parallel to the X-axis. Its angular momentum about the Z-axis

A. is zero
B. remains constant
C. goes in increasing
D. goes on decreasing

84. A particle undergoes uniform circular motion. About which point on the plane of the circle, will the angular momentum of the particle remain conserved?

A. Centre of the circle

B. On the circumference of the circle
C. Inside the circle
D. Outside the circle

85. Angular momentum of a body is defined as the product of
A. mass and angular velocity
B. centripetal force and radius
C. linear velocity and angular velocity
D. moment of inertia and angular velocity

86. What will happen to the weight of the body at the south pole, if the earth stops rotating about its polar axis ?
A. no change
B. increases
C. decreases but does not become zero
D. reduces to zero

87. If one moves from the surface of earth to moon, what will be the effect on its weight ?
A. weight of a person decreases continuously with height from the surface of earth
B. weight of a person increases with height from the surface of earth
C. weight of a person first decreases with height and then increases with height from the surface of earth
D. weight of a person first increases with height and then decreases with height from the surface of earth

88. One goes from the centre of the earth to a distance two third the radius of the earth, where will the acceleration due to gravity be the greatest?
A. at the centre of the earth
B. at a depth half the radius of the earth
C. at a depth one third the radius of the earth
D. at a depth two third the radius of the earth

89. Which of the following cannot be used for measuring time in a spaceship orbiting around the earth ?
A. atomic clock
B. quartz watch
C. electric clock
D. pendulum clock

90. At a point P, which is at a height of R metres from the surface of the earth, the gravitational potential will be (M = mass of the earth, R = radius of the earth)
A. $GM/2R$
B. $-GM/2R$
C. $-GM/R$
D. GM/R

91. A steel ball is floating in a trough of mercury. If we fill the empty part of the trough with water, what will happen to the steel ball?
A. it will continue in its position
B. it will move up
C. it will move down
D. it will execute vertical oscillations

92. A wooden block is floating in a trough of water. If the trough falls freely, then upward thrust on the wooden block will be
A. same as before
B. more than earlier
C. zero
D. equal to the weight of the block in air

93. If there were no gravity, which of the following will not be there for a fluid?
A. viscosity
B. surface tension
C. pressure
D. Archimede's upward thrust

94. A person is carrying a bucket in one hand and a fish in the other. If he puts fish in the bucket, how will the load carried by the person change?
A. no change
B. it will be more
C. it will be less
D. it will depend on the mass of the fish

95. A bird is sitting in a wire cage, which is hanging from a spring balance. How will the reading change when the bird flies inside the cage?
A. it will remain unchanged
B. it will be less than earlier
C. it will be more than earlier
D. it cannot be predicted

96. What makes a ship made of steel float, whereas a steel needle sinks in water?
A. viscosity
B. surface tension
C. power of its engine
D. None of these

97. For a floating body to be in stable equilibrium, where should its centre of buoyancy be located?
A. above the centre of gravity
B. below the centre of gravity
C. at the centre of gravity
D. it may be anywhere

98. A boat floating in a tank is carrying passengers. If the passengers drink water, how will it affect the water level of the tank?
A. it will go down
B. it will rise
C. it will remain unchanged
D. it will depend on atmospheric pressure

99. Sudden fall of pressure at a place indicates

A. storm
B. rain
C. fair weather
D. cold wave

100. Why the aeroplanes are made to run on the runway before take off?

A. it decreases friction
B. it decreases viscous drag of the air
C. it decreases atmospheric pressure
D. it provides required lift to the aeroplane

101. Which of the following is equivalent to Pa?

A. dyn $/cm^2$
B. bar
C. atm
D. None of these

102. Hydraulic brakes work on the basis of

A. Pascal's law
B. Bernoulli's principle
C. Poiseuille's law
D. Archimede's principle

103. Why is it easier to swim in sea water?

A. atmospheric pressure is highest at the sea level
B. sea water contains salt
C. density of sea water is higher than the ordinary water
D. because of some reason other than those mentioned above

104. A jet plane flies in air because

A. upthrust of air balances the weight
B. weight of the air displaced is equal to the weight of the aeroplane
C. gravity does not act on the aeroplane
D. of some reason other than those mentioned above

105. The unit of thrust is

A. Nm^{-1}
B. Nm^{-2}
C. Nm^{-2} s
D. N

106. An iron ball is heated. The percentage increase will be the largest in

A. diameter
B. surface area
C. volume
D. density

107. Two rods of length L_1 and L_2 are made of materials having coefficients of linear expansions as α_1 and α_2 respectively. If $L_1 - L_2$ is independent of temperature, then which of the following relations is correct?

A. $L_1\alpha_1 = L_2\alpha_2$
B. $L_1\alpha_2 = L_2\alpha_1$
C. $L_1L_2 = \alpha_1\alpha_2$
D. None of these

108. The area under the indicator diagram gives

A. heat gained or lost by the system
B. work done on the system or by the system
C. average kinetic energy of the particles of the system
D. None of these

109. A process in which the heat content of the system remains constant is called

A. isobaric
B. isochoric
C. isothermal
D. None of these

110. A process in which the volume remains constant is called

A. isobaric
B. isochoric
C. isothermal
D. None of these

111. Which of the following is not the property of both heat and work.

A. transient phenomenon
B. boundary phenomenon
C. path function
D. exact differential

112. An ideal gas expands freely in a perfectly rigid and insulated cylinder. Which of the following parameters connected with it varies?

A. temperature alone
B. internal energy alone
C. both temperature and internal energy
D. neither temperature nor internal energy

113. When heat is added to a system, which of the following is not possible?

A. internal energy of the system increases
B. work is done by the system
C. neither internal energy increases nor work is done by the system
D. internal energy increases and also work is done by the system

114. In which process the indicator diagram is straight line parallel to volume axis?

A. isobaric
B. isothermal
C. adiabatic
D. irreversible

115. The first law of thermodynamics is based on the law of conservation of

A. energy
B. mass
C. momentum
D. None of these

116. Thermodynamics is concerned with

A. measurement of heat
B. transfer of heat
C. change of state
D. None of these

117. Isothermal is a graph between (P is pressure, V is volume, T is absolute temperature)

A. P and T
B. P and V
C. V and T
D. PV and T

118. The first law of thermodynamics forbids interconversion of

A. heat and work
B. internal energy and work
C. potential energy and kinetic energy
D. None of these

119. In which of the following process all the three thermodynamic variables, that is pressure, volume and temperature can change?

A. isobaric
B. isothermal
C. isochoric
D. adiabatic

120. In which of the process, the internal energy of the system remains constant?

A. adiabatic
B. isochoric
C. isobaric
D. isothermal

121. The internal energy of a real gas is independent of

A. pressure
B. temperature
C. volume
D. None of these

122. The internal energy of a perfect gas is

A. wholly kinetic
B. wholly potential
C. sum of potential and kinetic energy of the molecules
D. difference of kinetic and potential energies of the molecules

123. A heat engine is a device to

A. convert work into heat
B. convert heat into work
C. increase the efficiency
D. transfer heat from lower to higher temperature

124. When the temperature difference between the source and the sink increases, the efficiency of the heat engine

A. increases
B. decreases
C. is not affected
D. may increase or decrease depending upon the nature of the working substance

125. In a Carnot heat engine the temperature of the working substance at the end of the cycle is

A. equal to that at the beginning
B. more than that at the beginning
C. less than that at the beginning
D. determined by the amount of heat rejected at the sink

126. Two mutually perpendicular simple harmonic vibrations have same amplitude, frequency and phase. When they superimpose, the resultant form of vibration will be

A. a straight line
B. a parabola
C. a circle
D. an ellipsoid.

127. A spring has a force constant K and a mass m is suspended from it. The spring is cut in half and the same mass is suspended from one of the halves. If the frequency of oscillation in the first case is α, then frequency in the second case will be

A. α
B. $\alpha/2$
C. $\alpha\sqrt{2}$
D. 2α.

128. A mass m is suspended from the two coupled spring connected in series. The force constant for springs are K_1 and K_2. The time period of the suspended mass will be

A. $T = 2\pi\sqrt{\dfrac{m}{K_1 - K_2}}$
B. $T = 2\pi\sqrt{\dfrac{m K_1 K_2}{K_1 - K_2}}$
C. $T = 2\pi\sqrt{\dfrac{m}{K_1 + K_2}}$
D. $T = 2\pi\sqrt{\dfrac{m(K_1 + K_2)}{K_1 K_2}}$

129. A spring of force constant K is cut into two pieces whose lengths are in the ratio 1 : 2. What is the force constant of the longer piece

A. $\dfrac{K}{2}$
B. $\dfrac{3K}{2}$
C. $2K$
D. $3K$

130. The vertical extension in a light spring by a weight of 1 kg suspended from the wire is 9.8 cm. The period of oscillation is

A. $20\,\pi$ sec
B. 2π sec
C. $2\pi/10$ sec
D. 200π sec

131. When a mass is attached to a spring, its length is increased by 20 cm. It is now further lowered and released. The time period is

A. $2\pi/7$ sec
B. 7 sec
C. 2πsec
D. enough data not available

132. A spring of force constant K is cut into three equal parts. The force constant of each part will be

A. K
B. 3 K
C. $K/3$
D. 9 K

133. The velocity of sound in oxygen at NTP is v. The velocity of sound in hydrogen at NTP will be

A. 4 v
B. $2\sqrt{2}$
C. 2 v
D. None of these

134. In which one of the following cases the jet aeroplane is flying at supersonic speed?

A. its sound makes 30° with the vertical, when the jet is passing over the head of the listener
B. its line of sight makes 30° with the vertical when sound appears to be coming vertically downwards
C. its sound makes 60° with the vertical, when sound appears to be coming vertically downwards
D. its line of sight makes 60° with the vertical, when sound appears to be coming vertically downwards

135. The pitch of the sound as detected by the observer is independent of
A. original frequency
B. the velocity of sound in the medium
C. relative velocity of source and observer
D. None of these

136. A source of sound moves towards a stationary listener. The apparent pitch of the sound is found to be higher than its actual value. This happens because
A. wavelength of sound waves decreases
B. wavelength of sound waves increases
C. the number of waves received by the listener increases
D. the number of waves received by the listener decreases

137. Radio waves of wavelength λ are sent from a radar towards an aeroplane. If the aeroplane is moving towards the radar station, the wavelength of the radiowaves, received after reflection from the aeroplane will be
A. λ
B. more than λ
C. less than λ
D. more or less than λ, depending on the speed of aeroplane

138. In case of vibrating string, the frequency of the first overtone is equal to frequency of the
A. fundamental note   B. first harmonic
C. second harmonic   D. None of these

139. The sound of minimum frequency emitted by a vibrating string is not termed as
A. first overtone   B. first harmonic
C. fundamental tone   D. None of these

140. If tension in the string is increased from 1 kN to 4 kN, other factors remaining unchanged, the frequency of the second harmonic will
A. be halved   B. remain unchanged
C. be doubled   D. become four times

141. Maximum value of electric intensity due to a charged sphere is at

A. centre
B. surface
C. infinity
D. None of these

142. For a material to behave as good conductor, which of the following conditions is a must?

A. each atom should have large number of electrons
B. each molecule should have large number of electrons
C. total number of electrons in it should be zero
D. None of these

143. What is the direction of the lines of force at any point on the equipotential surface?

A. parallel to it
B. normal to it
C. be inclined
D. None of these

144. Electric lines of force about a +ve point charge are

A. circular and clockwise
B. circular and anticlockwise
C. radial outwards
D. radial inwards

145. Electric potential is

A. scalar and dimensionless quantity
B. vector and dimensionless quantity
C. scalar and dimensional quantity
D. vector and dimensional quantity

146. Gauss's law helps in

A. determination of electric force between point charges
B. situations where Coulomb's law fails
C. determining electric potential due to symmetric charge distributions
D. determining electric potential due to symmetric charge distributions

147. Two thin and infinite parallel plates have uniform densities of charge $+\sigma$ and $-\sigma$. The electric field in the space outside the plates is

A. $\frac{\sigma}{2\varepsilon_0}$
B. $\frac{\sigma}{\varepsilon_0}$
C. $\frac{2\sigma}{\varepsilon_0}$
D. zero

148. Charge on a spherical conductor resides

A. at its surface
B. at its centre
C. throughout the body
D. None of these

149. Which of the following is discontinuous across the charged conducting surface?

A. electric field
B. electric potential

C. both electric field and potential
D. neither electric field nor electric potential

150. If the radius of a soap bubble is doubled, its capacitance will be
A. doubled
B. unchanged
C. halved
D. increased by 50%

151. The length of a conductor is doubled and its radius is halved, its resistance is
A. unchanged
B. doubled
C. quadrupled
D. eight times its value

152. The length of a conductor is doubled. Its conductance will be
A. unchanged
B. halved
C. doubled
D. quadrupled

153. Conductivity of a conductor depends upon
A. length
B. area of cross-section
C. volume
D. temperature

154. Identify the set in which all the three materials are good conductors of electricity
A. Cu, Ag and Au
B. Cu, Si and diamond
C. Cu, Hg and NaCl
D. Cu, Ge and Hg

155. Two unequal resistances are connected in parallel across a cell. Which of the following statement is true ?
A. current through smaller resistance is more
B. current through larger resistance is more
C. current is same through both the resistances
D. nothing is definite, as it depends upon the e.m.f. of the cell and the circuit conditions

156. Seebeck effect is inverse of
A. Peltier effect
B. Joule's effect
C. Thomson's effect
D. None of these

157. As the temperature of hot junction increases, the thermo emf
A. always increases
B. always decreases
C. may increase or decrease
D. neither increases nor decreases

158. Voltameter cannot be used to measure
A. current
B. electrochemical equivalent
C. potential difference
D. charge

159. What determines the emf between the two metals placed in an electrolyte?
A. relative position of metals in the electrochemical series
B. distance between them
C. strength of electrolyte
D. nature of electrolyte

160. Electric current is passed through the following solutions. In which case hydrogen will be liberated at the cathode?

A. sugar
B. sodium hydroxide
C. sulphuric acid
D. copper sulphate

161. A current carrying coil is bent sharply so as to convert it into a double loop both carrying a current in the same direction. If B is the initial magnetic field at the centre and if the current in the two coils is opposite to each other, the final magnetic field will be

A. zero
B. $2B$
C. $4B$
D. $8B$

162. A current carrying coil is bent sharply so as to convert it into a double loop both carrying a current in the same direction. If B is the initial magnetic field at the centre, then the final concentric magnetic field will be

A. zero
B. $2B$
C. $4B$
D. $8B$

163. Magnetic field at the centre of a circular loop of area A is B. The magnetic moment of the loop will be

A. $\dfrac{BA^2}{\mu_0 \pi}$
B. $\dfrac{BA^{3/2}}{\mu_0 \pi}$
C. $\dfrac{BA^{3/2}}{\mu_0 \pi^{1/2}}$
D. $\dfrac{2BA^{3/2}}{\mu_0 \pi^{1/2}}$

164. A beam of protons is moving parallel to a beam of electrons. Both the beams will tend to

A. repel each other
B. come closer
C. move more apart
D. either B. or C.

165. The mass of a proton is 1847 times that of electron. If an electron and a proton are injected in a uniform electric field at right angle to the direction of the field, with the same kinetic energy, then

A. the proton trajectory will be less curved than that of electron
B. both the trajectories will be straight
C. both the trajectories will be equally curved
D. the electron trajectory will be less curved than that of proton.

166. A uniform electric field and a uniform magnetic field are pointed in the same direction. If an electron is projected in the same direction, the electron

A. velocity will increase in magnitude
B. velocity will decrease in magnitude
C. will turn to its left
D. will turn to its right

167. A charge moving with velocity v in x-direction is subjected to a field of magnetic induction in the negative x-direction. As a result, the charge will

A. retard along x-axis

B. move along a helical path around x-axis

C. remain unaffected

D. starts moving in a circular path

168. Radius of curvature of a charged particle, in a uniform magnetic field, is directly proportional to

A. momentum of particle

B. intensity of the field

C. charge on the particle

D. energy of the particle

169. The work done by a magnetic field, on a moving charge is

A. zero because $\vec{F}$ acts parallel to $\vec{v}$

B. positive because $\vec{F}$ acts perpendicular to $\vec{v}$

C. zero because $\vec{F}$ acts perpendicular to $\vec{v}$

D. negative because $\vec{F}$ acts parallel to $\vec{v}$

170. A proton moving in a straight line enters a strong magnetic field along the field direction. How will its path and velocity change ?

A. path is circular but speed constant

B. path is same but velocity increases

C. path is same and velocity remains constant

D. path is same and motion is retarded

171. S.I. unit of magnetic permeability is

A. A-m

B. Am^2

C. H-m

D. H/m

172. Potential at any point on equatorial line of dipole is

A. $\mu_0 \; M/4\pi d^2$

B. $\mu_0 M/4\pi d^3$

C. zero

D. None of these

173. Force between two magnetic poles depends on

A. pole strength only

B. distance only

C. medium only

D. All the three above

174. The source of magnetic field is

A. isolated magnetic pole

B. static electric charge

C. current loop

D. None of these

175. If the distance between two similar poles of equal strength is doubled, to get the same repulsive force, the pole strength of each pole should be

A. increased by $\sqrt{2}$ times
B. halved
C. doubled
D. increased by 4 times

176. Tesla is a unit of

A. magnetic flux
B. electric flux
C. magnetic Induction
D. potential difference

177. Faraday's law of electromagnetic induction states that the induced e.m.f. in a circuit is

A. proportional to density of lines of force
B. inversely proportional to the rate of change of lines of force
C. proportional to the total magnetic field produced
D. directly proportional to the rate of change of lines of force

178. Lenz's law states that the direction of the induced e.m.f. in a conductor is such as to

A. move the conductor parallel to itself
B. generate a magnetic field parallel to the conductor
C. align the conductor parallel to earth's magnetic field
D. develop forces opposing the cause of the induced e.m.f.

179. The induced e.m.f. in a circuit according to Faraday's law of electromagnetic induction is

A. inversely proportional to the total number of lines of force through the circuit
B. inversely proportional to the rate of change of lines of force through the circuit
C. directly proportional to the rate of change of lines of force through the circuit
D. directly proportional to the total number of lines of force through the circuit

180. A moving conductor coil in a magnetic field produces an induced emf. This is in accordance with

A. Lenz's law
B. Faraday's law
C. Coulomb's law
D. Ampere's law.

181. The direction of induced emf during electromagnetic induction is given by

A. Faraday's law
B. Lenz's law
C. Maxwell's law
D. Ampere's law

182. The induced currents always produced expanding magnetic fields round their conductors in a direction that opposes the original magnetic field. This law is called.

A. Ohm's law
B. Kirchhoff's law
C. Lenz's law
D. Fleming's rule

183. A normal domestic electric supply is an alternating current whose average value is
A. zero
B. half the peak value
C. the peak value multiplied by π / 2
D. the peak value divided by π / 2

184. The root-mean square value of the alternating current is equal to
A. twice the peak vlaue
B. half the peak value
C. $\frac{1}{\sqrt{2}}$ times the peak value
D. equal to the peak value

185. An electric bulb in series with a large inductor when connected across a D.C. source take a little time before reaching a stable glow. If an iron core is inserted into the inductor , the delay will
A. increase
B. decrease
C. remain the same
D. may change in either direction depending upon the values of inductance and resistance.

186. Ray optics is valid when the characteristic dimensions are
A. much larger than wavelength of light
B. much smaller than wavelength of light
C. of the order of one millimetre
D. of same order as wavelength of light

187. The rectilinear propagation of light in a medium is due to
A. its short wavelength
B. its high frequency
C. its high velocity
D. the refractive index of medium.

188. A thick mirror produces a number of images of an object. Which of the image is the brightest?
A. first
B. second
C. third
D. last one

189. Two mirrors are kept at 60° to each other and a body is placed at middle. The total number of images formed is
A. six
B. four
C. five
D. three

190. The height of a man is 6 m. To see his full image the size of mirror is approximately
A. 2.5 m
B. 3 m
C. 6 m
D. 12 m

191. Evidence of the wave nature of light cannot be obtained from
A. reflection
B. Doppler effect
C. interference
D. diffraction

192. Newton proposed his corpuscular theory of light on the basis of
A. Planck's quantum theory
B. rectilinear propagation of light
C. refraction effect of photons
D. dispersion effect of light

193. Huygen's wave theory of light cannot explain
A. diffraction
B. interference
C. polarization
D. photoelectric effect.

194. According to Huygen's wave theory point on any wavefront may be regarded as
A. a photon
B. an electron
C. a new source of wave
D. neutron

195. Light propagates rectilinearly because of its
A. frequency
B. velocity
C. wavelength
D. wave nature

196. Two monochromatic light sources are said to be coherent if they have
A. same frequency.
B. constant relative phase difference.
C. a phase difference changing with time.
D. difference amplitude for their wave motion.

197. Interference occurs in which of the following waves?
A. Longitudinal
B. Transverse
C. Electro-magnetic
D. All of these

198. The phenomenon of interference of light was discovered by
A. Newton
B. Young
C. Fresnel
D. Huygen

199. As a result of an interference of two coherent waves energy is
A. increased
B. decreased
C. redistribution and distribution changes with time
D. redistribution and distribution does not change with time

200. To demonstrate the phenomena of interference we require
A. two sources which emit radiation of the same frequency
B. two sources which emit radiation of nearly the same frequency
C. two sources which emit radiation of the same frequency and have a definite phase relationship
D. two sources which emit radiation of different wavelength

201. Photoelectric effect can be explained by assuming that light
A. is a form of transverse waves
B. is a form of longitudinal waves
C. can be polarised
D. consists of quanta

202. In photoelectric effect, the photoelectric current
A. does not depend on photon frequency, but only on intensity of incident beam
B. depends both on intensity and frequency of incident beam
C. increases when frequency of incident photons increases
D. decreases when frequency of incident photons increases

203. Which one of the following is incorrect statement about a photon?
A. photon's rest mass is zero
B. photon's momentum is hν/c
C. photon's energy is hν
D. photons exert no pressure

204. Blue light can cause photoelectric emission from a metal, but yellow light cannot. If red light is incident on the metal, then
A. photoelectric current will increase
B. rate of emission of photoelectrons will decrease
C. no photoelectric emission will occur
D. energy of the photoelectrons will increase

205. When a photon collides with an electron which of the following characteristic of the photon increases?
A. energy
B. frequency
C. wavelength
D. None of these

206. Which of the following makes use of photoelectric effect?
A. television receiver
B. television camera
C. cathode Ray oscillograph
D. radar

207. The dynamic mass of the photon is given by
A. $\frac{h\nu}{c}$
B. $\frac{h\lambda}{c}$
C. $\frac{h}{c\lambda}$
D. $\frac{h}{c\nu}$

208. Which of the following characteristics of photoelectric effect supports the particle nature of radiations.
A. threshold frequency.
B. dependence of the velocity of photoelectron on frequency.
C. independence of velocity of photoelectrons on intensity of radiations.
D. instantaneous photoelectric emission.

209. The maximum energy of the electrons released in photocell is independent of
A. frequency of incident light
B. intensity of incident light
C. nature of cathode surface
D. None of these

210. Which of the following sources give discrete emission spectrum?
A. incandescent electric bulb
B. sun
C. mercury vapour lamp
D. candle

ANSWERS

1	2	3	4	5	6	7	8	9	10
B	A	A	A	C	D	A	C	B	A
11	12	13	14	15	16	17	18	19	20
A	B	A	D	A	C	B	C	C	D
21	22	23	24	25	26	27	28	29	30
D	D	C	B	B	A	C	D	B	D
31	32	33	34	35	36	37	38	39	40
D	C	B	B	C	D	C	C	D	D
41	42	43	44	45	46	47	48	49	50
B	B	A	A	B	B	A	B	D	D
51	52	53	54	55	56	57	58	59	60
C	A	C	A	D	C	C	B	A	B
61	62	63	64	65	66	67	68	69	70
C	C	D	B	D	B	A	A	C	C
71	72	73	74	75	76	77	78	79	80
C	A	A	B	C	B	A	C	D	C
81	82	83	84	85	86	87	88	89	90
D	A	B	A	D	A	C	C	D	B
91	92	93	94	95	96	97	98	99	100
B	C	D	A	B	D	C	C	A	D
101	102	103	104	105	106	107	108	109	110
D	A	C	D	D	C	A	B	D	B
111	112	113	114	115	116	117	118	119	120
B	C	C	A	A	B	B	D	D	D
121	122	123	124	125	126	127	128	129	130
A	A	B	A	A	A	C	D	B	C
131	132	133	134	135	136	137	138	139	140
A	B	A	D	D	A	C	C	A	C
141	142	143	144	145	146	147	148	149	150
B	D	B	C	C	C	D	A	A	A
151	152	153	154	155	156	157	158	159	160
D	B	D	A	A	D	C	C	A	C

161	162	163	164	165	166	167	168	169	170
A	C	D	D	C	B	C	A	C	C
171	172	173	174	175	176	177	178	179	180
D	C	D	A,C	C	C	D	D	C	B
181	182	183	184	185	186	187	188	189	190
B	C	D	C	A	A	D	B	C	B
191	192	193	194	195	196	197	198	199	200
A	B	C	C	D	B	D	B	C	C
201	202	203	204	205	206	207	208	209	210
B	D	D	C	C	B	C	A	B	C

Some Selected Explanatory Answers

18. $\left[\dfrac{\text{Force} \times \text{displacement}}{\text{time}}\right]$

$= \dfrac{[MLT^{-2}][M^0LT^0]}{[M^0L^0T]} = ML^2T^{-3}.$

26. Here $[\tan\theta] = [v^2/rg] = M^0L^0T^0$. Also, in the actual expression for the angle of banking of a road, there is no numerical factor involved. Therefore, the relation is both numerically and dimensionally correct.

27. The correct relation for time period of simple pendulum is $T = 2\pi\,(l/g)^{1/2}$. So, the given relation is numerically incorrect as the factor 2π is missing.

66. Generally it is a said that he does no work, but this is wrong because while he does no work against his weight (i.e. gravitational force, mg) but he definitely does work against frictional froce (μ mg). Students must understand it clearly. If he is walking towards, say, north, he, in fact, is pushing earth towards south which means frictional force is acting on him towards north.

67. Work done = 1/2 × stress × strain

= 1/2 × mg × ℓ

79. Since there is no friction at the contact surface (smooth horizontal surface) there will be no rolling. Hence, the acceleration of the centre of mass of the sphere will be independent of the position of the applied force F. Therefore, there is no relation between h and R.

84. $\vec{L} = \vec{r} \times \vec{p}$ Where $\vec{L}$ is angular momentum, r is position vector and $\vec{p}$ linear momentum.

$\therefore$ for $\vec{L}$ to be constant, the following 3 values should remain unchanged

1. $|\ \vec{r}\ |$
2. $|\ \vec{p}\ |$
3. direction of $\vec{r} \times \vec{p}$,which is $\perp$ to the plane containing. This happens only when it is calculated about the centre of the circle.

86. As weight of body on pole = mg and g does not change at pole due to rotation of earth, so there is no change in the weight of body.

87. The gravitational attraction on a body due to earth decreases with height and increases due to moon. At a certain height, it becomes zero and with further increase in height, the gravitational attraction of moon becomes more than that of earth.

88. The acceleration due to gravity at a depth d inside the earth is

$$g' = g\left(1 - \frac{d}{R}\right) = g\left(\frac{R-d}{R}\right) = g\frac{r}{R}$$

Where, $R - d = y$ = distance of a place from the centre of earth. Therefore $g' \propto r$.

91. The water will lie above the mercury. The steel ball will continue to float above the mercury and will be covered by water. The upthrust due to the water displaced will make the ball move up.

96. The ship is given special shape so that the weight of the water displaced is more than the weight of the ship.

100. The shape of the wings is such that the air running around them causes loss of pressure on the upper side. This, in accordance with Bernoulli's theorem causes lift.

107. Here $\Delta L_1 = \Delta L_2$.

That is $L_1\ (1 + \alpha_1 T) = L_2\ (1 + \alpha_2 T)$.

Which gives $L_1 - L_2 = (L_2\alpha_2 - L_1\alpha_1)\ T$.

Since $L_1 - L_2$ is independent of temperature.

Therefore: $L_2\alpha_2 - L_1\alpha_1 = 0$.

121. The internal energy of a real gas consists of KE and PE, which depend on temperature and volume.

124. $\eta = \frac{T_1 - T_2}{T_1}$. Hence $\eta \propto (T_1 - T_2)$

When $T_2 = 0\,k, \eta = 1 = 100\%$

126. $x = a \sin \omega t$ and $y = a \sin \omega t$

So $x = y$.

It will be a straight line equally inclined from X and Y-axis.

127. $v = \frac{1}{2\pi}\sqrt{\frac{K}{m}}$

and $v_1 = \frac{1}{2\pi}\sqrt{\frac{K_1}{m}} = \frac{1}{2\pi}\sqrt{\frac{2K}{m}} = \sqrt{2}\,v.$

128. The effective spring constant of two springs in series is;

$K = \frac{k_1 k_2}{k_1 + k_2}$. There period,

$T = 2\pi\sqrt{\frac{m}{K}} = 2\pi\sqrt{\frac{m(k_1 + k_2)}{k_1 k_2}}$

137. Here $v' = \frac{c}{c - 2u}v$. When the aeroplane approaches with velocity u.

Hence v' increases and so λ decreases.

147. Electric intensity due to a sheet of charge having surface density $\sigma/2\,\varepsilon_0$ That due to $-\sigma$ is $-\sigma/2\varepsilon_0$.

Total intensity

$\sigma/2\varepsilon_0 - (-\sigma/2\varepsilon_0) = \sigma/\varepsilon_0.$

150. When radius is doubled, the capacitance is also doubled. Since, the charge remains unchanged, therefore $V = q/C$ is halved.

155. When resistance are connected in parallel to a cell, the potential difference across each resistance is the same.

Current = Pot. diff./resistance.

161. The magnetic field due to current through one coil is equal and opposite to that due to other, hence the resultant magnetic field is zero.

162. As $$B = \frac{\mu_0}{4\pi}\frac{2\pi ni}{r}; \text{ so } B \propto \frac{n}{r}$$

Thus $$\frac{B_2}{B_1} = \frac{n_2}{n_1}\times\frac{r_1}{r_2} = \frac{2}{1}\times\frac{r}{r/2} = 4$$

or $$B_2 = 4B_1.$$

163. $$B = \frac{\mu_0}{4\pi}\frac{2\pi I}{r} = \frac{\mu_0 I}{2r} \text{ or } I = \frac{2Br}{\mu_0};$$

Also $$A = \pi r^2 \text{ or } r = \left(\frac{A}{\pi}\right)^{1/2}$$

Magnetic moment, $$M = IA = \frac{2Br}{\mu_0}A$$

$$= \frac{2BA}{\mu_0}\times\left(\frac{A}{\pi}\right)^{1/2} = \frac{2BA^{3/2}}{\mu_0\pi^{1/2}}$$

164. There will be an electrostatic force of attraction between beam of protons and beam of electrons and there will be magnetic attraction due to currents by virtue of motion of protons and electrons in the same direction and magnetic repulsion due to currents by virtue of motion of protons and electrons in the opposite direction.

165. Kinetic energy, $E_k = \frac{1}{2}mv^2$ or $mv^2 = 2E_k$.

Force on the charged particle in electric field $F = Eq$. Acceleration of the charged particle in the direction of electric field,

$a = Eq/m$

Taking the motion of charged particle at right angle to the initial direction of motion i.e., motion along the direction of electric field for the displacement y in the electric field.

$u = 0$, $a = Eq/m$, $t = t$, $s = y$.

As, $s = ut + \frac{1}{2}at^2$

$$\therefore y = 0\times t + \frac{1}{2}\frac{Eq}{m}t^2 = \frac{1}{2}\frac{Eq}{m}t^2 \quad ...(1)$$

If x is the length of region of electric field, then $t = x/v$

From (1), $y = \frac{1}{2}\frac{Eq}{m} \times \frac{x^2}{v^2} = \frac{1}{2}\frac{Eq\,x^2}{2E_k}$

As y is independent of m, hence both the trajectories will be equally curved.

166. When electron is moving along the direction of electric and magnetic field, it experience no force due to magnetic field, but experience force due to electric field, which is $\vec{F} = e\vec{E}$. It acts opposite to the direction of electric field, hence velocity of electron will decrease.

169. Force on moving charge while moving in magnetic field is;

$\vec{F} = q(\vec{v} \times \vec{B})$ where $\vec{F}$ is perpendicular to $\vec{v}$.

Work done/sec = $\vec{F} \cdot \vec{v} = Fv \cos 90° = 0$.

175. $F = \frac{\mu_0}{4\pi}\frac{mm}{r^2}$ = constant

When r is doubled, m.m should become 4 times or m should be doubled.

186. We know that wave optics is valid, when the size of the objects is of the order of wavelength of light. And the ray optics is valid when the size of the object is much larger than the wavelength of light.

187. It is actually due to uniformity of refractive index of the medium. In case of a optically heterogenous medium, the light ray will not go straight.

188. We know that first image is produced due to at the front surface and other images are produced due to multiple reflection at the front and rear surfaces. Since second image is produced due to reflection from rear and silvered point. Therefore it is brightest image.

192. On the basis of the rectilinear propagation of light Newton formulated his corpuscular theory of light because on its basis he could explain three things

(i) rectilinear propagation of light

(ii) reflection from a surface

(iii) refraction of light in an other medium.

CHEMISTRY

ATOMIC STRUCTURE

Atom and Molecule : The atom of an element is that smallest particle which takes part in chemical reaction but doesn't exist in free state.

Similarly the molecule of an element or compound is that smallest particle which doesn't take part in chemical reaction but exists in free state.

Main fundamental particles of an atom :

	Electron	*Proton*	*Neutron*
Inventor	J.J. Thomson	Goldstein	Chadwick
Charge	-1.6×10^{-19}C	1.6×10^{19} C	No charge
Mass	9.1×10^{-31} kg	1.67×10^{-27} kg	Nearly equal to proton

Rutherford's Atomic model

This model has following conclusions :

(*i*) In an atom there is a central massive part and it is called nucleus which is surrounded by the electrons and in this nucleus proton and neutron are packed together.

(*ii*) The atom is spherical and most of its part is empty.

(*iii*) The size of the nucleus is very small with comparison to the entire atom.

(*iv*) Rutherford predicted empirically that the electrons rotate in the various orbits around the nucleus while the electron and proton of the nucleus has a coulomb force of attraction which is equal to the centripetal force to remain the electron orbiting in the circular orbits.

Shortcoming of this model : According to the classical theory of electrodynamics every accelerated electron would radiate energy continuously around the nucleus under the influence of centripetal accelaration and ultimately electron would be spiralled out into the nucleus and the atom would collapse. But the atom is found to be stable. Thus Rutherford's model could not explain about the atom stability and it was not correct.

Bohr's Atomic model

Bohr provided the following new ideas on the basis of Planck's quantum theory called the postulates of Bohr's theory, which are as below–

(*i*) The centripetal force required for an orbiting electron is counter balanced by the electrostatical Coulombian force of attraction between the nucleus and the electron.

(*ii*) The electrons in an atom only revolve in a certain definite orbit in which energy is fixed and quantized. This orbit is stationary and in any such orbit electron doesn't radiate any energy although it is accelerated. Only those orbit are stable in which electrons rotate and the angular momentum of such orbits must be quantized which is equal to an integral multiple of $h/2\pi$.

(*iii*) Electrons of greater radii posses greater energy and vice-versa. But if any electron jumps from any higher orbit to any lower one then a quanta of energy appears to be radiated, while when an electron from lower orbit to higher orbit is raised then a quanta of energy appears to be absorpt. Thus energy emission or absorption from the electron's orbit is not continuous but descret only when any electron jumps from higher to lower and vice-versa.

Atomic Number (Z) : The number of protons or electrons of an atom is called atomic number of the element.

Mass Number (A) : In every atom there is a small central massive part called nucleus where almost masses of the atom is assumed to be concentrated.

Atomic Symbol of an element : $_zX^A$, where z = Atomic number, A = Mass number.

Shell or orbit : The electrons revolve in the various orbits with different and definite energies. These orbit or path of electrons is called shell.

Subshell or Sub orbit : A subshell is a three dimensional graphic plot of electronic wave function of every orbit in which various orbitals are found. It is represented by s, p, d, f. Maximum number of electrons in s, p, d and f are 2, 6, 10, 14 respectively. Various shell are K, L, M, N etc.

Orbital : An orbital is the three dimensional space around the nucleus of an atom where there is maximum probability of finding an electron.

Electronic Configuration : A comprehensive and proper distribution of the various electrons in various shell and subshells of any atom is called electronic configuration. Na(11) E.C. ($1s^2$, $2s^2\,2p^6$, $3s^1$), Mg(12) E.C. ($1s^2$, $2s^2\,2p^6$, $3s^2$)

Aufbau Principle : Aufbau is a German word which means to *build.* Hence Aufbau principle explained about the order of filling up of the atomic orbitals and thus gives the principle of building of atomic structure of elements with electrons. According to this principle the electrons are filled in atomic orbitals in order of their increasing energy.

An electron occupies the orbital of lowest energy first and when it is filled up completely with electrons there after remaining electrons are accommodated to the orbitals of the next higher energy. The orbital having highest energy is filled in last. The order of filling of atomic orbitals with electrons can be shown as below;

Thus according to Aufbau principle the order of energy levels of the various subshells—$1s < 2s < 2p < 3s < 3p < 4s < 3d < 4p < 5s < 4d < 5p < 6s < 4f < 5d < 6p < 7s < 5f$.

Quantum Numbers

The Quantum numbers are those number through which the position of electrons and their respective energies in various shells, subshells or orbitals are known.

To know the position of an electron and its corresponding energy; normally there are four parameters which are needed to describe it as below :

(*i*) The orbit number in which electron exists.
(*ii*) The suborbit or subshell of the orbit or shell in which electron resides.
(*iii*) The orbital of the subshell in which electron resides.
(*iv*) The electron which rotates in the orbital.

There are four quantum numbers—

(*i*) Principal Quantum Number
(*ii*) Azimuthal Quantum Number
(*iii*) Magnetic Quantum Number
(*iv*) Spin Quantum Number

(*i*) Principal Quantum Number : This quantum number which simply indicates orbit of an electron and its energy and it is represented by n (=1, 2, 3, ...), where n is integer. For $n = 1$, electron is said to be in normal state.

(*ii*) Azimuthal Quantum Numer : This quantum number which represents the angular momentum of the revolving electron and it is indicated by l. For principal quantum number n, l has all the values from 0 to $(n - 1)$.

(*iii*) Magnetic Quantum Number : This quantum number which indicates the direction of an orbit in space in a magnetic field and it is represented by m. The values of magnetic quantum number m depend on the value of l and its values are from $-l$ to $+ l$ including zero.

(*iv*) Spin Quantum Number : This quantum number represents spin of the electron. Quantum mechanically it has been observed that electrons have two types of spin—clock wise (+1/2) and anti clock wise (–1/2). In fact spinning electrons possess spin angular momentum and it is quantized. This spin quantum number has two values +1/2 and –1/2 and represented by s.

Quantum Number	Symbol	Contains
Principal Quantum Number	n	Orbit number and the corresponding energy of the electron
Azimuthal Quantum Number	l	Angular momentum of the revolving electron of subshell
Magnetic Quantum Number	m	Direction of an orbital in the space of magnetic field
Spin Quantum Number	s	Spin of the electron

Pauli's Exclusive Principle : The Pauli's exclusion principle states that—

No two electrons in an atom can have the same set of four quantum numbers and maximum a set of three quantum numbers for two electrons can be identical but the fourth quantum number must be different for them.

Thus according to this rule only following two sets of four quantum numbers are possible for the first orbit.

$$n = 1 \qquad n = 1$$
$$l = 0 \qquad l = 0$$
$$m = 0 \qquad m = 0$$
$$s = +\frac{1}{2} \qquad s = -\frac{1}{2}$$

Thus in the first orbit, only two electrons can be accommodated—one spinning in clock wise direction and other in anit-clock wise direction.

Hund's rule : This is also called law of maximum multiplicity and it states that—

Electrons have the general tendency to remain unpaired in an incompletely filled orbital so as to have maximum spin multiplicity, maximum stability and minimum energy.

Isotopes : The atoms which have equal atomic numbers but differnet mass numbers are called isotopes. Exam.: Protium ($_1H^1$), duterium ($_1H^2$) and tritium ($_1H^3$).

Isobars : The atoms which have equal mass numbers but different atomic numbers are called isobars. Example : Nitrogen ($_7N^{14}$) and Carbon ($_6C^{14}$).

Isotones : The atoms which have different atomic numbers and mass numbers but same number of neutrons are called isotones. Example : ($_{15}P^{31}$) and ($_{14}S^{30}$).

METALS & NON-METALS

Elements are pure form of substances. Chemical elements can be classified into metals, metalloids and non-metal.

On the basis of their physical and chemical properties, out of the 92 naturally occurring elements, about 70 are metals and 22 are non-metals. Some example of metals are — iron, copper, aluminium, zinc, sodium, gold, sulphur, tungsten, cadmium, nickel, uranium and mercury etc.

Examples of non-metals are — sulphur, iodine, bromine, chlorine, helium, oxygen, carbon, fluorine etc. Metalloids have some chemical and physical properties of metals and other properties of non-metals.

Example of metalloids are — silicon, germanium, arsenic which are also semiconductors.

Ore : An ore is a naturally occurring mineral from which one or more metals can be profitably extracted.

Metallurgy : It is the science of extracting metals from their ores and purifying them. Metallurgical processes may contain three main operations :

The metal is purified. After refining, some substances are added to give the desired properties to the final product.

Physical Properties of Metals

• Shiny appearance • Generally hard • Malleable • Ductile • Good conductors of heat • Good conductors of electricity • High melting points • Sonorous • High densities.

Chemical Properties of Metals

1. Metals combine with oxygen to form basic oxides.
2. Metals react with water to form metal hydroxide and evolve hydrogen gas.
3. Metals react with dilute acids to form metal salt and liberate hydrogen gas.
4. More reactive metal displaces a less reactive metal from its salt solution.

Physical Properties of Non-metals

• Brittle in nature • Non-ductile • Bad conductor of heat and electricity except Graphite • Non-lustrous and cannot be polished • Not strong and have low tensile strength • Soft *e.g.,* sulphur and phosphorus. Except Diamond • Low densities • Non-sonorous.

Chemical Properties of Non-metals

(1) Non-metals are electronegative in nature.

(2) Reaction of non-metals with oxygen.

Non-metals form active or neutral oxides.

$C + O_2 \rightarrow CO_2$ $\quad\quad$ $S + O_2 \rightarrow SO_2$

(3) Reaction of non-metals with water
Non-metals do not react with water or steam to evolve hydrogen gas.
(4) Non-metals do not react with dilute acids.
(5) A more reactive non-metal displaces a less reactive non-metal from its salt solution. $2NaBr(aq) + Cl_2(g) \rightarrow 2\ NaCl(aq) + Br_2(l)$ Bromine

Important Compounds of Metals (Ores)

Ore ***Oxides Ore***	**Formula**	**Ore** **of Metal**
Zincite	ZnO	Zinc
Haematite	Fe_2O_3	Iron
Magnetite	Fe_3O_4	Iron
Corundum	Al_2O_3	Aluminium
Cuprite	Cu_2O	Copper
Calcia	CaO	Calcium
Cassiterite	SnO_2	Tin
Pyrolusite	MnO_2	Manganese

Alloys

An alloy is generally a homogenous mixture of two or more metals prepared by mixing the components in the molten state. When one of the metals is mercury the alloy is called as **amalgam**.

Some important Alloys—

Alloys	**Composition**	**Uses**
Brass	*Cu*–70%, *Zn*–30%	In making wires, parts of machines, utensils etc.
Bronze	*Cu*–90%, *Sn*–10%	In making utensils, idols etc.
Artificial gold	*Cu*–90%, *Al*–10%	In making ornaments, idols etc.
Coins metal	*Cu*–95%, *Sn*–4%, *P*–1%	In making coins and costly idols.
Gun metal	*Cu*–88%, *Sn*–10%, *Zn*–2%	In making fire arms like gun, pistol, equipments of machines.
Bel metal	*Cu*–80%, *Sn*–20%	In making bels which are used in schools and temples.
Constanton	*Cu*–60%, *Ni*–40	In making wires.

Monal metal	Cu–28%, Fe–2%, Ni–70%	In making idols.
German silver	Cu–50%, Zn–35%, Ni–15%	In making utensils idols etc.
Dutch metal	Cu–80%, Zn–20%	In making parts of machines, devices etc.
Magnelium	Al–5%, Mg–95%	In making aircrafts and aeroplane.
Durelumine or Hydroleum	Al–95%, Mg–1%, Cu–4%	In making aircrafts pressure cookers etc.
Aluminium bronze	Al–10%, Cu–90%	In making utensils, coins, artificial ornaments, paint etc.
Nichrome	Ni, Fe, Cr, Mn	In making electric heater, good quality electric wires etc.
Solder	Pb–68%, Sn–32%	In welding metallic bodies, filling cracked metallic parts.
Alanko	Fe, Al, Ni, Co	In making magnet.
Manganese steel	Mn–14%, Fe–(80–50)%	In making lockers, fish plates of railway tracks, part of cutting machines etc.
Chromium steel	Cr–2.4%, C–1.5% Fe–(90–95%)	In making cutting machines, shaving blades, bullets of gun and pistol etc.

CARBON AND ITS COMPOUNDS

- Carbon is a non-metallic element, represented by the symbol C.
- All living things contain carbon. All the things that support life, such as proteins, fats, carbohydrates and vitamins contain carbon.
- Carbon had a unique property that it can join with other carbon atoms to form carbon - carbon bonds. This can result in the formation of compounds with long chains. This property is called Catenation.
- The name carbon is derived from the Latin word *carbo,* which means *charcoal.*
- Carbon constitutes only 0.03% of the earth crust.
- Carbon is present in coal and petroleum wood, coke, charcoal, saw dust, kerosene, alcohol, petrol, Liquefied Petroleum Gas (LPG), Compressed Natural Gas (CNG) and Gobbar Gas (Biogas).
- Carbon is present in the form of calcium carbonate ($CaCO_3$) in minerals like chalk, marble and limestone.

- Carbon also occurs in the form of CO_2 (0.03%) in the atmosphere.
- The exchange of carbon between the living and the non-living things by the processes of respiration and photosynthesis.
- The process of heating wood or coal in the absence of air is known as **destructive distillation**.
- Carbon exists mainly in two allotropic forms : Crystalline form and Non-crystalline or amorphous form.

Crystalline forms of Carbon

Diamond and graphite are the two crystalline forms of carbon.

DIAMOND

It is one of the purest forms of carbon. Diamond crystals found in nature are generally **octahedral** (eight faced). In diamond, each carbon atom is attached to four other carbon atoms by strong forces. This results in a three-dimensional rigid structure which makes the **hardest substance**.

Graphite

Graphite is black and slippery with a metallic lustre, a form of carbon. In graphite, each carbon is bonded to only three neighbouring carbon atoms in the same plane forming layers of hexagonal networks separated by larger distances.

Amorphous Carbon

Amorphous carbon has physical and chemical properties that may vary depending on its method of manufacture and conditions to which it is later subjected. Amorphous carbon burns relatively easily in air.

The important varieties of amorphous carbon are : (*i*) Charcoal, (*ii*) Coke, (*iii*) Carbon Black.

Coal

Coal is a mixture of compounds of carbon, hydrogen, oxygen and some free carbon.

The Unique properties of Carbon

Carbon is a non-metal in Group IV of the Periodic Table. It forms covalent compounds. The uniqueness of carbon lies in the versatility of that bonding.

- The carbon atoms can join to each other to form long chains.
- The carbon atoms in a chain can be linked by single, double or triple covalent bonds.
- Carbon atoms can also arrange themselves in rings.

Compounds of Carbon and Hydrogen

Hydrocarbons are compounds that contain only the elements of hydrogen and carbon. There are two basic groups of hydrocarbon : Aliphatics & Aromatics. In aliphatic hydrocarbons, the carbon atoms are usually linked in chains. Methane is an example of an aliphatic hydrocarbon. Its chemical formula is **CH_4**. Aromatic hydrocarbons are made up of rings. Toluene is an example of an aromatic hydrocarbon. Its chemical formula is $C_6H_5CH_3$.

General formula of Alkane : $C_n H_{2n+2}$

$n = 1$,	$C H_4$ —	(Methane)		$n = 5$,	$C_5 H_{12}$ —	(Pentane)
$n = 2$,	$C_2 H_6$ —	(Ethane)		$n = 6$,	$C_6 H_{14}$ —	(Hexane)
$n = 3$,	$C_3 H_8$ —	(Propane)		$n = 7$,	$C_7 H_{16}$ —	(Heptane)
$n = 4$,	$C_4 H_{10}$ —	(Butane)				

Radioactivity

Radioactive rays and its properties : Radioactive elements and their compounds by the process of nuclear spontaneous disintegration into smaller fragments emit invisible radiations and which were called Bacquerel rays, compose positively charged alpha-rays (α-rays), negatively charged beta-rays (β-rays) and electrically neutral gamma-rays (γ-rays). The radioactive rays α, β and γ were pronounced their name by Rutherford.

Properties of α-rays:

(*i*) α-rays are the streams of He^{++} ions which have mass of 4 a.m.u. and charge of 2 units that's why α-rays are called α-particles.

(*ii*) When α-particles are passed through an electric field and a magnetic field then these are deflected.

(*iii*) It has maximum power of ionisation through the gases.

(*iv*) Its velocity is less then that of light and it is equal to the $1/10^{th}$ of the velocity of light in vacuum (3×10^8 m/second)

(*v*) It has least penetrating power as compared to that of β and γ-rays.

Properties of β-rays :

(*i*) β-rays are streams of fast moving electrons.

(*ii*) Each β-particle is an electron having mass of $\frac{1}{1836}$ a.m.u. and the charge of -1 unit.

(*iii*) It has less power of ionisation through the gases as compared to α-rays.

(*iv*) Its velocity is equal to $(33 - 92)\%$ of the velocity of light.

(*v*) It has more penetrating power than α-rays and less penetrating power than γ-rays.

Properties of γ-rays :

(*i*) γ-rays are electro-magnetic radiations of high energy.
(*ii*) It is composed of photons (rest mass zero) of high energy.
(*iii*) It is electrically neutral and it is an electro magnetic wave thus it has velocity equal to the velocity of light in vacuum (3×10^8 m/second).
(*iv*) It has largest (maximum) penetrating power and it can pass through 8 cm of thick lead block and 25 cm of thickened iron sheet.

Types of radioactive elements

Elements which exhibit the phenomenon of radioactivity are called radioactive elements and these are of two types;

(*i*) **Natural radioactive elements:** The elements *Po* (84), *At* (85), *Rn* (86), *Fr* (87), *Ra* (88), *Ac* (89), *Th* (90), *Pa* (91) and *U* (92) are naturally occurring radioactive elements.
(*ii*) **Artificial radioactive elements :** The elements *Np*(93), *Pu*(94).....to Habnium, *Ha*(105) are radioactive elements which have been synthesized inside the nuclear laboratory. These are called artificial radioactive elements and also called transuranic elements.

Half life period of a radioactive element : Half life period of a radioactive element is the time during which half of the total number of atoms of the radioactive element disintegrate, and it is represented by $T_{\frac{1}{2}}$.

$$\text{Half life period}\left(T_{\frac{1}{2}}\right) \text{ of any element } = \frac{0.693}{\lambda}.$$

Where; λ is called disintegration constant or decay constant.

Characteristics of half life period :

(*i*) Every radioactive element has its own constant half life and thus different radioactive elements have different half lives.
(*ii*) Half life period of a radioactive element is independent of all external conditions such as temperature, pressure, mass etc.
(*iii*) A radioactive element can be detected by means of its half life period.
(*iv*) Smaller the half life period of a radioactive element, larger is its radioactivity and vice-versa.

$$\text{Average life } (T_{av}) = \frac{\text{sum of lives of all atoms}}{\text{Total number of atoms}} = \frac{\int_0^\infty t\,dn}{\int_0^\infty dn} = \frac{1}{\lambda}$$

$\Rightarrow T_{av} = \frac{1}{\lambda}$, where, λ = decay constant or disintegration constant.

Radioactive dating or Radio isotope dating : Naturally occuring radioactive isotopes have been very useful in dating (estimating age) the geological events. Thus the technique of detecting the amount or quantity of any radio isotope in the sample of the rock, dead plants or organism or in any bio residue to estimate and measure its actual or exact age is called Radioactivity or radio isotope dating.

Nuclear Fission : The process (or nuclear reaction) in which a heavy nucleus splits up into two nuclei of nearly comparable masses with tremendous release of energy and some free neutrons is called nuclear fission. Elements having a higher value of neutron to proton ratio are more likely to undergo fission.

Neutron induced fission of uranium is represented as below :

$$_{92}U^{235} + {}_0n^1 \rightarrow ({}_{92}U^{236}) \rightarrow {}_{56}Ba^{141} + {}_{36}Kr^{92} + 3{}_0n^1 + 200\,\text{MeV}.$$

(Slow neutron) (compound nucleus)

Nuclear Fusion : The process of combining two light nuclei to form a heavy nucleus with tremendous release of energy is known as nuclear fusion.

Similar to fission, in fusion an appearance of small mass difference takes place between the reactants and product and this mass difference transforms into nuclear energy by Einstein's mass energy equivalence relation; $\Delta E = \Delta mc^2$. Also like nuclear fission, in fusion lighter nuclei such as hydrogen, deutron, tritium and helium etc are involved. A typical nuclear fusion reaction occuring in sun is as below :

$${}_1H^1 + {}_1H^1 + {}_1H^1 + {}_1H^1 \rightarrow {}_2He^4 + 2e^+ + 24.7\text{ MeV}.$$

Chemical bonding : The binding force of the constituents atoms of the molecule to maintain a mutual atomic order and a definite but specific geometrical shape is called chemical bonding.

Types of chemical bonding : There are three types of chemical bonding- Electrovalent or Ionic bonding, covalent bonding and Co-ordinate covalent bonding.

Electrovalent or Ionic bonding : The bond formed by the result of the electron transfer from the one atom to another among the atoms is called electrovalent or ionic bonding.

Example :

$Na + Cl \rightarrow Na^+\ Cl^-$ $(NaCl)$

(2, 8, 1) (2, 8, 7) (2, 8) (2, 8, 8)

(*i*) These compounds have high m.p. and b.p. because of the presence of strong intermolecular forces of attraction in their solid states.

(*ii*) These compounds are non-volatile because of their high m.p. and b.p.

(*iii*) These compounds are generally soluble in water because they generally ionise in water, ions become heavily hydrated and they disappear in the intermolecular spaces of water molecules and dissolve.

(*iv*) These electrovalent compounds are insoluble in organic solvants, because the organic solvants are covalent compounds.

Covalent bonding : The bond formed by the result of sharing of electrons between two atoms in which atoms form the chemical bonding in such a way that form molecules achieve the permanent electronic structure of the inert gas, is called covalent bonding.

When a pair of electron is produced by electrons sharing in a hydrogen molecules by two hydrogen atoms then a single covalent bond is formed.

$H(\times\bullet)H \rightarrow H — H$

Co-ordinate covalent bonding : In co-ordinate covalent bonding the pair of electrons are obtained by only through single atom and in this bonding the atom which supplies electrons pair is called donar and the atom which takes such pair of electrons is called accepter. The electrons pair donated by the donor atom is called singlton pair.

CHEMICAL REACTION AND EQUATIONS

Chemical Reaction is a process in which some known substances are changed into new substance or new substances. The starting substances are called **reactants**. The new substances formed are called products. *e.g.*

Hydrogen +	Oxygen →	Water
(reactant)	(reactant)	(product)

Chemical Equation : A shorthand notation of describing an actual chemical reaction in terms of the symbols and formula along with the number of atoms and molecules of the reactant and products is called **chemical equation**.

Types of Chemical Equations

Based on the change the chemical reactions can be categorised as shown in the following chart :

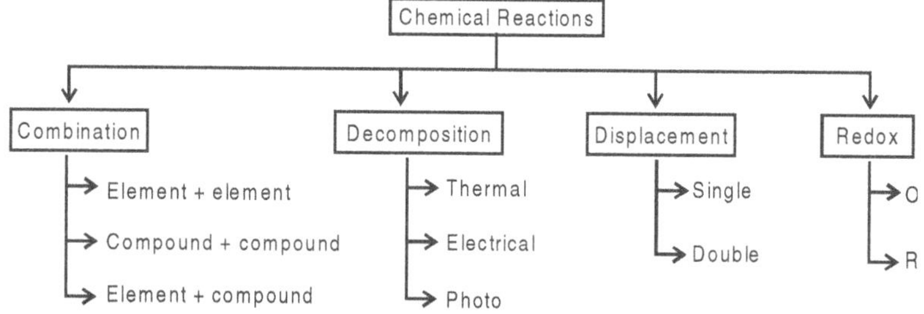

Oxidation : The oxidation is the chemical process in which either the ratio of electronegative atoms or radicals of any element or compound increases or the ratio of electropositive atoms or radicals of the element or compound decreases.

Example : $2Mg + O_2 \rightarrow 2MgO$, $C + O_2 \rightarrow CO_2$
$2H_2 + O_2 \rightarrow 2H_2O$, $2FeCl_2 + Cl_2 \rightarrow 2FeCl_3$.

Reduction : The reduction is the chemical process in which either the ratio of electropositive atoms or radicals of any element or compound increases or the ratio of electronegative atoms or radicals of the element or compound decreases.

$Cl_2 + H_2S \rightarrow 2HCl + S$
$2FeCl_3 + H_2 \rightarrow 2FeCl_2 + 2HCl$.

Oxidising agent : The atom which oxidises another atom or ion is called oxidising agent. An oxidising agent itself is reduced.

Reducing agent : Reducing agent is that which oxidises itself and reduces others. *e.g.* Na reduces Cl_2 but Na itself is oxidised. So, Na is reducing agent.

The oxidation number is defined as the charge which an atom appears to have when electrons are counted in ion, molecules or compounds.

Oxidation and Reduction in Terms of Oxidation Numbers

Oxidation refers to any chemical change involving **increase** in oxidation number where as the **reduction** refers to any chemical change involving **decrease** in oxidation number.

- **Atomic mass unit (amu)** : $\frac{1}{12}$th of mass of an atom of ^{12}C is called atomic mass unit. Its value is 1.6603×10^{-24} grams.
- **Relative atomic mass** : The mass of an atom of a substances relative to $\frac{1}{12}$th of the mass of a ^{12}C atom whose atomic mass is exactly 12 amu.

Mole : Collection of 6.023×10^{23} particles of definite formula/symbol is called **mole**. It is the unit to represent the amount of a substance.

Molar mass : The mass of 6.023×10^{23} particles of a substance is called molar mass.

Empirical formula : The simplest ratio of the atoms of the constituent elements of a compound is called its empirical formula.

Molecular formula : Actual number of all types of atoms of the constituent elements of a molecule is called its molecular formula.

$$\text{Molecular formula} = (\text{Empirical formula}) \times n$$

Boyle's law : The volume of the definite amount of any gas at constant temperature is inversely proportional to the pressure of the gas.

If at constant temperature the volume of the definite amount (mass) of the gas is V and its corresponding pressure be p then

$$V\alpha\frac{1}{p}or, V=K\frac{1}{p}$$

Where K is a proportionality constant.

$\Rightarrow pV = K$ (constant) $\Rightarrow p_1 \; V_1 = P_2V_2$

Thus at constant temperature the product of the pressure and volume remains constant.

Charle's law : The volume of the definite amount of any gas at constant pressure is directly proportional to the absolute temperature.

If at constant pressure the volume of the definite amount (mass) of the gas is V and its corresponding temperature (absolute) be T then

V $\propto$ T or, $\frac{V}{T}=K$, where; K is proportionality constant.

$$\Rightarrow \frac{V_1}{T_1}=\frac{V_2}{T_2}$$

Pressure's law : The pressure of the definite amount of any gas at constant volume is directly proportional to the absolute temperature.

If at constant volume the pressure of the definite amount (mass) of the gas is p and its corresponding temperature (absolute) be T then

p $\propto$ T or, $\frac{p}{T}=K$, where K is a proportionality constnat.

$$\Rightarrow \frac{p_1}{T_1}=\frac{p_1}{T_2}\Rightarrow p_1T_2=p_2T_1$$

Standard temperature and pressure (STP) or Normal temperature and pressure (NTP) : The temperature 0°C or 273K is called normal temperature or standard temperature. When in a barometer the mercury column is 760 mm then this atmospheric pressure is called normal pressure or standard pressure. This is equivalent to 1 atmospheric pressure. Thus 0°C temperature and 760 mm (76 cm) of Hg (mercury) is called STP or NTP.

Graham's law of diffusion : Graham in 1883 propounded a comprehensive theory regarding the rate of diffusion of gases and it is called Graham's law of diffusion stated as below;

At constant temperature and pressure the rate of diffusion of various gases are inversely proportional to the square root of the densities of the gases.

Thus if two gases have relative densities as d_1 and d_2 and their respective rates of diffusion be r_1 and r_2 then

$$r_1\propto\frac{1}{\sqrt{d_1}}, r_2\propto\frac{1}{\sqrt{d_2}}$$

$$\Rightarrow r_1 = \frac{k}{\sqrt{d_1}}, r_2 = \frac{k}{\sqrt{d_2}}$$

$$\Rightarrow \frac{r_1}{r_2} = \sqrt{\frac{d_2}{d_1}} \Rightarrow \text{rate of diffussion} \propto \frac{1}{\sqrt{\text{density}}}$$

Thereby, the lighter gases diffuse at faster rate and vice-versa.

Dalton's law of partial pressure : It states that the total pressure of the gaseous mixtures of a definite volume of these is equal to the sum of partial pressure of the component gases.

If there by three gases *A*, *B* and *C* whose partial pressures be p_A, p_B and p_C then according to Dalton's law of partial pressure total pressure (*p*) of the gas = $p_A + p_B + p_C$.

Avogadro's hypothesis : At equal temperature and pressure in equal volumes of all gases there are equal number of molecules.

If at equal temperature and pressure the gas has *V* volume and there be *n* mole gas then

V $\propto$ *n* i.e., volume of the gas is directly proportional to the no. of mole.

ACID, BASE & SALTS

Acid : According to Arrhenius's theory an acid is a compound which dissolved in water to give hydrogen ions (H^+). All Acids contain Hydrogen.

The Chemical formulas of some important Acids

Name of the Acid	*Chemical Formula*
Hydrochloric acid	HCl
Nitric acid	HNO_3
Sulphuric acid	H_2SO_4
Carbonic acid	H_2CO_3
Acetic acid	CH_3COOH
Formic acid	$HCOOH$
Sulphurous acid	H_2SO_3
Nitrous acid	HNO_2
Phosphoric acid	H_2PO_4
Boric acid	H_3BO_3
Hydrobromic acid	HBr
Hydroiodic acid	HI

Chloric acid	$HClO_3$
Tetraboric acid	$H_2B_4O_7$
Hydrocyanic acid	HCN
Oxalic acid	$H_2C_2O_4$
Chromic acid	H_2CrO_4
Dichromic acid	$H_2Cr_2O_7$
Thiosulfuric acid	$H_2S_2O_3$
Pyro-sulphuric acid	$H_2S_2O_7$
Per sulphuric	$H_2S_2O_8$

Base : A base is a compound which dissolved in water to give hydroxide ions (OH^-). The hydroxides of metals which dissolve in water are known as **alkalies**. Thus all soluble hydroxides are **alkalies**.

Indicators of Testing Acids and Bases

Indications	*Acid*	*Base*
Litmus paper	turns blue to red	turns red to blue
Methyl orange	pinkish red	yellow
Phenolphthalein	Colourless	Pink

Salts : A salt is a compound made from an acid when a metal takes the place of the hydrogen in the acid.

pH Scale : The hydrogen ion concentration of any acidic, alkaline, or neutral solution is expressed in term of pH. Thus pH value of any solution is defined on the logrithmic scale as negative of the logarithm of the hydrogen ion (H^+) concentration expressed in gm-molecule per liter.

Thereby $pH = -\log_{10} [H^+]$

pH value and hydrogen ion concentration [H⁺] :

$[H^+]$	1	10^{-2}	10^{-4}	10^{-6}	10^{-7}	10^{-8}	10^{-10}	10^{-12}	10^{-14}
pH	0	2	4	6	7	8	10	12	14

——————————— neutral ———————————

increasing acidity *increasing alkalinity*

Buffer solution : The solution whose acidity or alkalinity does not alter or remain intact after mixing acid or alkali in very small amount then its pH value does not change and it is called buffer solution.

There are two types of buffer solution—

(i) Acidic buffer : The solution which is the mixture composed from any weak acid and its salt is called acidic buffer.

Example : The mixture of the solution of acetic acid and sodium acetate, the mixture of the solution of boric acid and borax etc.

(*ii*) Basic buffer : The solution which is the mixture composed from any weak base and its salt is called basic buffer.

Examples : The mixture of the solution of ammonium hydroxide and ammonium chloride etc.

PERIODIC TABLE

Mendeleev's periodic table

1. Elements are arranged according to the increasing atomic weight.
2. The subgroups A and B are kept under same group.
3. There are 9 groups.
4. There is no any distinct dividing line between metals and non-metals.
5. Ordinary elements and transition elements are not separately exhibited.
6. Elements are not arranged on the basis of electronic configuration due to lack of it at that time.

Mosely's modern periodic table

1. Elements are arranged according to the increasing atomic number.
2. The subgroups A and B are kept separate.
3. There are 16 groups.
4. The places of metals and non-metal are separated and there is a distinctive line of division.
5. Ordinary elements and transition elements are separated.
6. Elements are arranged on the basis of electronic configuration.

Chief characteristics of the period (Modern periodic table)

(*i*) In the periodic table in any period from left to right the metallic properties of the elements decrease, while non-metallic properties increase.

(*ii*) In the periodic table in any period from left to right chemical reactivities of the elements firstly decrease then increase.

(*iii*) In the period the valency of the elements increases from 1 to 4, later diminishes and becomes 0.

(*iv*) In the period the number of valence electrons increase from left to right and increases from 1 to 8.

(*v*) Generally in the period the values of electron affinity increase from left to right.

(*vi*) Also in the period the values of electron negativity of the elements increase from left to right.

(*vii*) The values of ionization potential of the elements increase from left to right in the period.

(*viii*) The size or atomic radius of the elements decreases in the period from left to right.

(*ix*) The basic or alkaline characteristics of the oxides of the elements in the period decrease.

Chief Characteristics of the group (Modern periodic table) :

(*i*) The metallic properties of the elements in the group from top to bottom increase.

(*ii*) The chemical reactivities of the metallic elements increase in the group from top to bottom, while the chemical reactivities of the non-metallic elements decrease in the group from top to bottom.

(*iii*) The valency of the elements of any particular group is same for all elements.

(*iv*) The number of valence electrons are same for all elements kept in a group.

(*v*) The values of the electron affinity of the elements decrease from top to bottom in the group.

(*vi*) Generally the values of electron negativity of the elements in the group decrease from top to bottom.

(*vii*) The values of ionization potential of the elements decrease from top to bottom in the group.

(*viii*) The size or atomic radius of the elements increases from top to bottom in the group.

Chemical formulae, commercial name of chemical compounds

Commercial Name	*Chemical Compounds*	*Chemical formulae*
Common salt	Sodium chloride	$Nacl$
Baking soda	Sodium bicarbonate	$NaHCO_3$
Washing soda	Sodium carbonate	$Na_2CO_3.10H_2O$
Caustic soda	Sodium hydroxide	$NaOH$
Borax	Sodium borate	$Na_2B_4O_7$. $10H_2O$
Globour salt	Sodium sulphate	Na_2SO_4. $10H_2O$
Potash alum	Potassium aluminium sulphate	K_2SO_4. $Al_2(SO_4)_3.24H_2O$
Bleaching powder	Calcium oxy dichloride	$Ca(OCl)$ Cl or $CaOCl_2$
Lime water	Calcium hydroxide	$Ca(OH)_2$

Gypsom	Calcium sulphate	$CaSO_4.2H_2O$
Plaster of paris	Calcium sulphate hemihydrate	$CaSO_4.\ 1/2H_2O$
Chalk or Marble	Calcium carbonate	$CaCO_3$
Laughing gas	Nitrous oxide	N_2O
Letharg	Lead oxide	PbO
Galena	Lead sulphide	PbS
Red vermillian	Lead peroxide	pb_3O_4
Acid of salt	Hydrogen chloride	HCl
	Nitric acid	HNO_3
Water gas	Mixture of carbon monoxide and hydrogen	$CO + H_2$
Bauxite	Hydrates alumina	$Al_2O_3\ .\ 2H_2O$
Solid ice	Solid carbondioxide	CO_2
Lunar caustic	Silver nitrate	$AgNO_3$
Calomel	Mercuric chloride	Hg_2Cl_2
Vermilian	Mercuric sulphide	HgS
Heavy water	Duetereum oxide	D_2O
Heavy hydrogen	Duetereum	D
Silica	Silicon dioxide	SiO_2
Lithopone	Mixture of zinc sulphide and barium sulphate	$ZnS + BaSO_4$
Producer gas	Mixture of carbon monoxide and nitrogen gas	$CO + N_2$
Marsh gas	Methane	CH_4
Vinegar	dilute solution of acetic acid	CH_3COOH
Starch	–	$C_6H_{10}O_5$
TNB	Tri Nitro Benzene	$C_6H_3(NO_2)_3$
Juice of grapes	Glucose	$C_6H_{12}O_6$
Feron	Dichloro difluoro carbon	CF_2CL_2
Urea	Carbamyde	NH_2CONH_2
Chloroform	Tri chloro methane	$CHCl_3$
Iodoform	Tri iodo methane	CHI_3
Pyrine	Carbon tetra chloride	CCl_4
Phenol	Hydroxy benzene or carbolic acid	C_6H_5OH
MIC	Methyl isocyanate	CH_3NC

MULTIPLE CHOICE QUESTIONS

1. A gas behaves like an ideal gas at
A. High pressure and low temperature
B. Low pressure and high temperature
C. High pressure and high temperature
D. Low pressure and low temperature

2. Which of the following quantity is the same for all ideal gases at the same temperature?
A. The kinetic energy of 1 mol
B. The kinetic energy of 1 g
C. The number of molecules in 1 mol
D. Both A and C

3. Which of the following graph represents Boyle's law?

A. 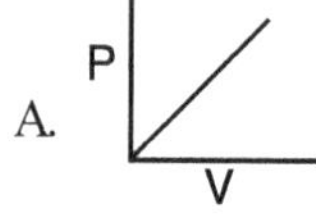

B. 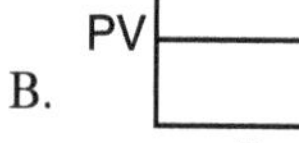

C. 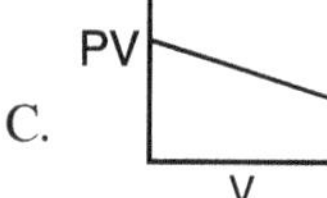

D. 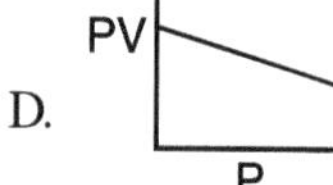

4. Which of the following statements are *correct* on the basis of Charle's law?
A. The volume of an ideal gas can never be zero
B. At zero pressure, all molecular motion ceases in a gas, and it does not exert any pressure on the walls of the container.
C. It is not possible to attain absolute zero.
D. All of these

5. According to the kinetic theory of gases,
A. The pressure exerted by a gas is proportional to the mean square velocity of the molecules.
B. The pressure exerted by the gas is proportional to the root mean square velocity of the molecules.
C. The root mean square velocity is inversely proportional to the temperature
D. Both B and C

6. Indicate which of the following statements are *correct*?

A. At constant temperature, the Kinetic Energy (KE) of all gas molecules will be the same

B. At constant temperature, the Kinetic Energy (KE) of different molecules will be different

C. At constant temperature, the Kinetic Energy (KE) will be greater for heavier gas molecules

D. At constant temperature, the Kinetic Energy (KE) will be less for heavier gas molecules.

7. The temperature at which real gases obey the ideal gas laws over a wide range of pressure is called

A. Critical temperature
B. Inversion temperature
C. Boyle's temperature
D. Reduced temperature

8. Real gases approach ideal gas behaviour at

A. Low temperature and low pressure

B. Low temperature and high pressure

C. High temperature and high pressure

D. High temperature and low pressure

9. According to kinetic theory of gases, for a diatomic molecule

A. The pressure exerted by the gas is proportional to the mean velocity of the molecule.

B. The pressure exerted by the gas is propotional to the root mean square velocity of the molecules.

C. The root mean square velocity of the molecule is inversely proportional to the temperature.

D. The mean translational kinetic energy of the molecules is proportional to the absolute temperature.

10. At constant volume, for a fixed number of moles of a gas, the pressure of the gas increases with rise of temperature due to

A. Increase in average molecular speed

B. Increased rate of collisions amongst molecules

C. Increase in molecular attraction

D. Decrease in mean free path

11. The construction of an electron microscope is based on

A. de Broglie's principle
B. Heisenberg's principle
C. Bohr's theory
D. Rutherford concept

12. Which of the following statements does not make a part of Bohr's model of atom?

A. The electron in the orbit nearest to the nucleus is in the lowest energy.

B. Energy of an electron in an orbit is quantized.
C. Electrons revolve around nucleus in orbits of definite energy.
D. Electron can jump from one orbit to another on its own.

13. The nature of anode rays depends upon
A. Nature of gas filled in the discharge tube
B. Nature of electrode
C. Nature of discharge tube
D. None of these

14. Which of the following is main cause of late discovery of neutron
A. Neutron is highly unstable particle
B. Neutron in nucleus moves very fast
C. Neutron is chargeless particle
D. All of these

15. If a radioactive substance is kept in a vessel and is subjected to very high temperature and pressure, its rate of radioactive disintegration will
A. Increase B. Decrease
C. Remain uncharged D. Decrease very slightly

16. The magnetic quantum number specifies
A. Shape and size of an orbital
B. Distance of an orbital from nucleus
C. Orientations of a sub-shell in the space
D. Number of electrons in an orbit

17. The splitting of atomic spectral lines in the applied electric field is known as
A. Zeeman effect B. Compton effect
C. Stark effect D. Newman effect

18. Rutherford's experiment, on scattering of α-particles, showed for the first time that the atom has
A. Electrons B. Protons
C. Nucleus D. Neutrons

19. Which of the following does not characterise X-rays?
A. The radiation can ionize gases
B. It causes ZnS to fluresence
C. Deflected by electric and magnetic fields
D. Have wavelengths shorter than UV-rays.

20. When greater number of excited hydrogen atoms reach the ground state, then
A. more number of lines are found in Lyman series
B. the intensity of lines in Balmer series increases

C. the intensity of lines in Lyman series increase

D. both the intensity and number of lines in Lyman series increases

21. Which of the following aqueous solutions remain neutral after electrolysis?

A. $CuSO_4$ B. $AgNO_3$

C. K_2SO_4 D. NaCl

22. During the purification of copper by electrolysis

A. The anode are made of copper ore

B. Pure copper is deposited on the cathodes, with evolution of hydrogen at the anode

C. The impurities such as Ag, Au, Zn and Fe go into solution

D. The voltage is carefully controlled to prevent the deposition of Zn and Fe at the cathode

23. In an electrochemical process, a salt bridge is used

A. To maintain electroneutrality in each solution

B. To complete the circuit so that current can flow

C. As an oxidizing agent

D. As a colour indicator

E. A and B

24. Which one of the following statements is not applicable to electrolytic conductors?

A. No products show up at the elctrodes

B. Ions are responsible for carrying the current

C. Show a positive temperature coefficient for conductance

D. A single stream of electrons flows from cathode to anode

25. The electric charge for electrode deposition of one gram equivalent of a substance is

A. One ampere per second B. 96500 coulombs per second

C. One ampere for one hour D. Charge on one mole of electrons

26. One the basis of position in the electrochemical series, the metal which does not displace hydrogen from water and acids is

A. Hg B. Al

C. Pb D. Ba

27. The amount of an ion discharged during electrolysis is not dependent of

A. Resistance of solution

B. Time

C. Current strength

D. Electrochemical equivalent of the element

28. The calomel electrode is a

A. Standard hydrogen electrode
B. Reference electrode
C. Platinum electrode
D. Mercury electrode

29. An unit of charge is

A. Volt
B. Ampere
C. Coulomb
D. None

30. Metals can be prevented from rusting by

A. Connecting iron to more electropositive metal cathodic protection
B. Connecting iron to more electropositive metal anodic protection
C. Connecting iron to less electropositive metal anodic protection
D. Connecting iron to less electropositive metal cathodic protection

31. The rate of a reactant does not depend upon

A. Pressure
B. Temperature
C. Concentration
D. Catalyst

32. For a zero order reaction

A. The reaction rate is double when the initial concentration is doubled
B. The time for half change is half the time taken for completion of the reaction
C. The time for half change is independent of the intial concentration
D. The time for completion of the reaction is independent of the initial concentration.

33. For an endothermic reaction, where ΔH represents the enthalpy of the reaction in kJ/mole the minimum energy for the energy of activation will be

A. Less than ΔH
B. Zero
C. More than ΔH
D. Equal to ΔH

34. Which of the following is not a characteristic of a catalyst?

A. It changes the equilibrium constant
B. It alters the reaction path
C. It increases the rate of reaction
D. It increases the average K.E. of the molecules

35. According to adsorption theory of catalysis, the speed of the reaction increases because

A. The concentration of reactant molecules at the active centres of the catalyst becomes high due to absorption
B. In the process of adsorption the activation energy of the molecules becomes large
C. Adsorption produces heat which increases the speed of the reaction
D. All of these

36. The raw material used in Solvay process for manufacture of sodium carbonate comprises

A. Sodium chloride and carbon dioxide

B. Ammonia and carbon dioxide

C. Sodium chloride, limestone and ammonia

D. Sodium chloride, limestone and carbon dioxide

37. Alkali metal atoms show the oxidation states

A. + 1 B. + 2

C. – 1 D. – 2

38. The degree of hydration of alkali metal ions are in the order

A. $Li^+ > Na^+ > K^+ > Rb^+ > Cs^+$ B. $Li^+ > Rb^+ > Cs^+ > Na^+ > K^+$

C. $Rb^+ > Cs^+ > Li^+ > Na^+ > K^+$ D. $Na^+ > K^+ > Li^+ > Rb^+ > Cs^+$

39. Alkali metals react with hydrogen forming ionic hydrates. The reactivity of alkali metals with hydrogen decreases in the order

A. Li > Na >K > Rb > Cs B. Na > K > Rb > Cs > Li

C. Rb > Cs > Li > Na > K D. Cs > Rb > K > Na > Li

40. Which of the following alkali metals is used in photoelectric cells?

A. Na B. K

C. Li D. Cs

41. A solution of sodium metal in liquid ammonia is blue and is a strong reducing agent due to the presence of

A. Sodium atoms B. Sodium hydride

C. Sodium amide D. Solvated electrons

42. Soda ash is

A. $Na_2CO_3.H_2O$ B. $NaHCO_3$

C Na_2CO_3 D. NaOH

43. Sodium thiosulphate is used in photography to

A. Convert metallic silver to silver salt

B. Reduce silver bromide to silver salt

C. Remove unreduced silver

D. Remove undecomposed AgBr as a soluble silver thiosulphate complex

44. Sodium carbonate reacts with SO_2 in an aqueous medium to give

A. Na_2SO_4 B. $NaHSO_4$

C. Na_2SO_3 D. $NaHSO_3$

45. In a nuclear reactor, molten sodium is used to

A. Absorb neutrons for controlling the chain reaction

B. Absorb the heat generated by nuclear fission

C. Slow down fast neutrons

D. Extract radioisotopes produced in the reactor

46. Addition of excess KCN to an aqueous solution of $CuSO_4$ gives

A. $Cu(CN)_2$
B. $K_2[Cu(CN)_4]$
C. $K_3[Cu(CN)_4]$
D. $K[Cu(CN)_2]$

47. Sodium thiosulphate is prepared by

A. Boiling an Na_2SO_3 solution with S in an acidic medium
B. Boiling an NaOH solution with S
C. Boiling Na_2SO_3 with S in an alkaline medium
D. B & C

48. Dolomite is

A. $MgCO_3$
B. $MgCO_3.CaCO_3$
C. MgO
D. $CaSO_4$

49. Plaster of Paris is

A. $CaSO_4.2H_2O$
B. $(CaSO_4)_2.H_2O$
C. $CaSO_4.MgO$
D. $CaSO_4.5H_2O$

50. Epsom salt is

A. $MgSO_4.7H_2O$
B. $Na_2SO_4.10H_2O$
C. $MgCO_3.CaCO_3$
D. $Al_2O_3.H_2O$

51. The main constituent of bones is

A. CaF_2
B. $CaSO_4$
C. $Ca_3(PO_4)_2$
D. $CaSO_4$

52. In comparison to alkali metals, alkaline earth metals are

A. Less reactive
B. Less basic
C. More reactive
D. Less reducing
E. B & D

53. The most electropositive among the alkaline earth metals is

A. Beryllium
B. Barium
C. Magnesium
D. Calcium

54. The order of solubility of the sulphates of alkaline earth metals in water is

A. Be > Mg > Ca > Sr > Ba
B. Mg > Be >> Ba > Ca > Sr
C. Be > Ca > Mg > Ca >> Sr
D. Mg > Ca > Ba >> Be > Sr

55. Neutrons are produced by

A. Ra
B. Ba
C. Sr
D. Be

56. Which of the following can adsorb largest volume of hydrogen gas?

A. Finely divided platinum
B. Finely divided nickel
C. Colloidal solution of palladium
D. Colloidal Hydroxide

57. A basic oxide will be formed by the element:

A. K
B. S
C. P
D. Kr

58. An acidic oxide is produced by the element:

A. Na
B. C
C. Ca
D. H

59. Which among the following is most reactive metal:

A. aluminium
B. copper
C. tin
D. calcium

60. The least reactive metal among the following is:

A. sodium
B. silver
C. copper
D. lead

61. The metals which can produce amphoteric oxides are:

A. sodium and aluminium
B. zinc and potassium
C. calcium and sodium
D. aluminium and zinc

62. The elements whose oxides can turn litmus solution blue are:

A. carbon and sulphur
B. sodium and carbon
C. potassium and magnesium
D. magnesium and sulphur

63. A metal less reactive and another metal more reactive than hydrogen are:

A. aluminium and lead
B. iron and magnesium
C. copper and tin
D. copper and mercury

64. An element reacts with oxygen to give a compound with a high melting point. This compound is also soluble in water. The element is likely to be:

A. calcium
B. carbon
C. silicon
D. iron

65. Which of the following metal exists in the liquid state?

A. Na
B. Ag
C. Cr
D. Hg

66. Two metals lighter than water are

A. Al, Mg
B. Al, Mn
C. Pb, Mg
D. CO, Mn

67. Temporary hardness of water is due to the presence of

A. Magnesium bicarbonate
B. Calcium chloride
C. Magnesium sulphate
D. Calcium carbonate

68. Which statement is true?

A. Aluminium is the most abundant metal in the earth's crust.

B. Oxygen is the most abundant non-metal in the earth's crust.

C. Ammonia (NH_3) and methane (CH_4) are covalent hydrides
D. All of these

69. Which of the following is a metal?
A. Potassium
B. Sulphur
C. Argon
D. Diamond

70. Which of the following has metallic as well as non-metallic character?
(*i*) Arsenic
(*ii*) Antimony
(*iii*) Lead
A. (*i*) Only
B. (*ii*) Only
C. (*i*) and (*ii*) Only
D. (*i*), (*ii*) and (*iii*)

71. Malachite is an ore of
A. copper
B. iron
C. zinc
D. silver

72. Cryolite is an ore of
A. aluminium
B. iron
C. silicon
D. None of these

73. Copper glance is represented by
A. Cu_2S
B. Cu_2O
C. $CuCO_3$
D. None of these

74. Saturated solution of sodium chloride is
A. crystal
B. brine
C. lime stone
D. soda ash

75. Which metal can melt even in our hand?
A. Gallium
B. Sodium
C. Nickel
D. None of these

76. Which of the following is used in making printer's ink, shoe polish, black varnish and point?
A. Lamp black
B. Bone black
C. Carbon black
D. None of these

77. Which is an example of amorphous carbon?
A. charcoal
B. coke
C. lamp black
D. All of these

78. A gas which burns with blue flame is
A. CO
B. O_2
C. N_2
D. CO_2

79. Diamonds are brought to the earth's surface by
A. igneous rocks
B. kimberlite rocks
C. sedimentary rocks
D. None of these

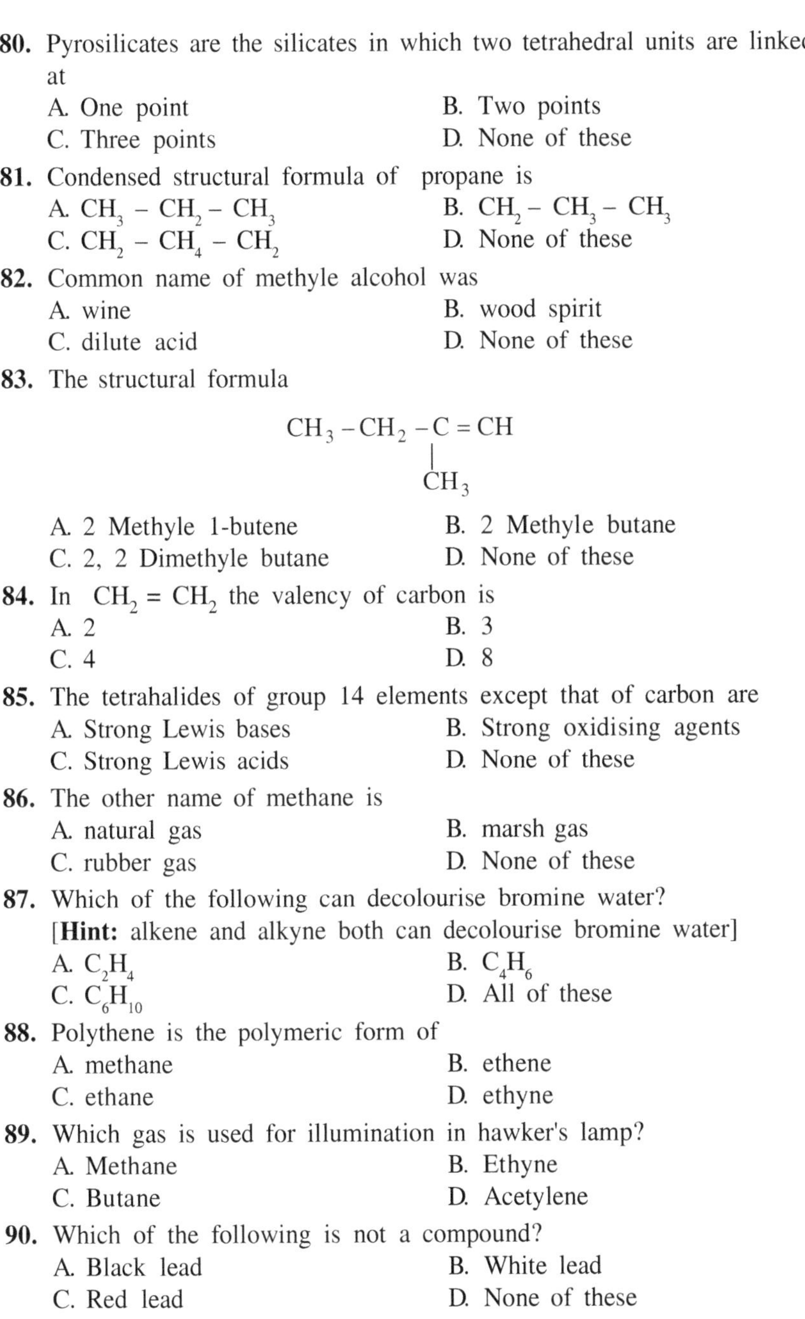

80. Pyrosilicates are the silicates in which two tetrahedral units are linked at

A. One point B. Two points

C. Three points D. None of these

81. Condensed structural formula of propane is

A. $CH_3 - CH_2 - CH_3$ B. $CH_2 - CH_3 - CH_3$

C. $CH_2 - CH_4 - CH_2$ D. None of these

82. Common name of methyle alcohol was

A. wine B. wood spirit

C. dilute acid D. None of these

83. The structural formula

$$\begin{array}{c} CH_3 - CH_2 - \underset{\displaystyle CH_3}{\underset{|}{C}} = CH \end{array}$$

A. 2 Methyle 1-butene B. 2 Methyle butane

C. 2, 2 Dimethyle butane D. None of these

84. In $CH_2 = CH_2$ the valency of carbon is

A. 2 B. 3

C. 4 D. 8

85. The tetrahalides of group 14 elements except that of carbon are

A. Strong Lewis bases B. Strong oxidising agents

C. Strong Lewis acids D. None of these

86. The other name of methane is

A. natural gas B. marsh gas

C. rubber gas D. None of these

87. Which of the following can decolourise bromine water?
[**Hint:** alkene and alkyne both can decolourise bromine water]

A. C_2H_4 B. C_4H_6

C. C_6H_{10} D. All of these

88. Polythene is the polymeric form of

A. methane B. ethene

C. ethane D. ethyne

89. Which gas is used for illumination in hawker's lamp?

A. Methane B. Ethyne

C. Butane D. Acetylene

90. Which of the following is not a compound?

A. Black lead B. White lead

C. Red lead D. None of these

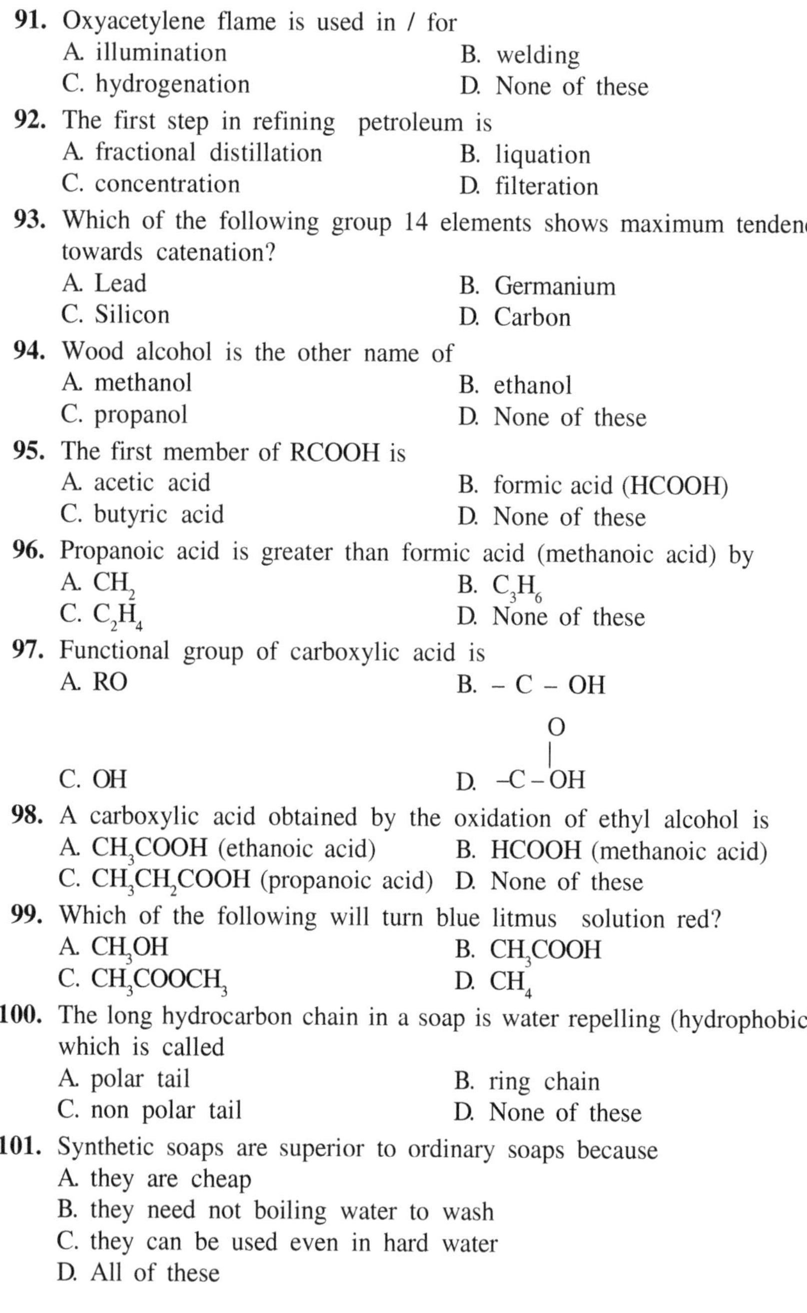

91. Oxyacetylene flame is used in / for

A. illumination
B. welding
C. hydrogenation
D. None of these

92. The first step in refining petroleum is

A. fractional distillation
B. liquation
C. concentration
D. filteration

93. Which of the following group 14 elements shows maximum tendency towards catenation?

A. Lead
B. Germanium
C. Silicon
D. Carbon

94. Wood alcohol is the other name of

A. methanol
B. ethanol
C. propanol
D. None of these

95. The first member of RCOOH is

A. acetic acid
B. formic acid (HCOOH)
C. butyric acid
D. None of these

96. Propanoic acid is greater than formic acid (methanoic acid) by

A. CH_2
B. C_3H_6
C. C_2H_4
D. None of these

97. Functional group of carboxylic acid is

A. RO
B. – C – OH
C. OH
D. $-C-\overset{\overset{O}{|}}{OH}$

98. A carboxylic acid obtained by the oxidation of ethyl alcohol is

A. CH_3COOH (ethanoic acid)
B. HCOOH (methanoic acid)
C. CH_3CH_2COOH (propanoic acid)
D. None of these

99. Which of the following will turn blue litmus solution red?

A. CH_3OH
B. CH_3COOH
C. CH_3COOCH_3
D. CH_4

100. The long hydrocarbon chain in a soap is water repelling (hydrophobic), which is called

A. polar tail
B. ring chain
C. non polar tail
D. None of these

101. Synthetic soaps are superior to ordinary soaps because

A. they are cheap
B. they need not boiling water to wash
C. they can be used even in hard water
D. All of these

102. Detergents are sodium salts of a long chain

A. benzene sulphonic acids
B. alkyl hydrogen sulphate
C. Both of these
D. None of these

103. Which glass has the highest percentage of lead

A. Soda glass
B. Jena glass
C. Flint glass
D. Pyrex glass

104. Rubber is hardened for making tyres by

A. adding H_2
B. adding carbon black
C. saturating it
D. All of these

105. Preshrink cotton is called

A. natural cotton
B. terycotton
C. sanforized cotton
D. None of these

106. The element with atomic number 26 will be found in group

A. 2
B. 8
C. 6
D. 10

107. Which of the following ion is not isoelectronic with O^{2-}

A. N^{3-}
B. Na^+
C. F^-
D. Ti^+

108. Which gases were unknown at the time of Medeleef?

A. Oxygen
B. Noble gases
C. CO_2
D. None of these

109. Of the given alkali metals, the one with smallest size is

A. Rb
B. Cs
C. K
D. Na

110. The valency of noble gases is generally

A. zero
B. one
C. three
D. two

111. Which of the following iso-electronic ions has lowest I.E.?

A. K^+
B. Ca^{2+}
C. Cl^-
D. S^{2-}

112. Which of the following is the property of a group?

A. The elements in the same group have similar outer electronic configuration
B. Their atomic size increases on moving down the group
C. Their melting and boiling points changes in a regular manner
D. All of these

113. Which of the following is an alkaline earth metal?

A. Magnesium
B. Calcium
C. Both of these
D. None of these

114. An element X belongs to the group III and IInd period of the periodic table. Which property will it have

A. Liquid most metallic
B. Gaseous and basic
C. Solid non-metallic
D. Solid less metallic

115. Element X has electronic configuration 2,8,1 and Y has 2,8,7. Which one will have high electron affinity?

A. X
B. Y
C. Both X and Y
D. None of these

116. In the table calcium lies above barium. Which one is more reactive?

A. Calcium
B. Barium
C. Both are equally reactive
D. Nothing could be predicted

117. Which element of 2nd period forms most acidic oxide?

A. fluorine
B. nitrogen
C. boron
D. carbon

118. Which of the following non-metals belongs to the halogen family?

A. Fluorine
B. Chlorine
C. Bromine
D. All of these

119. Which of the following statements is true?

A. Cations are smaller in size than neutral atoms
B. Horizontal rows in the table are called periods
C. On going across the periods atomic size of the element decreases
D. All to these

120. Which element has least atomic diameter?

A. F
B. Fe
C. Cl_2
D. Na

121. Atmospheric pollutant is

A. CO_2
B. CO
C. O_2
D. N_2

122. Biodegradable pollutant is

A. Domestic waste
B. DDT
C. Mercury salt
D. Aluminium foil

123. Water pollution is mainly due to

A. Agricultural discharges
B. Sewage and other wastes
C. Industrial effluents
D. All of the above

124. Photochemical smog always contain

A. O_3
B. CO
C. CO_2
D. CH_4

125. Result of ozone hole is

A. Green house effect
B. UV rays reaching the earth
C. Global warming
D. Acid rain

126. Atmosphere of big/meteropolitian cities is polluted most by

A. Automobile exhaust
B. Pesticide residue
C. Household waste
D. Radioactive fall out

127. Carbon monoxide is a pollutant as it

A. Inactivates nerves
B. Inhibits glycolysis
C. Combines with oxygen
D. Combines with haemoglobin and replaces O_2

128. Chief air pollutant which is likely to deplete ozone layer is

A. Oxygen
B. Fluorsive
C. Nitrogen oxides and chlorofluorocarbons
D. All of them

129. Gas released during *Bhopal Gas tragedy* was

A. Potassium isothiocyanate
B. Calcium chloride
C. Methyl isocyanate
D. Hydrogen sulphide

130. Air pollutant that produce photochemical oxidants include

A. CO_2, CO & SO_2
B. Nitrous oxide, nitric oxide & nitric acid
C. Oxygen, chlorine & nitric acid
D. Ozone, chlorine & sulphur dioxide

131. Chlorofluorocarbon release a chemical harmful to ozone is

A. Iodine
B. Hydrocarbons
C. Chorine
D. Fluorine

132. DDT is

A. Biodegradable pollutant
B. Nondegradable pollutant
C. An antibiotic
D. None of these

133. Most hazardous metal pollutant of automobile exhaust is

A. Mercury
B. Lead
C. Cadmium
D. Copper

134. Increasing skin cancer and high mutation rate are due to

A. Acid rain
B. Ozone depletion
C. CO pollution
D. CO_2 pollution

135. Environmental pollution affects
A. Biotic components
B. Plants only
C. Man only
D. Biotic & abiotic components of environment

136. Sewage water is purified by
A. Micro orgnisms
B. Light
C. Fishes
D. Aquatic plants

137. Ultra violet light causes
A. Formation of pyrimidines
B. Sticky metaphores
C. Sticky anaphores
D. Destruction of hydrogen bonds between complementary DNA strands.

138. Burning of fossil fuels is the main source of pollution due to
A. Nitrogen oxide
B. Nitric oxide
C. Nitrous oxide
D. Sulphur dioxide

139. Ultraviolet radiation from sun causes a reaction that produces
A. Fluorides
B. Carbon monoxide
C. Sulphur dioxide
D. Ozone

140. Which of the following is **not** a pollutant from exhaust of motor vehicle?
A. Hydrocarbons
B. Fly ash
C. NO_x
D. CO

141. *Taj Mahal* is threatened by pollution from
A. Chlorine
B. Sulphur dioxide
C. Hydrogen
D. Oxygen

142. Which one is the most toxic?
A. Carbon
B. SO_2
C. CO
D. CO_2

143. The electronic structures of four elements A, B, C and D are
A. $1s^2$
B. $1s^2, 2s^2\ 2p^2$
C. $1s^2, 2s^2\ 2p^5$
D. $1s^2\ 2s^2\ 2p^6$
The tendency to form electrovalent bond is greatest in (A) (B) (C) (D).

144. Covalent compounds are soluble in

A. Polar solvents

B. Non-polar solvents

C. Concentrated acids

D. Strong bases only

145. Which of the following is purest covalent bond?

A. H – Cl　　B. Cl – Cl

C. C – Cl　　D. Na – Cl

146. The compound which contains both ionic and covalent bonds is

A. CH_4　　B. H_2

C. KCN　　D. KCl

147. The maximum covalency of an element of the atomic number 7 is

A. 2　　B. 3

C. 4　　D. 5

148. In a double bond connecting two atoms, there is a sharing of

A. 2 electrons　　B. 4 electrons

C. 1 electron　　D. All electrons

149. Iron is tougher than sodium because

A. Iron atoms are smaller

B. Iron atoms are more closely packed

C. Metallic bonds are stronger in iron

D. All of the above

150. The mode of hybridization of carbon in CO_2 is

A. sp　　B. sp^2

C. sp^3　　D. None

ANSWERS

1	**2**	**3**	**4**	**5**	**6**	**7**	**8**	**9**	**10**
B	D	B	D	D	A	C	D	D	C
11	**12**	**13**	**14**	**15**	**16**	**17**	**18**	**19**	**20**
A	D	A	C	C	C	C	C	C	C
21	**22**	**23**	**24**	**25**	**26**	**27**	**28**	**29**	**30**
C	D	E	D	D	A	A	B	C	A
31	**32**	**33**	**34**	**35**	**36**	**37**	**38**	**39**	**40**
A	B	C	A	A	C	A	A	A	D
41	**42**	**43**	**44**	**45**	**46**	**47**	**48**	**49**	**50**
D	C	D	D	B	C	D	B	B	A

51	52	53	54	55	56	57	58	59	60
C	E	D	A	A	C	A	B	D	B
61	**62**	**63**	**64**	**65**	**66**	**67**	**68**	**69**	**70**
D	C	C	A	D	A	A	D	A	C
71	**72**	**73**	**74**	**75**	**76**	**77**	**78**	**79**	**80**
A	A	A	B	A	A	D	A	B	A
81	**82**	**83**	**84**	**85**	**86**	**87**	**88**	**89**	**90**
A	B	A	C	C	B	D	B	D	A
91	**92**	**93**	**94**	**95**	**96**	**97**	**98**	**99**	**100**
B	A	D	A	B	C	D	A	B	C
101	**102**	**103**	**104**	**105**	**106**	**107**	**108**	**109**	**110**
C	C	C	B	C	B	D	B	D	A
111	**112**	**113**	**114**	**115**	**116**	**117**	**118**	**119**	**120**
D	D	C	C	B	B	A	D	D	A
121	**122**	**123**	**124**	**125**	**126**	**127**	**128**	**129**	**130**
B	A	D	A	B	A	D	C	C	B
131	**132**	**133**	**134**	**135**	**136**	**137**	**138**	**139**	**140**
B	B	B	B	D	A	D	D	D	B
141	**142**	**143**	**144**	**145**	**146**	**147**	**148**	**149**	**150**
B	C	C	B	B	C	C	B	C	A

❍❍❍

1308

GENERAL KNOWLEDGE

INDIA

Facts About India

(1) **Area** = 32, 87,263 sq. km.

(2) **Land Frontier** = 15, 200 km

(3) **Total Coast line** = 7516.6 km

(4) **Population (2011 census)** = 1,21,08,54,977 (62,32,70,258 males and 58,75,84,719 females)

(5) **Average Density of Population:** 382 per sq. km.

(6) **Total Literacy** = 73.0%

(i) Male literacy = 80.9%

(ii) Female literacy = 64.6%

(7) **India is** -

(i) 7th largest country in the world in area.

(ii) 2nd largest populous country in the world.

(iii) home of more than 16 per cent of world population (2011 census) and accounts for 2.42 per cent of the total world area.

(8) **India's neighbour's**

(i) in the north – China, Nepal and Bhutan

(ii) in the east – Myanmar (Burma)

(iii) Bangladesh lies wedged between India's north-eastern States and West Bengal

(iv) in the west and north-west – Pakistan

(v) in the south – Sri Lanka

(9) India's States and Union Territories

(i) India has 29 States and 7 Union Territories.

STATES OF INDIA

State	Capital	Principal Language(s)	Area in (sq. km)	Population 2011
1	2	3	4	5
1. Andhra Pradesh	Hyderabad	Telugu, Urdu	1,60,205	4,93,86799
2. Arunachal Pradesh#	Itanagar	Monpa, Miji, etc.	83,743	1383727
3. Assam	Dispur[1]	Assamese, Bengali	78,438	31205576
4. Bihar	Patna	Hindi	94,163	104099452
5. Chhattisgarh	Raipur	Hindi	1,35,192	25545198
6. Goa	Panaji	Konkani, Marathi	3,702	1458545
7. Gujarat	Gandhi Nagar	Gujarati	1,96,024	60439692
8. Haryana	Chandigarh	Hindi	44,212	25351462
9. Himachal Pradesh	Simla	Hindi, Pahari	55,673	6864602
10. Jammu & Kashmir	Srinagar[2]	3	2,22,236[4-5]	12541302
11. Jharkhand	Ranchi	Hindi	79,714	32988134
12. Karnataka	Bengaluru	Kannada	1,91,791	61095297
13. Kerala	Thiruvananthapuram	Malayalam	38,863	33406061
14. Madhya Pradesh	Bhopal	Hindi	3,08,000	72626809
15. Maharashtra	Mumbai	Marathi	3,07,713	112374333
16. Manipur	Imphal	Manipuri	22,327	2855794
17. Meghalaya	Shillong	Khasi, Garo, English	22,429	2966889
18. Mizoram	Aizawl	Mizo, English	21,081	1097206
19. Nagaland	Kohima	6	16,579	1978502
20. Odisha	Bhubaneswar	Odiya	1,55,707	41974218
21. Punjab	Chandigarh	Punjabi	50,362	27743308
22. Rajasthan	Jaipur	Hindi, Rajasthani	3,42,239	68548437
23. Sikkim	Gangtok	7	7,096	610577

24.	Tamil Nadu	Chennai	Tamil	1,30,058	72147030
25.	Tripura	Agartala	8	10,491	3673917
26.	Uttarakhand	Dehradun (Provisional)	Hindi	53,483	10086292
27.	Uttar Pradesh	Lucknow	Hindi, Urdu	2,40,928	199812341
28.	West Bengal	Kolkata	Bengali	88,752	91276115
29.	Telangana	Hyderabad	Telugu, Urdu	1,14,840	3,51,93,978
UNION TERRITORIES					
1.	Andaman & Nicobar Islands	Port Blair	9	8,249	380581
2.	Chandigarh	Chandigarh	Hindi, Punjabi, English	114	1055450
3.	Dadar & Nagar Haveli	Silvassa	Gujarati and Hindi	491	343709
4.	Daman & Diu	Daman	Gujarati	112	243247
5.	Delhi	Delhi	Hindi, Urdu, Punjabi	1,483	16787941
6.	Lakshadweep	Kavaratti	Malayalam	32	64473
7.	Pudducherry	Pudducherry	Tamil, French, Telugu English and Malayalam	490	1247953

1. Pragjyotishpur will be the new capital of Assam; **2.** In winter the capital shifts to Jammu; **3.** Kashmiri, Dogri, Gujri, Urdu, Balti, Dadri, Pahari, Ladakhi, Punjabi; **4.** Includes 78,114 sq km under illegal occupation of Pakistan, 5,180 sq. km illegaly handed over by Pakistan to China and 37,555 sq km under illegal occupation of China; **5.** The population figure excludes population of area under unlawful occupation of Pakistan and China. **6.** Angami, Ao, Chang, Konyak, Lotha, Sangtam, Semaand Chakhesang; **7.** Bhutia, Nepali, Lepcha and Limbu; **8.** Bengali, Kakborak and Manipuri, **9.** Hindi, Nicobarese, Bengali, Malayalam, Tamil & Telugu. # This State enjoys special status on traditional and customary laws.

Note: The figures are based on Final Census of India 2011.

States:

(i)	Largest in population	: Uttar Pradesh (about 19.9 crore)
(ii)	Smallest in population	: Sikkim (about 6 lakh)
(iii)	Largest in area	: Rajasthan (about 3.4 Lakh sq. km)
(iv)	Smallest in area	: Goa (3702 sq. km)
(v)	Highest density of population	: Bihar (1106)
(vi)	Lowest density of population	: Arunachal Pradesh (17)
(vii)	First to achieve 100% rural electrification	: Haryana
(viii)	First to achieve total Literacy	: Kerala
(ix)	Lowest percentage of literacy	: Bihar (61.8%)
(x)	With high number of females than males	: Kerala (1084 females for 1000 males)

Union Territories

(i)	Largest in population	: Delhi (over 1.6 crore)
(ii)	Smallest in population	: Lakshadweep (over 64 thousand)
(iii)	Largest in area	: Andaman & Nicobar Islands (8249 sq. km)
(iv)	Smallest in area	: Lakshadweep (32 sq. km)
(v)	Highest density of population	: Delhi (11,320)
(vi)	Lowest density of population	: Andman & Nicobar Islands (46)
(vii)	Highest percentage of Literacy	: Lakshadweep (91.8%)
(viii)	Lowest percentage of Literacy	: Dadra & Nagar Haveli (76.2%)

National Flag:

(1) It is horizontal tricolour.

(2) Three equal horizontal strips : *(a)* Deep saffron at the top
: *(b)* White in the middle
: *(c)* Dark Green at the bottom.

(3) Ratio of width to length : 2:3.

(4) In the centre of the white stripe : a wheel in navy blue.

(5) Number of spokes in the wheel : 24.

(6) The wheel is a replica of the wheel on the capital of the Ashoka Pillar at Sarnath.

(7) The National Flag was adopted *(i)* by the Constituent Assembly of India, *(ii)* on July 22, 1947.

(8) Its use and display are regulated by a code.

National Emblem:

(1) National Emblem is an adaptation from the Sarnath Lion Capitol of Ashoka.
(2) It depicts three lions.
(3) A wheel appears in relief in the centre of the abacus with a bull on the right and a horse on the left.
(4) Below the abacus appear *Satyameva Jayate* in the devanagari script.
(5) *Satyameva Jayate* has been taken from Mundaka Upanishad.
(6) *Satyameva Jayate* means "Truth Alone Triumphs."
(7) The National Emblem was adopted by the Government of India on January 26, 1950.

National Anthem:

(1) *Jana-gana-mana* composed by Rabindranath Tagore is our national anthem.
(2) The Constituent Assembly of India adopted it as the national anthem on January 24, 1950.
(3) It was first sung on December 27, 1911 at the Calcutta Session of the Indian National Congress.
(4) It was first published under caption 'Bharat Vidhata' in January 1912 in the magazine named *'Tatva Bodhini'*.
(5) Playing time of the full version of the national anthem is approximately 52 seconds.
(6) *Vande Mataram*, composed by Bankim Chandra Chatterjee has an equal status with *Jana-gana-mana.*
(7) It was first sung at the 1896 session of the Indian National Congress.
(8) This song occurs in the novel *Anand Math,* written by Bankim Chandra Chatterjee.

National Calendar

(1) India's National Calendar is based on *Saka* Era.
(2) It was adopted and introduced on March 22, 1957.
(3) It has a normal year of 365 days.
(4) *Chaitra* is the first month and *Phalguna* is the last month of the year.
(5) 1 *Chaitra* falls on March 22 in a normal year and on March 21 in a leap year.

National Animal and National Bird

(1) Tiger is the national animal of India.
(2) Peacock is the national bird of India.

History of India – Some Facts

1. The discovery of the Indus Valley Civilisation was made in 1921.

2. The main centres of the Indus Valley Civilisation were – Harappa, Mohenjodaro, Kali Bangan, Luthal, etc.

3. The Aryans came into India from Central Asia and settled first in *Sapta Sindhu.*
4. The Indus Valley Civilisation was urban whereas the Aryan Civilisation was rural.
5. The Vedas are four: *(i)* Rig Ved, *(ii)* Yajur Ved, *(iii)* Sam Ved, and *(iv)* Atharva Ved.
6. Of the four Vedas, Rig Ved is the oldest.
7. Jainism and Buddhism were founded during the 6th century B. C.
8. Jainism was founded by Lord Mahavir whereas Buddhism was founded by Lord Buddha.
9. Buddha was born at Lumbini.
10. Buddhism got maximum state patronage from Ashoka.
11. Buddha delivered his first sermon at Sarnath (near Varanasi)
12. Megasthenese was the Greek ambassador to the Court of Chandragupta Maurya.
13. The capital of the Mauryan Empire was Pataliputra.
14. Kanishka was the most important Kushana ruler who ruled from Purushpur (Peshawar).
15. Gupta Period is known as the Golden Age of ancient India.
16. Ashoka vowed never to wage a war (after his victory in Kalinga War) and converted himself to Buddhism.
17. Chinese Buddhist monk Hiuen Tsang visited India during the reign of Harshavardhana.
18. Sind (in India) was the first victim of Arab invasion.
19. Mahmud Ghaznavi plundered Somnath temple in 1026.
20. Mohammad Ghori defeated Prithviraj Chauhan in the second battle of Tarain.
21. Qutb-ud-din Aibak was the first Muslim ruler of India.
22. Razia Begum was the first woman who sat on the throne of Delhi Sultanate.
23. The founder of the Mughal Empire in India was Babar.
24. First battle of Panipat (1526) laid the foundation of Mughal rule in India.
25. Akbar was the greatest of the conquerors, administrators and empire builders amongst the Mughal rulers.
26. *Din-e-Ilahi* was a religious sect founded by Akbar.
27. Akbar founded Fatehpur Sikri and constructed beautiful buildings there.

28. Shahjehan died as a prisoner in the jail.

29. Aurangzeb had to face a great challenge from the Marathas.

30. The English established their first factory at Surat in 1615.

31. Portuguese were the first European traders to come to India.

32. Robert Clive was the real founder of British power in India.

33. It was Robert Clive who set up double government in Bengal.

34. Lord Wellesley followed the policy of Subsidiary Alliance to make Indian rulers as subordinate allies of the British power in India.

35. Lord William Bentinck abolished the *Sati* system.

36. During the tenure of William Bentinck English was made medium of instruction in India.

37. The last Governor General of British India was Lord Canning.

38. Lord Dalhousie sowed the seeds of 1857 Sepoy Mutiny.

39. Doctrine of Lapse was used against the Indian rulers by Lord Dalhousie.

40. Warren Hastings introduced the Permanent Settlement of land revenue in Bengal.

41. Lord Curzon partitioned Bengal in 1905.

42. The Sepoy Mutiny of 1857 started from Meerut on May 10, 1857.

43. The glorious leaders of the Revolt of 1857 were – Nana Saheb, Rani Lakshmi Bai of Jhansi, Mughal Emperor Bahadur Shah II Zafar, Kunwar Singh and Tantia Tope.

44. Indian National Congress was founded by A.O. Hume in 1885.

45. Netaji Subhash Chandra Bose founded the Indian National Army (INA) at Singapore.

46. Jallianwala Bagh massacre took place at Amritsar in 1919.

47. Indian National Congress put forth the demand of Complete Independence in 1929.

48. Swadeshi movement became very popular during mass agitation against Partition of Bengal (1905).

49. Gandhiji's Dandi March is associated with the salt law.

50. 'Quit India' slogan was given by the Indian National Congress in 1942.

51. Indian Muslim League was founded in 1906.

52. India achieved Independence in 1947 during the tenure of Lord Mountbatten.

53. With the Partition of India the British Rule ended; two "Independent States" India and Pakistan were created; Mountbatten became the first Governor-General of Free India in 1947.

54. Assassination of Mahatma Gandhi (January 30, 1948) by Nathu Ram Godse; Kashmir acceded to India; C. Rajgopalachari took over as the first Indian Governor-General (1948).

55. Integration of the Princely States into the Indian Union (1948-50).

56. Indian Constitution was signed and adopted on November 26, 1949.

57. India became Sovereign Republic (January 26, 1950). Sardar Patel died (December 15, 1950); Dr. Rajendra Prasad became the first President of India (1950).

India's Armed Forces

1. President of India is the Supreme Commander of the Armed Forces of India.
2. Union Cabinet is responsible for national defence.
3. Operational control of the armed forces is exercised by the Ministry of Defence.
4. The armed forces consist of three services namely: *(i)* Army, *(ii)* Navy and *(iii)* Air Force.
5. The three services function under their respective Chiefs of Staff namely: *(i)* Chief of the Army Staff, *(ii)* Chief of the Naval Staff and *(iii)* Chief of the Air Staff.

Army

1. Army Headquarters is in New Delhi.
2. Army is organised into Six operational Commands, *viz.* *(i)* Southern, *(ii)* Eastern, *(iii)* Western, *(iv)* Central, *(v)* Northern and *(vi)* South Western.
3. Army has also a training Command in Shimla (Himachal Pradesh).
4. Each Command is under a General Officer Commanding-in-Chief.
5. Army consists of a number of arms and services such as *(i)* Armoured Corps, *(ii)* Regiment of Artillery, *(iii)* Corps of Air Defence, *(iv)* Army Aviation Corps, *(v)* Corps of Engineers/Signals, *(vi)* Infantry, *(vii)* Army Medical/ Nursing Corps, *(viii)* Army Education Corps, *(ix)* Corps of Military Police etc.

Navy

1. Navy Headquarters is in New Delhi.
2. The Navy has 3 commands – *(i)* Western, *(ii)* Eastern, and *(iii)* Southern.
3. Each Command is headed by a Flag Officer Commanding-in-Chief.
4. The Western and the Eastern Commands are operational commands with their fleets while the Southern Command is responsible for all training activities of Indian Navy.

5. Fleets of Indian Navy comprise warships, submarines, aircraft carriers, etc.
6. There are two major naval bases at Mumbai and Vishakhapatnam.
7. Coast Guard was constituted in 1978 with its headquarters at New Delhi. It is responsible for defence and security of India's marine interests and assets.

Air Force

1. Air Force Headquarters is in New Delhi.
2. Air Force is organised into 5 operational Commands — *(i)* Western Air Command, *(ii)* South-Western Air Command, *(iii)* Central Air Command, *(iv)* Eastern Air Command, and *(v)* Southern Air Command.
3. There are two functional commands — *(i)* Maintenance Command, and *(ii)* Training Command.
4. Air Force fleet consists of fighter bombers, fighters, Transport, Interceptors and logistic aircrafts and helicopters. Strike aircrafts are MIG-21, MIG-23, MIG-25, MIG-27 and Jaguar, Air Defence Aircrafts are MIG 29, Mirage-2000. Transport fleet consists of AN-32, Boeing - 737, HS-748. Helicopters are — MI-8, MI-17, Chetak/Cheetah.
5. Chetak/Cheetah helicopters are manufactured by HAL.

Commissioned Ranks in Defence Services

Army	*Navy*	*Air Force*
General	Admiral	Air Chief Marshal
Lieutenant-General	Vice-Admiral	Air Marshal
Major-General	Rear-Admiral	Air Vice-Marshal
Brigadier	Commodore	Air Commodore
Colonel	Captain	Group Captain
Lieutenant-Colonel	Commander	Wing Commander
Major	Lt. Commander	Squadron Leader
Captain	Lieutenant	Flight Lieutenant
Lieutenant	Sub-Lieutenant	Flying Officer

Non-Commissioned and Junior Commissioned Ranks in Defence Services

Army	*Navy*	*Air Force*
Subedar Major	Master Chief Petty Officer I	Master Warrant Officer
Subedar	Master Chief Petty Officer II	Warrant Officer
Naik Subedar	Chief Petty Officer	Junior Warrant Officer
Havildar	Petty Officer	Sergeant
Naik	Leading Sailor I	Corporal
Lance Naik	Leading Sailor II	Leading Aircraftsman
Jawan	Sailor	Aircraftsman

Training Institutions:

(i) ***Training Institutions for Army:*** National Defence Academy, Khadakwasla; The National Defence College, New Delhi; The Indian Military Academy, Dehra Dun; Defence Service Staff College, Wellington; Armed Forces Medical College, Pune; The Officers Training School, Chennai; Army Ordnance Corps School, Jabalpur; Army Defence College, Pune; College of Defence Management, Secunderabad; The School of Artillery, Deolali; Military College of Telecommunication Engineering, Mhow and The College of Military Engineering, Kirkee.

(ii) ***Training Institutions for Navy:*** INS Shivaji, Lonavala; INS Valsura, Jamnagar; INS Vendruthy, Kochi; INS Chilka, Odisha; INS Satavahan, Vishakhapatnam; INS Garuda, Kochi; INS Mandovi, Goa; INS Dronacharya, Kochi and INS Hamla, Malad (Mumbai).

(iii) ***Training Institutions for Air Force*:** Air Force Academy, Hyderabad; Fighter Training Wing, Hakim; Elementary Flying School, Bidar; Air Force Technical College, Jalahalli; College of Air Warfare, Secunderabad; Air Force Administrative College, Coimbatore and Institute of Aviation Medicine, Bengaluru.

Defence Production Undertakings: There are eight public sector enterprises under the Department of Defence Production:- 1. Hindustan Aeronautics Ltd. (HAL); 2. Bharat Electronics Ltd. (BEL); 3. Bharat Earth Movers Ltd. (BEML); 4. Mazagon Dock Ltd. (MDL); 5. Garden Reach Shipbuilders & Engineers Ltd. (GRSE); 6. Goa Shipyard Ltd. (GSL); 7. Bharat Dynamics Ltd. (BDL); 8. Mishra Dhatu Nigam Ltd. (MIDHANI).

Second Line of Defence:

(a) Territorial Army: Organised in 1949.

(b) Border Security Force: Set up in 1965.

(c) Home Guards : Organised in 1962.

(d) N.C.C. (National Cadet Corps)

N.C.C., the premier youth organisation of the country was established in 1948 (15th July). Its motto is "Unity and Discipline" and its aims are:

1. To develop qualities of character, courage, comradeship, discipline, leadership, secular outlook, spirit of adventure, sportsmanship.
2. NCC is headed by a Director General NCC, located at New Delhi.
3. NCC consist of 3 divisions—(i) Senior division for college student, (ii) Junior division for secondary school boys and girls, and (iii) Girls division.
4. The senior and junior divisions are composed of three wings: Army, Navy and Air Force.

Miscellaneous Facts

Indian Missiles: *(i)* Prithvi – Surface to surface
(ii) Nag – Anti-Tank
(iii) Trishul – Surface to air
(iv) Akash – Surface to air
(v) Agni – Air to air
(vi) Brahmos – Supersonic Cruise Missile (It is a product of India-Russia Cooperation)

Main Battle Tank: Arjun

First Indigenous Tank: Vijayanta

Multi-barrel Rocket System: Pinaka

Indian Transport System

1. Railways

(i) Indian Railway System is our country's biggest national undertaking.

(ii) It is largest in Asia and the second largest in the world.

(iii) As on March 31, 2017, the total route length was 67,368 km.

(iv) Indian Railway is organised into 17 zones.

(v) Gatiman Express is the fastest train in India with a permissible speed of 160 km per hour.

(vi) The first Shatabdi Express was introduced on July 10, 1988 between New Delhi and Jhansi.

(vii) *Locker on Wheels* is a service introduced in Feb. 1995 for passengers of Shatabdi Express trains with 100% guaranteed delivery on the same day.

(viii) There are six main production units under the Indian Railways: (1) Chittaranjan Locomotive Works (West Bengal), (2) Diesel Locomotive Works (Varanasi, Uttar Pradesh), (3) Diesel Component Works (Patiala, Punjab), (4) Integral Coach Factory (Perambur, Tamil Nadu), (5) Rail Coach Factory (Kapurthala, Punjab), (6) Wheel & Axles Plant, Yelahanka (Bangalore, Karnataka).

Miscellaneous Facts

1. The first train in India was introduced between Mumbai and Thana, a stretch of 34 km on April 16, 1853.
2. The first electric train was opened in February 1925 on Mumbai sub-urban railway on Mumbai VT-Kurla branch line.
3. As on 31-3-2017 the electrified route was about 47.09 per cent of the route km.
4. The largest rail platform in India is at Gorakhpur (1355.4 mt.), Uttar Pradesh.

5. The longest railway tunnel is Banihal–Qazigund tunnel (J&K, 11 km).
6. At present Indian Railways have 17 zones.
7. The largest marshalling yard is at Mughalsarai.
8. The third class in the Indian Railways was abolished in 1974.
9. The Railways have more than 1.32 million employees.
10. The steam engines are being phased out and diesel and electric locomotives are being introduced.
11. India's first Metro Railway was opened in Calcutta (now Kolkata) on Oct. 24, 1984.
12. *Palace on Wheels* is Rajasthan's prestigious tourist train.
13. Computer reservation is 95%.

2. Shipping

1. Shipping Corporation of India came into being in 1961.
2. Four major shipyards in the public sector are: *(i)* Garden Reach Shipbuilders & Engineers Ltd, Kolkata, *(ii)* Mazagon Dock Ltd, Mumbai, *(iii)* Hindustan Shipyard Ltd, Vishakhapatnam, *(iv)* Cochin Shipyard, Cochin.
3. The major ports on Western Coast are: Kandla, Mumbai, Mormugao, New Mangalore, Cochin and Nhava Sheva (Jawaharlal Nehru Port).
4. The major ports on Eastern Coast are: Tuticorin, Chennai, Vishakhapatnam, Paradip and Kolkata-Haldia.
5. In respect of shipping tonnage, India ranks second in Asia and fifteenth in the world.
6. The first passenger ship built in India is Harshavardhana.

3. Civil Aviation:

1. All air routes and air companies in India were nationalised in 1953.
2. Air India Corporation and Indian Airlines Corporation were established in 1953.
3. In 1994, these Corporations were converted into public limited companies and private sector was allowed in the field.
4. Jet Airways, Jetlite Airlines, Go Airlines, Kingfisher Airlines, Spicejet Ltd, Paramount Airways and IndiGo are private carriers.
5. In India main International Airports are:

   (i) Mumbai, *(ii)* Kolkata, *(iii)* Delhi, *(iv)* Chennai, *(v)* Thiruvananthapuram, *(vi)* Ahmedabad.
6. Vayudoot was set up in January 1981.
7. Helicopter Corporation of India (*Pavan Hans*) was inaugurated on October 15, 1985.

Communications

1. Akashvani and Doordarshan

1. All India Radio was named *Akashvani* in 1957.

2. Akashvani covers 91.37% area and 99.13% of the population of India.

3. *Vividh Bharati* service was started in 1957.

4. Sponsored Programmes were introduced in May 1970.

5. Television in India was started in Delhi on September 15, 1959.

6. Doordarshan was separated from Akashvani in 1976.

7. Doordarshan turned commercial from January 1, 1976.

8. Satellite technology came into operation in 1975.

9. Doordarshan National Programme was introduced on August 15, 1984.

10. International Channel of Doordarshan was started on March 14, 1995.

2. Post-Telecommunications

(i) Postal Department was set up in 1854.

(ii) Money Order service was introduced in 1880.

(iii) Air Mail Service started in 1911.

(iv) PIN Code system started in 1972.

(v) Speed Post was introduced in 1986.

(vi) Satellite Money Order service started in December 1994.

Scientific Research

(i) Atomic Energy Commission was set up in 1948.

(ii) Atomic Power Stations are located at : *(a)* Tarapore (Maharashtra), *(b)* Rawathbhata (Rajasthan), *(c)* Kalpakkam (Tamil Nadu), *(d)* Narora (UP), *(e)* Kakrapara (Gujarat), *(f)* Kaiga (Karnataka) and *(g)* Kudankulam (Tamil Nadu).

(iii) The first heavy water plant was set up in 1961 in Nangal.

(iv) India coducted her first underground atomic explosion at Pokhran (Rajasthan) on May 18, 1974.

(v) Space Commission was set up in 1972.

(vi) Squadran Leader Rakesh Sharma became the first Indian to go into Space on April 3, 1984.

(vii) Department of Ocean Development was set up in July 1981.

(viii) *Dakshin Gangotri and Maitri* are the two stations set up by India in Antarctica.

Planning

(1) Planning Commission was constituted in March 1950. 'NITI Aayog' replaced it from January 1, 2015.

(2) Prime Minister is the Chairman of the NITI Aayog.

(3) The Five-Year Plans are finally approved by the National Development Council.

(4) The 12th Five-Year Plan started in 2012.

(5) The First Five-Year Plan started in 1951.

Finance

(1) Finance Commission is appointed by the President of India.

(2) Finance Commission is appointed every 5 years.

(3) All currency notes are issued by the Reserve Bank of India.

(4) One rupee notes are issued by the Ministry of Finance.

(5) Decimal system of coins was introduced in India from April 1, 1957.

(6) 14 major banks were nationalised in July 1969.

(7) Reserve Bank of India is the Central Bank of India.

(8) The largest commercial bank in public sector is State Bank of India.

(9) Life Insurance Corporation of India was set up in September 1956.

(10) Unit Trust of India (UTI) was set up in 1964.

Wildlife Sanctuaries and National Parks

Wildlife Sanctuaries & National Parks	*State*
Kanha National Park	Madhya Pradesh
Shivpuri National Park	Madhya Pradesh
Kaziranga Sanctuary	Assam
Manas Sanctuary	Assam
Hazaribagh National Park	Jharkhand
Ghana Bird Sanctuary	Rajasthan
Sariska Game Sanctuary	Rajasthan
Corbett National Park	Uttarakhand
Chandraprabha Sanctuary	Uttar Pradesh
Rangathittoo Bird Sanctuary	Karnataka
Bandipur Sanctuary	Karnataka
Vendanthangal Bird Sanctuary	Tamil Nadu
Mudumalai Sanctuary	Tamil Nadu
Periyar Sanctuary	Kerala

Eravikulam Rajmallay National Park	Kerala
Sultanpur Bird Sanctuary	Haryana
Todoba National Park	Maharashtra
Semlipal National Park	Odisha
Nal Sarovar Bird Sanctuary	Gujarat
Rohia National Park	Himachal Pradesh
Jaldapara Sanctuary	West Bengal

Agriculture, Industries and Minerals

I. Agriculture

Crop	*Chief Producers*
Wheat	Punjab, Haryana and UP
Rice	West Bengal
Rubber	Kerala
Tea	Asom and West Bengal
Cotton	Maharashtra
Sugar	UP
Tobacco	Andhra Pradesh
Cashew nut	Kerala
Pulses	UP, Bihar and Madhya Pradesh

II. Industries

Places	*Associated with Industries*
Khetri	Copper
Raniganj & Jheria	Coal
Durgapur	Steel
Ahmedabad	Cotton Textiles
Barauni	Oil Refinery
Nepanagar	Newsprint
Sindri	Fertilisers
Anand	Dairy
Avadi	Heavy Vehicle Factory
Dalmia Nagar	Cement
Digboi	Oil wells
Katni	Cement
Koyali	Petro-Chemicals
Narora	Atomic Power Station
Nangal	Fertilisers

Nasik	Currency Note Press
Obra	Thermal Power Station
Pimpri	Antibiotic Drugs
Renukoot	Aluminium plant
Sivakasi	Match Box and Fire works
Hoshangabad	Security Paper Mills

III. Minerals

Minerals	*States*
Coal	Jharkhand
Iron	Jharkhand
Mica	Jharkhand
Gold	Karnataka (Kolar)
Uranium	Jharkhand
Diamond	Madhya Pradesh (Panna)

Constitution of India

(1) Constitution of India came into force on January 26, 1950.

(2) President of India is elected for a term of five years.

(3) Sessions of Parliament are summoned by President.

(4) Vice-President of India is the ex-offico Chairman of Rajya Sabha.

(5) Lok Sabha is elected for a term of five years.

(6) Speaker, Lok Sabha is elected by the members of Lok Sabha.

(7) Council of Ministers is appointed by the President on the recommendation of the Prime Minister.

(8) The Union Council of Ministers is responsible to Lok Sabha.

(9) Rajya Sabha is a permanent body and cannot be dissolved.

(10) Members of Rajya Sabha have a term of 6 years.

(11) Judges of Supreme Court are appointed by the President.

(12) State Governors are appointed by the President.

President

The President is the Constitutional head of the Republic of India. He is more or less the titular head of the executive. Really speaking, he is the constitutional head but not the real executive.The real power is vested in the hands of the Council of Ministers.

Qualifications: (*i*) Indian citizen, (*ii*) age not less than 35 years, (*iii*) should have qualification for election to Lok Sabha, (*iv*) should not hold any office of profit, (*v*) should not be a Member of Parliament or State Legislature.

Powers: He makes appointments to all the constitutional posts. He can address either House of Parliament and dissolve Lok Sabha. All Bills passed by Parliament must receive his assent to become an Act. He issues ordinances when Parliament is not in session. No Money Bill can be introduced in Lok Sabha without his recommendation. He can grant pardon, reprieve or remit punishment and he can commute death sentences, can declare national emergency, state emergency and financial emergency.

Term and Emolument: The President holds the office for a period of five years. He is eligible for re-election. He draws a fixed salary. He is also entitled to rent free official residence called Rashtrapati Bhawan.

Vice-President

The Vice-President acts as the ex-officio Chairman of the Council of States (Rajya Sabha). He is elected by an electoral college consisting of the members of both Houses of Parliament in accordance with the system of proportional representation by means of the single transferable vote. He must be a citizen of India, not less than 35 years of age, and should be eligible for election as a member of the Council of States. Disputes in connection with election of a president or a vice-president are to be a dealt with in accordance with Article-71. Such disputes shall be decided by the Supreme Court.

Prime Minister

The constitution lays down that there shall be a Council of Ministers headed by the Prime Minister to aid and advise the President in the exercise of his functions. The Prime Minister is the head of the Cabinet. Other Ministers are appointed by the President on his advice. He is the leader of the majority party in the Lok Sabha.

First in India

First Person to get Nobel Prize	Rabindranath Tagore (1913)
First President of Indian Republic	Dr. Rajendra Prasad
First Prime Minister	Pt. Jawaharlal Nehru

First Woman Prime Minister	Smt. Indira Gandhi
First Woman President	Pratibha Patil
First President of the Indian National Congress	W.C. Banerjee
First Woman Governor of a State	Smt. Sarojini Naidu
First Woman Chief Minister of a State	Smt. Sucheta Kripalani
First Indian President of the International Court of Justice	Dr. Nagendra Singh
First Indian in the British Parliament	Dadabhai Naoroji
First Field Marshal	S.H.F.J. Manekshaw
First Indian to conquer Mt. Everest	Tenzing Norgay
First Indian Cosmonaut	Rakesh Sharma
First Indian to address UN General Assembly in Hindi	Atal Bihari Vajpayee
First Indian to get Special Oscar Award	Satyajit Ray
First Indian Satellite	Aryabhatta
First person to get Bharat Ratna	C. Rajagopalachari
First Woman to get Bharat Ratna	Smt. Indira Gandhi
First Governor-General of Free India	C. Rajagopalachari

Largest, Highest, Biggest & Longest in India

Highest Gate way	Buland Darwaja (Fatehpur Sikri, Agra)
Highest Dam	Tehri Dam on Bhagirathi river in Uttarakhand (855 f.)
Highest Tower (minar)	Qutub Minar (Delhi)
Highest Waterfall	Gersopa Waterfall (Karnataka)
Highest Peak	K-2*
Highest Civilian Award	Bharat Ratna
Highest Rainfall	Mowsyrnam near Cherapunji (Meghalaya)
Highest Literacy	Kerala
Largest lake (Fresh Water)	Wular lake (Kashmir)
Largest Dome	Gol Gumbaj (Bijapur)
Biggest Cattle Fair	Sonepur Fair (Bihar)
Biggest Mosque	Jama Masjid (Delhi)
Longest Platform	Gorakhpur (Uttar Pradesh)
Longest River Bridge	Bhupen Hazarika Bridge (Assam)
Oldest Mountain Range	Aravali Range

Important Architectures, Monuments and Places of Interest

Meenakshi Temple	Madurai (Tamil Nadu)
Khajuraho Temple	Madhya Pradesh

* Highest peak in the world is Mount Everest, which is in Nepal, K-2 is the second highest peak in the world.

Lingaraja Temple	Bhubaneswar (Odisha)
Jagannath Temple	Puri (Odisha)
Gateway of India	Mumbai (Maharashtra)
Buland Darwaja	Fatehpur Sikri (UP)
Victory Tower	Chittorgarh (Rajasthan)
Gol Gumbaj	Bijapur (Karnataka)
Golden Temple	Amritsar (Punjab)
Dilwara Temples	Mt. Abu (Rajasthan)
Sarnath Temple	Varanasi (UP)
Rameshwaram	Tamil Nadu
Amarnath Temple	Jammu & Kashmir
Sambhar Lake	Rajasthan
Dal Lake	Srinagar (Jammu & Kashmir)
Thumba (Rocket Launching Station)	Kerala
Sriharikota (Satellite Launching Station)	Andhra Pradesh
Ajanta and Ellora Caves	Aurangabad (Maharashtra)
Taj Mahal	Agra (UP)
Char Minar	Hyderabad (Telangana)
Sabarmati	Ahmedabad (Gujarat)
Sanchi (Stupa)	Madhya Pradesh
Vivekanand Rock	Tamil Nadu (near Kanyakumari)

Samadhis

Name	***Associated with***
Rajghat	Mahatma Gandhi
Shantivan	Jawahar Lal Nehru
Samta Sthal	Jagjivan Ram
Vijayghat	Lal Bahadur Shastri
Shakti Sthal	Indira Gandhi
Vir Bhumi	Rajiv Gandhi

Important Towns on River Banks

Town	***River***	***Town***	***River***
Agra	Yamuna	Ahmedabad	Sabarmati
Allahabad	Confluence of Ganga & Yamuna	Kolkata	Hooghli
		Cuttack	Mahanadi
Ayodhya	Saryu	Kanpur	Ganga

Town	River	Town	River
Kota	Chambal	Delhi	Yamuna
Serivrangapatnam	Cauveri	Hardwar	Ganga
Ujjain	Chhipra	Jabalpur	Narmada
Vijayawada	Krishna	Dibrugarh	Brahamputra
Sambalpur	Mahanadi	Srinagar	Jhelum
Nasik	Godavari	Surat	Tapti
Mathura	Yamuna	Varanasi	Ganga
Lucknow	Gomati	Guwahati	Brahamputra
Patna	Ganga	Vijaywada	Krishna

Nicknames of Rivers and Cities

Bengal's Sorrow	Damodar River
City of Palaces	Kolkata
Gateway of India	Mumbai
Land of Five Rivers	Punjab
Pink City	Jaipur
Blue Mountains	Nilgiri Hills

Important Days

National Youth Day	January 12
Army Day	January 15
Republic Day	January 26
Martyr's Day	January 30
National Science Day	February 28
Independence Day	August 15
Teacher's Day	September 5
Mahatma Gandhi's Birthday	October 2
Air Force Day	October 8
Energy Conservation Day	October 14
National Intergration Day	October 31
Children's Day	November 14
Navy Day	December 4
Flag Day	December 7

Books and Authors

Ain-e-Akbari	Abul Fazl
Anand Math	Bankim Chandra Chatterjee

Arthasastra	Kautilya
Chidambara	Sumitranandan Pant
Devdas	Sarat Chandra Chatterjee
Discovery of India	Jawaharlal Nehru
Geet Govind	Jaya Dev
Geetanjali	Rabindranath Tagore
Godan	Munshi Prem Chand
Idols	Sunil Gavaskar
India Divided	Dr. Rajendra Prasad
India Wins Freedom	Abul Kalam Azad
Kamayani	Jaishankar Prasad
Mahabharat	Ved Vyas
My Experiments with Truth	Mahatma Gandhi
Ramayan	Valmiki
Ram Charit Manas	Tulsidas
Saket	Maithili Sharan Gupta
Pancha Tantra	Vishnu Sharma

Important Slogans & Quotations

Slogans

Dilli Chalo	Netaji Subhash Chandra Bose
Jai Jawan Jai Kisan	Lal Bahadur Shastri
Garibi Hatao	Indira Gandhi
Quit India	Mahatma Gandhi

Quotations

Swarajya is my birth right and I shall have it.	*Bal Gangadhar Tilak*
Give me blood, I shall give you freedom.	*Subhas Chandra Bose*

Popular Names

Popular Name	*Real Name*
Iron Man	Sardar Vallabhbhai Patel
Bapu, Father of Nation	Mahatma Gandhi
Chachaji	Jawaharlal Nehru
Gurudev	Rabindranath Tagore
Lokmanya	Bal Gangadhar Tilak
Netaji	Subhas Chandra Bose
Punjab Kesari	Lala Lajpat Rai

Popular Name	*Real Name*
Mahamana	Madan Mohan Malviya
Baba Saheb	Dr. B.R. Ambedkar
Grand Old Man of India	Dada Bhai Naoroji
Lok Nayak	Jay Prakash Narain
Nightingale of India	Sarojini Naidu
Bal, Pal, Lal	Bal Gangadhar Tilak, Bipin Chandra Pal, Lala Lajpat Rai

Festivals (Regional)

Festival	*State*
Teej	Rajasthan
Vaisakhi	Punjab and Haryana
Ganesh Chaturthi Puja	Maharashtra
Durga Puja	West Bengal
Onam	Kerala
Pongal	Tamil Nadu and Andhra Predesh
Lohri	Punjab & Haryana
Bhageli Bihu	Assam
Ugadi	Karnataka

Popular Dances

Bharat Natyam	Tamil Nadu
Kathakali	Kerala
Kathak	North India
Manipuri	Manipur
Odissi	Orissa
Kuchipudi	Andhra Pradesh
Bhangra	Punjab
Bihu	Assam
Garba	Gujarat
Ghoomar	Rajasthan

National Honours & Awards

I. Civilian Awards

1. **Bharat Ratna:** This is India's highest civilian award. It is given for exceptional work in art, literature, science, sport and recognition of public service

of the highest order. Government servants are not eligible for it.

2. **Padma Vibhushan:** This award is given for exceptional and distinguished service in any field, including service rendered by Government servants.
3. **Padma Bhushan:** This award is given for distinguished service of a high order in any field, including service rendered by Government servants.
4. **Padma Shri:** This award is given for distinguished service in any field, including service rendered by Government servants.

II. Gallantry Awards

1. **Param Vir Chakra:** The highest award for bravery or some daring and pre-eminent act of valour of self-sacrifice in the presence of the enemy, whether on land, at sea or in the air.
2. **Mahavir Chakra:** It is the second highest decoration and is awarded for acts of conspicuous gallantry in the presence of the enemy, whether on land, at sea or in the air.
3. **Vir Chakra:** It is the third in order of awards given for acts of gallantry in presence of enemy, whether on land, at sea or in the air.
4. **Ashok Chakra:** This medal is awarded for the most conspicuous bravery or some daring or pre-eminent act of valour or self-sacrifice on land, at sea or in the air but not in the presence of enemy.
5. **Vishistha Sewa Medal:** It is awarded to personnel of all the three Services in class I, II and III in recognition of distinguished service of the "most exceptional" and "exceptional" and a "high" order respectively. Prefixes *Parma* and *Ati* added before first two categories of medals respectively.
6. **Jeewan Raksha Padak:** Awarded for meritorious acts or a series of acts of human nature displayed in saving life from drowning, fire and rescue operations in mines etc.

III. Other awards

Awards	***Related to***
Jnanpith Award	Outstanding contribution to Indian Literature.
Dada Saheb Phalke Award	Outstanding contribution to Indian cinema (films).
Arjuna Awards	Given to sportspersons who distinguish themselves in different sports disciplines.
Dronacharya Awards	Given to outstanding Indian Sports Coaches.
Bhatnagar Awards	Given for important contribution to any field of science.
Krishi Pandit Award	It is given to agriculturist showing maximum per acre production.

Sports

Cups and Trophies

Cricket: Ranji Trophy—National Championship, C.K. Naidu Trophy, Asia Cup, Ashes (Australia-England), Baria Trophy (Inter University), Benson & Hedges, Sharjah Cup, Nehru Gold Cup.

Hockey: Rangaswamy Trophy—National Championship, Agha Khan Cup, Indira Gold Cup, Jawaharlal Nehru Gold Cup, Obaidullah Gold Cup, Sultan Ajlan Shah Cup, Beighton Cup, Champions Trophy, Lady Ratan Tata Trophy (Women), Sindhya Gold Cup, Asia Cup.

Football: Santosh Trophy—National Championship, Durand Cup, DCM Trophy, IFA Shield, Rovers Cup, Subroto Mukherji Cup (Inter School), Scissors Cup, Federation Cup, Kalinga Cup, Airlines Gold Cup, Merdeka, Asia Cup, Jules Rimet Trophy—World Cup.

Badminton: Rahimtoola Cup, Chadha Cup, Thomas Cup—World Championship Men, Uber Cup—World Championship Women.

Table Tennis: Corbillion Cup (Women), Asia Cup, Swaythling Cup (Men).

Lawn Tennis: Davis Cup, Wimbledon Trophy.

Golf: Walker Cup.

Billiards: Arthur Walker Trophy.

Sport Terms

Badminton: Mixed doubles; Deuce; Drop; Smash; Let; Foot work; Setting.

Base Ball: Pitcher; Put out; Strike; Home; Bunt.

Billiards: Cue; Jigger; Pot; Break; In Baulk; In Off; Corom; Cannons.

Boxing: Upper cut; Round; Punch; Bout; Knock down; Hitting below the belt; Ring.

Bridge: Finesse; Dummy; Revoke; Grand Slam; Little Slam; No Trump; Rubber.

Chess: Bishop, Gambit; Checkmate; Stalemate.

Cricket: L.B.W. *(leg before wicket)*; Creases, Popping-creases; Stumped; Bye; Leg-Bye; Googly; Hat-trick; Maiden over; Drive; Bowling; Duck; Follow on; No ball; Leg Break; Gulley; Silly point; Cover point; Hit-wicket; Late-cut; Slip; Off-spinner; Leg-spinner; In-swing; Night watchman.

Football: Off side; Block; Drop-kick; Penalty-kick (or *goal kick*); Corner-kick; Free-kick; Dribble; Thrown-in; Foul.

Golf: Boggy; Foursome; Stymic; Tee; Put; Hole; Niblic; Caddie; Links; The green; Bunker.

Hockey: Carried; Short Corner; Bully; Sticks; Off side; Roll in; Striking Circle; Under-cutting; Dribble.
Horse racing: Jockey; Punter.
Polo: Bunker; Chukker; Mallet.
Tennis: Back hand drive; Volley; Smash; Half-volley; Deuce; Service; Let; Grand Slam.

Facts About UNO

- UNO officially came into existence on October 24, 1945.
- UNO headquaters are located at New York.
- UN Charter was signed on June 26, 1945 by 50 countries at San Francisco.
- Objectives of the UN are:-
  (1) Security, (2) Welfare, (3) Protection of Human Rights
- UN Flag is light blue in colour and emblazoned in white in its centre is the UN symbol – a polar map of the world embraced by twin olive branches open at the top.
- UN is financed by the contibution from member countries.
- UN membership is open to all peace-loving countries. New members are admitted by the General Assembly on the recommendation of the Security Council.
- The six major organs of the UNO are:
  (1) General Assembly
  (2) Security Council
  (3) Economic and Social Council
  (4) Trusteeship Council
  (5) International Court of Justice
  (6) Secretariat
- The General Assembly meets once a year.
- The General Assembly elects its President for a year.
- The General Assembly passes the entire budget of the UN.
- The Security Council has 15 members – 5 permanent members and 10 non-permanent members.
- The permanent members of the Security Council are – USA, UK, Russia, France and China.
- The non-permanent members of the Security Council are elected by the General Assembly for a term of 2 years.

- The right to veto is available to only 5 permanent members of the Security Council.
- Presidency of the Security Council is held for one month in rotation by member states in the English alphabetical order of their names.
- The Secretary General of the UNO is appointed on the recommendation of the Security Council.
- The International Court of the Justice has 15 Judges elected by the General Assembly and the Security Council sitting independently.
- The term of office of the Judges of the International Court of Justice is 9 years.
- The seat of the International Court of Justice is the Hague (Netherlands).
- The official languages of the UN are – English, French, Chinese, Russian, Arabic and Spanish. However, the languages mostly used are English and French.
- The International Labour Organisation (ILO) was established in 1919. Its headquarters are located at Geneva (Switzerland).
- The Food and Agriculture Organisation (FAO) has its headquarters at Rome (Italy).
- The United Nations Educational, Scientific and Cultural Organisation (UNESCO) with its headquarters at Paris (France) seeks to promote peace through international collaboration in education for all.
- Taiwan is not member of the UNO.
- At present 193 countries are members of the UNO.

Years Observed by the UNO

1972: International Book Year; ***1973:*** Copernicus Year; ***1974:*** World Population Year; ***1975:*** International Women's Year; ***1979:*** International Year of the Child; ***1981:*** International Year of Disabled; ***1983:*** World Communication Year; ***1985:*** International Youth Year; ***1986:*** International Year of Peace; ***1987:*** International Year of Shelter for the Homeless; ***1990:*** International Literacy Year; ***1992:*** International Space Year; ***1993:*** International Year for World's Indigenous People; ***1994:*** International Year of Family; ***1995:*** International Year of Tolerance; ***1999:*** International Year of Older Persons; ***2000:*** International Year of the Culture of Peace; ***2001:*** Internation Year of Volunteer; ***2002:*** International Year of Ecotourism; ***2003:*** International year of Fresh Water; ***2004:*** International year of Rice; ***2005:*** International year of Sport and Physical Education; ***2006:*** International year of deserts and desertification; ***2008:*** International Year of Potato; ***2009:*** International Year of Astronomy; ***2010:*** International Year of Bio-Diversity; ***2011:*** International Year of Forest; ***2012:*** International Year of Cooperatives; ***2013:***International Year of Water Cooperation; ***2014:*** International Year of Family Farming; ***2015:*** International Year of Soils; ***2016:*** International Year of Pulses; ***2017:*** International Year of Sustainable Torism for Development; ***2019:*** International Year of Indigenous Languages.

National Games of Some Countries

USA	Baseball
Australia	Cricket
Canada	Ice Hockey
Spain	Bull Fighting

Britain	Cricket
India	Hockey
Japan	Jujitsu

– Olympic Games are held every four years.

– Asian Games are held every four years.

Capitals & Currencies of Countries

Country	*Capital*	*Currency*
Afghanistan	Kabul	Afghani
Algeria	Algiers	Dinar
Angola	Luanda	New Kwanza
Argentina	Buenos Aires	Peso
Austria	Vienna	Euro
Azerbaijan	Baku	Ruble
Bangladesh	Dhaka	Taka
Belgium	Brussels	Euro
Bhutan	Thimpu	Ngultrum
Bosnia	Sarajevo	Dinar
Brazil	Brasillia	Cruzeiro
Bulgaria	Sofia	Lev
Byelorussia	Minsk	Ruble, Zaichik
Cambodia	Phnom-Penh	Riel
Canada	Ottawa	Dollar
Chile	Santiago	Peso
China	Beijing	Yuan
Colombia	Bogota	Peso
Congo	Brazzaville	Franc
Croatia	Zegerb	Dinar
Cuba	Havana	Peso
Cyprus	Nicosia	Pound
Czech	Prague	Crown
Denmark	Copenhagen	Krone
Egypt	Cairo	Pound
Ethiopia	Addia Ababa	Birr
Finland	Helsinki	Euro
France	Paris	Euro

Country	*Capital*	*Currency*
Germany	Berlin	Euro
Ghana	Accra	Cedi
Greece	Athens	Euro
Hong Kong	Victoria	Dollar
Hungary	Budapest	Forints
India	New Delhi	Rupee
Indonesia	Jakarta	Rupiah
Iran	Tehran	Rials
Iraq	Baghdad	Dinar
Ireland	Dublin	Euro
Israel	Jerusalem	Shekel
Italy	Rome	Euro
Jamaica	Kingston	Dollar
Japan	Tokyo	Yen
Jordan	Amman	Dinar
Kazakhstan	Alma Ata	Ruble
Kenya	Nairobi	Shilling
Korea (S)	Seoul	Won
Korea (N)	Pyongyang	Won
Kuwait	Kuwait City	Dinar
Laos	Vientiane	Kip
Lebanon	Beirut	Pound
Libya	Tripoli	Dinar
Malaysia	Kuala Lumpur	Ringgit
Maldives	Male	Rufiyya
Mauritius	Port Louis	Rupee
Mexico	Mexico City	Peso
Morocco	Rabat	Dirham
Mozambique	Maputo	Metical
Myanmar (Burma)	Nay Pyi Taw	Kyat
Nepal	Kathmandu	Rupee
Netherlands	Amsterdam	Euro
New Zealand	Wellington	Dollar
Nigeria	Abuja	Naira
Norway	Oslo	Kroner
Oman	Muscat	Rial

Country	*Capital*	*Currency*
Pakistan	Islamabad	Rupee
Phillippines	Manila	Peso
Poland	Warsaw	Zloty
Portugal	Lisbon	Euro
Romania	Bucharest	Leu
Russia	Moscow	Ruble
Saudi Arabia	Riyadh	Rial
South Africa	Capetown (Legislative) Pretoria (Administrative)	Rand
Spain	Madrid	Euro
Sri Lanka	Colombo	Rupee
Sweden	Stockholm	Krona
Switzerland	Berne	Swiss Francs
Syria	Damascus	Pound
Taiwan	Taipei	Dollar
Tanzania	Dodoma	Shilling
Thailand	Bangkok	Baht
Turkey	Ankara	Lira
United Arab Emirates	Abu Dhabi	Dirham
U.K.	London	Pound Sterling
U.S.A.	Washington	Dollar
Uzbekistan	Tashkent	Ruble
Vietnam	Hanoi	Dong
Zimbabwe	Harare	Dollar
Zaire	Kinshasa	Zaire
Zambia	Lusaka	Kwacha

Nicknames of Countries, Lakes and Cities

China's Sorrow	Hwang-Ho
Cockpit of Europe	Belgium
Dark Continent	Africa
Empire City	New York
Eternal City/City of Seven Hills	Rome
Forbidden City	Lhasa (Tibet)
Gift of the Nile	Egypt
Hermit Kingdom	Korea

Holy Land	Jerusalem (Palestine)
Island of Cloves	Zanzibar
Key to the Mediterranean	Gibraltar
Land of Maple Leaf/Lillies	Canada
Land of the Rising Sun	Japan
Land of the Thousand Lakes	Finland
Land of Golden Fleece	Australia
Land of Kangaroo	Australia
Land of Midnight Sun	Norway
Land of the White Elephants	Thailand
Manchester of the Orient	Osaka (Japan)
Playground of Europe	Switzerland
Queen of the Adriatic	Venice (Italy)
Roof of the world	Pamirs
Sickman of Europe	Turkey
Sugar Bowl of the World	Cuba
Venice of the North	Stockholm (Sweden)

Important Days

Women's Day, International	March 8
Consumers' Rights Day, World	March 15
Disabled Day, World	March 15
Health Day, World	April 7
May Day, World	May 1
Red Cross Day, World	May 8
Commonwealth Day	May 24
No Tobacco Day, World	May 31
Environment Day, World	June 5
International Yoga Day	June 21
International Day against Drug abuse and illicit Trafficking	June 26
Population Day, World	July 11
Hiroshima Day	August 6
Literacy Day, World	September 8
Ozone Day, World	September 16
Tourism Day, World	September 27
Habitat Day, World	October 3
Standards Day, World	October 14

Food Day, World	October 16
U.N. Day, World	October 24
Human Rights Day, World	December 10

Important Towns on River Banks

Town	*River*	*Town*	*River*
Alexandria	Nile	Lisbon	Tagus
Bangkok	Chao Phraya	London	Thames
Baghdad	Tigris	Madrid	Menzanares
Belgrade	Danube	Moscow	Moskwa
Berlin	Spree	New York	Hudson
Bonn	Rhine	Paris	Seine
Budapest	Danube	Prague	Vltava
Buenos Aires	La Plata	Quebec	St. Lawrence
Cairo	Nile	Rome	Tiber
Dublin	Liffey	St. Louis	Mississippi
Karachi	Indus	Sydney	Darling
Khartoum	Nile	Vienna	Danube
Lahore	Ravi	Warsaw	Vistula
Leh	Indus	Washington	Potomac

Major Producers of Crops, Minerals and Industrial Goods

Items of Production	*Country*
Aluminium	China
Coal	China
Coffee	Brazil
Copper	Chili
Cotton	China
Gold	China
Grapes	Italy
Iron ore	Australia
Jute	India, Bangladesh
Manganese	South Africa
Diamond	Russia
Rice	China

Items of Production	*Country*
Rubber	Thailand
Silver	Mexico, Peru
Steel	China
Sugar	Brazil
Tea	China, India
Tin	China
Wheat	China, India
Wool	Australia
Mica	China

First in the World

First Chinese visitor to India	Fahien
First foreign invader of India	Alexander, the Great (Greek)
First person to climb Mt. Everest	Tenzing Norgay (Indian)
First atom bomb dropped at	Hiroshima (Japan)
First man in the space	Yuri Gagarin (former USSR)
First woman in the space	Valentina Tereshkova (former USSR)
First person to land on the moon	Neil Armstrong (USA)
First person to climb Mt. Everest twice	Nawang Gombu
First President of the USA	George Washington
First woman Prime Minister	Sirimavo Bandaranaike (Sri Lanka)
First person to swim across English Channel	Mathew Webb
First woman to swim across English Channel	Gertrude Caroline Ederle
First woman to climb Mt. Everest	Junko Tabei (Japan)
First test-tube Baby	Louise Brown (UK; 1978)
First person to reach South Pole	R. Amundsen (Norway)
First person to reach North Pole	Robert Peary (USA)

Famous Books and Authors

Aesop's Fables	Aesop
Comedy of Errors, Julius Caesar, Merchant of Venis, Hamlet, As you Like it	William Shakespeare
Apple Cart, Doctor's Dilemma	G.B. Shaw
A Tale of Two Cities	Charles Dickens

Das Kapital	Karl Marx
Good Earth	Pearl S. Buck
Indica	Megasthenese
Light of Asia	A. Arnold
Lajja	Taslima Nasreen
Long Walk to Freedom	Nelson Mandela
Man Eaters of Kumayun	Jim Corbett
Mein Kampf	Adolf Hitler
Mother	Maxim Gorky
Paradise Lost	John Milton
The Satanic Verses	Salman Rushdie
The Moor's Last Sigh	Salman Rushdie
Shahnama	Firdausi
Rubaiyat	Omar Khayyam
Unto the Last	John Ruskin
War and Peace	Leo Tolstoy
Wealth of Nations	Adam Smith

Some Famous Quotations

Abraham Lincoln	Government of the People, by the people and for the people.
Neil Armstrong	A single step for a man, a giant leap for the mankind.
John Milton	Better to reign in Hell than to serve in the Heaven.
William Shakespeare	Cowards die many times before their death; The valiant never taste of death but once.
Napoleon Bonaparte	Give us good mothers and I shall give you good nation.
Goldsmith	Where wealth accumulates, men decay.
John F. Kennedy	We do not fear to negotiate, but we do not negotiate out of fear.

Important Official Residences

Buckingham Palace (London)	King/Queen of Britain
10, Downing Street (London)	Prime Minister, Britain
Elysee Palace (Paris)	President, France
Rashtrapati Bhawan (New Delhi)	President, India
White House (Washington)	President, USA
Vatican (Rome)	Pope
7, Race Course (New Delhi)	Prime Minister, India

Wonders of the World

Seven Wonders of the Ancient World : *(1)* the Pyramids of Egypt, built in approximately 2700 BC; *(2)* the Hanging Gardens at Babylon; *(3)* the temple of Artemis at Emphesus; *(4)* the statue of Zeus at Olympia; *(5)* the tomb of Mausolus at Halicarnassus, built in nearly 350 BC; *(6)* the Colossus of Rhodes, built in nearly 280 BC; *(7)* the Pharos Lighthouse at Alexandria.

Seven Wonders of the Medieval World : *(1)* the Colosseum of Rome; *(2)* the Great Wall of China; *(3)* the Porcelain Tower of Nanking; *(4)* the Mosque at St. Sophia (Constantinople); *(5)* Stonehenge; *(6)* the Catacombs of Rome; *(7)* the Leaning Tower of Pisa.

Seven New Wonders of the World : *(1)* Taj Mahal of Agra (India); *(2)* Pyramid at Chichen Itza (Mexico); *(3)* Machu Picchu (Peru); *(4)* Statue of Christ The Redeemer (Brazil); *(5)* Great Wall of China; *(6)* Roman Colosseum, Italy; *(7)* Ruins of Petra, Jordan.

Symbols and Signs

Red Triangle	Family Planning
Red Cross	Hospital (or medical aid)
Lotus	Culture and Civilization
Olive Branch	Peace
Red Light	Danger; Traffic signal for 'stop'
Green Light	Traffic signal for 'go'
Black arm-band	Sign of mourning or protest
Dove	Peace
Two bones crossing each other diagonally with a skull in the upper quadrant	Danger
Flag upside down	Distress
Flag flown at half mast	National mourning
Red Flag	Revolution
White Flag	Truce
Wheel	Progress
Two hands protecting a lamp	Life Insurance Corporation of India
V (letter)	Victory

Names of Parliaments of Some Countries

Country	*Name of the Parliament*
Afghanistan	Shora
Canada	Parliament: Senate (Upper House); House of Commons (Lower House)
China	National People's Congress
Denmark	Folketing

Country	*Name of the Parliament*
Germany	Bundestag (Lower House); Bandesrat (Upper House)
Iceland	Althing
India	Sansad : Lok Sabha (Lower House); Rajya Sabha (Upper House)
Iran	Majlis
Israel	Knesset
Japan	Diet
Korea (North)	Supreme People's Assembly
Mongolia	Great People's Khural
Nepal	National Panchayat
Netherlands	The States General
Norway	Storting
Poland	Sejm
Russia	Federation Council (Upper House); Duma (Lower House)
Spain	Cortes
Sweden	Riksdag
UAR	Darul Avam
U.K.	Parliament: House of Commons (Lower); House of Lords (Upper)
USA	Congress: Senate (Upper House); House of Representatives (Lower House)

Highest, Biggest, Largest, Longest, etc. in the World

Animal, *tallest*	Giraffe
Bird, *largest*	Ostrich
Canal, *longest*	Suez canal
Church, *largest*	St. Peter's Church (Rome)
City, *largest in population*	Tokyo (Japan)
Continent, *largest*	Eurasian Landmass (Europe and Asia)
smallest	Australia
Country, *largest*	
(i) in population	China
(ii) in area	Russia
Smallest	Vatican

Desert, *largest*	Sahara (N. Africa)
Gulf, *largest*	Gulf of Mexico
Island, *biggest*	Greenland
Lake, *largest*	Caspian Sea
largest (fresh water)	Superior Lake (USA—Canada border)
Mountain, *highest peak*	Mt. Everest
Ocean, *largest and deepest*	The Pacific Ocean
Place, *rainiest*	Mowsyrnam near Cherapunji (Meghalaya)
Planet, *biggest*	Jupiter
brightest	Venus
nearest to the sun	Mercury
Railway Line, *longest*	Trans-Siberian Railway
River, *longest*	*(i)* Nile (6670 km) *(ii)* Amazon (6570 km)
Building, *tallest*	Burj Khalifa, Dubai (2010), 818 m
Tower, *tallest*★	Guangzhou TV Tower, China (2010), 2001 ft.
Waterfall, *highest*	Salto-Angel (Venezuela)

★ C.N. Tower, Toronto, Canada (1815 ft) is now second in the world

INVENTIONS AND DISCOVERIES

IMPORTANT INVENTIONS

Name of Invention	*Inventor*	*Nationality*	*Year*
Aeroplane	Orville & Wilbur Wright	U.S.A	1903
Ball-Point Pen	John J. Loud	U.S.A.	1888
Barometer	Evangelista Torrcelli	Italy	1644
Bicycle	Kirkpatrick Machmillan	Britain	1839-40
Bifocal Lens	Benjamin Franklin	U.S.A.	1780
Car (Petrol)	Karl Benz	Germany	1888
Celluloid	Alexander Parkes	Britain	1861
Cinema	Nicolas and Jean Lumiere	France	1895
Clock (mechanical)	I-Hsing & Liang Ling-Tsan	China	725
Diesel Engine	Rudolf Diesel	Germany	1895
Dynamo	Hypolite Pixii	France	1832
Electric Lamp	Thomas Alva Edison	U.S.A.	1879
Electric Motor (DC)	Zenobe Gramme	Belgium	1873
Electric Motor (AC)	Nikola Tesla	U.S.A.	1888
Electromagnet	William Sturgeon	Britain	1824
Electronic Computer	Dr. Alan M Turing	Britain	1943
Film (moving outlines)	Louis Prince	France	1885
Film (musical sound)	Dr. Le de Forest	U.S.A.	1923
Fountain Pen	Lewis E. Waterman	U.S.A.	1884

Name of Invention	*Inventor*	*Nationality*	*Year*
Gramophone	Thomas Alva Edison	U.S.A.	1878
Helicopter	Etienne Oehnichen	France	1924
Jet Engine	Sir Frank Whittle	Britain	1937
Laser	Charles H. Townes	U.S.A.	1960
Lift (Mechanical)	Elisha G. Otis	U.S.A.	1852
Locomotive	Richard Trevithick	Britain	1804
Machine Gun	James Puckle	Britain	1718
Microphone	Alexander Graham Bell	U.S.A.	1876
Microscope	Z. Janssen	Netherlands	1590
Motor Cycle	G. Daimler	Germany	1885
Photography (on film)	John Carbutt	U.S.A.	1888
Printing Press	Johann Gutenberg	Germany	1455
Razor (safety)	King C. Gillette	U.S.A.	1895
Refrigerator	James Harrison & Alexander Catlin	U.S.A.	1850
Safety Pin	Walter Hunt	U.S.A.	1849
Sewing machine	Barthelemy Thimmonnier	France	1829
Ship (steam)	J.C. Perier	France	1775
Ship (turbine)	Hon. Sir C. Parsons	Britain	1894
Skyscraper	W. Le Baron Jenny	U.S.A.	1882
Slide Rule	William Oughtred	Britain	1621
Steam Engine(condenser)	James Watt	Britain	1765
Steel Production	Henry Bessemer	Britain	1855
Steel (stainless)	Harry Brearley	Britain	1913
Submarine	David Bushnell	U.S.A.	1776
Tank	Sir Ernest Swinton	Britain	1914
Telegraph	M. Lammond	France	1787
Telegraph Code	Samuel F.B. Morse	U.S.A.	1837
Telephone (perfected)	Alexander Graham Bell	U.S.A.	1876
Television (mechanical)	John Logie Baird	Britain	1926
Television (electronic)	P.T. Farnsworth	U.S.A.	1927
Thermometer	Galileo Galilei	Italy	1593
Transformer	Michael Faraday	Britain	1831
Transistor	Bardeen, Shockley & Brattain	U.S.A.	1948
Washing Machine (elect.)	Hurley Machine Co.	U.S.A.	1907
Zip-Fastener	W.L. Judson	U.S.A.	1891

GEOGRAPHICAL EXPLORATIONS/DISCOVERIES

Place	*Explorer/Discoverers*	*Nationality*	*Year*
America	Christopher Columbus	Italy	1492
Hawaii Islands (Sandwich Islands)	Captain James Cook	England	1778
Newfoundland	John Cabot	England	1497

Place	*Explorer/Discoverers*	*Nationality*	*Year*
New Zealand	Abel Janszoon Tasman	Holland	1642
North Pole	Robert Peary	U.S.A.	1909
Sea Route to India (via Cape of Good Hope)	Vasco da Gama	Portugal	1498
South Pole	Ronald Amundsen	Norway	1911

IMPORTANT DISCOVERIES

Discovery	*Discoverer*	*Nationality*	*Year*
Aluminium	Hans Christian Oerstedt	Denmark	1827
Atomic number	Henry Moseley	England	1913
Atomic structure of matter	John Dalton	England	1803
Chlorine	C.W. Scheele	Sweden	1774
Electromagnetic induction	Michael Faraday	England	1831
Electromagnetic waves	Heinrich Hertz	Germany	1886
Electromagnetism	Hans Christian Oersted	Denmark	1920
Electron	Sir Joseph Thomson	England	1897
General theory of relativity	Albert Einstein	Switzerland	1915
Hydrogen	Henry Cavendish	England	1766
Law of electric conduction	Georg Ohm	Germany	1827
Law of electromagnetism	Andre Ampere	France	1826
Law of falling bodies	Galileo	Italy	1590
Laws of gravitation & motion	Isaac Newton	England	1687
Laws of planetary motion	Johannes Kepler	Germany	1609-19
Magnesium	Sir Humphry Davy	England	1808
Neptune (Planet)	Johann Galle	Germany	1846
Neutron	James Chadwick	England	1932
Nickel	Axel Cronstedt	Sweden	1751
Nitrogen	Daniel Rutherford	England	1772
Oxygen	Joseph Priestly	England	1772
	C.W. Scheele	Sweden	
Ozone	Christian Schonbein	Germany	1839
Pluto (Planet)	Clyde Tombaugh	U.S.A.	1930
Plutonium	G.T. Seaborg	U.S.A.	1940
Proton	Ernest Rutherford	England	1919
Quantum Theory	Max Planck	Germany	1900
Radioactivity	Antoine Henery Bacquerel	France	1896
Radium	Pierre and Marie Curie	France	1898
Silicon	Jons Berzelius	Sweden	1824
Special theory of relativity	Albert Einstein	Switzerland	1905
Sun as centre of solar system	Copernicus	Poland	1543
Uranium	Martin Klaproth	Germany	1789
Uranus (Planet)	William Herschel	England	1781
X-rays	Willhelm Roentgen	Germany	1895

ABBREVIATIONS

A.D.: Anno Domini (in the year of our Lord)
A.H.Q.: Air Head Quarters: Army Head Quarters
A.I.: Air India, Artificial Intelligence
A.I.D.S.: Acquired Immune Deficiency Syndrome
A.I.I.M.S.: All India Institute of Medical Sciences
A.M.: Ante Meridiem (before noon), Amplitude Modulation
A.S.L.V.: Augmentated Satellite Launch Vehicle
B.C.: Before Christ, Backward Class
B.S.F.: Border Security Force
C.B.I.: Central Bureau of Investigation
C.D.S.: Combined Defence Services
C-in-C.: Commander-in-Chief
CTBT: Comprehensive Test Ban Treaty
DoT: Department of Telecommunication
E. & O.E.: Errors and Omission Excepted
FAX: Fascimile Exchange
FDI: Foreign Direct Investment
F.I.R.: First Information Report
G.A.T.T.: General Agreement on Tariffs and Trade
G.M.T.: Greenwich Mean Time
H.R.D.: Human Resource Development
I.C.A.R.: Indian Council of Agricultural Research
I.L.O.: International Labour Organisation
I.M.F.: International Monetary Fund
I.S.R.O.: Indian Space Research Organisation
LASER: Light Amplification by Stimulated Emission of Radiation
L.I.C.: Life Insurance Corporation (of India)
N.A.S.A.: National Aeronautics and Space Administration (of U.S.A.)
N.C.C.: National Cadet Corps
N.C.E.R.T.: National Council of Educational Research and Training
N.D.A.: National Defence Academy
N.H.R.C.: National Human Rights Commission
P.I.N.: Postal Index Number
P.M.: Post Meridiem (afternoon); Prime Minister
P.S.U.: Public Sector Undertaking
P.T.I.: Press Trust of India
P.W.D.: Public Works Department
R.B.C.: Red Blood Corpuscles
R.B.I.: Reserve Bank of India
S.O.S.: Save our Souls
S.S.B.: Service Selection Board
U.N.O.: United Nations Organisation
U.N.E.S.C.O.: United Nations Educational, Scientific and Cultural Organisation
V.I.P.: Very Important Person
W.H.O.: World Health Organisation

COMMON TERMS

Adult Franchise: It is a voting right conferred on every adult, without distinction, to elect any candidate he or she may choose.

By-election: It is the special election to a seat tendered vacant during the running term of an elected person (by death, resignation, disqualification).

Coalition: It is a temporary union of political parties for special purpose. It is formed either deal with some crisis situation or when no party is able to secure absolute majority in a legislature.

Coup d' Etat: It is a sudden change of government by force, brought about by those who already hold some governmental or military power.

Federation: It is a political unit on which a number of smaller political units devolve certain power over themselves and their citizens and to which they usually entrust the conduct of their foreign affairs.

Fili buster: It is a parliamentary device of long winded speeches, not necessarily relevant to obstruct, delay or bargain over a measure under consideration for voting.

Impeachment: It is a prosecution of a very high public officials by the legislature for alleged offences otherwise beyond the normal reach of law.

Lame-ducks: These are the members of the Parliament who failed to get re-elected.

Martial Law: It is an administration of a certain area passing into the hands of military authorities superseding all civil law.

Mid-term election: It is an election to the legislature before completion of its full term usually, because of dissolution.

Ombudsman: A vigilance officer who hears citizens complaints against the government.

Plebiscite: Direct vote of electors on a political issue of importance.

Proportional Representation: An electrical system under which a legislature reflects the strength of the various political parties among the electorate at large, it has several form.

Question Hour: Session of legislature usually beings with question hour in which members can ask questions on any aspect of administration. Each member is allowed a quota of five questions per day.

Ratification: The formal adoption by a state of a treaty signed by its representatives. It is effected by an exchange of documents, embodying their formal adoption of the treaty between the states concerned.

Referendum: A reference of a particular political question to the electorate for a direct decision by popular vote.

Republic: This is a form of government by people and for people.

Secession: Formal withdrawal from an organisation such as party, church or state. A session from a state is often preceded by a revolt.

Separation: A belief that a particular group or area should be separated from the larger organisation of which it forms a part applied to political movements that advocate independence.
Snap Vote: A vote taken unexpectedly without voters having been briefed in advance.
Supplementary question: Question asked in parliament based on answer to the main question.
Veto: The right to reject.
Zero Hour: Time allotted in the House every day for miscellaneous business, *i.e.*, call attention notice, question on official statements and adjournment motion.
Solid Smoke: Aerogels are known as solid smoke. They are composite materials-the-lightest solid known. They are made of silica, alumina and carbon. It can weigh lesser than the same volume of air. A lump of this frozen smoke the size of a man would weigh less than half-a-kilogram, but could bear the weight of a car.
Super acids: Acids are substances capable of giving hydrogen ions for chemical reaction. An acid is called a super acid if it is stronger than 100% sulphuric acid, the strongest classical acid which is also considered to be a super acid. Super acids are a trillion times stronger than the dilute sulphuric acid used to kill bacteria in swimming pool which spreads just a few ions through a large volume of water and yet the solution is weakly acid.
Neutrons: Uncharged sub atomic particle, mass approximately equal to that of the proton, which enters into the structure of atomic nuclei.
Superliquid: Helium may well be the strongest element in the universe. For poorly understood reasons, at very low temperatures it becomes a superfluid, a substance that flows without friction.
Cypher: Cypher is a prototype car-size flying machine with a global positioning satellite receiver and radar tied into a remote laptop computer. All an operator has to do is to indicate on a computer map where he wants his machine to go and immediately it plots a route, takes off and navigates itself.
Galaxies: Galaxies are huge congregations of stars held together by force of gravity. They are so big that they have some times been called islands universes. They are so big that they have some times been called islands universes. It seems to be scattered in space. It tend to be grouped together into clusters, and some clusters appear to be grouped into superclusters.
The Milky Way: The Milky Way is our home galaxy. A peculiar feature of this galaxy is a bright band of light that runs almost in a perfect circle through it. Milky way belongs to a cluster of some 24 galaxies called the local group.
Black Hole: Strange things happen to a star at the end of its life of its mass is more than three times the mass of the sun. It will collapse, becoming more and more compact. The collapse continues until the star becomes so dense that

nothing, not even light, can escape from its gravity. Hence, the object is dark and can't be viewed directly.

Asteroids: They are rocky debris upto 1000 km in diameter, although most are much smaller. They are remains from the nebulac, out of which the Solar System formed. Most of them orbit the sun in the asteroid belt, which lies between the orbit of Mars and Jupiter.

Comets: Comets may originate in a huge cloud called the Oort cloud that is supposed to surround Solar System. When first viewed through a telescope the bright head of a comet, called coma, looks like a hazy dot. Comets have very low density. It can move into new orbits.

Meteors: As the earth travels in its orbit around the Sun, it continually encounters meteoroides head on. On a clear, dark night one may see more than 10 meteors/hours. Sometimes an unusually large number of small meteors can be seen in rapid succession perhaps more than 50/hour. Such a display is called a meteorids.

Lithosphere: The lithosphere is the top crust of the Earth on which our continents and ocean basins rest. It is the thickest in the continental regions where it has an average thickness of 40 km and thinest in the oceans where it may have a maximum thickness of 10 to 12 km. It constitutes about 1% of the Earth's volume and 0.4% of its mass.

Mountains: Mountains are conventionally divided into four type, according to their male of origin: fold mountains, Block mountains, Volcanic mountains and Residual mountains.

Richter Scale: The Richter is a logarithmic scale, devised in 1935 by geophysicist Charles Richter, for representing the energy released by earthquake. A figure of 2 is barely perceptible, which an earthquake measuring over 5 may be destructive.

Earthquakes: The earthquake is a shaking of the ground. Caused by the sudden breaking and shifting of large sections of the Earth's rocky outer shell. A severe earthquake may release energy 10,000 times as great as that of the first atomic bomb. Earthquake can trigger landslides that causes great damage and loss of life.

Volcanos: Volcano is an opening in the Earth's surface through which lava, hot gases, and rock fragments erupt. Such an opening forms when melted rock form deep within the earth blasts through the surface.

Desert: Desert is a part of Earth's surface that is too dry to support plant or animal life and is usually sparsely inhabited or uninhabited by man.

Hydrosphere: It is estimated that the hydrosphere contains about 1,460,000 cubic km of water of this 97.3% is in the oceans and inland seas. The rest 2.7% is formed as glaciers and ice caps, fresh water lakes, rivers and underground water.

RELIGIONS FOUNDERS AND FOLLOWERS

Religion	Founder	Followers
Christianity	Jesus Christ	Christians
Islam	Prophet Mohammed	Muslims
Hinduism	Aryans	Hindus
Buddhism	Gautama Buddha	Buddhists
Judaism	Prophet Moses	Jews
Zoroastrianism	Zaratushtra	Parsis
Sikhism	Guru Nanak	Sikhs
Jainism	Mahavira	Jains

GEOGRAPHY

Soils

Types of Soils

Sandy Soil: It contains sand in large quantity.
Clay Soil: It contains a good quantity of clay.
Black Soil: It is formed by disintegration of basalt rocks.
Yellow Soil: It is deposited by winds from deserts.

Rocks

Types of Rocks

(a) **Igneous Rocks :** These are formed by cooling of hot masses of the earth. *e.g.*, granite and basalt rocks.
(b) **Aqueous Rocks :** These are formed by the action of water and have layers of clay, chalk or sandstone.
(c) **Sedimentary Rocks :** These are formed by layers of sediments which are brought by rivers.
(d) **Organic Rocks :** These are formed by remains of plants and animals.

Mountains

Types of Mountains

Fold Mountains : These mountains are mainly made up of folded strata of sedimentary rocks. These rocks are folded when they are compressed. These are the highest mountains of the world. The Alps, the Himalayas and Rockies are fold mountains.

Block Mountains : These are parts of the earth's crust which have been uplifted due to the earth's movement along the line of weakness called faults.

Residual Mountains : These are formed by the differences in the rates of erosion.

Volcanic Mountains : These mountains are formed by accumulation of material erupted from the interior of the earth.

MOUNTAINPEAKS

Name	Country	Range	Height (m)	Dt. of first ascent
Mt. Everest	Nepal-Tibet	Himalayas	8,848	May 29, 1953
K-2 (Godwin Austin)	India	Karakoram	8,611	July 31, 1954
Kanchenjunga	Nepal-India	Himalayas	8,598	May 25, 1955
Lhotse	Nepal-China	Himalayas	8,511	May 18, 1956
Makaly	Tibet-Nepal	Himalayas	8,481	May 15, 1955
Dhaulagiri-I	Nepal	Himalayas	8,172	May 13, 1960
Nanga Parbat	India	Himalayas	8,124	July 03, 1953
Nanda Devi	India	Himalayas	7,817	Aug. 29, 1960

MAJOR PORTS

There are 13 major ports and about 200 non-major ports along the coast line of (about 7,516.6 km.) India. The major ports on the west coast of India are Mumbai, Kandla, Mormugao, New Mangaluru, Kochin and Jawaharlal Nehru port at Nhava Sheva. On the east coast, the major ports are Tuticorin, Chennai, Visakhapatnam, Paradip and Kolkata (Haldia).

INDIAN LANGUAGES

There are 22 national languages recognized by the Indian Constitution and these are spoken in over 1600 dialects. India's official language is Hindi in the Devanagri script. However, English continues to be the official working language. The country has a wide variety of local languages and in many cases the State boundaries have been drawn on linguistic lines. Besides Hindi and English, the other languages recognised in the Indian Constitution are Assamese, Bengali, Gujarati, Kannada, Nepali, Kashmiri, Konkani, Sanskrit, Sindhi, Tamil, Malayalam, Marathi, Punjabi, Odiya, Telugu, Urdu, Bodo, Maithili, Santhali and Dogri.

Some Indian languages have evolved from the Indo-European group of languages and these were the languages of the Aryans who invaded India. This set is known as the Indic group of languages. The other set of languages are Dravidian and are native to South India, though a distinct influence of Sanskrit and Hindi is evident in these languages.

BATTLES AND WARS IN INDIA

War	*Year*	*Result*
Battle of Kalinga	(261 B.C.)	Ashoka defeated the king of Kalinga
Second battle of Tarain	(1192 A.D.)	Muhammad Gori defeated Prithviraj Chauhan
First battle of Panipat	(1526 A.D.)	Babar defeated Ibrahim Lodi
Battle of Khandawa	(1527 A.D.)	Babar defeated Rana Sanga
Battle of Chausa	(1539 A.D.)	Shershah Suri defeated Humayun and became ruler of Delhi
Second Battle of Panipat	(1556 A.D.)	Akbar defeated Hemu

War	Year	Result
Battle of Talikota	(1565 A.D.)	Allied forces of Bijapur, Bidar, Golkunda and Ahamadnagar defeated the King of Vijay Nagar
Battle of Haldighati	(1576 A.D.)	Rana Pratap was defeated by Akabar
Battle of Palasey	(1757 A.D.)	British forces defeated Nawab of Bengal Sirajudoulla
Battle of Wandiwash	(1760 A.D.)	British forces defeated the French
Third battle of Panipat	(1761 A.D.)	Maratha were defeated by Ahmad Shah Abadali
Battle of Buxar	(1764 A.D.)	British forces defeated the combined forces of Mir Quasim. Shah Alam Mughal empire and Awadh's Nawab
Third Anglo-Maratha War	(1792 A.D.)	Maratha were conclusively defeated
Fourth Anglo-Mysore War	(1799 A.D.)	Tipu Sultan died fighting the British forces
Second Anglo-Sikh War	(1848 A.D.)	British forces annexed Punjab from Sikh rulers
Indo-China War	(1962 A.D.)	China attacked India unilaterally and annexed some area
Indo-Pak War	(1965 A.D.)	Pakistan attacked India but had to suffer severe setbacks
Indo-Pak War	(1971 A.D.)	Pak declear war against India.

Short Biography of Historical Personalities

Aurobindo Ghosh (1872-1950): He began his life as ICS officer but became a revolutionary. He played an important role during partition of Bengal. He was among the first Indian leaders to demand independence. He was tried for waging war against the state but the British could not prove their allegations. Later, he became a philosopher and thinker. He went to Pondicherry and lived rest of his life in Aurobindo Ashram.

Chandra Shekhar Azad (1906-1931): He was one of the leading revolutionary of Indian freedom struggle who showed exemplary courage at very young age. Once when he was arrested, he said his name was Azad, father's name was Swatantrata and his residence was jail. He was a member of Azad Hindustan Socialist Republic Party which carried out several acts like Kakori dacoity, bomb blast in assembly, Saunders's murder etc. He was killed in an encounter.

Sardar Bhagat Singh (1907-1931): He was another great revolutionary. He spread the spirit of nationalism throughout the country. He was involved in killing of English officer Saunders. He, along with Battukeshwar Dutt, decided to throw a bomb in the Central Assembly to draw attention of Lawmakers towards their demand. After throwing bomb, they did not run away and made patriotic slogans. Later, Rajguru and Sukhdev were also arrested on the doubt of being involved in the case. Bhagat Singh, Rajguru and Sukhdev were hanged in Lahore Jail on March 23, 1931.

Lokmanya Bal Gangadhar Tilak (1856-1920): He was a great Indian freedom fighter who revived the festival in memory of Shivaji and Ganesh festival to make people interested in nationalistic activities. He started "Kesri" and "Maratha" newspapers to spread the message. He belonged to the extremist wing and did not believe in the politics of petitions and passing resolutions. He coined the slogan that "Swaraj is our birthright".

Subhash Chandra Bose (1897-1945): He started his life as an ICS officer but quit it, joined the national movement. He joined the Congress and took strong stand against the British rule. He was elected President of the Congress in 1938 and 1939 but due to differences with Gandhiji, he resigned from the post. He launched Forward Bloc. After the start of Second World War, the Congress initially was not in favour of taking strong position against the British but he announced a non-cooperation movement. He was put under house arrest but he escaped from there to Germany. He tried to form an armed force against the British. He came to Singapore and with the help of Indians living in South-East Asia, he launched Azad Hind Fauj (INA). It marched towards India, with the slogan "Delhi Chalo". It liberated Andaman and Nicobar Islands. It reached upto Kohima but setbacks to Japan and Germany in World War forced INA to slow down the march. Subhash Chandra Bose is known as Netaji. His death has been shrouded with mystery.

Acharya Vinoba Bhave (1895-1982): His full name was Vinayak Narhari Bhave. He was a self-taught multilinguist and was proficient in Hindi scriptural books Gandhiji had great faith in him and chose him for managing the Wardha Ashram, and participating in the famous 'Dandi March'. He started the Bhoodan movement to bring about fundamental social and economic changes in society by peaceful means.

Baba Kharak Singh: He was the Grand Old Man of Punjab during the freedom struggle. He urged the Sikhs to throw in their lot with the Congress against imperialism. He took active part in the Gurudwara liberation movement. The British Government, afraid of indomitable will and spirit of sacrifice, put him in jail for a long time but he continued his efforts for the freedom of the country.

Sardar Patel (1875-1950): He is known in history as the "Iron Man of India". His real name was Vallabhbhai Patel. He began his political career in Kheda district of Gujarat by launching "no tax" campaign. He led the peasants agitation against an increase in land revenue at Bardoli and won a signal victory. Gandhiji described him as the "Sardar". He was a very able negotiator and played a vital role in discussions with the British Government. He was a trusted lieutenant of Gandhiji. He joined interim government as a minister Incharge of Home Affairs and Information and Broadcasting and played important role in uniting the country and maintaining order. In independent India, he became the Deputy Prime Minister and accomplished the tough task of integrating various States in India.

Raja Rammohan Roy (1772-1833): He was the pioneer of social and religious reforms in the country. He was a scholar in English, Sanskrit and Persian. He was close to the Englishmen. He opposed the Sati system in the country and worked for its abolition. He established Brahamo Samaj. He wrote several books. He asked the British to introduce reforms in India.

Objective General Knowledge

History

1. 'Abhinav Bharat' was organized by
   A. Bhai Parmanand
   B. Khudiram Bose
   C. Vir Savarkar
   D. None of these
2. The ancient name of Bengal was
   A. Kamrupa B. Vasta
   C. Gauda D. Vallabhi
3. Ashoka belonged to:
   A. Maurya dynasty
   B. Gupta dynasty
   C. Kushan dynasty
   D. Saka dynasty
4. Morish traveller, Ibn Batutah, came to India during the time of
   A. Ala-ud-din Khilji
   B. Firoz Shah Tughluq
   C. Balban
   D. Muhammad-bin-Tughluq
5. The relics of Indus Valley Civilisation indicates that the main occupation of the people was
   A. Agriculture
   B. Cattle rearing
   C. Commerce
   D. Hunting
6. The Mahabalipuram temples were built by the king of .... dynasty
   A. Gupta
   B. Chola
   C. Pallava
   D. Kushana
7. The first telegraph line between Calcutta (Kolkata) and Agra was opened in
   A. 1852 B. 1853
   C. 1854 D. 1855
8. The first discourse of Buddha in Sarnath is called
   A. Mahabhiniskraman
   B. Mahaparinirvana
   C. Mahamastakabhisheka
   D. Dharmachakrapravartan
9. The political and cultural centre of the Pandyas was
   A. Vengi
   B. Madurai
   C. Kanchipuram
   D. Mahabalipuram
10. What is the correct chronological order of the dynasties in which they invaded India?
    1. Huns 2. Kushanas
    3. Aryans 4. Greeks
    A. 4, 3, 2, 1 B. 3, 4, 2, 1
    C. 4, 2, 3, 1 D. 3, 4, 1, 2
11. Who wrote Mitakshara, a book of Hindu law?
    A. Nayachandra
    B. Amoghvarsa
    C. Vijnaneswara
    D. Kumban
12. Gupta empire declined in the fifth century A.D. as a consequence of
    A. Chalukya raids
    B. Greek invasion
    C. Hun invasion
    D. Pallava raids

13. Who founded the Hindu Shahi dynasty of Punjab?
A. Vasumitra
B. Kallar
C. Jayapala
D. Mahipala

14. The main external threat to the Sultanate of Delhi was posed by the
A. Mughals
B. Afghans
C. Iranians
D. None of these

15. Who among the following was a leading exponent of Gandhian thoughts?
A. J.L. Nehru
B. M.N. Roy
C. Vinoba Bhave
D. Jayaprakash Narayan

16. Who were the immediate successors of the Imperial Mauryas in Magadha?
A. Kushanas
B. Pandyas
C. Satvahanas
D. Sungas

17. Both Mahavira and Buddha preached during the reign of
A. Ajatashatru
B. Bimbisara
C. Nandivardhan
D. Uday

18. Jahangiri Mahal is located in
A. Delhi
B. Fatehpur Sikri
C. Agra Fort
D. Sikandara

19. The main contribution of the Chola dynasty is in the field of
A. Systematic provincial administration
B. A well planned revenue system
C. A well organised central government
D. An organised local self government

20. Who founded the philosophy of Pustimarga?
A. Chaitanya
B. Nanak
C. Surdas
D. Ballabhacharya

21. Which of the following battles changed the destiny of a Mughal ruler of India?
A. Haldighati
B. Panipat II
C. Khanwah
D. Chausa

22. "The Vedas contain all the truth" was interpreted by
A. Swami Vivekanand
B. Swami Dayanand
C. Swami Shraddhanand
D. S. Radhakrishnan

23. Match the colums

Column I	Column II
(*a*) Second Battle of Panipat	1. Decline of Vijayanagar empire
(*b*) Second Battle of Tarain	2. British rule in India
(*c*) Battle of Talikota	3. Turkish rule in India
(*d*) Battle of Plassey	4. Mughal rule in India
	5. Slave dynasty in India

Codes:

	(*a*)	(*b*)	(*c*)	(*d*)
A.	2	3	4	1
B.	3	1	2	4
C.	5	3	2	1
D.	4	3	1	2

24. Babur entered India for the first time from the west through

A. Kashmir B. Sind

C. Punjab D. Rajasthan

25. Which was the first among the following?

A. Doctrine of Lapse

B. Subsidiary Alliance

C. Permanent Settlement

D. Double Government

26. The name of Lord Cornwallis is associated with the

A. Dual government

B. Maratha wars

C. System of subsidiary

D. Permanent settlement

27. Sir Charles Wood's Despatch of 1854 dealt with

A. Administrative reforms

B. Social reforms

C. Economic reforms

D. Educational reforms

28. Which of the following pairs is correct?

A. Ashvaghosa — Vikramaditya

B. Banabhatta — Harshvardhan

C. Harisena — Kanishka

D. Kalidasa — Samudragupta

29. 4th July, 1776 is important in world history because

A. battle fo Plassey started

B. Sea route to India was discovered

C. English King Charles II was executed

D. American Congress adopted the Declaration of Independence

30. Rawlatt Act was passed in the year

A. 1917 B. 1919

C. 1921 D. 1923

31. The court language of Delhi Sultanate was

A. Urdu B. Persian

C. Hindi D. Arabic

32. Where did Buddha attain Mahaparinirvana?

A. Kushinagar

B. Kapilvastu

C. Pava

D. Kundagramma

33. In Afghanistan, two towering Buddha statues were destroyed at

A. Kandahar B. Yakaolong

C. Bamiyan D. Mazar-i-Sharif

34. Kalibangan, the Indus Valley site is in

A. Rajasthan

B. Gujarat

C. Madhya Pradesh

D. Uttar Pradesh

35. Which of the following materials was mainly used in the manufacture of harappan seals?

A. Terracota B. Bronze

C. Copper D. Iron

36. The Grand Trunk Road in India was got constructed by

A. Ashoka B. Shershah Suri

C. Akbar D. Humayun

37. 'Tripitaka' is the religious book of the

A. Jains B. Buddhists

C. Sikhs D. Hindus

38. Which among the following states was forced to merge itself with the Union of India after 1947?
A. Hyderabad
B. Kashmir
C. Patiala
D. Mysore

39. Alexander the Great died in 323 B.C. in
A. Persia
B. Babylon
C. Macedonia
D. Taxila

40. Who gave the slogan—"Jai Hind"?
A. Subhash Chandra Bose
B. Jawaharlal Nehru
C. Moti Lal Nehru
D. Mahatma Gandhi

41. The most glorious king of the Chola dynasty who conquered Ceylon was
A. Rajaraja I
B. Rajaraja II
C. Rajendra Chola
D. Gangai Konda Chola

42. Name the Chera King known as the "Red Chera", who built a temple for Kannagi?
A. Elara
B. Karikala
C. Senguttuvan
D. Nedenjerai Alan

43. The first Indian ruler to accept Subsidiary Alliance offered by Lord Wellesley in 1798 was
A. Nawab of Oudh
B. Nizam of Hyderabad
C. Nawab of Carnatic
D. King of Mysore

44. The first Viceroy of India was
A. Lord Hastings
B. Lord Canning
C. Lord Minto
D. Lord Curzon

45. The Satavahanas formerly worked as local officials under the
A. Nandas B. Mauryas
C. Cholas D. Cheras

46. Who was the first woman President of the Indian National Congress?
A. Sarojini Naidu
B. Bhikaji Cama
C. Annie Besant
D. Vijaya Lakshmi Pandit

47. During the Indian Freedom Struggle, who of the following founded the Parathana Samaj?
A. Atmaram Pandurang
B. Gopal Hari Deshmukh
C. Ishwar Chandra Vidyasagar
D. Keshav Chandra Sen

48. Which one of the following periodicals was published by Mahatma Gandhi during his stay in South Africa?
A. Afrikanes
B. Indian Opinion
C. India Gazette
D. Navjivan

49. During the Civil Disobedience Movement, who led the 'Red Shirts' of North-Western India?
A. Abul Kalam Azad
B. Khan Abdul Ghaffar Khan
C. Mohammad Ali Jinnah
D. Shaukat Ali

50. Match List-I with List-II and select the correct answer using the codes given below the lists—

List-I
(Name of the Author)

(a) Abul Fazal
(b) Nizamuddin Ahmed
(c) Krishnadeva Raya
(d) Kalhana

List-II
(Name of the Book)

1. Tabqat-i-Akbari
2. Akbarnama
3. Rajatarangini
4. Amuktamalyada

Codes:

	(a)	*(b)*	*(c)*	*(d)*
A.	2	4	1	3
B.	3	1	4	2
C.	2	1	4	3
D.	3	4	1	2

51. Which one of the following pairs is not correctly matched?

A. Sheikh Shihab-ud-din Suharawardi — Sufi Saint
B. Chaitanya Maha Prabhu — Bhakti Saint
C. Minhaj-us Siraj — Founder of Sufi order
D. Lalleshwari — Bhakti Saint

52. Who of the following kings was an ardent follower of Jainism?

A. Bimbisara
B. Mahapadma Nanda
C. Kharavela
D. Pulakesin II

53. To which dynasty did Ashoka belong?

A. Vardhana B. Maurya
C. Kushan D. Gupta

54. Which one of the following battles was fought between Babar and the Rajputs in 1527?

A. The First Battle of Panipat
B. The Battle of Khanwah
C. The Battle of Ghagra
D. The Battle of Chanderi

55. Aryabhat,ta and Varahamihira belong to which age?

A. Guptas B. Cholas
C. Mauryas D. Mughals

56. Consider the· following statements about Amir Khusro:

1. He was a disciple of Nizamuddin Auliya.
2. He was the founder of both Hindustani classical music and Qawwali.

Which of the statements given above is/are correct?

A. 1 only
B. 2 only
C. Both 1 and 2
D. Neither 1 nor 2

57. Panini, the first Grammarian of Sanskrit language in India, lived during the

A. 2nd Century B.C.
B. 6th-5th Century B.C.
C. 2nd Century A.D.
D. 5th-6th Century A.D.

58. Who among the following was associated with the foundation of Ghadar party?

A. Lala Lajpat Rai
B. Lala Hardayal
C. C.R. Das
D. Bipin Chandra Pal

59. The Treaty of Bassein (1802) was signed between

A. Madhav Rao and the British
B. Baji Rao II and the British
C. Mahadji Scindia and the British
D. Holkar and the British

60. The words 'Satyameva Jayate' in the State Emblem of India, have been adopted from which one of the following?

A. Brahma Upanishad
B. Mudgala Upanishad
C. Maitreyi Upanishad
D. Mundaka Upanishad

61. Match List-I with List-II and select the correct answer using the codes given below the lists—

List-I
(Symbol)

(*a*) Elephant
(*b*) Tree
(*c*) Empty Throne
(*d*) Horse

List-II
(Important event of life of Buddha)

1. Renouncement of worldly pleasures
2. Birth of Buddha
3. Enlightenment
4. Representation of royalty

Codes:

	(*a*)	(*b*)	(*c*)	(*d*)
A.	2	4	3	1
B.	3	1	4	2
C.	3	4	1	2
D.	2	3	4	1

62. When was Mahatma Gandhi, the father of the nation, born?

A. 1889 B. 1859
C. 1869 D. 1879

63. Chinese pilgrim Hiuen-Tsang came to and lived in India under whose rule?

A. Harshavardhan
B. Chandragupta Maurya
C. Ashok
D. Samudragupta

64. Who had founded the Slave dynasty in India?

A. Qutb-ud-din Aibak
B. Iltutmish
C. Mohammed Gauri
D. Balban

65. Which British Governor-General had started the *Doctrine of Lapse* policy in India?

A. Lord William Bentinck
B. Lord Dalhousie
C. Lord Canning
D. Lord Hardinge

66. "Liberty is our birth right, we shall seize it." Who said it?

A. Bhagat Singh
B. Ramprasad Bismil
C. Bal Gangadhar Tilak
D. Mahatma Gandhi

67. The most important Sufi shrine in India is located at

A. Pandua
B. Bidar
C. Ajmer
D. Shahjahanabad

68. The 'Ajivikas' were a

A. Sect contemporary to the Buddha
B. Breakaway branch of the Buddhists
C. Sect founded by Charvaka
D. Sect founded by Shankaracharya

69. The Indian Universities were first founded during the time of
A. Macaulay
B. Warren Hastings
C. Lord Canning
D. Lord William Bentinck

70. One of the following was ***not*** involved in the Chittagong Armoury Raid, 1934. Who was he?
A. Kalpana Dutt
B. Surya Sen
C. Pritilata Woddedar
D. Dinesh Gupta

71. Which of the following is associated with Sufi saints?
A. Tripitaka B. Dakhma
C. Khanqah D. Synagogue

72. Which Indian statesman used these, magic words, "Long years ago we made a tryst with destiny, and now the time comes when we shall redeem our pledge ... "?
A. Mohandas Karamchand Gandhi
B. Sardar Vallabhbhai Patel
C. Netaji Subhas Chandra Bose
D. Jawaharlal Nehru

73. In which century did French Revolution begin?
A. 16th century
B. 17th century
C. 18th century
D. 19th century

74. Under whose patronage was the Khandariya Mahadeo Temple at Khajuraho built?
A. Solankis
B. Rashtrakutas
C. Tomaras
D. Chandellas

75. During the period of which of the following was 'Panchtantra' written?
A. Nandas B. Mauryas
C. Guptas D. Sungas

76. Who wrote the book called Kitab-i-Nauras?
A. Amir Khusro
B. Badauni
C. Ibrahim Adil Shah II
D. Ala-ud-din Bahmani

77. Who among the following, Mughal rulers granted the English Company *Dewani* over Bengal, Bihar and Orissa, by Treaty of Allahabad?
A. Ahmad Shah
B. Alamgir II
C. Shah Alam II
D. Akbar Shah II

78. During the Indian freedom struggle, what accusation was made against Master Amir Chand, Awadh Bihari, Bal Mukund and Basant Kumar Biswas?
A. Assassination of the Commissioner of Poona
B. Throwing a bomb on Viceroy's procession in Delhi
C. Attempt to shoot the Governor of Punjab
D. Looting an armoury in Bengal

79. Which of the following pairs is/are correctly matched?
1. Regulating Act : Hastings
2 Widow Remarriage Act : Bentinck
3. Vernacular Press Act : Lytton

Select the correct answer using the codes given below:

A. 1 only B. 2 and 3

C. 1 and 3 D. 1, 2 and 3

80. Which among the following is referred to as the Montague-Chelmsford Reforms?

A. Indian Council Act, 1909

B. Government of India Act, 1919

C. Rowlatt Act

D. Government of India Act, 1935

81. Consider the following statements:

1. Lord Cornwallis introduced the Permanent Land Settlement in Bengal.
2. Lord Wellesley introduced the Subsidiary Alliance system.

Which of the statements given above is/are correct?

A. 1 only

B. 2 only

C. Both 1 and 2

D. Neither 1 nor 2

82. Who was the Governor-General when the Revolt of 1857 started?

A. Lord Canning

B. Lord Cornwallis

C. Lord Dalhousie

D. Lord Ellenborough

83. Which of the following pairs is correctly matched?

A. Mahatma Gandhi : Home Rule

B. Annie Besant : Non-Cooperation Movement

C. Jawaharlal Nehru : Khilafat Movement

D. Lala Hardayal : Hindustan Ghadar Party

84. For which of the following movements did Mahatma Gandhi give the slogan "Do or Die"?

A. Kheda Satyagraha

B. Non-Cooperation Movement

C. Civil Disobedience Movement

D. Quit India Movement

85. Who among the following was the founder of the Servants of India Society?

A. Bal Gangadhar Tilak

B. Dadabhai Naoroji

C. Gopal Krishna Gokhale

D. Lala Lajpat Rai

86. Which of the following pairs is ***not*** correctly mathced?

A. Lord Wellesley : Subsidiary Alliance

B. Lord Dalhousie : Doctrine of Lapse

C. Lord Ripon : Vernacular Press Act

D. Lord Curzon : Partition of Bengal

87. Which of the following territories was outside the boundaries of the Mughal Empire during the reign of Akbar?

A. Khandesh B. Kabul

C. Bijapur D. Kashmir

88. Which Sultan of Delhi enforced a strict market control system during his time?

A. Ala-ud-din Khilji

B. Mohammad-bin-Tughlaq

C. Firoz Shah Tughlaq

D. Bahlol Lodi

89. Which of the following pairs is ***not*** correctly matched?

A. Kautilya : Arthashastra

B. Hala : Gathasaptasati

C. Banabhatta: Buddha Charita

D. Kalidasa : Abhijnana Shakuntalam

90. With which of the following countries is the famous 'October Revolution' associated?

A. China B. Cuba

C. France D. Russia

91. Who is the author of "Das Kapital"?

A. Karl Marx

B. Friedrich Engels

C. Joseph Stalin

D. Vladimir Lenin

92. Who was the Commander of the American forces during the American War of Independence?

A. Alexander Hamilton

B. Thomas Jefferson

C. George Washington

D. Major Samuel Shaw

93. Who fought the Battle of Buxar?

A. Humayun and Sher Shah Suri

B. Ahmad Shah Abdali and Marathas

C. English and Mir Kasim

D. English and Marathas

94. Who of the following started the newspaper 'Samvad Kaumudi' in the early 19th century?

A. Ishwar Chandra Vidyasagar

B. Keshav Chandra Sen

C. Raja Rammohan Roy

D. Satyendranath Tagore

95. Match List-I (Movements) with List-II (Leaders) and select the correct answer using the codes given below the lists:

List-I (Movements)	**List-II (Leaders)**
A. Home Rule movement	1. Maulana Abul Kalam Azad
B. Bhudan movement	2. Bal Gangadhar Tilak
C. Aligarh movement	3. Sayyid Ahmad Khan
D. Khilafat movement	4. Vinoba Bhave

Codes:

	(a)	*(b)*	*(c)*	*(d)*
A.	1	4	3	2
B.	2	4	3	1
C.	2	3	4	1
D.	1	3	4	2

96. When the Moroccan traveller Ibn Batutah visited India, who was the Delhi Sultan?

A. Jalaluddin Khilji

B. Ala-ud-din Khilji

C. Giasuddin Tughlaq

D. Muhammad-bin Tughlaq

97. The Lingaraja Temple built during the medieval period is at

A. Bhubaneswar

B. Khajuraho

C. Madurai

D. Mount Abu

98. Which of the following is Considered as an encyclopaedia of Indian medicine?

A. Charakasamhita

B. Lokayata

C. Brihatsamhita
D. Suryasiddhanta

99. Which of the following is not included in the 'eight-fold path' of Buddhism?
A. Right Speech
B. Right Contemplation
C. Right Desire
D. Right Conduct

100. During India's freedom struggle, the 'Sepoy Mutiny' started from which of the following places?
A. Agra B. Gwalior
C. Jhansi D. Meerut

Geography

101. Match List-I (Historical Site) with List-II (State) and select the correct answer using the codes given below the lists:

List-I (Historical Site)	List-II (State)
(*a*) Shore temple	1. Karnataka
(*b*) Bhimbetka	2. Tamil Nadu
(*c*) Kesava temple (Hoysala (Monuments)	3. Kerala
(*d*) Hampi	4. Madhya Pradesh
	5. Rajasthan

Codes :

	(*a*)	(*b*)	(*c*)	(*d*)
A.	3	5	2	1
B.	2	4	1	1
C.	3	4	2	2
D.	2	5	1	4

102. Where are the maximum numbers of major ports located in India?
A. Maharashtra
B. Kerala
C. Goa
D. Tamil Nadu

103. Match List-I (Beach Resort) with List-II (State) and select the correct answer using the codes given below the lists:

List-I (Beach Resort)	List-II (State)
(*a*) Digha	1. Kerala
(*b*) Covelong	2. West Bengal
(*c*) Cherai	3. Maharashtra
(*d*) Murud-Janjira	4. Tamil Nadu

Codes :

	(*a*)	(*b*)	(*c*)	(*d*)
A.	2	4	1	3
B.	3	1	4	2
C.	2	1	4	3
D.	3	4	1	2

104. Match List-I (Produce) with List-II (Major Producer State) and select the correct answer using the codes given below the lists:

List-I (Produce)	List-II (Major Producer State)
(*a*) Rubber	1. Andhra Pradesh
(*b*) Soyabean	2. Tamil Nadu
(*c*) Groundnut	3. Madhya Pradesh
(*d*) Wheat	4. Kerala
	5. Uttar Pradesh

Codes :

	(*a*)	(*b*)	(*c*)	(*d*)
A.	4	1	2	5
B.	5	3	1	4
C.	4	3	1	5
D.	5	1	2	4

105. Match List-I (Railway Zone) with List-II (Headquarters) and select the correct answer using the codes given below the lists:

List-I (Railway Zone)	**List-II (Headquarters)**
(*a*) East-Central Railway	1. Hubli
(*b*) North-Western Railway	2. Allahabad
(*c*) North-Central Railway	3. Hajipur
(*d*) South-Western Railway	4. Jabalpur
	5. Jaipur

Codes :

	(*a*)	(*b*)	(*c*)	(*d*)
A.	3	5	2	1
B.	2	1	4	5
C.	3	1	2	5
D.	2	5	4	1

106. Match List-I (Wildlife Sanctuary) with List-II (State) and select the correct answer using the codes given below the lists:

List-I (Wildlife Sanctuary)	**List-II (State)**
(*a*) Bhitar Kanika	1. Andhra Pradesh
(*b*) Pachmarhi	2. Karnataka
(*c*) Pocharam	3. Madhya Pradesh
(*d*) Sharavathi	4. Orissa
	5. Uttar Pradesh

Codes :

	(*a*)	(*b*)	(*c*)	(*d*)
A.	4	2	1	3
B.	1	3	5	2
C.	4	3	1	2
D.	1	2	5	3

107. Which one of the following is ***not*** a tributary of the river Godavari?

A. Koyna B. Manjra
C. Pranhita D. Wardha

108. Which one of the following is the correct statement?

A. Spring tides occur on the full moon day only
B. Neap tides occur on the new moon day only
C. The West coast of India experiences tides four times a day
D. Tides do not occur in the gulfs

109. Which one of the following pairs is ***not*** correctly matched?

	City	**River**
A.	Ahmedabad:	Sabarmati
B.	Hyderabad :	Musi
C.	Lucknow :	Gomti
D.	Surat :	Narmada

110. Match List-I (Famous Place) with List-II (Country) and select the correct answer using the codes given below the lists:

List-I (Famous Place)	List-II (Country)
(*a*) Alexandria	1. Turkey
(*b*) Blackpool Pleasure Beach	2. Great Britain
(*c*) Constantinople	3. Italy
(*d*) Florence	4. Greece
	5. Egypt

Codes :

	(*a*)	(*b*)	(*c*)	(*d*)
A.	1	3	4	2
B.	5	2	1	3
C.	1	2	4	3
D.	5	3	1	2

111. Match List-I (Institute) with List-II (City) and select the correct answer using the codes given below the lists:

List-I (Institute)	List-II (City)
(*a*) Rashtriya Sanskrit Vidyapeeth	1. Hyderabad
(*b*) Maharishi Sandipani Rashtriya Veda Vidhya Pratishthan	2. Varanasi
(*c*) Central Institute of Indian Languages	3. Mysore
(*d*) Central Institute of English and Foreign Languages	4. Tirupati
	5. Ujjain

Codes :

	(*a*)	(*b*)	(*c*)	(*d*)
A.	2	3	1	5
B.	4	5	3	1
C.	2	5	3	1
D.	4	3	1	5

112. Consider the following statements:

1. Kaziranga National park is a World Heritage Site recognised by the UNESCO
2. Kaziranga National Park is a home to sloth bear and hoolock gibbon.

Which of the statements given above is/are correct?

A. 1 only
B. 2 only
C. Both 1 and 2
D. Neither 1 nor 2

113. Which country among the following is the biggest producer of cotton?

A. China
B. India
C. Indonesia
D. USA

114. Where is the Holy Shrine of Imam Ali in Najaf located?

A. Saudi Arabia
B. Iraq
C. Iran
D. Kuwait

115. Match List-I (Institute) with List-II (Location) and select the correct answer using the codes given below the lists:

List-I (Institute)	List-II (Location)
(*a*) Indian Institute of Public Administration	1. Faridabad

(*b*) V.V. Giri National Labour Institute	2. Bangalore
(*c*) National Institute of Financial Management	3. NOIDA
(*d*) National Law School of India University	4. Mumbai
	5. Delhi

Codes :

	(*a*)	(*b*)	(*c*)	(*d*)
A.	1	2	4	3
B.	5	3	1	2
C.	1	3	4	2
D.	5	2	1	3

116. Which river feeds "Tehri dam"?
A. Alaknanda
B. Bhagirathi
C. Gandak
D. Ghaghara

117. Which of the following winds are known as "Anti-trade winds"?
A. Chinook
B. Cyclones
C. Typhoons
D. Westerlies

118. Geostationary orbit is at a height of
A. 6 km
B. 1000 km
C. 3600 km
D. 36000 km

119. The orbits of planets around the Sun can be
A. Elliptic and parabolic
B. Parabolic and hyperbolic
C. Circular and hyperbolic
D. Circular and elliptic

120. What is Super Nova?
A. A black hole
B. A dying star
C. An asteroid
D. A comet

121. Which State is irrigated by the Gang Canal?
A. Uttar Pradesh
B. Bihar
C. West Bengal
D. Rajasthan

122. Among the following Indian cities, which one is located most southward?
A. Hyderabad
B. Visakhapatnam
C. Panaji
D. Belgaum

123. Match List I (National Highway) with List II (Connected Cities) and select the correct answer using the codes given below the Lists:

List-I (National Highway)	**List-II (Connected Cities)**
A. NH 3	1. Delhi-Lucknow
B. NH 4	2. Agra-Bikaner
C. NH 11	3. Agra-Mumbai
D. NH 24	4. Chennai-Thane (Mumbai)

Codes :

	(*a*)	(*b*)	(*c*)	(*d*)
A.	3	1	2	4
B.	2	4	3	1
C.	3	4	2	1
D.	2	1	3	4

124. Match List-I (Defence Institute) with List-II (City) and select the correct answer using the codes given below the Lists:

List-I (Defence Institute)	List-II (City)
(*a*) College of Defence Management	1. Panchmarhi
(*b*) Army Air Defence College	2. Bengaluru
(*c*) Army Supply Corps (ASC) Centre and College	3. Secunderabad
(*d*) Army Education Corps (AEC) Training College and Centre	4. Gopalpur

Codes :

	(*a*)	(*b*)	(*c*)	(*d*)
A.	3	4	2	1
B.	1	2	4	3
C.	3	2	4	1
D.	1	4	2	3

125. Which of the following are Defence Public Sector Undertakings?

1. Goa Shipyard Limited
2. The Bharat Dynamics Limited
3. Mishra Dhatu Nigam Limited

Select the correct answer using the codes given below:

A. 1 and 2 B. 2 and 3
C. 1 and 3 D. 1, 2 and 3

126. Which one of the following pairs is ***not*** correctly matched?

A. Gol Gumbaz : Hyderabad
B. Tomb of Itmad-ud-daula : Agra
C. Tomb of Sher Shah : Sasaram
D. Tomb of Rani Rupmati : Ahmedabad

127. Where is the Baglihar Hydroelectric Project located?

A. Firozepur District of Punjab
B. Doda District of Jammu and Kashmir
C. Faridkot District of Punjab
D. Baramulla District of Jammu and Kashmir

128. Match List-I (Temple/Cathedral) with List-II (Place) and select the correct answer using the code given below the Lists:

List-I (Temple/Cathedral)

(*a*) Brihadeswara Temple
(*b*) Vishwanatha Temple
(*c*) Kamakhya Temple
(*d*) Santhom Cathedral

List-II (Place)

1. Guwahati
2. Chennai
3. Thanjavur
4. Khajuraho

Codes :

	(*a*)	(*b*)	(*c*)	(*d*)
A.	3	2	1	4
B.	1	4	3	2
C.	3	4	1	2
D.	1	2	3	4

129. Match List-I (World Heritage Site) with List-II (State) and select the correct answer using the code given below the Lists:

List-I (World Heritage Site)

(*a*) Manas Wildlife Sanctuary
(*b*) Mahabodhi Temple Complex
(*c*) Group of Monuments, Pattadakal
(*d*) Nandadevi National Park

List-II (State)

1. Bihar
2. Uttarakhand
3. Asom
4. Karnataka

Codes :

	(*a*)	(*b*)	(*c*)	(*d*)
A.	2	4	1	3
B.	3	1	4	2
C.	2	1	4	3
D.	3	4	1	2

130. Consider the following statements:

1. Black soils occur mainly in Maharashtra, Western Madhya Pradesh and Gujarat.
2. Alluvial soils are confined mainly to the northern plains.

Which of the statements given above is/are correct?

A. 1 only
B. 2 only
C. Both 1 and 2
D. Neither 1 nor 2

131. What is the new name of the old colony of Northern Rhodesia?

A. Zambia B. Zimbabwe
C. Uganda D. Tanzania

132. Which is the smallest (in area) of the following Union Territories?

A. Chandigarh
B. Dadra and Nagar Haveli
C. Daman and Diu
D. Lakshadweep

133. The Sundarbans or the 'Mangrove' forests are found in

A. Kutch Peninsula
B. Western Ghats
C. Konkan Coast
D. Deltaic West Bengal

134. On which river has the Hirakud dam been built?

A. Mahanadi
B. Godavari
C. Cauvery
D. Periyar

135. Where is "Ground Zero"?

A. Greenwich
B. New York
C. Indira Point
D. Sriharikota

136. The maximum concentration of scheduled caste population is in the

A. Indo-Gangetic Plains
B. North-East India
C. Western Coast
D. Eastern Coast

137. When was the first passenger train run in India?

A. January 1848
B. April 1853
C. May 1857
D. April 1852

138. Which is the major area where 'Garba' dance form is common?

A. Maharashtra B. Gujarat
C. Rajasthan D. Punjab

139. Where is India's most prized tea grown?

A. Jorhat B. Darjeeling

C. Nilgiris D. Mannar

140. Which is the largest cotton growing State in India?

A. Maharashtra

B. Madhya Pradesh

C. Andhra Pradesh

D. Gujarat

141. Which one of the following is the first shipyard of India?

A. Cochin

B. Visakhapatnam

C. Mazagaon

D. Paradeep

142. Which of the following Indian States is the largest producer of Cardamom?

A. Kerala

B. Tamil Nadu

C. Karnataka

D. Jammu & Kashmir

143. Vikram Sarabhai Space Centre is located in

A. Peenya

B. Ahmedabad

C. Thiruvananthapuram

D. Dehradun

144. The Sardar Sarovar Dam is associated with

A. Tapti river valley project

B. Mahanadi river valley project

C. Narmada project

D. Bhakra-Nangal project

145. In which of the following states in India is the bird, Great Indian Bustard found?

A. Rajasthan

B. Bihar

C. Karnataka

D. Andhra Pradesh

146. The Indian state with smallest population is

A. Sikkim

B. Arunachal Pradesh

C. Goa

D. Mizoram

147. On which of the following rivers Nasik is situated?

A. Ganges

B. Krishna

C. Godavari

D. Cauvery

148. Atacama Desert is in

A. South America

B. North America

C. South Africa

D. Russia

149. Which place in India is a reference for determining Indian Standard Time?

A. Delhi B. Allahabad

C. Kolkata D. Mumbai

150. Which of the following does not share a boarder with India?

A. Pakistan

B. Bangladesh

C. Burma

D. Afghanistan

151. The Dachigam Wildlife Sanctuary is in

A. Himachal Pradesh

B. Asom

C. Jammu & Kashmir

D. Karnataka

152. How many days does the moon take to complete 1 revolution around the earth?

A. $26\frac{1}{3}$ days

B. $27\frac{1}{3}$ days

C. $24\frac{1}{3}$ days

D. $28\frac{1}{2}$ days

153. A high growth rate of population is characterised by

A. High birth and high death rates

B. High birth and low death rates

C. Low birth and low death rates

D. Low birth and high death rates

154. The Indian Sub-continent was originally a part of

A. Jurassic-land

B. Angara-land

C. Aryavarta

D. Gondwana-land

155. The tropical grassland is called

A. Pampas B. Llanas

C. Savanah D. Veld

156. The atmosphere is heated mainly by

A. Insolation

B. Conduction

C. Radiation

D. Convection

157. Which one of the following countries is the largest producer of uranium in the world?

A. Canada B. South Africa

C. Namibia D. USA

158. Which of the following methods does not help in conserving soil fertility and moisture?

A. Contour ploughing

B. Dry farming

C. Strip cropping

D. Shifting agriculture

159. Mudumalai Wildlife Sanctuary is located in the State of

A. Kerala

B. Karnataka

C. Tamil Nadu

D. Andhra Pradesh

160. The narrow stretch of water connecting two seas is called

A. Bay B. Peninsula

C. Isthmus D. Strait

161. The topography of plateau is ideal for

A. Cultivation

B. Forestry

C. Mining

D. Generation of hydel power

162. Naga Khasi and Garo hills are located in

A. Purvanchal Ranges

B. Karakoram Ranges

C. Zaskar Ranges

D. Himalayas Ranges

163. In which of the following States, Jawahar Tunnel is located?

A. Himachal Pradesh

B. Jammu & Kashmir

C. Uttarakhand

D. Goa

164. Where was India's first submarine museum established?
A. Kochi
B. Panjim
C. Visakhapatnam
D. Mumbai

165. Which two countries are connected by an under-water tunnel?
A. England and Spain
B. Malaysia and Singapore
C. England and Belgium
D. France and England

166. Which of the following is correctly matched with regard to thermal power projects?
A. Korba — Uttar Pradesh
B. Ramagundam — Tamil Nadu
C. Talcher — Andhra Pradesh
D. Kawas — Gujarat

167. Sundarbans of Eastern India is an example of
A. Forest Ecosystem
B. Mangrove Ecosystem
C. Grassland Ecosystem
D. Marine Ecosystem

168. The deepest trench of the world—'The Mariana Trench' is located in the
A. Indian Ocean
B. Atlantic Ocean
C. Arctic Ocean
D. Pacific Ocean

169. Which of the following is a landlocked sea?
A. Timor Sea
B. Arafura Sea
C. Greenland Sea
D. Aral Sea

170. Match the dams and the states in which they are situated:

	Dam	**State**
(*a*)	Hirakud	1. Chhattisgarh
(*b*)	Mettur	2. Orissa
(*c*)	Mahanadi	3. Karnataka
(*d*)	Almatti	4. Tamil Nadu

Codes :

	(*a*)	(*b*)	(*c*)	(*d*)
A.	3	2	4	1
B.	2	4	1	3
C.	1	3	2	4
D.	4	1	3	2

171. Which of the following territories does not have a border with Arunachal Pradesh?
A. Asom
B. Nagaland
C. Bhutan
D. Manipur

172. Which of the following 'rivers does ***not*** originate in the Indian territory?
A. Mahanadi
B. Brahamaputra
C. Ravi
D. Chenab

173. Land and sea-breezes occur due to
A. Conduction
B. Convection
C. Radiation
D. Tides

174. Which of the following is ***not*** correctly matched with regard to Project Tiger Reserves?
A. Sariska — Alwar
B. Valmiki — Hazaribagh
C. Pench — Garhwal
D. Nagarjunasagar — Sri Sailam

175. Trade winds blow from the
A. Equatorial low pressure
B. Polar high pressure
C. Subtropical high pressure
D. Subpolar low pressure

176. Most of the Indians belong to which of the following racial stocks?
A. Caucasoid
B. Negroid
C. Australoid
D. Mongoloid

177. Which of the following signifies the American Indians living in the US?
A. Bushmen
B. Alpine
C. Amerindus
D. Mestizoes

178. Which region is most famous for citrus fruits?
A. Deserts
B. Monsoon regions
C. Temperate grasslands
D. Mediterranean regions

179. The leading sulphur producing country in the world is
A. USA B. Russia
C. Japan D. Mexico

180. The largest producer of mercury is
A. USA B. Canada
C. China D. Spain

181. The largest amount of saffron comes from
A. Uttar Pradesh
B. Tamil Nadu
C. Jammu and Kashmir
D. Kerala

182. The boundary between Germany and Poland is called the
A. Hindenberg Line
B. Maginot Line
C. Durand Line
D. 17th Parallel

183. The boundary between North and South Korea is marked by the
A. Radcliffe Line
B. 38th Parallel
C. 49th Parallel
D. 17th Parallel

184. Which countries are separated by the 49th Parallel?
A. France and Germany
B. USA and Mexico
C. USA and Canada
D. Russia and China

185. Echo-sounding is the technique applied to
A. Measure the depth of the sea
B. Measure the amplitude of sound waves
C. Record earthquake waves
D. Record the density of air in the atmosphere

186. On which of the rivers is the famous Kariba Dam situated?
A. Nile B. Niger
C. Zambezi D. Amazon

187. The northernmost limit of India is
A. 36°4' N latitude
B. 37°8' N latitude
C. 37°6' N latitude
D. 36°12' N latitude

188. The length of India's coastline is about
A. 4,500 km
B. 5,900 km
C. 7,000 km
D. 7,516 km

189. The total area of India is about
A. 31 lakh sq km
B. 33 lakh sq km
C. 320 lakh sq km
D. 35 lakh sq km

190. Where is the Gulf of Mannar located?
A. West of Gujarat
B. East of Tamil Nadu
C. West of Kerala
D. South of Kanyakumari

191. The Sivaliks stretch between
A. Indus and Sutlej
B. Potwar Basin and Teesta
C. Sutlej and Kali
D. Sutlej and Teesta

192. The territorial waters of India extend up to
A. 12 nautical miles
B. 6 nautical miles
C. 15 nautical miles
D. 10 nautical miles

193. The deepest lake in the world is
A. Pushkar Lake
B. Lake Superior
C. Victoria Lake
D. Baikal Lake

194. Simlipal Tiger Reserve is located at
A. Assam
B. Gujarat
C. Orissa
D. Bihar

195. Which of the following rivers flow through a rift valley?
A. Ganga
B. Narmada
C. Brahmaputra
D. Krishna

196. What is the most important characteristic of the islands (Indian) located in the Arabian Sea?
A. They are all very small in size
B. They are all of coral origin
C. They have a very dry climate
D. They are extended parts of the mainland

197. The Thar Desert is believed to be expanding. The most suitable way to check it would be by
A. Afforestation
B. Artificial rain
C. Canal irrigation
D. Using the area for cattle rearing

198. Which one is a land-locked State?
A. Gujarat
B. Andhra Pradesh
C. West Bengal
D. Bihar

199. Which area in India gets the summer monsoon?
A. The Himalayas
B. The Eastern Ghats
C. The Western Ghats
D. The Indo-Gangetic plains

200. In which of the following areas is maximum precipitation received from the summer monsoon?
A. The Coromandel coast

B. The North-Eastern hilly region
C. The Central Indian hills
D. The Western Himalayas

Indian Polity and Constitution

201. Which Schedule of the Constitution lists the languages recognised by it?
A. Eighth Schedule
B. Sixth Schedule
C. Seventh Schedule
D. Ninth Schedule

202. Which of the following Union Territories has a Chief Minister?
A. Andaman and Nicobar Islands
B. Puducherry
C. Chandigarh
D. Dadra and Nagar Haveli

203. Who among the following administers the Oath of Office to the President of India?
A. The Vice-President of India
B. The Chief Justice of India
C. The Chairman of Rajya Sabha
D. The Prime Minister

204. Parliament of India consists of
A. Directly elected members only
B. Directly elected and nominated members
C. Directly elected and indirectly elected members
D. Directly elected, indirectly elected and nominated members

205. In a Unitary Government
A. All powers are vested in the Centre
B. Powers are divided between the Centre and the States under a Constitution
C. Powers are divided by mutual consent of the Centre and the States through Parliamentary statute
D. The Judiciary must be independent

206. Article 360 of the Constitution of India relates to
A. National Emergency
B. Emergency in a State
C. To conduct Parliament Elections
D. Financial Emergency

207. Panchayati Raj was recommended by
A. Sarkaria Commission
B. Fazlali Commission
C. Balwantrai Mehta Committee
D. Rajamannar Committee

208. Name the first woman Governor of an Indian State
A. Padmaja Naidu
B. Lakshmi N. Menon
C. Sarojini Naidu
D. Sucheta Kriplani

209. Gangtok is the capital of
A. Nagaland
B. Meghalaya
C. Sikkim
D. Arunachal Pradesh

210. Who appoints the Chief Justice of a High Court in India?

A. The President of India
B. The Governor of the State concerned
C. The Chief Justice of the Supreme Court
D. An Appointment Committee in the Union Ministry of Law

211. In India, how did the Planning Commission come into existence?
A. By an Act of Parliament
B. By an executive order
C. Under the provisions of the Constitution
D. As an attached office of the Union Ministry of Finance

212. Which is the first executive tier of the Panchayati Raj system from below?
A. Gram Sabha
B. Gram Panchayat
C. Mandal Parishad
D. Panchayat Samiti

213. After the Constitution of India, came into force, when did the Parliament enact the Untouchability (Offences) Act?
A. 1953 B. 1954
C. 1955 D. 1956

214. Which of the following pairs is ***not*** correctly matched?

	State/U.T.		High Court
A.	Goa	—	Bombay
B.	Andaman and Nicobar Islands	—	Calcutta
C.	Sikkim	—	Guwahati
D.	Puducherry	—	Madras

215. The procedure for the Amendment of the Constitution of India is given under
A. Article 315
B. Article 358
C. Article 360
D. Article 368

216. Which of the following Articles of the Constitution of India has provision for the President to proclaim emergency?
A. Article 352
B. Article 355
C. Article 356
D. Article 360

217. Which of the following offices is held during the pleasure of the President of India?
A. Vice-President
B. Chief Justice of India
C. Governor of a State
D. Chairman of the Union Public Service Commission

218. Article 370 of the constitution is applicable to the state of
A. Nagaland
B. Mizoram
C. Manipur
D. Jammu & Kashmir

219. In the parliamentary practices when did the "Zero-hour" interventions emerge in India?
A. 1952 B. 1962
C. 1972 D. 1982

220. "Vote on Account" means legislative vote
A. On the Appropriation Bill
B. On the Finance Bill

C. On the accounts and audit report submitted by the CAG
D. Authorising expenditure in respect of the demands for grants pending the passing of the Appropriation Bill

221. Which of these words is not in the preamble of the constitution of India?
A. Socialist
B. Sovereign
C. Secular
D. Public Welfare

222. Which of the following has ***not*** been mentioned in the Indian Constitution as a Right?
A. Political and Social Rights
B. Educational Rights
C. Economic Rights
D. Religious Rights

223. Which one of the following is ***not*** stated in the Preamble of the Indian Constitution?
A. Justice
B. Fraternity
C. Adult franchise
D. Equality of status

224. In framing the Constitution of India, from which country did we borrow the scheme of the federal set up?
A. U.S.A. B. U.K.
C. Canada D. Switzerland

225. Who among the following was ***not*** a member of the Constituent Assembly set up in July 1946?
A. Dr. Rajendra Prasad
B. K.M. Munshi
C. Mahatma Gandhi
D. Abul Kalam Azad

226. Which article of the Indian Constitution provides for the institution of Panchayati Raj?
A. Art. 36 B. Art. 39
C. Art. 40 D. Art. 48

227. Which of the following is a bulwark of personal freedom?
A. Mandamus
B. Habeas Corpus
C. Quo Warranto
D. Certiorari

228. Who is the highest civil servant of the Union Government?
A. Attorney-General
B. Cabinet Secretary
C. Home Secretary
D. Principal Secretary to the Prime Minister

229. Article 1 of the Constitution declares India as
A. Federal State
B. Quasi-Federal State
C. Unitary State
D. Union of States

230. Which functionary can be invited to give his opinion in the Parliament?
A. Attorney-General of India
B. Chief Justice of India
C. Chief Election Commissioner of India
D. Comptroller and Auditor-General of India

231. Which of the following countries has an Unwritten Constitution?
A. USA B. UK
C. Pakistan D. India

232. The Drafting Committee of the Constitution, including the chairman, comprised of

A. Seven members
B. Five members
C. Nine members
D. Three members

233. Which one of the following exercised the most profound influence on the Indian Constitution?

A. The Government of India Act 1935
B. The US Constitution
C. British Constitution
D. The UN Charter

234. Which one of the following features was borrowed by the Indian Constitution from the British Constiution?

A. Parliamentary system of government
B. Rule of Law
C. Law-making procedure
D. All the above

235. India borrowed the idea of a federal system with a strong centre from

A. USA B. Canada
C. Australia D. New Zealand

236. The emergency provisions of the constitution of India were greatly influenced by

A. The Government of India Act 1935
B. The Weimar Constitution of Germany
C. The Constitution of United States
D. The Constitution of Canada

237. India borrowed the idea of Directive Principles of State Policy from the Constitutions of

A. The Weimar Republic of Germany
B. The Republic of Ireland
C. The South Africa
D. None of the above

238. If the President wishes to tender his resignation before the expiry of his normal term, he has to address the same to

A. The Vice-President of India
B. The Speaker of Lok Sabha
C. The Chief Justice of India
D. The Election Commission

239. Who among the following got the Bharat Ratna Award before becoming the President of India?

A. Dr. Zakir Hussain
B. Dr. Rajendra Prasad
C. V.V. Giri
D. Dr. S. Radhakrishnan

240. The Council of Ministers is collectively responsible to

A. The President of India
B. The Parliament
C. The Prime Minister
D. The Rajya Sabha

241. The office of the Prime Minister of India

A. Has been created by the Constitution
B. Is extra-constitutional growth
C. Has been created by a Parliamentary Statute
D. Is the combination of all the above

242. The minimum age at which a person can be appointed Prime Minister of India?
A. 21 years B. 25 years
C. 30 years D. 35 years

243. The first Amendment of the constitution was made in the year:
A. 1950 B. 1949
C. 1954 D. 1958

244. Which of the following is the maximum time limit of 'Zero Hour' during the Parliament session in India?
A. 30 minutes
B. One hour
C. Two hours
D. None of the above

245. Who among the following summons the joint session of Lok Sabha and Rajya Sabha?
A. Speaker
B. Chairman of Rajya Sabha
C. President
D. Minister of Parliamentary Affairs

246. Which of the following is India's Contribution to parliamentary system of democracy?
A. Zero Hour
B. Cut Motion Resolution
C. Adjournment Motion
D. Guillotine

247. The total number of members in the Legislative Council of a State cannot exceed
A. one-fourth of the total number of members in the Legislative Assembly
B. one-third of the total number of members of the legislative Assembly
C. one-sixth of the total number of members of the Legislative Assembly
D. No such limit has been fixed

248. Sikkim was made an integral part of India under the
A. 42nd Amendment
B. 40th Amendment
C. 39th Amendment
D. 36th Amendment

249. The number of Anglo-Indians who can be nominated by the President to the Lok Sabha is
A. 2 B. 3
C. 4 D. 5

250. Money Bills can be introduced in the State Legislature with the prior consent of
A. the Speaker
B. the Chief Minister
C. the Governor
D. the President

Economy

251. The apex bank for industrial credit in India is
A. RBI B. NABARD
C. ICICI D. IDBI

252. The prominent function of the Central Statistical Organisation is
A. To determine the money supply
B. To collect national income estimates
C. To collect employment details
D. To determine prices

253. Planning and control are related in such a way that

A. Planning precedes control

B. Control precedes planning

C. Both are concurrent

D. Both go hand in hand with each other in a cyclical manner

254. 'Gresham's Law' states that

A. Good money drives away bad money out of circulation

B. Bad money drives away good money out of circulation

C. Good money promotes bad money in the system

D. Bad money promotes good money in the system

255. National income refers to

A. Money value of goods and services produced in a country during a year

B. Money value of stocks and shares of a country during a year

C. Money value of capital goods produced by a country during a year

D. Money value of consumer goods produced by a country during a year

256. Which of the following taxes is/ are lived by the Union and collected and appropriated by the States?

A. Service tax

B. Stamp duties

C. Estate duty

D. Passenger and goods tax

257. Which of the following is ***not*** shared by the Centre and the States?

A. Income tax

B. Excise duty

C. Corporation duty

D. Sales tax

258. Expenditure on which of the following is ***not*** considered as an investment in the theory of income determination?

A. Factory construction

B. A computer

C. Increase in stocks of unsold goods

D. Stocks or shares in a joint stock company

259. With what aspect of commerce are "Bull" and "Bear" associated?

A. Banking

B. E-Commerce

C. International trade

D. Stock market

260. FDI means—

A. Foreign Direct Investment

B. Full Dog Cost

C. Full Direct Cost

D. Finance Institute

261. If the tax rate increases with the higher level of income, it shall be called

A. Proportional tax

B. Progressive tax

C. Lump sum tax

D. Regressive tax

262. In India, one-rupee coins and notes and subsidiary coins are issued by
A. The Reserve Bank of India
B. The Central Government
C. The State Bank of India
D. The Unit Trust of India

263. Which is the highest body that approves Five-Year Plans in the country?
A. NITI Aayog
B. Union Cabinet
C. National Development Council
D. Parliament

264. Prime cost is equal to
A. Variable cost plus administrative cost
B. Variable cost plus fixed cost
C. Variable cost only
D. Fixed cost only

265. New capital issue is placed in
A. Secondary market
B. Grey market
C. Primary market
D. Black market

266. Bank deposits that can be withdrawn without notice are called
A. Account payee deposits
B. Fixed deposits
C. Variable deposits
D. Demand deposits

267. An expenditure that has been made and cannot be recovered is called
A. Variable cost
B. Opportunity cost
C. Sink cost
D. Operational cost

268. The practice of selling goods in a foreign country at a price below their domestic selling price is called
A. 'Diplomacy'
B. 'Discrimination'
C. 'Dumping'
D. 'Double pricing'

269. Who propounded the 'market law'?
A. Adam Smith
B. J.B. Say
C. T.R. Malthus
D. Dravid Ricardo

270. National income is based on the
A. total revenue of the state
B. production of goods and services
C. net profit earned and expenditure made by the state
D. the sum of all factors of incomes

271. 'Utility' in economics means the capacity to
A. provide comforts
B. earn an income
C. satisfy human wants
D. satisfy human motives

272. Labour welfare does not include
A. education facilities
B. health facilities
C. housing facilities
D. quick promotion in job

273. 'Sellersmarket' denotes a situation where
A. Commodities are available at competitive rates
B. Demand exceeds supply

C. Supply exceeds demand
D. Supply and demand are evenly balanced

274. "Legal Tender Money" refers to
A. Cheques
B. Drafts
C. Bills of exchange
D. Currency notes

275. The sum total of incomes received for the services of labour, land or capital in a country is called
A. Gross domestic product
B. National income
C. Gross domestic income
D. Gross national income

276. The measurement of poverty line is based on the criteria of
A. Their dwelling houses
B. The nature of employment
C. Coloric consumption
D. Level of education

277. Capital is that wealth
A. Which is used for the production of wealth
B. Which is kept in boxes and lockers
C. Which is buried in the land
D. Which is stored for consumption

278. The poverty line has been defined in the
A. Seventh Five–Year Plan
B. Sixth Five–Year Plan
C. Eight Five–Year Plan
D. Fifth Five–Year Plan

279. Perfect market means there are
A. Many sellers and many buyers
B. A few sellers and a few buyers
C. A few sellers and many buyers
D. A few buyers and many sellers

280. A hard currency is the one
A. Whose external value is increasing
B. Which can be acquired only with official permission
C. Which can be obtained only against sale of gold
D. Which is really accepted in international transactions

281. Which of the following is not a Central Government Tax?
A. Income Tax
B. Customs
C. Land Revenue
D. Corporation Tax

282. Who is called the father of White Revolution?
A. Dr. Kurien Verghese
B. Nanjunda Swamy
C. M.S. Swaminathan
D. U.R. Rao

283. The major source of revenue in India is through
A. Direct Taxes
B. Indirect Taxes
C. Internal Borrowings
D. External Borrowings

284. The Reserve Bank of India was established in
A. 1927 B. 1935
C. 1947 D. 1949

285. Finance Commission is appointed by
- A. Prime Minister
- B. President of India
- C. Ministry of Finance
- D. None of these

286. Which of the following groups suffer the most from inflation?
- A. Debtors
- B. Creditors
- C. Business class
- D. Holders of real assets

287. Which one of the following is not an example of indirect tax?
- A. Sales tax
- B. Excise duty
- C. Customs duty
- D. Expenditure tax

288. The major aim of devaluation is to
- A. Encourage imports
- B. Encourage exports
- C. Encourage both exports and imports
- D. Discourage both exports and imports

289. Which of the following is a cash crop?
- A. Wheat
- B. Rice
- C. Sugarcane
- D. Maize

290. NAFED is connected with
- A. Animal husbandry
- B. Conservation of fuels
- C. Agricultural marketing
- D. Agricultural implements

291. Which Commission replaced Planning Commission in 2015?
- A. NIYAM Aayog
- B. NAGRIK Aayog
- C. NITI Aayog
- D. None of these

292. The one-rupee notes bear the signatures of the
- A. Governor, Reserve Bank of India
- B. Secretary, Ministry of Finance
- C. Deputy Governor, Reserve Bank of India
- D. Joint Secretary, Ministry of Finance

293. Whose approval is necessary before the Five-Year Plan can start?
- A. The Finance Minister
- B. National Development Council
- C. The Prime Minister
- D. Parliament

294. NABARD stands for
- A. National Bank of Agriculture and Regional Development
- B. National Bank for Agriculture and Rural Development
- C. National Bureau of Aeronautical Research and Development
- D. None of these

295. 'Bottle neck inflation' means
- A. No rise in prices despite increase in aggregate demand
- B. Rise in prices without increase in the aggregate demand

C. Decline in prices due to increase in aggregate demand
D. None of these

296. The main cause of International Trade is
A. Equal cost difference
B. Absolute cost difference
C. Comparative cost difference
D. Equal and comparative cost difference

297. Which one of the following taxes is not shared by the Central Government with the States?
A. Union excise duties
B. Customs duty
C. Income tax
D. Estate duty

298. A dualistic economy is one in which
A. both rich and poor people co-exist side by side
B. it has both foreign trade and internal trade
C. industry and agriculture exist side by side
D. modern sector and traditional sector exist side by side

299. Whose signatures are found on the 10 rupee note in India?
A. Prime Minister of India
B. President of India
C. Finance Minister of India
D. Governor, Reserve Bank of India

300. "Green Revolution" began in India during the year
A. 1967-68 B. 1966-67
C. 1968-69 D. 1969-70

General Science

301. Deep blue colour is imparted to glass by the presence of
A. Cobalt Oxide
B. Cupric Oxide
C. Ferrous Oxide
D. Nickel Oxide

302. Which of the following fibres is least prone to fire?
A. Nylon B. Cotton
C. Rayon D. Terry Cott

303. Which of the following is used as a filler in rubber tyres?
A. Carbon black
B. Coal
C. Coke
D. Graphite

304. Which of the following alloys is used for making magnets?
A. Duralumin
B. Stainless Steel
C. Alnico
D. Magnalium

305. Which of the following elements is obtained from sea weeds?
A. Argon
B. Sulphur
C. Vanadium
D. Iodine

306. Where are Mesons found?
A. Cosmic rays
B. X-rays
C. γ-rays
D. Laser beams

307. Milk tastes sour when kept in the open for sometime due to the formation of
A. Lactic acid
B. Citric acid
C. Acetic acid
D. Carbonic acid

308. Polythene is industrially prepared by the polymerisation of
A. Methane
B. Styrene
C. Acetylene
D. Ethylene

309. Which of the following chemicals responsible for the depletion of ozone layer in the atmosphere?
A. Nitrous oxide
B. Carbon dioxide
C. Chlorofluorocarbons
D. Sulphur dioxide

310. Plants die in winter by frost because
A. There is no transpiration
B. No photosynthesis takes place at such low temperatures
C. Respiration ceases at such low temperatures
D. Of desiccation and mechanical damage to tissues

311. Which of the following is ***not*** a constituent of chlorophyll?
A. Hydrogen
B. Magnesium
C. Carbon
D. Calcium

312. Which is the chief nitrogenous waste in humans?
A. Ammonia
B. Urea
C. Uric acid
D. Ammonium nitrate

313. Which is the largest living bird?
A. Peacock B. Ostrich
C. Dodo D. Turkey

314. Hormones are normally absent in
A. Rat B. Monkey
C. Bacteria D. Cat

315. Dengue fever is caused by
A. Fungi B. Bacteria
C. Protozoa D. Virus

316. Which of the following is considered to be good cholesterol?
A. VLDL B. LDL
C. HDL D. Triglycerides

317. "Thalassaemia" is a hereditary disease affecting
A. Blood B. Kidney
C. Lungs D. Heart

318. Which of the following is a proper food chain showing a producer, a herbivore and the carnivore?
A. Grass-Insect-Elephant
B. Plants-Rabbit-Tiger
C. Fish-Insect-Whale
D. Tiger-Rabbit-Owl

319. Aspirin is
A. Methoxy Benzoic acid
B. Methyl Salicylate
C. Acetyl Salicylic acid
D. Phenyl Salicylate

320. The medical instrument sphygmomanometer is used to examine
A. hormonal activity
B. brain tumor
C. the functions of intestine
D. blood pressure

321. Onion is a modified form of
A. stem B. root
C. leaves D. fruit

322. Weight of the body
A. remains the same everywhere on the earth's surface
B. is maximum at the poles
C. is maximum at the equator
D. is more on mountains than plains

323. Most of the nutrients are absorbed into blood through
A. large intestine
B. mouth
C. small intestine
D. abdomen

324. The path of Halley's comet in its orbit around the Sun is
A. circular
B. elliptical
C. parabolic
D. hyperbolic

325. Atoms of the same element having the same atomic number but different atomic weights are called
A. Isotopes B. Polymers
C. Isomers D. Isobars

326. The chief constituent of gobar gas is
A. Nitrogen
B. Ethane
C. Hydrogen
D. Methane

327. Law of heredity was put forward by
A. Mendel B. Mendeleev
C. Pavlov D. Koch

328. A device used for converting a.c. into d.c. is called
A. Transformer
B. Rectifier
C. Induction oil
D. Dynamo

329. An antibiotic is
A. A chemical synthesised by a human cell against a micro-organism
B. A chemical synthesised by a micro-organism against another micro-organism
C. A substance produced by blood cells against bacteria
D. A substance produced by blood cells against infection

330. Which one of the following can be synthesized by Liver?
A. Vitamin-A
B. Vitamin-E
C. Vitamin-D
D. Vitamin-K

331. Fluid part of blood devoid of corpuscles is called
A. Tissue fluid
B. Plasma
C. Serum
D. Lymph

332. Heart murmur indicates a
A. Defective valve
B. Poor oxygenation
C. Dislocation of the heart
D. Improper development of muscles

333. The language used in writing the scientific name of animals is
A. French B. Latin
C. German D. Dutch

334. Energy of Ultra-violet rays is greater than
A. Infra-red rays

B. Gamma rays
C. X-rays
D. Cosmic rays

335. By-product obtained by soap-industry is
A. Caustic soda
B. Glycerol
C. Naphthalene
D. Caustic potash

336. Ripe grapes contain
A. Fructose
B. Sucrose
C. Galactose
D. Glucose

337. Polythene is polymer of
A. Ethylene
B. Propylene
C. Acetylene
D. Aniline

338. Which one of the following is pure water?
A. Rain water
B. Filter water
C. Tubewell water
D. Distilled water

339. Which silver salt is used for making film for photography?
A. Silver bromide
B. Silver chloride
C. Silver sulphate
D. Silver nitrate

340. To an astronaut sky appears
A. White
B. Rich blue
C. Light blue
D. Dark

341. The instrument used to measure the speed of the wind is
A. Altimeter
B. Anemometer
C. Chronometer
D. Dosimeter

342. Who defined the law of gravitation?
A. Newton B. Archimedes
C. Galileo D. Faraday

343. The metal used to make lightning conductors is
A. Iron B. Aluminium
C. Copper D. Zinc

344. 'IC' in computers stands for
A. Integrated Charge
B. Integrated Current
C. Integrated Circuits
D. Internal Circuits

345. A hydrogen balloon floats up because of
A. Air pressure decreases with decrease in height
B. Air pressure decreases with decrease in weight
C. Weight of the balloon is less than the weight of air displaced by it
D. The pressure inside the balloon is more than the pressure outside it

346. In a rechargeable cell what kind of energy is stored within the cell?
A. Electrical energy
B. Potential energy
C. Chemical energy
D. Kinetic energy

347. M.R.I. stands for
A. Metered Resonance imaging
B. Magnetic Resonance Imaging

C. Magnetic Reaction Imaging
D. Metered Reaction Imaging

348. The American space shuttle which exploded in space killing astronaut Kalpana Chawla, was known as
A. Challenger
B. Columbia
C. Discovery
D. Columbus

349. For determination of the age of which among the following is carbon dating method used?
A. Fossils
B. Rocks
C. Trees
D. A and B

350. Which is the hottest planet in the Solar System?
A. Jupiter B. Saturn
C. Venus D. Uranus

State

351. Telangana became India's 29th State in
A. 2014 B. 2013
C. 2012 D. 2011

352. In which State would you find Jim Corbett National Park?
A. Assam
B. Uttar Pradesh
C. Maharashtra
D. Uttarakhand

353. Jharia mines are situated in which of the following States?
A. Jharkhand
B. West Bengal
C. Bihar
D. Odisha

354. 'Sardar Sarovar' project is in which of the following States?
A. Rajasthan
B. Madhya Pradesh
C. Uttar Pradesh
D. Gujarat

355. The new name of Rajasthan canal is
A. Gandhi canal
B. Indira Gandhi canal
C. Jawahar canal
D. Subhash canal

356. Which of the following lakes in Rajasthan is saline?
A. Ana Sagar
B. Pichola
C. Sambhar
D. Jaisamand

357. In which state is the district of Udham Singh Nagar situated?
A. Punjab
B. Uttarakhand
C. Uttar Pradesh
D. Rajasthan

358. Which amongst the following States has the highest population density as per census 2011?
A. Kerala
B. Madhya Pradesh
C. Uttar Pradesh
D. Bihar

359. Which one among the following states is smallest in area?
A. Andhra Pradesh
B. Gujarat
C. Karnataka
D. Tamil Nadu

360. In which State is Nalsarovar Bird Sanctuary located?

A. Maharashtra
B. Odisha
C. Gujarat
D. Rajasthan

361. Which of the following is the 28th State of India?
A. Jharkhand
B. Uttarakhand
C. Chhattisgarh
D. Gorkhaland

362. In which State is Ghana Bird Sanctuary located?
A. U.P.
B. M.P.
C. Assam
D. Rajasthan

363. Which of the following States does not have border with China?
A. Uttarakhand
B. U.P.
C. H.P.
D. Sikkim

364. What is the capital of the State of Chhattisgarh?
A. Raipur
B. Patna
C. Jamshedpur
D. Bokaro

365. With which State would you associate the festival of Dev Devali?
A. Bihar
B. West Bengal
C. Uttar Pradesh
D. Maharashtra

366. Areawise, which is the smallest State in India?
A. Goa B. Sikkm
C. Manipur D. Tripura

367. The capital of Lakshadweep is
A. Aizwal B. Port Blair
C. Kavaratti D. Agartala

368. The famous Kanha Wildlife Sanctuary is located in the State of:
A. Assam
B. Bihar
C. Madhya Pradesh
D. Karnataka

369. Which one of the following State is most populous?
A. Odisha
B. Uttar pradesh
C. Maharashtra
D. Bihar

370. Bhangra is a folk dance of
A. Punjab
B. Madhya Pradesh
C. Odisha
D. Assam

371. Kaziranga Animals Sanctuary is situated in the State of
A. Assam
B. Uttar Pradesh
C. Madhya Pradesh
D. Rajasthan

372. Konark temple is situated in the State of
A. Odisha
B. Kerala
C. Madhya Pradesh
D. Andhra Pradesh

373. The State which produces maximum Uranium in India is
A. Rajasthan
B. Kerala
C. Jharkhand
D. West Bengal

374. Lumbini, the birth place of Gautam Buddha is in
A. Bihar B. Sikkim
C. Nepal D. Uttar Pradesh

375. Which of the following is the least densely populated State?
A. Sikkim
B. Meghalaya
C. Mizoram
D. Arunachal Pradesh

376. "Dudhawa National Park" is situated in
A. Madhya Pradesh
B. Bihar
C. Uttar Pradesh
D. Karnataka

377. Sandal wood is found in
A. Tamil Nadu
B. Himachal Pradesh
C. Karnataka
D. Maharashtra

378. The chief producer of 'Jute' in India is
A. West Bengal
B. Karnataka
C. Tamil Nadu
D. Asom

379. The Ghat and Bhor Ghat are the important passes in
A. Kerala
B. Maharashtra
C. Gujarat
D. Rajasthan

380. The famous monolithic statue of Jain Saint Bahubali is situated in the state of
A. Andhra Pradesh
B. Bihar
C. Karnataka
D. Tamil Nadu

381. Which state of India is the largest exporter of marine products?
A. Andhra Pradesh
B. Gujarat
C. Kerala
D. Maharashtra

382. After Uttar Pradesh, which State leads in the production of sugarcane?
A. Bihar
B. Andhra Pradesh
C. Maharashtra
D. Tamil Nadu

383. Goa was liberated from the Portuguese in
A. 1964 B. 1961
C. 1963 D. 1962

384. The State which accounts for more than 90 per cent of total rubber production in India is
A. Karnataka
B. Kerala
C. Tamil Nadu
D. Andhra Pradesh

385. Which one of the following States has no common border with UP?
A. Punjab
B. Haryana
C. Madhya Pradesh
D. Uttarakhand

386. Name the State in which the Hirakud Dam is located?
A. Orissa B. Karnataka
C. U.P. D. Gujarat

387. Panna in Madhya Pradesh is associated with
A. Manganese
B. Mica
C. Copper
D. Diamond

388. The holy city Hardwar is in which of the State?

A. Uttar Pradesh
B. Haryana
C. Bihar
D. Uttarakhand

389. According to the census of 2011 the only State in India that shows excess of females over males is

A. Uttar Pradesh
B. Kerala
C. Maharashtra
D. Jammu and Kashmir

390. Which States share the Tungabhadra multipurpose project?

A. Karnataka and Madhya Pradesh
B. Orissa and Madhya Pradesh
C. Andhra Pradesh and Karnataka
D. Tamil Nadu and Andhra Pradesh

Organisations

391. The headquarter of World Trade Organisation (WTO) is located at

A. Rome
B. New York
C. Geneva
D. Washington DC

392. Which of the following countries is not a member of SAARC?

A. Nepal
B. China
C. Pakistan
D. India

393. Where is SAARC secretariat situated?

A. Islamabad
B. Colombo
C. New Delhi
D. Kathmandu

394. What is the activity of the INTERPOL?

A. Central record keeping agency of the international crimes
B. Investigative agency of the UN
C. An organisation to coordinate the police activities of the participating nations
D. A terrorist outfit

395. The six official languages of the UN are Russian, Chinese, English, French, Spanish and

A. Hindi
B. Urdu
C. Arabic
D. Japanese

396. What does SAPTA stands for?

A. South Asian Preferential Trade Agreement
B. South Asian Post Trade Agreement
C. SAARC Preferential Trade Agreement
D. SAARC Prevention Trade Agreement

397. The Association of South East Asian Nations (ASEAN) has its headquarters at

A. Manila
B. Jakarta
C. Kuala Lumpur
D. Bangkok

398. The normal term of office of UN Secretary General is
A. 3 years
B. 4 years
C. 5 years
D. 6 years

399. Which of the following countries is not a member of the G-7 Group?
A. France
B. Italy
C. Spain
D. Germany

400. Which of the following is NOT a permanent member of the UN Security Council?
A. Germany
B. France
C. Great Britain
D. China

401. The first Secretary General of the United Nations was:
A. Mrs. Vijay Lakshmi Pandit
B. Trygve Lie
C. Dag Hammarskjoeld
D. U. Thant

402. Who was the first Indian to be the President of U.N. General Assembly?
A. Natwar Singh
B. V.K. Krishna Menon
C. Smt. Vijay Lakshmi Pandit
D. Romesh Bhandari

403. Where is the headquarters of the International Court of Justice?
A. The Hague (Netherlands)
B. Paris (France)
C. Rome (Italy)
D. Washington (U.S.A)

404. How many Judges are there in the International Court of Justice?
A. 9 B. 10
C. 11 D. 15

405. When was the United Nations Organisation founded?
A. 20th October, 1945
B. 11th, November, 1944
C. 24th October, 1945
D. 26th June, 1945

406. The headquarters of the Organisation of Petroleum Exporting Countries is at
A. Teheran
B. Vienna
C. Abu Dhabi
D. Doha

407. How many members does the Security Council of UN have?
A. Ten B. Fifteen
C. Sixteen D. Twenty

408. Which country is not a member of ASEAN?
A. Indonesia
B. Cambodia
C. Singapore
D. Philippines

409. Where is the Head Quarter of Asian Development Bank?
A. Washington
B. Manila
C. Paris
D. Canberra

410. The headquarters of the U.N.O. is located in
A. Washington
B. New York
C. Philadelphia
D. Chicago

Awards

411. 'Pulitzer' prizes are awarded to Americans for excellence in
A. Films
B. Social work
C. Journalism
D. Medicine

412. When was the Nobel Prize started?
A. 1901 B. 1905
C. 1934 D. 1900

413. 'Bharat Ratna' Award was given for the first time in
A. 1956 B. 1957
C. 1952 D. 1954

414. Saraswati Samman is awarded by
A. K.K. Birla Foundation
B. Government of India
C. Bharatiya Jnanpith
D. Sahitya Academy

415. Who was the first Asian to win a Nobel Prize?
A. Hideki Yuka
B. Har Gobind Khurana
C. C.V. Raman
D. Rabindranath Tagore

416. The highest Gallantry Award given in India is
A. Ashok Chakra
B. Mahavir Chakra
C. Param Vir Chakra
D. None of these

417. On which day every year National Awards for Teachers are announced?
A. September 5
B. November 14
C. November 19
D. August 15

418. Dronacharya Awards are given
A. to outstanding athletes
B. to outstanding coaches
C. for best performance in archery
D. for invention in science

419. Dr. C.V. Raman was awarded Nobel Prize in
A. Chemistry
B. Literature
C. Physics
D. Medicine

420. The first recipient of Rajiv Gandhi Khel Ratna Award is
A. Leander Paes
B. Viswanathan Anand
C. Kapil Dev
D. Limba Ram

421. The highest civilian award of India is
A. Bharat Ratna
B. Padam Vibhushan
C. Padam Bhushan
D. Padma Shri

422. Which of the following Indians awarded 'Legion D Award', the highest civilian award of France?
A. Satyajit Ray
B. Pandit Ravi Shankar
C. Lok Nayak Jayaprakash
D. J.L. Nehru

423. Dhanvantari Awards are given for the best performance in the field of
A. Medical Sciences
B. Nuclear Sciences
C. Economics
D. Space Research

424. Nobel Prizes are not given for which of the following fields?
A. Music B. Chemistry
C. Peace D. Physics

425. Dadasaheb Phalke Award is given for:
A. drama B. social welfare
C. films D. literature

426. In which year Nehru Award for International Understanding was instituted?
A. 1969 B. 1984
C. 1964 D. 1966

427. Who among the following has not been awarded the Bharat Ratna?
A. Indira Gandhi
B. Mahatma Gandhi
C. Sardar Patel
D. Radhakrishnan

428. Which one of the following is the second highest Civilian award in India?
A. Padma Shri
B. Bharat Ratna
C. Padma Bhushan
D. Padma Vibhushan

429. 'Victory Medal' is awarded in:
A. the USA
B. the UK
C. Russia
D. France

430. National film Awards were instituted in the year
A. 1954 B. 1950
C. 1961 D. 1969

431. In which year was the Nobel Prize for Economics announced for the first time?
A. 1969 B. 1901
C. 1919 D. 1970

432. Borlaug Award was instituted for recognising outstanding contribution in the field of
A. agriculture
B. ecology
C. journalism
D. medicine

433. Jesse Owens Global Award is given in the field of
A. Literature
B. Journalism
C. Science
D. Sports

434. Noble Alfred Bernhard after whom Nobel Prizes are given was
A. Engineer
B. Chemist
C. Both (A) and (B)
D. Doctor

435. Who was the first winner of Nehru Award for International Understanding?
A. Martin Luther King
B. Mother Teresa
C. U. Thant
D. Dr. Jonas Salk

Sports

436. In which International Championship, 'Thomas Cup' is given
A. Football
B. Cricket
C. Badminton
D. Tennis

437. 'Gambit' is related to which among the followings sports?
A. Carrom B. Bridge
C. Chess D. Billiards

438. The term 'Grandmaster' is used in which of these games?
A. Chess B. Judo
C. Bridge D. Karate

439. In the game of Volleyball, the number of players on each side is
A. Eight B. Five
C. Seven D. Six

440. The term "Cue" is associated with which game?
A. Hockey B. Football
C. Billiards D. Cricket

441. With which game is Geet Sethi Associated?
A. Basketball
B. Snooker
C. Chess
D. Tennis

442. How many players are there in each side in the game of Netball?
A. 7 B. 6
C. 9 D. 11

443. 'Uber Cup' is associated with which of the following?
A. Tennis B. Badminton
C. Chess D. Cricket

444. Where is the annual Australian Open Tennis tournament held?
A. Sydney B. Melbourne
C. Canberra D. Brisbane

445. The Olympic Motto is
A. Health is wealth
B. Promote Universal brotherhood
C. Faster, higher, stronger
D. Excellence is the goal

446. The term 'Tee' is associated with which of the following sports?
A. Polo B. Table Tennis
C. Golf D. Judo

447. Which Indian sportsman is known as Hockey Wizard throughout the world?
A. A.B. Subbiah
B. Jude Felix
C. Dhyan Chand
D. Ajitpal Singh

448. When did India become World Cricket champion?
A. 1980 B. 1982
C. 1983 D. 1986

449. "Googly" is associated with:
A. Cricket B. Table-Tennis
C. Hockey D. Billiards

450. With which game are the terms bull's eye, muzzle and plug associated?
A. Shooting B. Solitaire
C. Billiards D. Rowing

451. Who is the first Indian to take a hat trick in an international test?
A. Kapil Dev
B. Jasu Patel
C. Harbhajan Singh
D. B.S. Chandrashekhar

452. Who was declared by wisden as " The Best Indian Bowler of the Century" (20th Century)?
A. Kapil Dev
B. B.S. Chandrashekhar

C. B.S. Bedi
D. Subhash V. Gupte

453. " Jab" and "Parry" are terms used in which sport?
A. Wrestling
B. Boxing
C. Billiards
D. Weightlifting

454. India's national game is
A. Football B. Cricket
C. Tennis D. Hockey

455. Davis Cup is associated with the sport of
A. Tennis B. Football
C. Cricket D. Hockey

456. The term 'breast stroke' is associated with:
A. Skating
B. Croquet
C. Swimming
D. Rifle Shooting

457. What is the National Game of the USA?
A. Cricket B. Baseball
C. Soccer D. Billiards

458. Roger Federer is associated with
A. Hockey B. Lawn Tennis
C. Golf D. Badminton

459. 'Merdeka Cup' is associated with
A. Golf B. Football
C. Squash D. Hockey

460. Who among the following has become the first woman in the world to swim across seven seas?
A. Shikha Tandon
B. Bula Chowdhury
C. Amanda Beard
D. Arti Saha

Books

461. The famous book 'Geet Govind' is written by
A. Banabhatt
B. Jaydev
C. Mirabai
D. Kalidas

462. 'Ain-e-Akbari' was written by
A. Farista B. Ibn Batuta
C. Abul Fazal D. Birbal

463. Who wrote " Vande Mataram"?
A. Rabindra Nath Tagore
B. Sumitra Nandan Pant
C. Bankim Chandra Chatterji
D. Vivekanand

464. Who among the following is the author of 'Das Kapital'?
A. Lenin
B. J.M. Keynes
C. Robert Owen
D. Karl Marx

465. 'Panchatantra' was written by
A. Jai Dev
B. Ved Vyas
C. Bhavbhuti
D. Vishnu Sharma

466. Patanjali is well known for the compilation of
A. Yoga Sutra
B. Panchatantra
C. Brahma Sutra
D. Ayurveda

467. Who among the following has written the book, 'The Wings of Fire: An Autobiography'?
A. K.R. Narayan
B. Sobha De

C. A.B. Vajpayee
D. A.P.J. Abdul Kalam

468. Who compiled the 'Adi Granth'?
A. Guru Nanak
B. Guru Ramdas
C. Guru Arjun
D. Guru Gobind Singh

469. The famous book 'Anandmath' was authored by
A. Rabindranath Tagore
B. Bankim Chandra Chattopadhyaya
C. Sarojini Naidu
D. Sri Aurobindo

470. Which one of the following pairs is ***not*** correctly matched?
A. Mudrarakshasa : Visakhadatta
B. Rajtarangini : Kalhana
C. Kadambari : Bana Bhatta
D. Ratnavali : Bilhana

471. 'Harry Potter and the Deathly Hallows' is written by
A. Robert Ludlum
B. J.K. Rowling
C. Sidney Sheldon
D. Spencer Johnson

472. 'Arthashastra' was written by
A. Kalidas
B. Kautilya
C. R.K. Narayan
D. Bana Bhatta

473. Name the author of book ''The Post Office (Dak Ghar)''?
A. R.K. Narayan
B. Rabindra Nath Tagore
C. Prem Chand
D. Krishan Chandra

474. Who wrote the nursery rhyme, ''Twinkle, twinkle, little star''?
A. Lovelace
B. Ann Taylor
C. William Ross Wallace
D. William Shakespeare

475. Ashtadhyayi is a book written by
A. Panini
B. Patanjali
C. Vishnu Sharma
D. None of these

476. 'Prithviraj Raso' was written by:
A. Kalhan
B. Chand Bardai
C. Bhavbhuti
D. Bhule Shah

477. The book 'Prison Diary' was written by
A. Mahatma Gandhi
B. V.D. Savarkar
C. Jai Prakash Narayan
D. Morarji Desai

478. ''Runs and Ruins'' is written by
A. Nawab Pataudi
B. Vivian Richards
C. Clive Lloyd
D. Sunil Gavaskar

479. Who is the author of the book, 'The God of small Things'?
A. Ali Sardar Jafri
B. Vikram Chandra
C. Padma Seth
D. Arundhati Roy

480. India-2020 is a book written by
A. Montek Singh Ahluwalia
B. A.P.J. Abdul Kalam
C. G. Ganeshan
D. Indra Kumar Gujral

Computer

481. Which one of the following has earned the title "Father of Modern Computer"?
A. Blaise Pascal
B. Charles Babbage
C. Herman Hollerith
D. Jack Kilby

482. Which one of the following is the first generation computer?
A. UNIVAC-1
B. EDVAG
C. IBM 1201
D. IBM 1104

483. Which one of the following is a hardware?
A. Integrated circuit
B. Compiler
C. DOS
D. FORTRAN

484. What is the measuring unit of memory?
A. Watt B. Words
C. Bit D. None of these

485. How many bits are there in one byte?
A. 1 B. 2
C. 8 D. 1024

486. Digital computers deal with
A. discrete quantities
B. physical quantities
C. both discrete and physical quantities
D. neither discrete nor physical quantities

487. What is nibble?
A. A group of 2 bits
B. A group of 4 bits
C. A group of 8 bits
D. A group of 12 bits

488. Which one of the following is not a package?
A. BASIC
B. dBase
C. Pagemaker
D. Wordstar

489. Who invented the punched card?
A. Jack Kilby
B. John Napier
C. Gottfried Leibnitz
D. None of these

490. Which of the following does not represent an I/O device?
A. Speaker which beeps
B. Plotter
C. Joystick
D. ALU

491. A set of instructions is called a
A. compiler B. program
C. assembler D. information

492. Data is a collection of
A. raw material
B. number of alphabets
C. facts and entities relevant to user
D. input material for a computer

493. Which one of the following is part of the CPU?
A. Memory
B. Compiler
C. Control unit
D. Joystick

494. Which one of the following is not a system software?
A. Operating system
B. Compiler

C. Assembler
D. Software for railway reservation

495. What are the main limitations of computers?
A. Lack of decision-making power
B. Zero IQ
C. Lack in innovations
D. All the above

496. What do you understand by IPO cycle?
A. Information and Programming Operations cycle
B. Innovating and Programming Operations cycle
C. Input-Program-Output cycle
D. None of these

497. Calculations are made in computer with the help of its
A. Memory
B. ALU
C. CU
D. Input device

498. Results are obtained from computer through its
A. input unit
B. output unit
C. CPU
D. memory

499. Who, among the following invented the method of logarithm?
A. John Napier
B. Blaise Pascal
C. Joseph Jacquard
D. Charles Babbage

500. The modern age of data processing began with the completion of the computer
A. Analytical Engine
B. Napier's 'Logs' and 'Bones'
C. ENIAC
D. Leibnitz's Calculator

Miscellaneous

501. Who is called the First Citizen of India?
A. President of India
B. Prime Minister of India
C. Mahatma Gandhi
D. Dr. B.R. Ambedkar

502. Panini was a famous scholar of
A. Language and grammar
B. Ayurveda
C. Astronomy
D. Biology

503. Which of the following is not a mineral?
A. Slate
B. Limestone
C. Coal
D. Calcite

504. The state of rising prices due to an enhancement in the quantity of money in circulation, is termed as
A. Inflation
B. Deflation
C. Demonetisation
D. Devaluation

505. Name the minerals that are essential for bone and teeth formation in human
A. Calcium and Phosphorus
B. Magnesium and Potassium
C. Sodium and Iron
D. Iodine and Sulphur

506. Ripe mangoes contain
A. Vitamin A
B. Vitamin B
C. Vitamin C
D. Vitamin E

507. In which one of the following places, the boiling point of water is the highest?
A. Dead Sea
B. Mt. Everest
C. Nile Delta
D. Sunderbans Delta

508. The primary colours used in a colour TV are
A. Green, Yellow, Violet
B. Violet, Red, Orange
C. Blue, Green, Red
D. Blue, Geen, Violet

509. Which one of the following is not a Fundamental Right guaranteed by the Indian Constitution?
A. Freedom to manage religious affairs
B. Free and compulsory education up to primary stage
C. Prohibition of employment of children in factories
D. Freedom to propagate religion

510. The chief merit of a federal government is that it
A. Ensures a strong government at the centre
B. Integrates national unity with regional autonomy
C. Keeps a check on the multiparty system
D. Is very less expensive

511. The first Assamese to become the President of India was
A. Saiyeda Anowara Taimur
B. Gopinath Bordoloi
C. Fakhruddin Ali Ahmed
D. Syed Abdul Malik

512. Match List I with List II and select the correct answer using the codes given below the lists:

List-I	List-II
(*a*) Amjad Ali Khan	1. Flute
(*b*) Bismillah Khan	2. Sarod
(*c*) Hari Prasad Chaurasia	3. Tabla
(*d*) Alla Rakha	4. Shehnai

Codes:

	(*a*)	(*b*)	(*c*)	(*d*)
A.	2	1	3	4
B.	4	2	1	3
C.	2	4	1	3
D.	1	2	3	4

513. A dentist's mirror is a
A. Cylindrical mirror
B. Plane mirror
C. Convex mirror
D. Concave mirror

514. Which of the following is the largest producer of raw silk?
A. Asom
B. Karnataka
C. Andhra Pradesh
D. Jammu and Kashmir

515. The Gandhara School of Sculpture was a blend of
A. Indian and Greek styles
B. Indian and Persian styles
C. Purely Indian in origin
D. Indian and South East Asian style

516. Which one of the following languages is used in Tripura?
A. Hindi B. Mizo
C. Khasi D. Bengali

517. How many schedules are there in the Constitution of India?
A. Eight B. Ten
C. Twelve D. Fourteen

518. The term 'cloning' is related with
A. Environment
B. Genetics
C. Space technology
D. Trade

519. The planet nearest to the Earth is
A. Jupiter B. Venus
C. Mercury D. Mars

520. Hard water can be used in
A. Boilers
B. Textile industry
C. Paper industry
D. Drinking

521. Ras Leela, Yaosang, Lai Haraoba are the festivals of
A. Assemese people
B. Karbi people
C. Manipuri people
D. Bodo people

522. The Tigris river flows mainly through
A. Turkey B. Syria
C. Iraq D. Iran

523. ''India is a secular State''. It means that the Indian State
A. Favours irreligious citizens
B. Favours the religions of the majority community
C. Favours the religions of the minority community
D. Favours no particular religion

524. The second largest linguistic unit in India is
A. Tamil B. Hindi
C. English D. Telugu

525. The oldest inhabitants of India are considered to be
A. Mongoloids
B. Negritos
C. Indo-Aryan
D. Mediterranean

526. The International Date Line passes through
A. Malacca Strait
B. Gibraltar Strait
C. Bering Strait
D. Florida Strait

527. The last three digits of a PIN code represent
A. Zone
B. Subzone
C. Sorting District
D. Mailing route

528. Which state has the largest number of sugar mills?
A. Punjab
B. Haryana
C. Tamil Nadu
D. Uttar Pradesh

529. The first oil well in India was dug at
A. Bombay High
B. Moran
C. Digboi
D. Naharkatiya

530. Which of the following is ***not*** a rabi crop?
A. Wheat B. Maize
C. Mustard D. Gram

531. The state with the largest area under waste land is
A. Gujarat
B. Madhya Pradesh
C. Jammu and Kashmir
D. Rajasthan

532. Mixed farming involves
A. Growing more than one crop on a farm
B. Growing specialised crops
C. Growing crops and keeping livestock
D. Intensive and extensive agriculture

533. The country with the highest population density is
A. China B. Bangladesh
C. India D. France

534. When the first metal came into being, it was used for
A. Pot making
B. House-building
C. Clearing jungles
D. Making wheels

535. To whom does Vasudeva-Krishna address all his teachings in the Bhagvad Gita?
A. Arjuna
B. Duryodhana
C. Yudhishthira
D. The common people

536. Who raised the simple slogan 'Do or Die' for the Quit India Movement?
A. Mahatma Gandhi
B. Subhash Chandra Bose
C. Jawahar Lal Nehru
D. J.B. Kripalani

537. The salary and perquisities of the Prime Minister of India are decided by the
A. Constitution
B. Cabinet
C. Parliament
D. President

538. At what age can one exercise the right to vote in the general elections?
A. 18 years B. 21 years
C. 25 years D. 19 years

539. The Supreme Court was set up
A. By an act of Parliament
B. By the Constitution
C. Under the Government of India Act, 1935
D. By the Presidential order

540. A party to be recognised as a National Party must be in at least_____states.
A. Three B. Four
C. Five D. Six

541. Which of the following places is well known for the embroidery form of ''Chikankari''?
A. Hyderabad
B. Jaipur
C. Bhopal
D. Lucknow

542. Match the following

Folk form	**States where popular**
(*a*) Heer song	1. Bengal
(*b*) Bhatiali song	2. Punjab

(*c*) Garba dance 3. U.P.

(*d*) Raas dance 4. Gujarat

	(*a*)	(*b*)	(*c*)	(*d*)
A.	1	2	3	4
B.	1	3	2	4
C.	2	1	4	3
D.	2	3	4	1

543. Which is the most ancient musical instrument of India?
A. Flute B. Tabla
C. Veena D. Sitar

544. Who was the pioneer of the Bengal School of Art?
A. Nandlal Bose
B. B.C. Sanyal
C. Jamini Roy
D. Abanindranath Tagore

545. The proposed sea-route "Sethu Samudram" is a canal through which of the following sea-lanes?
A. Gulf of Mannar
B. Malacca Strait
C. Gulf of Kutch
D. Andaman and Nicobar Islands

546. The English established their first factory in India at
A. Bombay (Mumbai)
B. Surat
C. Sutanati
D. Madras (Chennai)

547. Which one of the following is a political right?
A. Right to freedom
B. Right to contest elections
C. Right to equality before law
D. Right to life

548. The main function of the judiciary is
A. Law formulation
B. Law execution
C. Law adjudication
D. Law application

549. 'Sakshat' is
A. A missile
B. An artificial satellite
C. A railway project
D. A website

550. Who started the first English newspaper in India?
A. Bal Gangadhar Tilak
B. Raja Rammohan Roy
C. J.A. Hickey
D. Lord William Bentinck

551. Mahatma Gandhi's autobiography—'My Experiments with Truth' was originally written in—
A. English B. Hindi
C. Marathi D. Gujarati

552. Who commanded the army of Bahadur Shah Zafar in 1857 revolt in Delhi ?
A. Azimulla
B. General Bakht Khan
C. Haqim Ahsanulla
D. Khan Bahadur

553. People greet one another in French language with—
A. GutenTag
B. Bonjour
C. Ahlan Wasahlan
D) None of these

554. Which among the following is ***not*** a correct match—
A. Thomas Cup—Badminton
B. Rovers Cup—Hockey
C. Deodhar Trophy—Cricket
D. Durand Cup—Football

555. What is Gene ?
A. A segment of RNA, DNA and Histone
B. A segment of DNA and RNA
C. A segment of DNA
D. A segment of DNA and Histone

556. Water pollution is mainly caused by-
A. Pesticides
B. NH_3
C. Industrial waste
D. Detergent

557. In the constitution of India, India has been described as—
A. A federation
B. A secular of federation
C. A quasi-federal organization
D. A union of states

558. Damodar Valley Project is sponsored by West Bengal and—
A. Orissa
B. Jharkhand
C. U.P.
D. All the above

559. Which among the following is a riverine port ?
A. Cochin B. Kolkata
C. Kanca D. Mormugao

560. Budapest is the capital of—
A. Haiti
B. Honduras
C. Hungary
D. Czech Republic

561. Among the following, which state capital is not situated near the bank of a river ?
A. Lucknow B. Patna
C. Bombay D. Kolkata

562. Which is the storehouse of salt in human body ?
A. Liver B. Skin
C. Kidneys D. Neck

563. Pyorrhoea affects which part of the body ?
A. The gums
B. The teeth
C. Salivary glands
D. Lips

564. Who was the author of 'Geet Govind' ?
A. Vidyapati B. Jayadeva
C. Magha D. Sriharsha

565. Thermocole is made from—
A. Polystyrene
B. Perspex
C. Polythene
D. Teflon

566. Printing for the blind was invented by—
A. Berliner
B. N.R.Finsen
C. Louis Braile
D. J. L. Baird

567. Which is the heaviest flying bird?
A. Bustard
B. Penguin
C. Ostrich
D. Vulture

568. Economic development of a country is directly based on—
A. Natural resources
B. Capital formation
C. Availability of market
D. None of these

569. The term Ikebana is associated with which country ?
A. Thailand B. Japan
C. England D. Australia

570. The largest irrigation canal in India is called the—
A. Yamuna canal
B. Sirhind canal
C. Lower Baridoab canal
D. Indira Gandhi canal

571. Horns of most mammals are made of—
A. Bones B. Cartilage
C. Keratin D. Chitin

572. Rigveda is divided into how many Mandals ?
A. 10 mandals
B. 7 mandals
C. 15 mandals
D. 20 mandals

573. The constitution of UNO is known as—
A. Peace agreement
B. Magna Carta
C. Declaration
D. Charter

574. December 10 is observed as—
A. World Mental Health Day
B. World Sight Day
C. World Red Cross Day
D. Human Rights Day

575. The Durand Line is the international border between—
A. Afghanistan and Pakistan
B. Iran and Syria
C. India and Bangladesh
D. India and Nepal

576. Washington is situated at the bank of—
A. Vistula B. Moskava
C. Potomac D. Tagus

577. The term 'Rook' is linked with—
A. Golf B. Archery
C. Chess D. Badminton

578. 'Fan', a widely spoken language of the world belongs to—
A. Laos B. Kenya
C. Tibet D. Myanmar

579. Which among the following is matched incorrectly ?
A. Mahatma Gandhi — Bapu
B. Lajpat Rai — Punjab Kesari
C. C.F. Andrews— Deshabandhu
D. Subhash Chandra Bose — Netaji

580. Supreme Court in India was established in Calcutta in :
A. 1771 B. 1774
C. 1775 D. 1776

581. The first radio-programme in India was broadcast by Radio Club of Bombay in:
A. 1924 B. 1923
C. 1926 D. 1927

582. In India, the first state to institute a Human Rights Commission is :
A. A.P. B. Kerala
C. W. Bengal D. Rajasthan

583. The 'Vikram Sarabhai Space Centre is located at :
A. Bangalore
B. Hyderabad
C. Chennai
D. Thiruvananthapuram

584. The first film actor to be nominated to Rajya Sabha was :
A. Ashok Kumar
B. Dilip Kumar
C. Jeevan
D. Prithviraj Kapoor

585. The first Indian Institute of Technology was set up in India in 1950 at :

A. Kolhapur B. Kanpur

C. Kharagpur D. Bangalore

586. Which state has the maximum forest cover amongst all Indian States and Union Territories?

A. T.N. B. A.P.

C. M.P. D. U.P.

587. Manas Wildlife Sanctuary housing tigers is in:

A. Sikkim

B. Asom

C. Karnataka

D. Arunachal Pradesh

588. Who wrote 'Long Walk To Freedom' ?

A. Nelson Mandela

B. Aung San Su Kyi

C. Abraham Lincoln

D. Moti Lal Nehru

589. The currency of Bhutan is :

A. Lote B. Rupiah

C. Ngultrum D. Shekel

590. Who discovered X-rays in 1895 ?

A. Mackintos

B. B. Certois

C. Belard

D. Prof. Roentgen

591. The melting point of iron is :

A. 1600°C B. 1535°C

C. 1765°C D. 1650°C

592. The headquarters of European Union is :

A. Rome B. Paris

C. Brussels D. Dublin

593. Commonwealth Day is observed by Member Countries on :

A. 26 August

B. 24 May

C. 27 December

D. 29 January

594. IMF (International Monetary Fund) was established in :

A. 1950 B. 1965

C. 1945 D. 1980

595. The distance covered by wheeled vehicle is measured by :

A. Sextant

B. Odometer

C. Speedometer

D. Stroboscope

596. Diphtheria, a disease, attacks :

A. Lungs B. Eyes

C. Gums D. Throat

597. Phrenology is the study of :

A. Language

B. Teeth

C. Skull and brain

D. Nerves

598. If the President of India wants to submit his resignation, to whom, would he submit his resignation?

A. Speaker of the Lok Sabha

B. Chief Justice of Supreme Court

C. Vice President

D. Prime Minister

599. Rose is the national emblem of :

A. Italy B. Iran

C. Israel D. Iraq

600. 'Akash' is India's—

A. Air to air missile

B. Anti-tank guided missile

C. Surface to surface missile

D. Surface to air missile

601. Tapti river originates from :
A. Amarkantak
B. Panchmarhi
C. Trimbakeshwar
D. Satpura range

602. The first municipal corporation in India was established in Madras in :
A. 1687 B. 1699
C. 1685 D. 1690

603. RAW (Research and Analysis Wing) works under:
A. Ministry of Home
B. Ministry of Personnel
C. PMO
D. Cabinet Secretariat

604. The first spacecraft sent by Europe to the moon is :
A. Atlantis B. Discovery
C. Odyssey D. SMART-I

605. Siyam is the old name of :
A. Vietnam B. Thailand
C. Myanmar D. Laos

606. The number of states which do not touch international boundary and are completely landlocked is :
A. 3 B. 7
C. 5 D. 6

607. Which state of India touches the boundary of most other states?
A. A.P. B. M.P.
C. Asom D. U.P.

608. Which of the Mughal rulers promoted painting most?
A. Babar B. Akbar
C. Jahangir D. Shahjahan

609. The subject matter of the fourth schedule of the Constitution of India is :
A. Administration of tribal areas
B. Forms of oath or Affirmation
C. Languages
D. Allocation of seats of the Rajya Sabha to states

610. Vice-President is the part of :
A. Legislature
B. Executive
C. Rajya Sabha
D. None of these

ANSWERS

1	**2**	**3**	**4**	**5**	**6**	**7**	**8**	**9**	**10**
C	C	A	D	C	C	B	D	B	B
11	**12**	**13**	**14**	**15**	**16**	**17**	**18**	**19**	**20**
C	C	C	D	C	D	B	C	D	D
21	**22**	**23**	**24**	**25**	**26**	**27**	**28**	**29**	**30**
B	B	D	B	D	D	D	B	D	B
31	**32**	**33**	**34**	**35**	**36**	**37**	**38**	**39**	**40**
B	A	C	A	A	B	B	B	A	A
41	**42**	**43**	**44**	**45**	**46**	**47**	**48**	**49**	**50**
C	C	B	B	B	C	A	B	B	C
51	**52**	**53**	**54**	**55**	**56**	**57**	**58**	**59**	**60**
C	C	B	B	A	C	B	B	B	D

61	**62**	**63**	**64**	**65**	**66**	**67**	**68**	**69**	**70**
D	C	A	A	B	C	C	A	C	D
71	**72**	**73**	**74**	**75**	**76**	**77**	**78**	**79**	**80**
C	D	C	D	C	C	C	B	C	B
81	**82**	**83**	**84**	**85**	**86**	**87**	**88**	**89**	**90**
C	A	D	D	D	C	C	A	C	D
91	**92**	**93**	**94**	**95**	**96**	**97**	**98**	**99**	**100**
A	C	C	C	B	D	A	A	C	D
101	**102**	**103**	**104**	**105**	**106**	**107**	**108**	**109**	**110**
B	D	A	C	A	C	A	A	D	B
111	**112**	**113**	**114**	**115**	**116**	**117**	**118**	**119**	**120**
B	C	A	B	B	B	D	D	D	B
121	**122**	**123**	**124**	**125**	**126**	**127**	**128**	**129**	**130**
D	C	C	A	D	A	D	C	B	C
131	**132**	**133**	**134**	**135**	**136**	**137**	**138**	**139**	**140**
B	D	D	A	B	A	B	B	B	D
141	**142**	**143**	**144**	**145**	**146**	**147**	**148**	**149**	**150**
B	A	C	C	A	A	C	A	B	D
151	**152**	**153**	**154**	**155**	**156**	**157**	**158**	**159**	**160**
C	B	B	C	C	D	A	D	C	D
161	**162**	**163**	**164**	**165**	**166**	**167**	**168**	**169**	**170**
B	D	B	C	D	D	B	D	D	B
171	**172**	**173**	**174**	**175**	**176**	**177**	**178**	**179**	**180**
D	B	B	C	C	C	A	D	A	C
181	**182**	**183**	**184**	**185**	**186**	**187**	**188**	**189**	**190**
C	A	B	C	B	C	C	D	B	D
191	**192**	**193**	**194**	**195**	**196**	**197**	**198**	**199**	**200**
D	A	D	C	B	B	A	D	D	C
201	**202**	**203**	**204**	**205**	**206**	**207**	**208**	**209**	**210**
A	B	B	D	A	D	C	C	C	A
211	**212**	**213**	**214**	**215**	**216**	**217**	**218**	**219**	**220**
B	B	C	C	D	A	C	D	B	D
221	**222**	**223**	**224**	**225**	**226**	**227**	**228**	**229**	**230**
D	C	C	A	C	C	B	A	D	A
231	**232**	**233**	**234**	**235**	**236**	**237**	**238**	**239**	**240**
B	A	A	A	A	B	B	A	D	B
241	**242**	**243**	**244**	**245**	**246**	**247**	**248**	**249**	**250**
D	B	A	B	C	C	B	D	A	C
251	**252**	**253**	**254**	**255**	**256**	**257**	**258**	**259**	**260**
D	B	D	B	A	B	C	D	D	A

261	262	263	264	265	266	267	268	269	270
B	A	C	C	C	D	C	C	B	B
271	**272**	**273**	**274**	**275**	**276**	**277**	**278**	**279**	**280**
C	D	B	D	D	C	A	D	A	D
281	**282**	**283**	**284**	**285**	**286**	**287**	**288**	**289**	**290**
C	A	B	B	B	B	D	B	C	C
291	**292**	**293**	**294**	**295**	**296**	**297**	**298**	**299**	**300**
C	B	D	B	B	C	B	D	D	A
301	**302**	**303**	**304**	**305**	**306**	**307**	**308**	**309**	**310**
A	B	A	C	D	A	A	D	C	A
311	**312**	**313**	**314**	**315**	**316**	**317**	**318**	**319**	**320**
D	C	B	C	D	C	A	B	C	D
321	**322**	**323**	**324**	**325**	**326**	**327**	**328**	**329**	**330**
A	B	C	B	A	D	A	B	B	D
331	**332**	**333**	**334**	**335**	**336**	**337**	**338**	**339**	**340**
B	A	B	A	C	C	A	A	D	D
341	**342**	**343**	**344**	**345**	**346**	**347**	**348**	**349**	**350**
B	A	B, C	C	C	C	B	B	A	C
351	**352**	**353**	**354**	**355**	**356**	**357**	**358**	**359**	**360**
A	D	A	D	B	C	B	D	D	C
361	**362**	**363**	**364**	**365**	**366**	**367**	**368**	**369**	**370**
A	D	B	A	D	A	C	C	B	A
371	**372**	**373**	**374**	**375**	**376**	**377**	**378**	**379**	**380**
A	A	C	C	D	C	C	A	B	C
381	**382**	**383**	**384**	**385**	**386**	**387**	**388**	**389**	**390**
D	C	B	B	A	A	D	D	B	C
391	**392**	**393**	**394**	**395**	**396**	**397**	**398**	**399**	**400**
C	B	D	C	C	A	B	C	C	A
401	**402**	**403**	**404**	**405**	**406**	**407**	**408**	**409**	**410**
B	C	A	D	C	B	B	B	B	B
411	**412**	**413**	**414**	**415**	**416**	**417**	**418**	**419**	**420**
C	A	D	A	D	C	A	B	C	B
421	**422**	**423**	**424**	**425**	**426**	**427**	**428**	**429**	**430**
A	A	A	A	C	C	B	D	A	A
431	**432**	**433**	**434**	**435**	**436**	**437**	**438**	**439**	**440**
A	A	D	B	C	C	C	A	D	C
441	**442**	**443**	**444**	**445**	**446**	**447**	**448**	**449**	**450**
B	A	B	B	C	C	C	C	A	A
451	**452**	**453**	**454**	**455**	**456**	**457**	**458**	**459**	**460**
C	B	B	D	A	C	B	B	B	B

461	462	463	464	465	466	467	468	469	470
B	C	C	D	D	A	D	C	B	D
471	**472**	**473**	**474**	**475**	**476**	**477**	**478**	**479**	**480**
B	B	B	B	B	B	C	D	D	B
481	**482**	**483**	**484**	**485**	**486**	**487**	**488**	**489**	**490**
B	A	A	D	C	A	B	A	D	D
491	**492**	**493**	**494**	**495**	**496**	**497**	**498**	**499**	**500**
B	C	C	D	D	D	B	B	A	A
501	**502**	**503**	**504**	**505**	**506**	**507**	**508**	**509**	**510**
A	A	C	A	A	A	A	C	C	B
511	**512**	**513**	**514**	**515**	**516**	**517**	**518**	**519**	**520**
C	C	D	A	A	D	C	B	B	A
521	**522**	**523**	**524**	**525**	**526**	**527**	**528**	**529**	**530**
C	C	D	D	B	C	C	D	C	C
531	**532**	**533**	**534**	**535**	**536**	**537**	**538**	**539**	**540**
D	C	B	A	A	A	C	A	B	B
541	**542**	**543**	**544**	**545**	**546**	**547**	**548**	**549**	**550**
D	C	A	D	A	B	B	C	D	C
551	**552**	**553**	**554**	**555**	**556**	**557**	**558**	**559**	**560**
D	B	B	B	C	C	D	B	B	C
561	**562**	**563**	**564**	**565**	**566**	**567**	**568**	**569**	**570**
C	B	A	B	A	C	A	B	B	D
571	**572**	**573**	**574**	**575**	**576**	**577**	**578**	**579**	**580**
C	A	D	D	A	C	C	D	C	B
581	**582**	**583**	**584**	**585**	**586**	**587**	**588**	**589**	**590**
B	C	D	D	C	C	B	A	C	D
591	**592**	**593**	**594**	**595**	**596**	**597**	**598**	**599**	**600**
B	C	B	C	B	D	C	C	B	D
601	**602**	**603**	**604**	**605**	**606**	**607**	**608**	**609**	**610**
B	A	D	D	B	C	D	C	D	B

1904

www.ingramcontent.com/pod-product-compliance
Ingram Content Group UK Ltd.
Pitfield, Milton Keynes, MK11 3LW, UK
UKHW021708190726
13853UKWH00001B/464

9 789387 918245